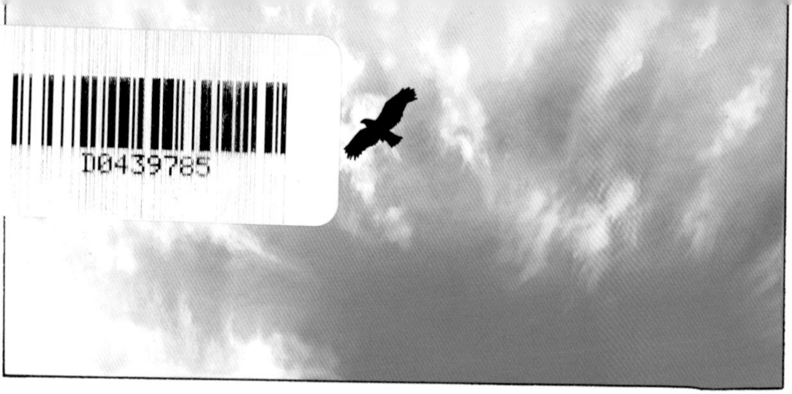

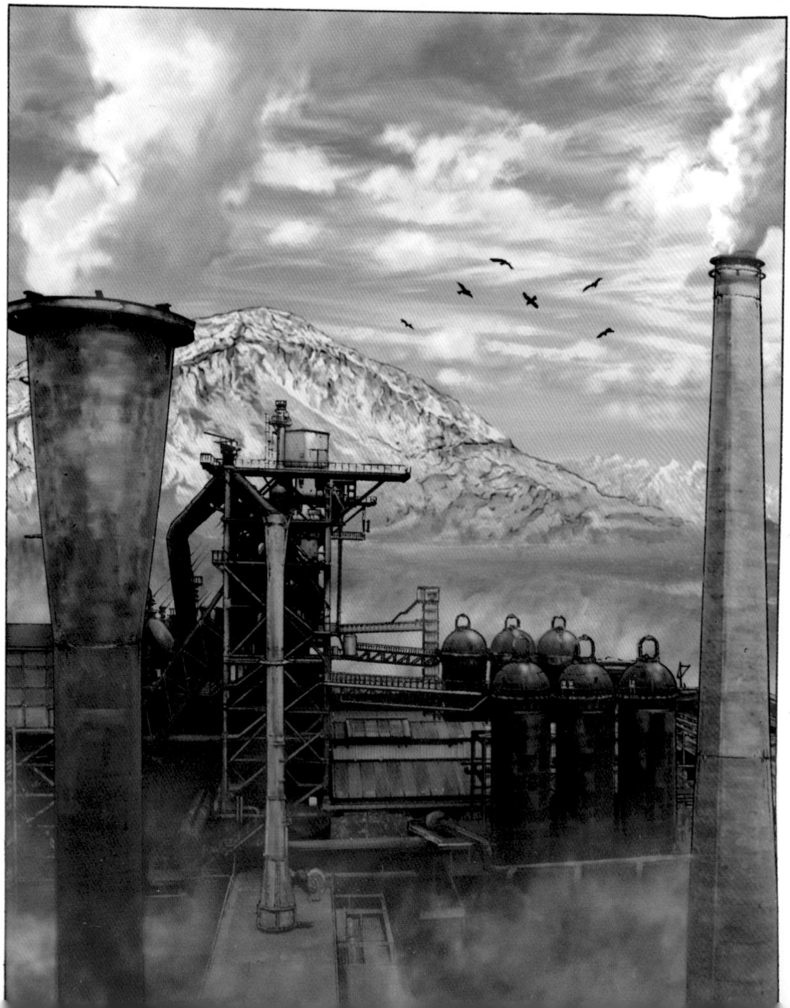

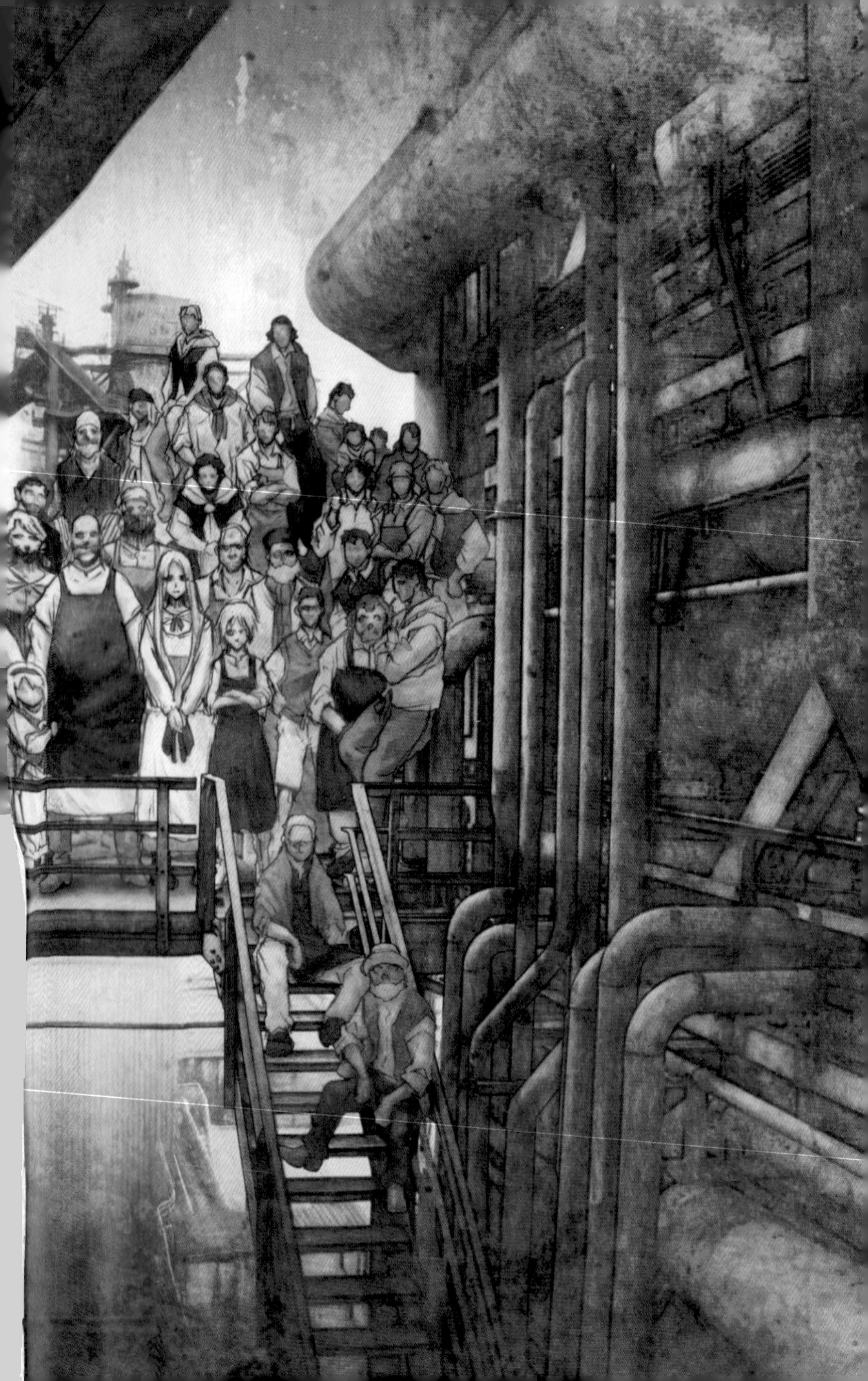

ATTACK on TITAN 8

BEFORE THE FALL

Based on "Attack on Titan"
created by Hajime Isayama
Story by: Ryo Suzukaze
Art by Satoshi Shiki
Character Designs by: Thores Shibamoto

Contents:

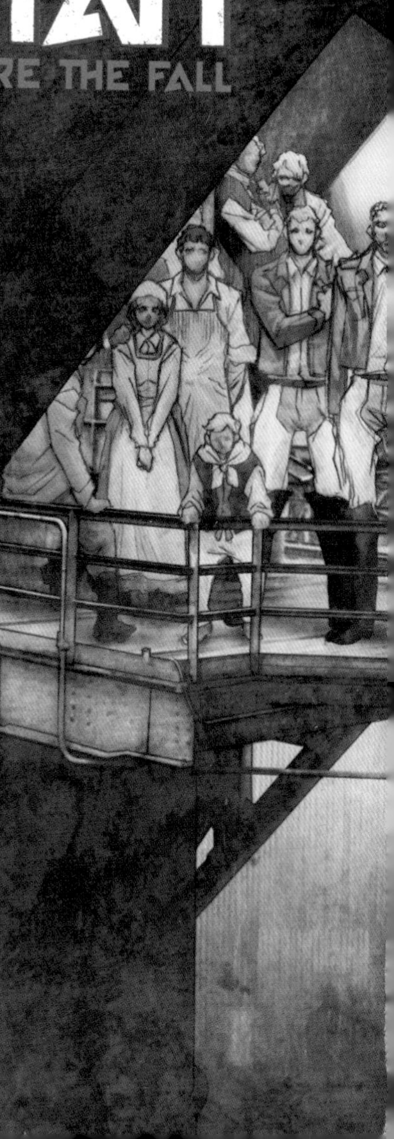

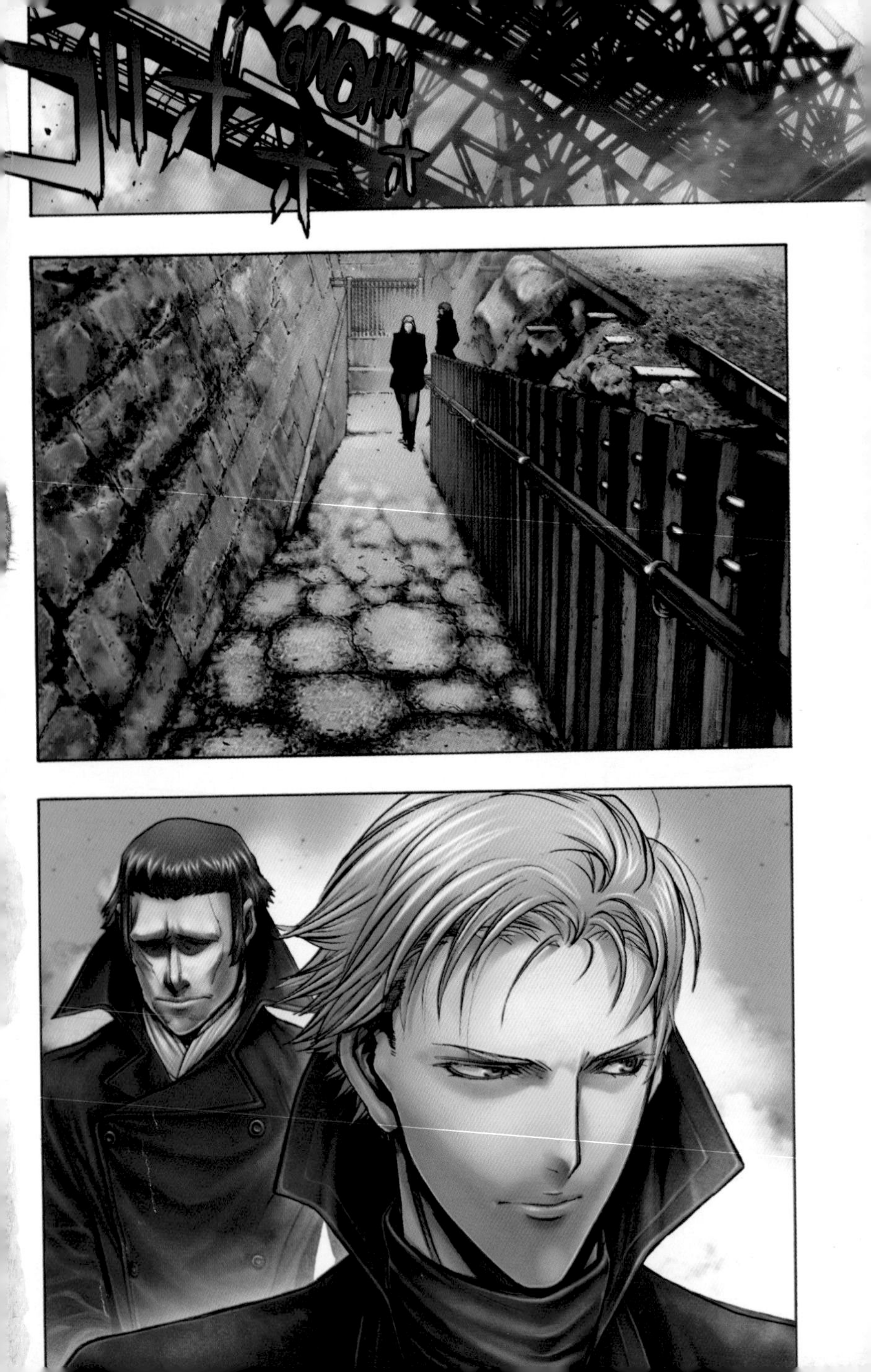
GWOHH

Before the Fall Character Profiles

Kuklo

A 15-year-old boy born from a dead body packed into the vomit of a Titan, which earned him the moniker, "Titan's Son." He is fascinated with the Device as a means to defeat the Titans. The protagonist of this story.

Sharle Inocencio

First daughter of the Inocencios, a rich merchant family within Wall Sheena. When she realized that Kuklo was a human, she taught him to speak and learn. Currently an apprentice craftsman under Xenophon in the industrial city.

Xavi Inocencio

Head of the Inocencio family and Sharle's brother. Member of the Military Police in Shiganshina District.

Cardina Baumeister

Kuklo's first friend in the outside world, and his companion in developing the Device.

Jorge Pikale

Training Corps instructor. A former Survey Corps captain who was hailed as a hero for defeating a Titan.

Carlo Pikale

Jorge's son and current captain of the Survey Corps. After they battled Titans together, he has great respect for Kuklo.

Xenophon Harkimo

Foreman at the industrial city. He took over development of the Device from its inventor, Angel.

Gloria Bernhart

Captain of the Military Police in Shiganshina District. A powerful MP officer with a cold, tactical mind.

The Story So Far

When a Titan terrorized Shiganshina District and left behind a pile of vomit, a baby boy was miraculously born of a pregnant corpse. This boy was named Kuklo, the "Titan's Son," and was treated as a sideshow freak. Eventually the wealthy merchant Dario Inocencio bought Kuklo to serve as a punching bag for his son, Xavi. Meanwhile, Xavi's sister Sharle decided to teach him the words and knowledge of humanity when she learned he was human and not the son of a Titan. Two years later, Kuklo escaped from the mansion along with Sharle, who was being forced into a marriage she did not desire.

In Shiganshina District, the Survey Corps was preparing for its first expedition outside of the wall in 15 years. Kuklo wanted to see a Titan to confirm that he was indeed a human being. He left Sharle behind and snuck into the expedition's cargo wagon. As he hoped, the Survey Corps ran across a Titan, but it was far worse of a monster than he expected. The group suffered grievous losses, but thanks to Captain Carlo and Kuklo's idea, they eventually retreated safely behind Wall Maria. Kuklo helped the Survey Corps survive, but inside the walls he was greeted by the Military Police, who wanted the "Titan's Son" on charges of murdering Dario. In prison, he met Cardina, a young man jailed over political squabbles. They hoped to escape to safety when exiled beyond the Wall, but found themselves surrounded by a pack of Titans. It was through the help of Jorge, former Survey Corps Captain and first human to defeat a Titan, that the two boys escaped with their lives. The equipment that Jorge used was the very "Device" that was the key to defeating the Titan those 15 years ago.

Kuklo and Cardina escaped the notice of the MPs by hiding in the Industrial City, where they found Sharle. It is there that the three youngsters learned the truth of the ill-fated Titan-capturing expedition 15 years earlier, and swore to uphold the will of Angel, the inventor of the Device. Next, Kuklo and Cardina headed back to Shiganshina to test out a new model of the Device developed by Xenophon, Angel's friend and rival. Unbeknownst to either side, the young men passed another carriage on the road to the industrial city bearing Xavi, now a new MP under secret orders from Gloria, Captain of the Shiganshina Military Police.

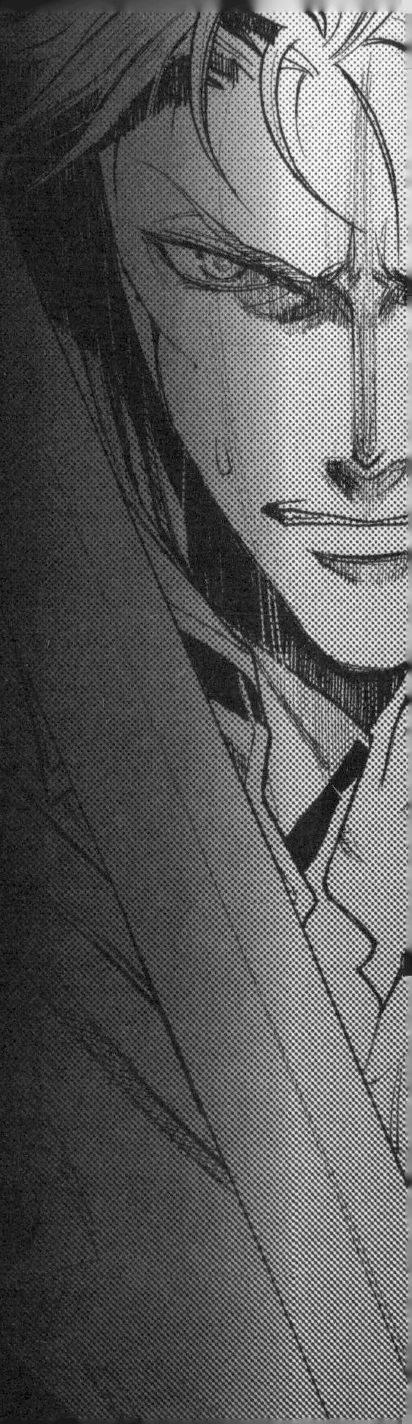

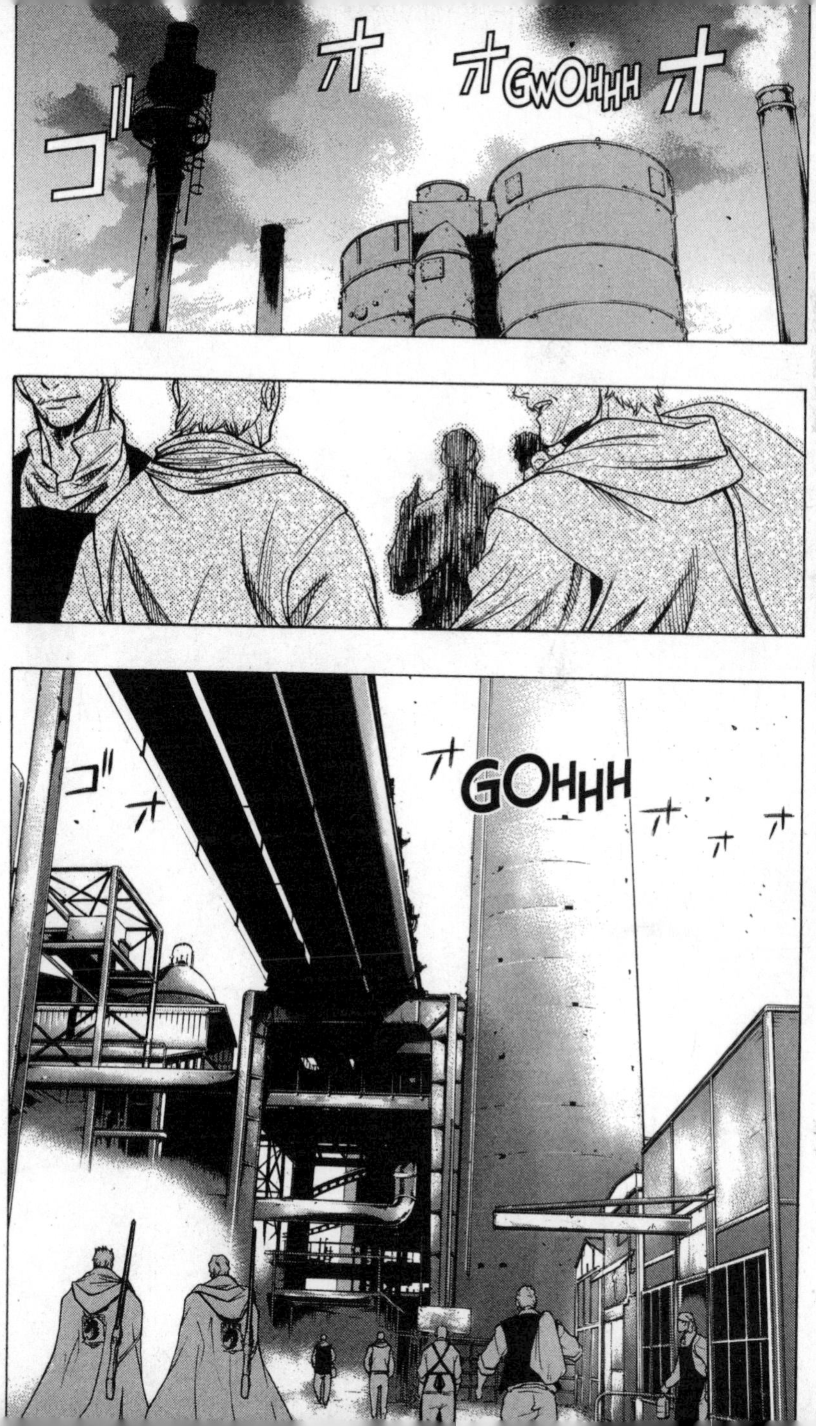
ゴオオオ
GWOHHH
ゴオオオオオ
GOHHH

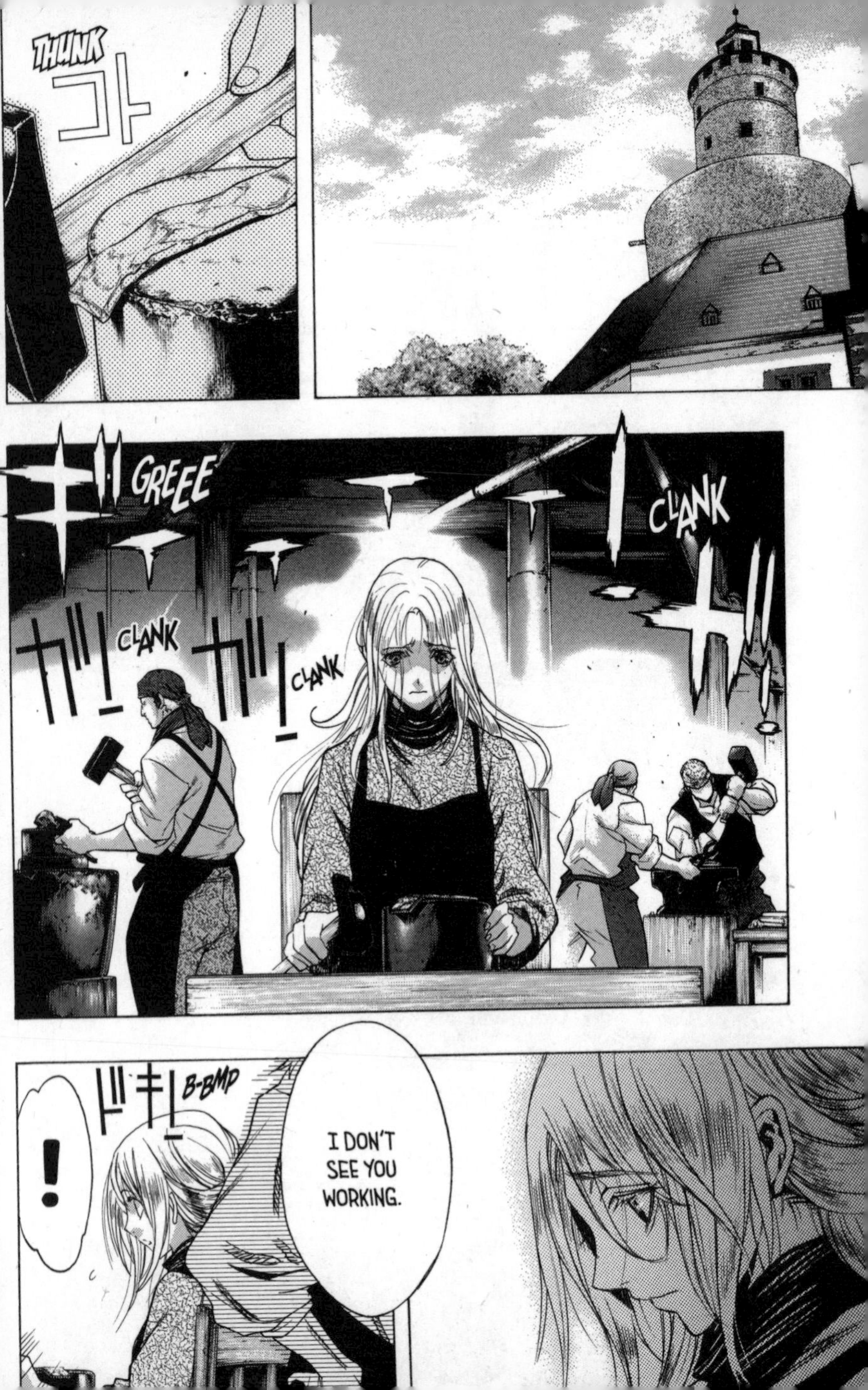
THUNK
コト
CLANK
GREEE
CLANK
ガッ
CLANK
ガッ
I DON'T SEE YOU WORKING.
!
ドキ
B-BMP

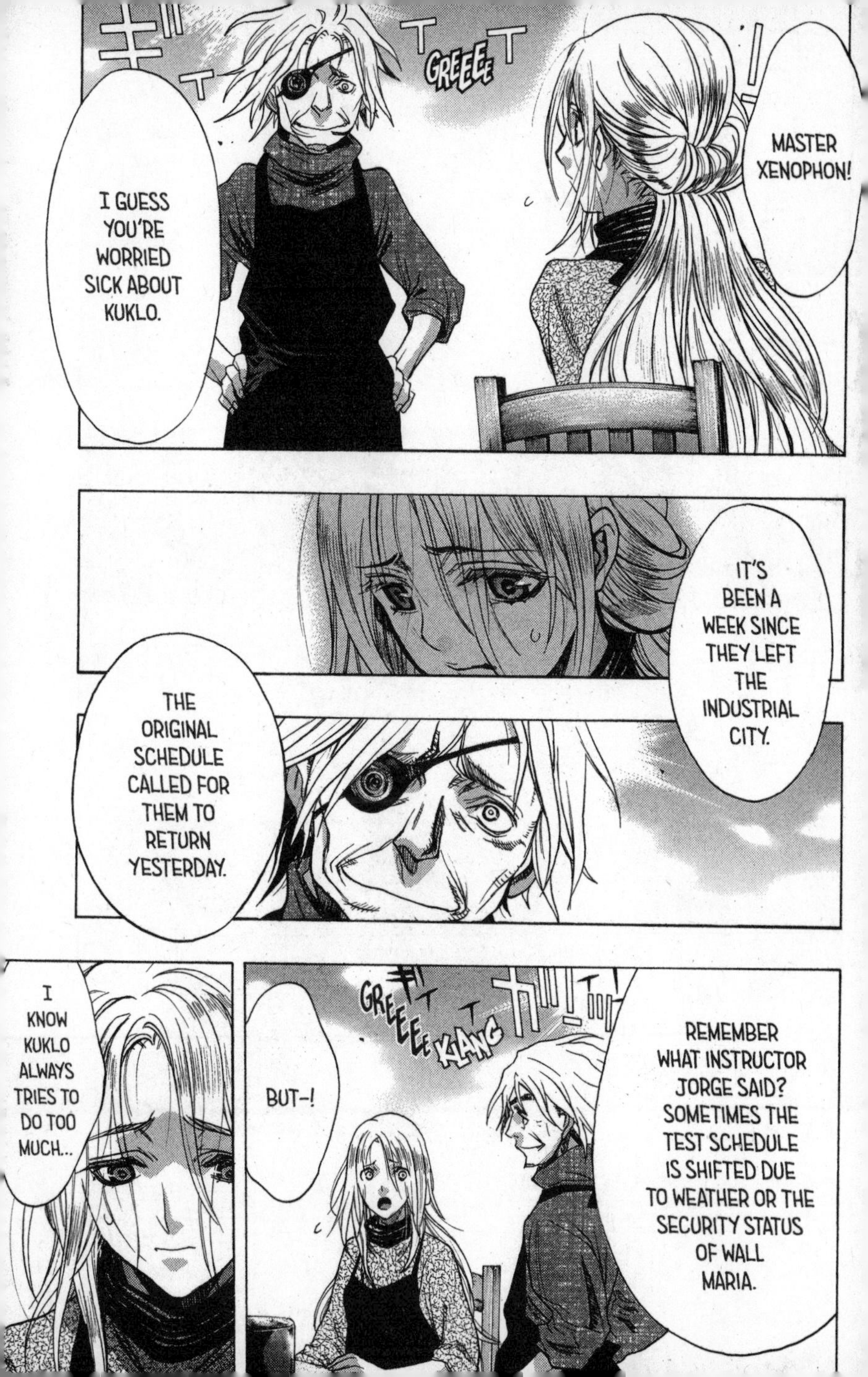
GREEEE
MASTER XENOPHON!
I GUESS YOU'RE WORRIED SICK ABOUT KUKLO.
IT'S BEEN A WEEK SINCE THEY LEFT THE INDUSTRIAL CITY.
THE ORIGINAL SCHEDULE CALLED FOR THEM TO RETURN YESTERDAY.
GREEEEE KLANG
REMEMBER WHAT INSTRUCTOR JORGE SAID? SOMETIMES THE TEST SCHEDULE IS SHIFTED DUE TO WEATHER OR THE SECURITY STATUS OF WALL MARIA.
BUT-!
I KNOW KUKLO ALWAYS TRIES TO DO TOO MUCH...

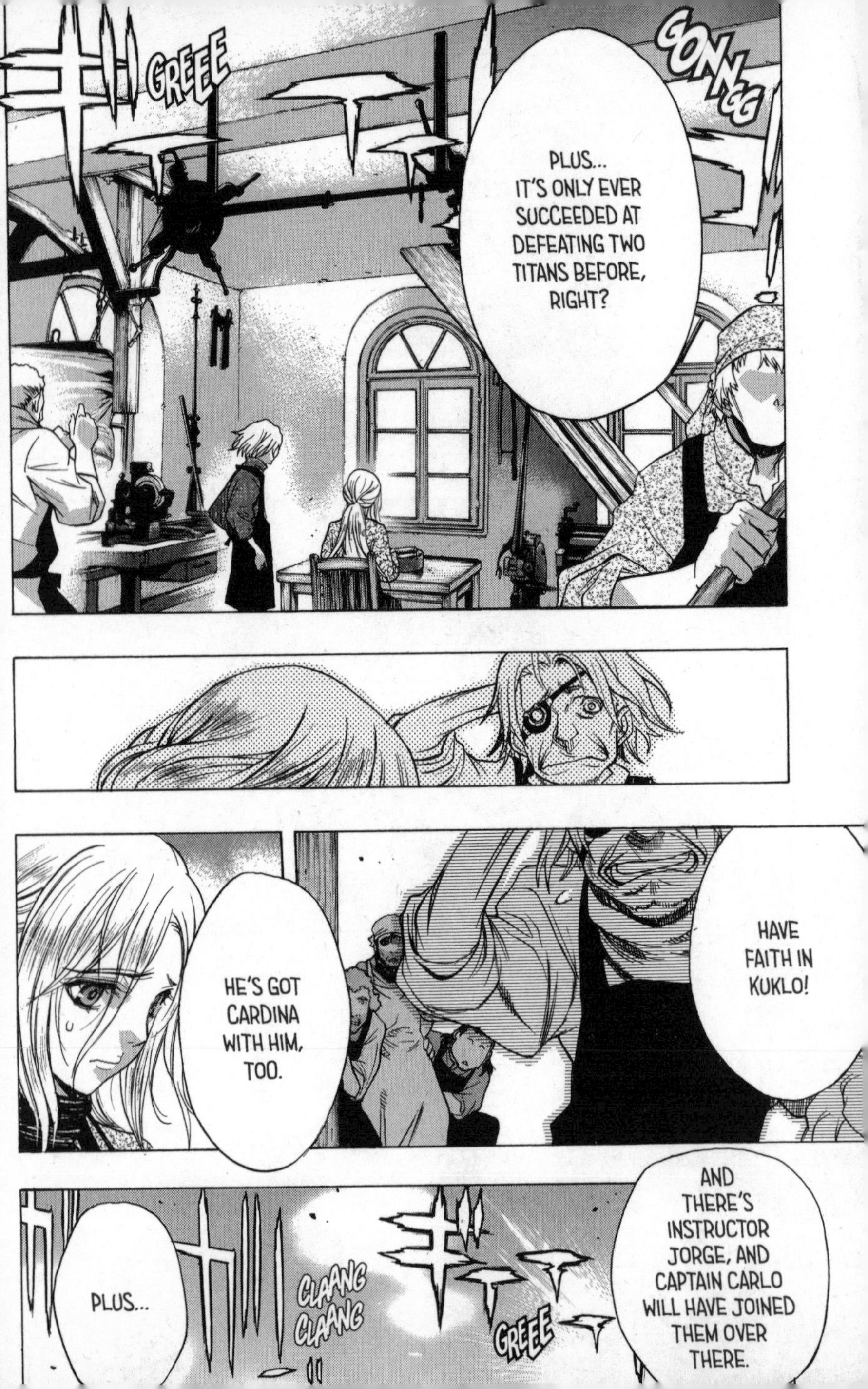
GONNGG
PLUS... IT'S ONLY EVER SUCCEEDED AT DEFEATING TWO TITANS BEFORE, RIGHT?
GREEE
HAVE FAITH IN KUKLO!
HE'S GOT CARDINA WITH HIM, TOO.
AND THERE'S INSTRUCTOR JORGE, AND CAPTAIN CARLO WILL HAVE JOINED THEM OVER THERE.
GREEE
CLAANG CLAANG
PLUS...

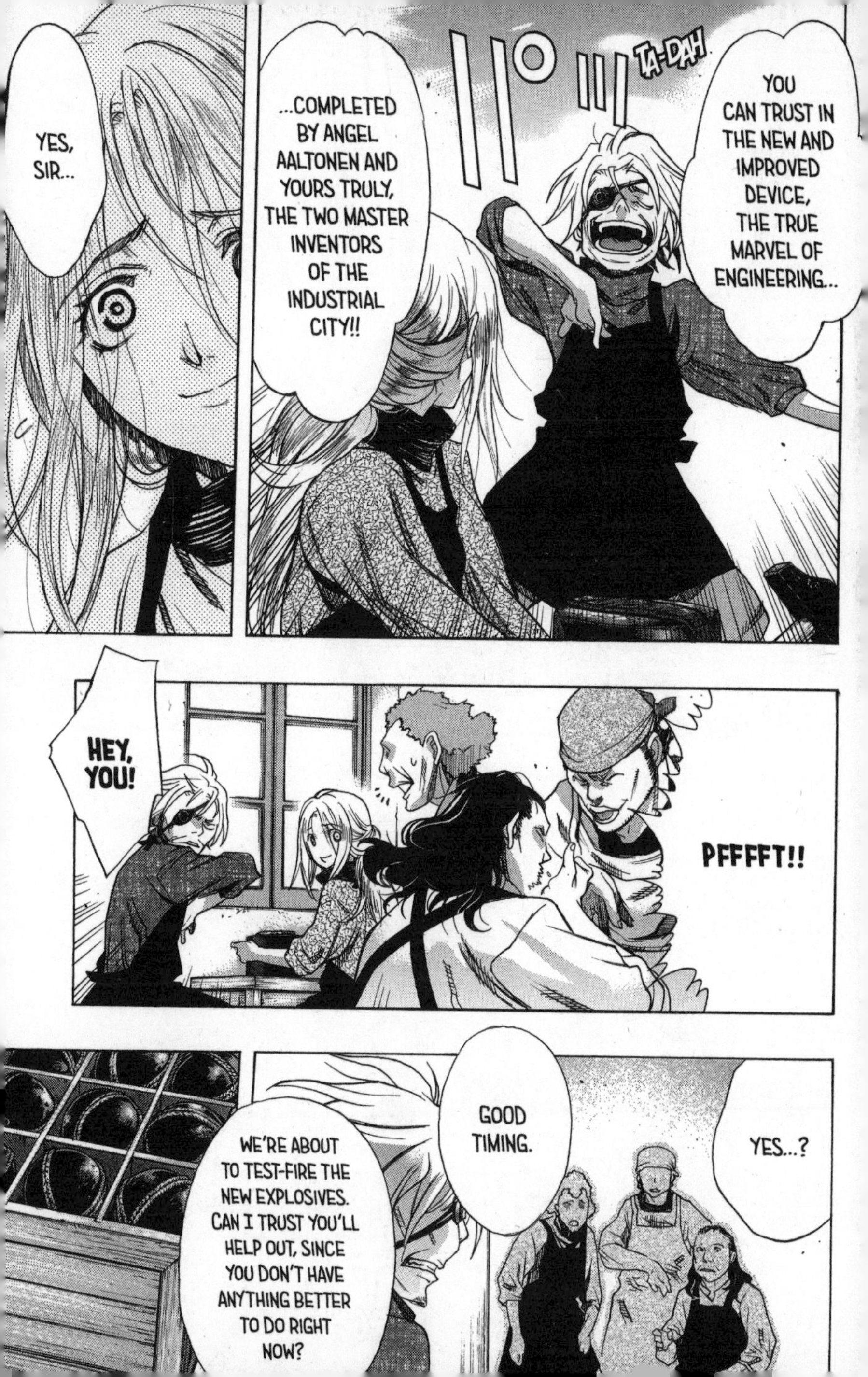
YOU CAN TRUST IN THE NEW AND IMPROVED DEVICE, THE TRUE MARVEL OF ENGINEERING...
TA-DAH
...COMPLETED BY ANGEL AALTONEN AND YOURS TRULY, THE TWO MASTER INVENTORS OF THE INDUSTRIAL CITY!!
YES, SIR...
PFFFFT!!
HEY, YOU!
YES...?
GOOD TIMING.
WE'RE ABOUT TO TEST-FIRE THE NEW EXPLOSIVES. CAN I TRUST YOU'LL HELP OUT, SINCE YOU DON'T HAVE ANYTHING BETTER TO DO RIGHT NOW?

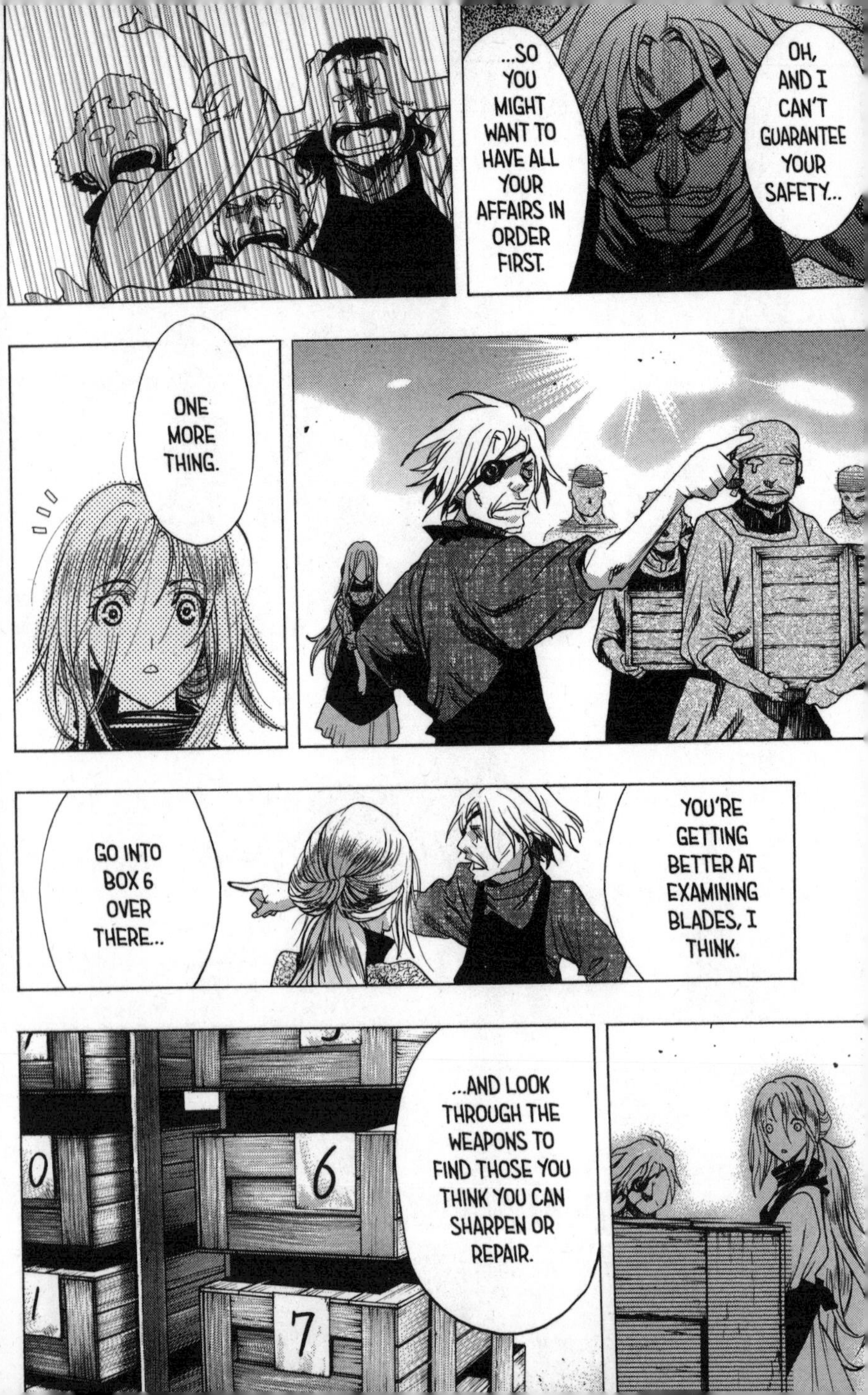
OH, AND I CAN'T GUARANTEE YOUR SAFETY...
...SO YOU MIGHT WANT TO HAVE ALL YOUR AFFAIRS IN ORDER FIRST.
ONE MORE THING.
YOU'RE GETTING BETTER AT EXAMINING BLADES, I THINK.
GO INTO BOX 6 OVER THERE...
...AND LOOK THROUGH THE WEAPONS TO FIND THOSE YOU THINK YOU CAN SHARPEN OR REPAIR.

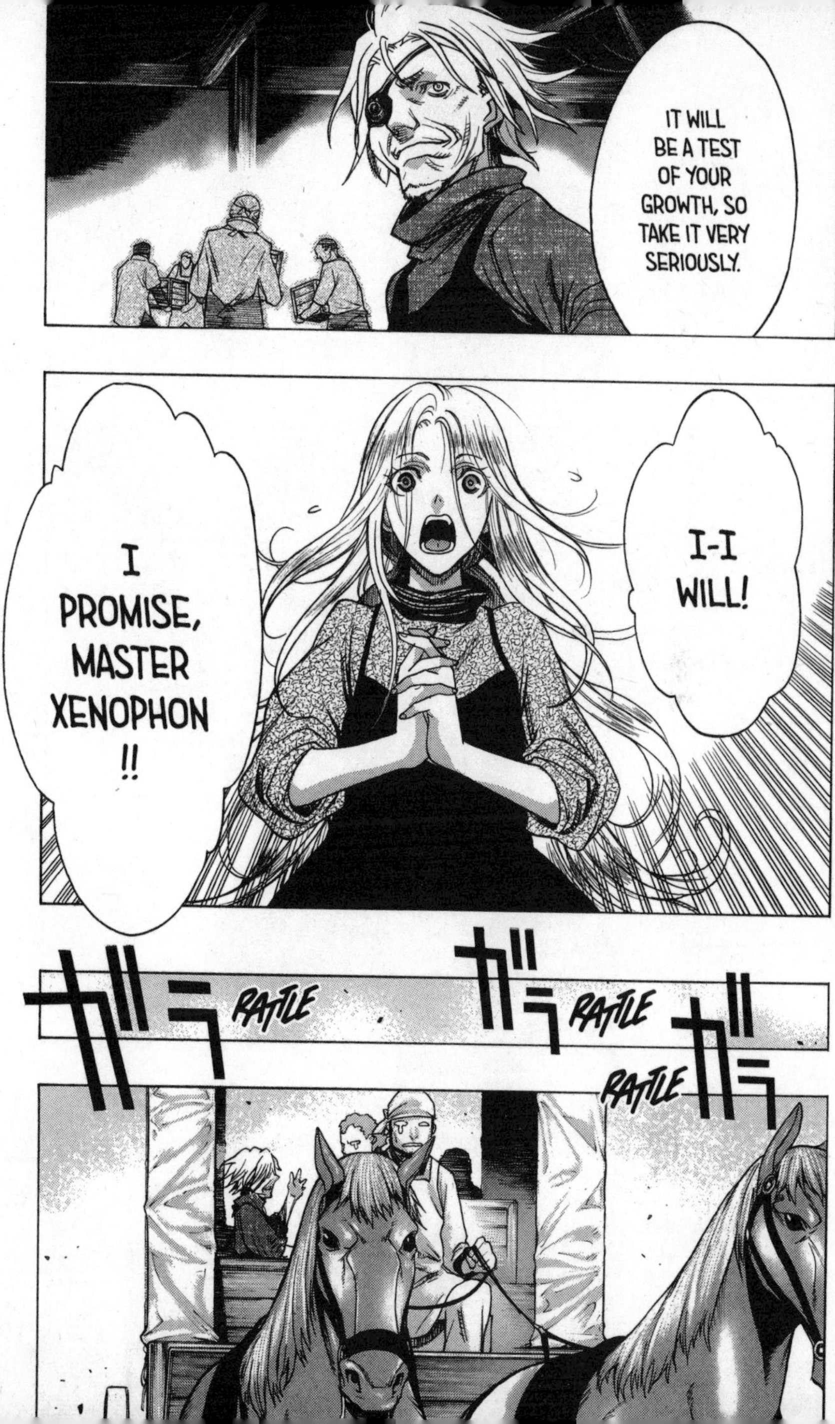
IT WILL BE A TEST OF YOUR GROWTH, SO TAKE IT VERY SERIOUSLY.
I-I WILL!
I PROMISE, MASTER XENOPHON !!
ガラ
RATTLE
ガラ
RATTLE
ガラ
RATTLE

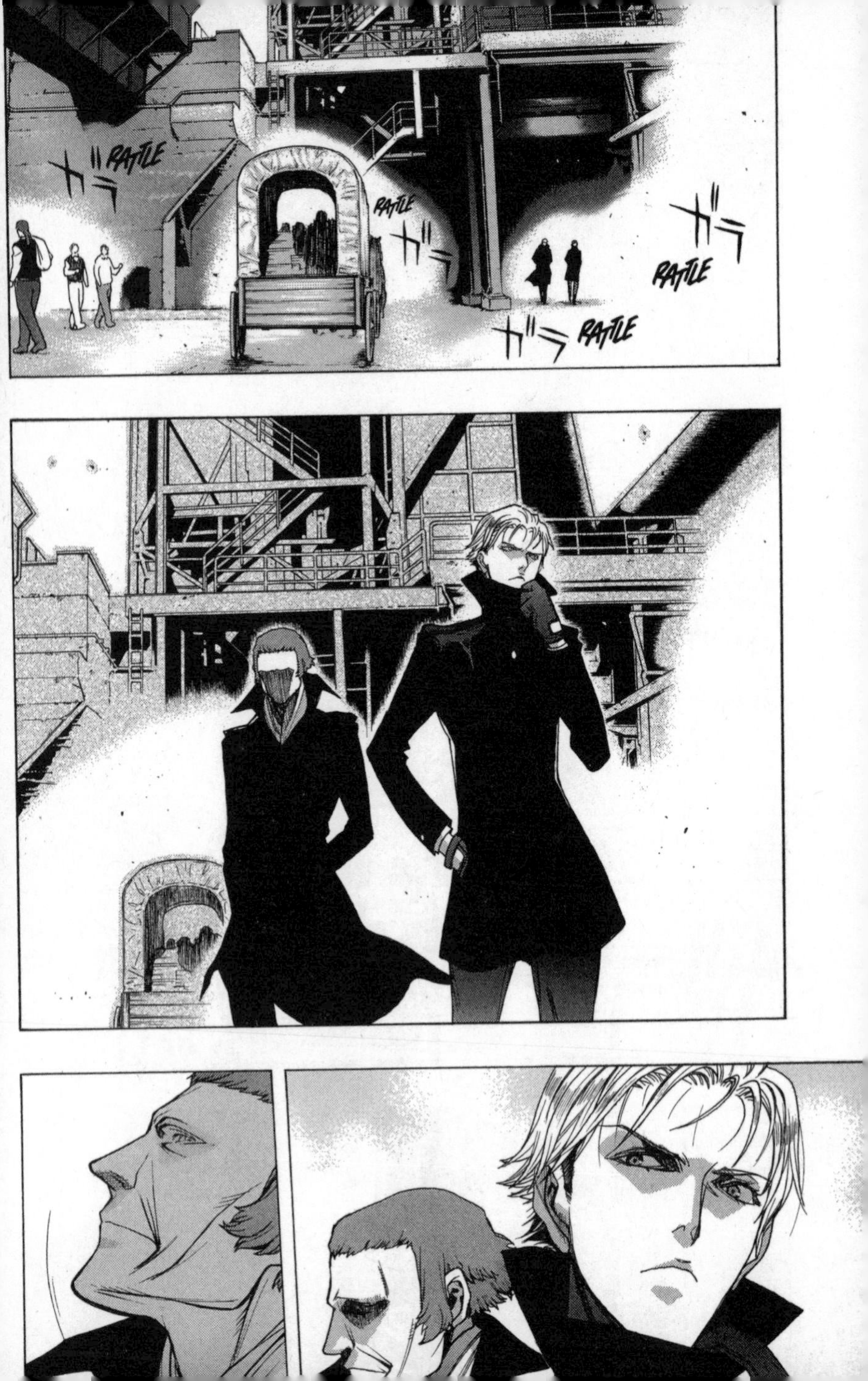
ガラ RATTLE
ガラ RATTLE
ガラ RATTLE
ガラ RATTLE

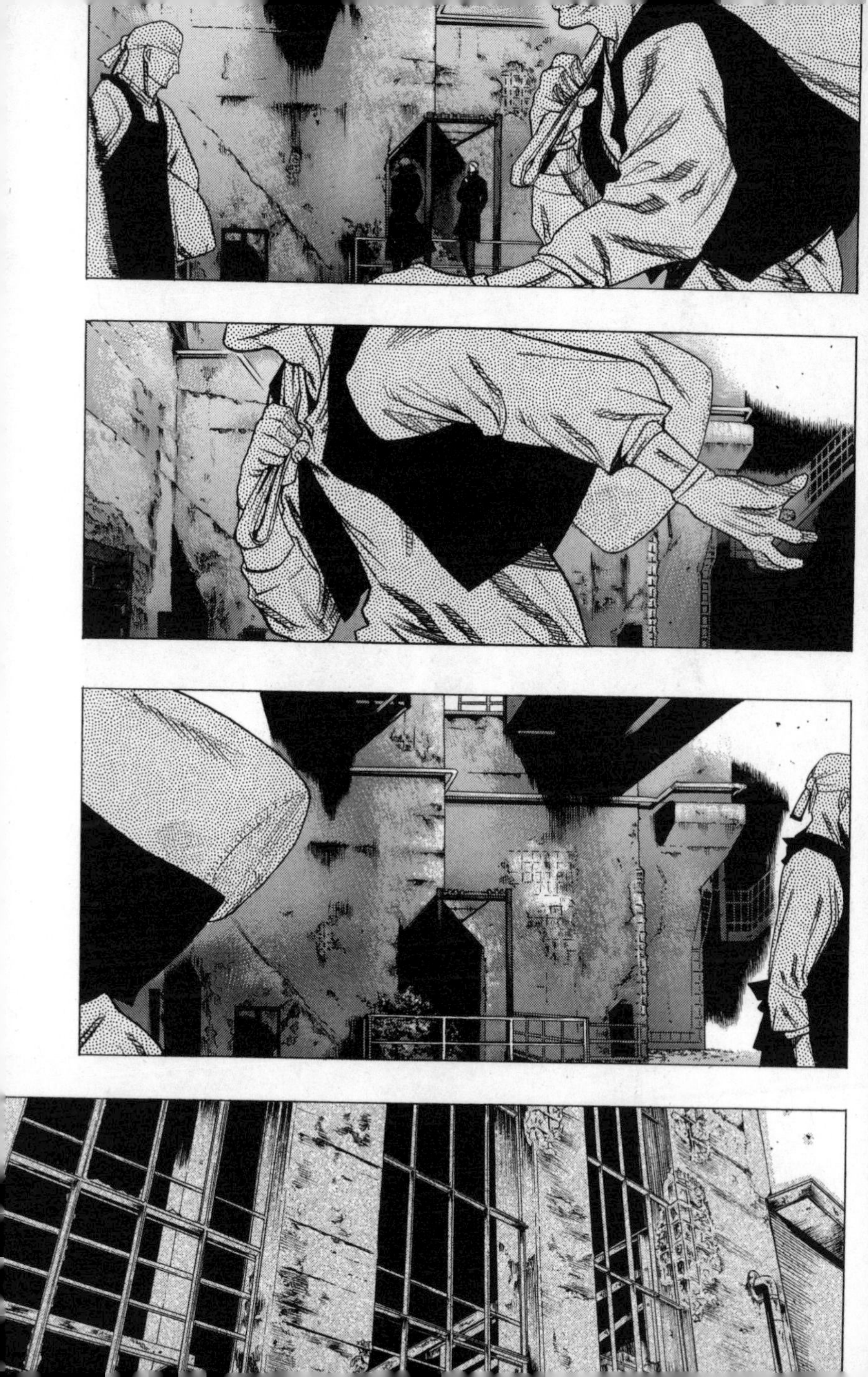

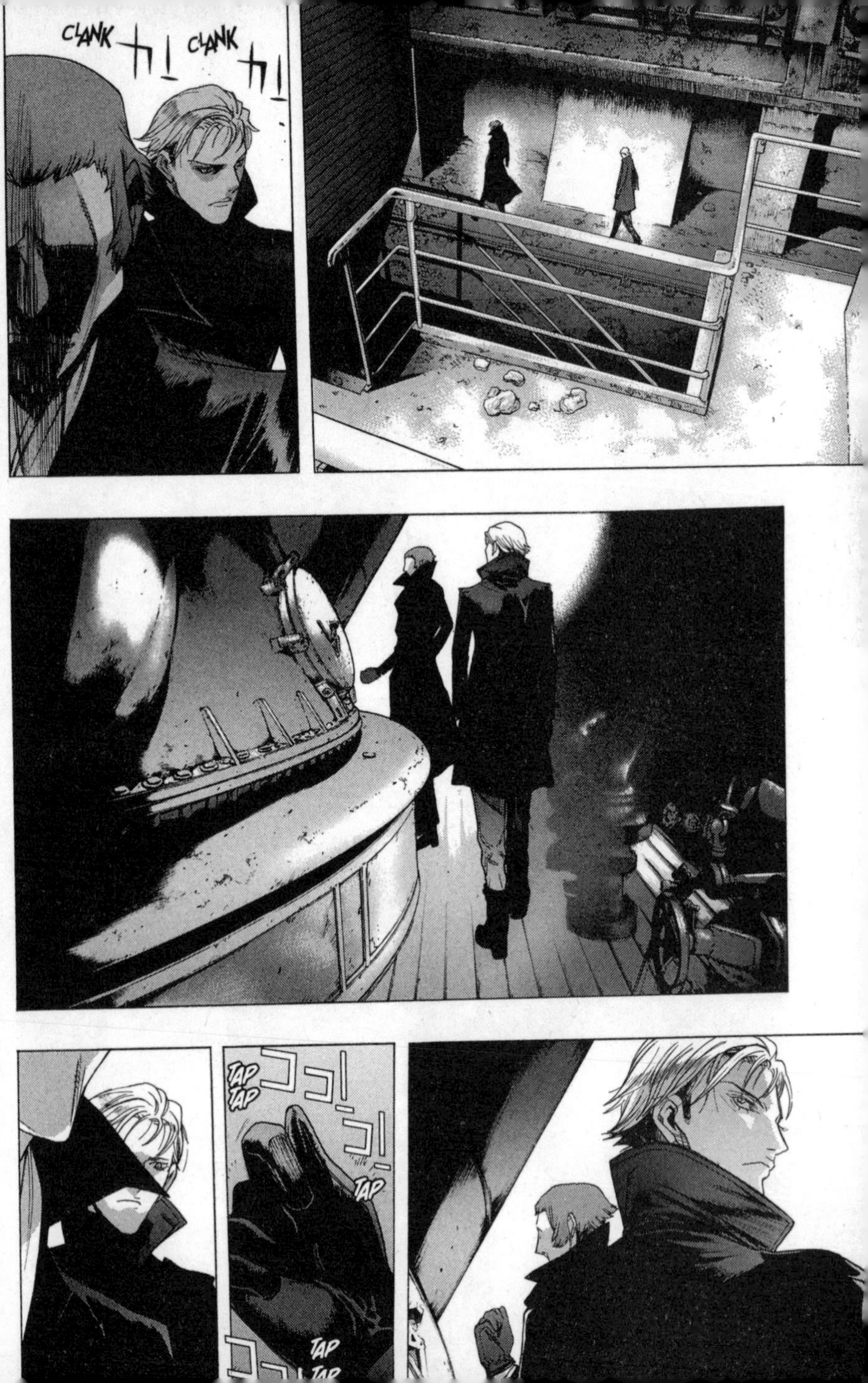
CLANK
CLANK
TAP TAP
TAP
TAP TAP

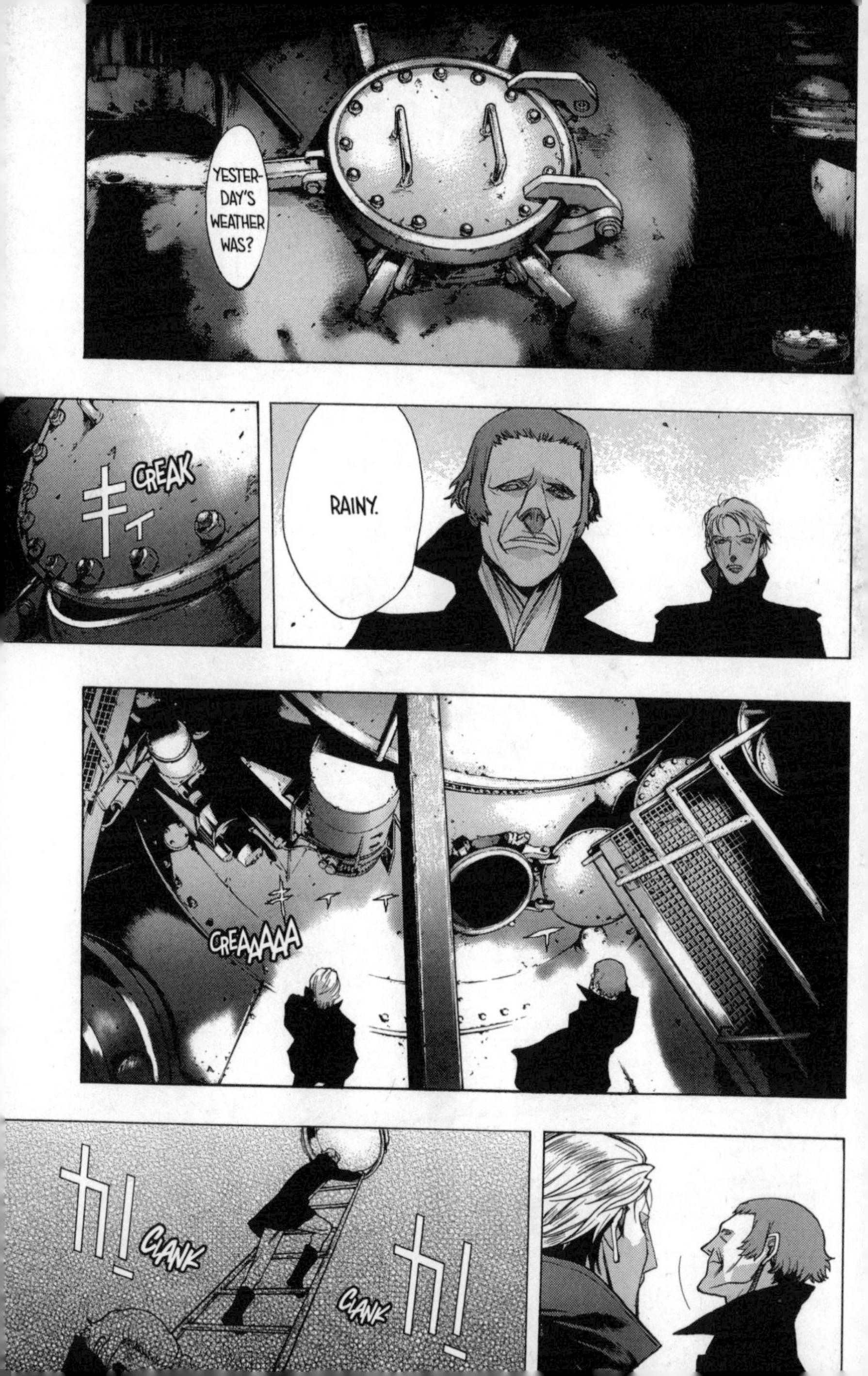
YESTER-DAY'S WEATHER WAS?
RAINY.
キイ
CREAK
CREAAAAA
カ!
CLANK
カ!
CLANK

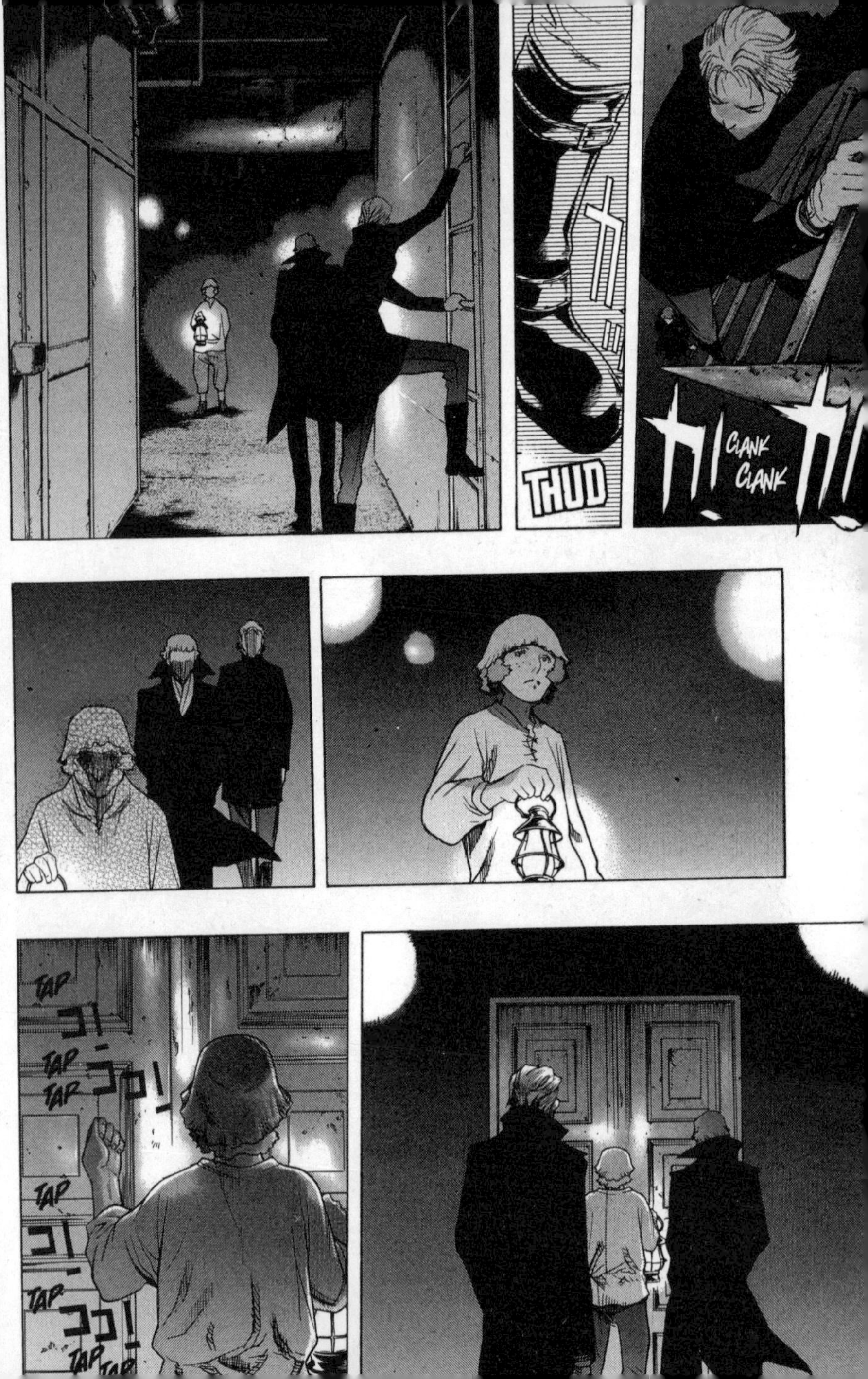
CLANK CLANK
THUD
TAP
TAP TAP
TAP
TAP
TAP TAP

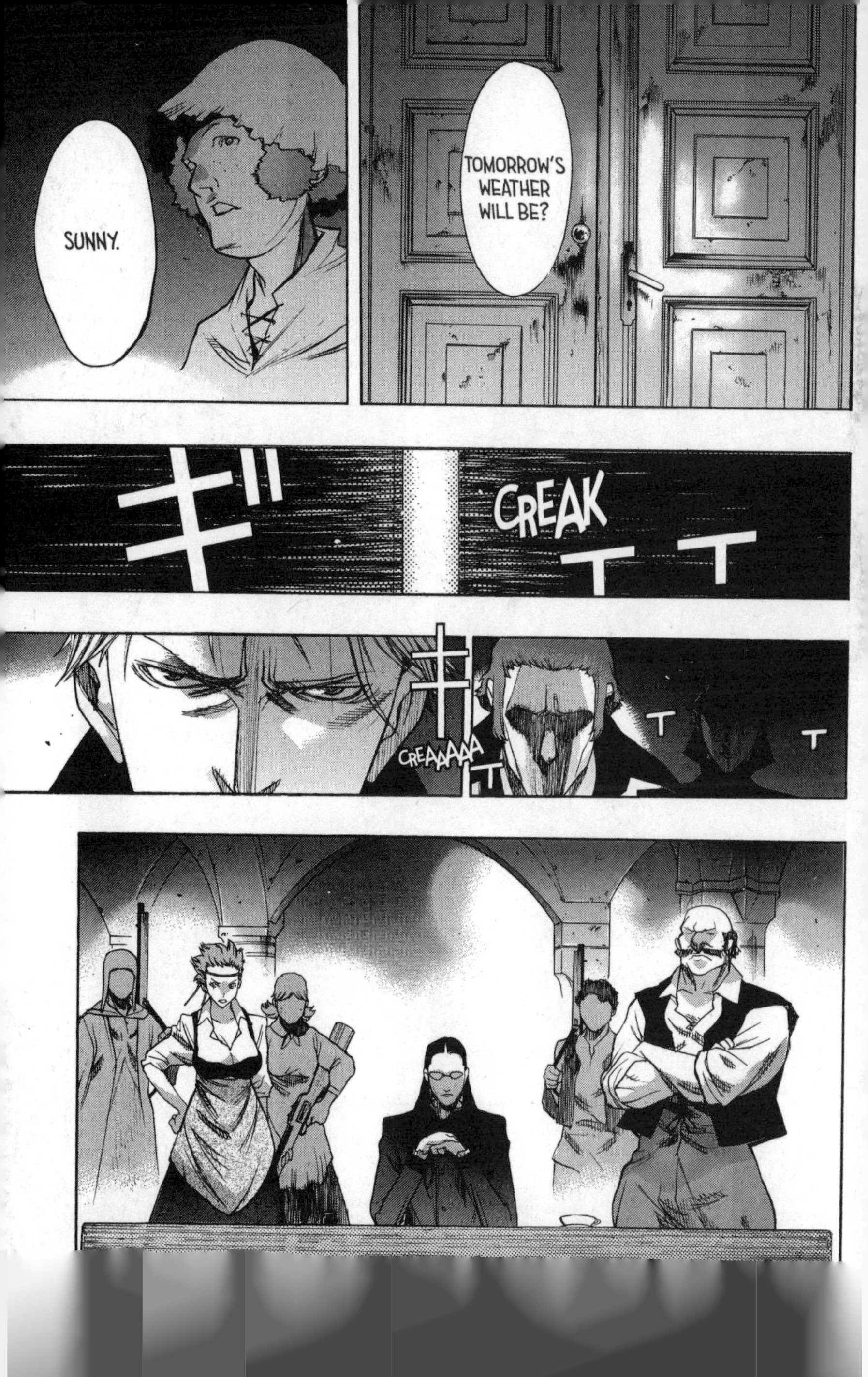
TOMORROW'S WEATHER WILL BE?
SUNNY.
CREAK
ギ
T T
ギ
T T
CREAAAAA
T

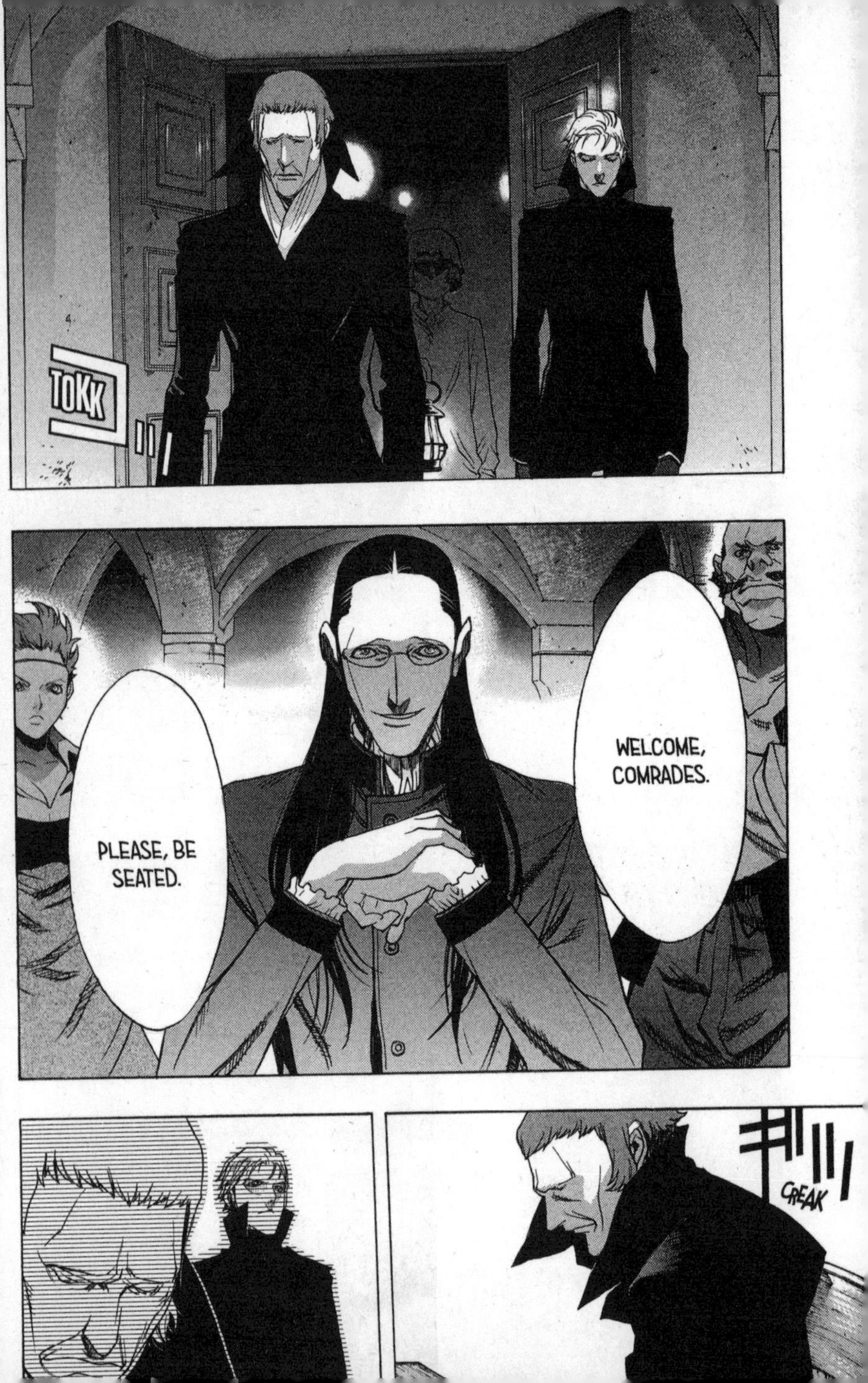
TOKK
WELCOME, COMRADES.
PLEASE, BE SEATED.
CREAK

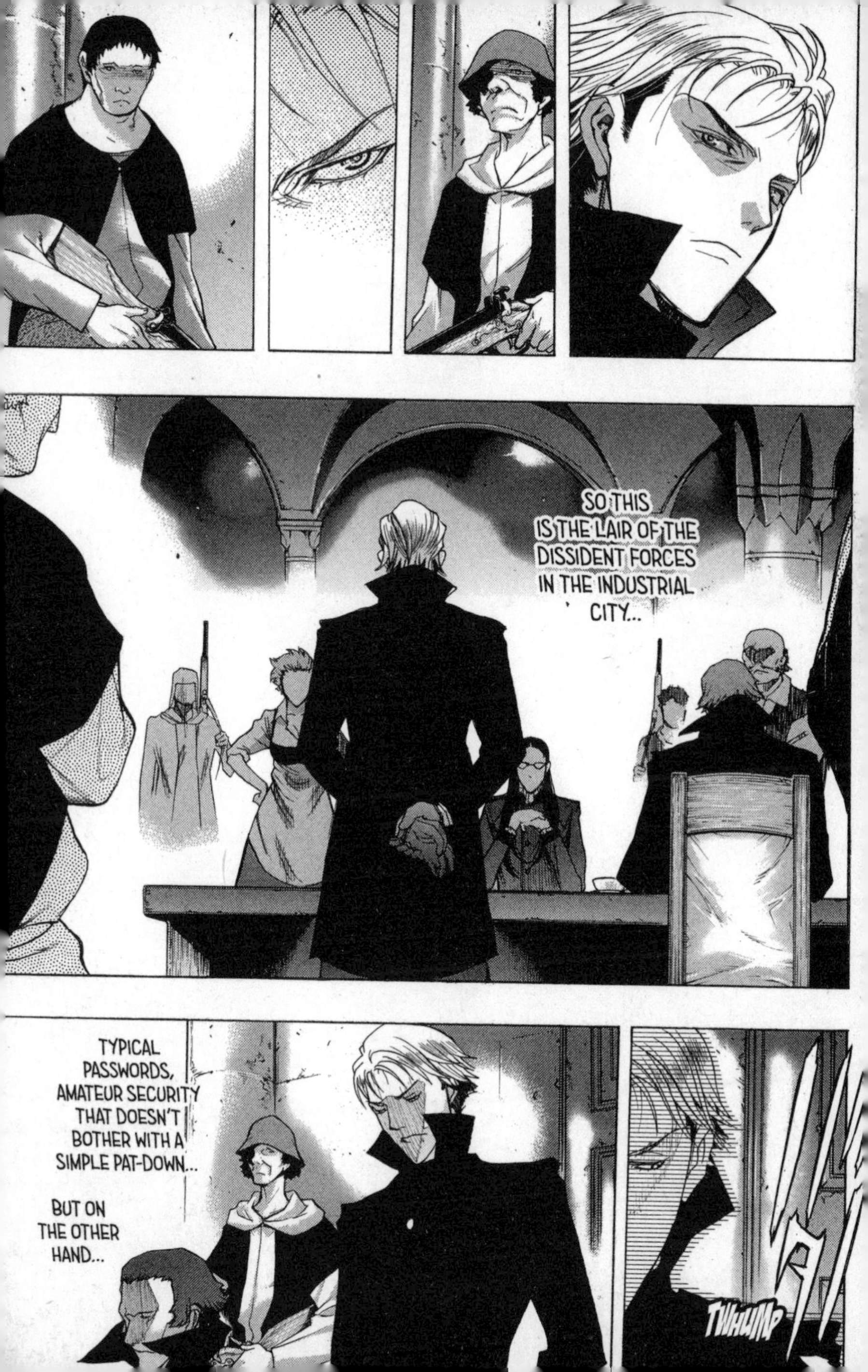
SO THIS IS THE LAIR OF THE DISSIDENT FORCES IN THE INDUSTRIAL CITY...
TWHUMP
TYPICAL PASSWORDS, AMATEUR SECURITY THAT DOESN'T BOTHER WITH A SIMPLE PAT-DOWN...
BUT ON THE OTHER HAND...

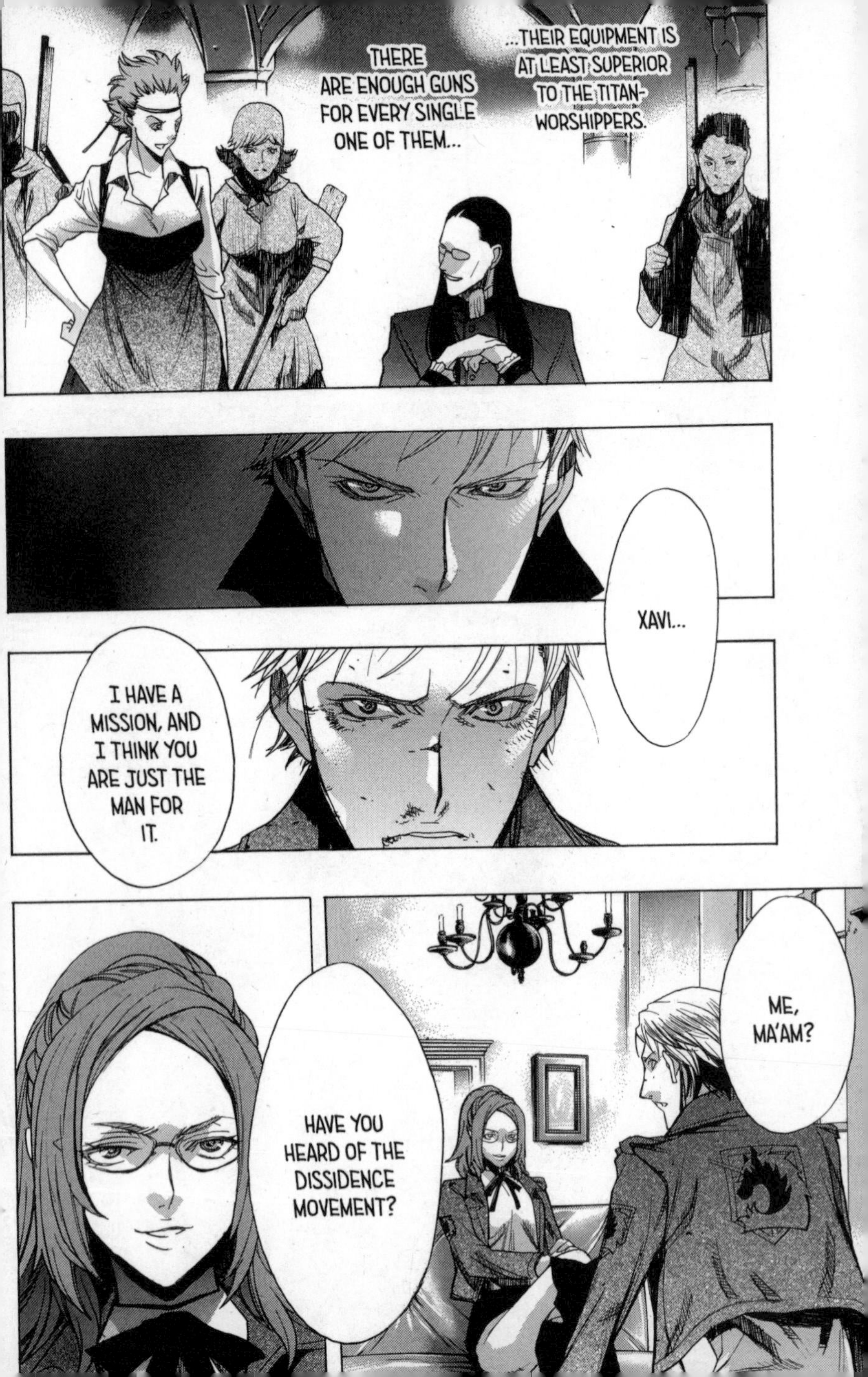
...THEIR EQUIPMENT IS AT LEAST SUPERIOR TO THE TITAN-WORSHIPPERS.
THERE ARE ENOUGH GUNS FOR EVERY SINGLE ONE OF THEM...
XAVI...
I HAVE A MISSION, AND I THINK YOU ARE JUST THE MAN FOR IT.
ME, MA'AM?
HAVE YOU HEARD OF THE DISSIDENCE MOVEMENT?

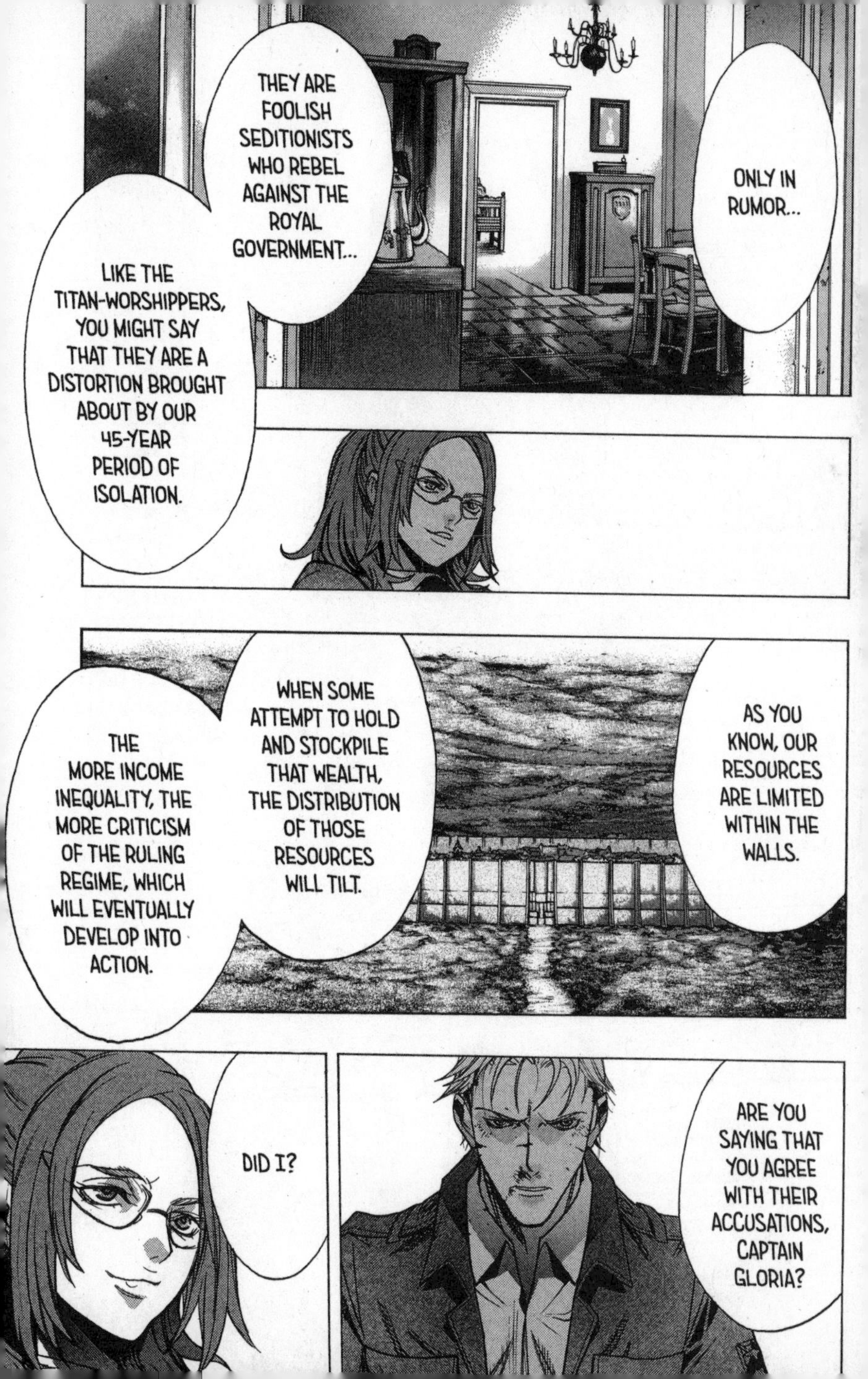
ONLY IN RUMOR...
THEY ARE FOOLISH SEDITIONISTS WHO REBEL AGAINST THE ROYAL GOVERNMENT...
LIKE THE TITAN-WORSHIPPERS, YOU MIGHT SAY THAT THEY ARE A DISTORTION BROUGHT ABOUT BY OUR 45-YEAR PERIOD OF ISOLATION.
AS YOU KNOW, OUR RESOURCES ARE LIMITED WITHIN THE WALLS.
WHEN SOME ATTEMPT TO HOLD AND STOCKPILE THAT WEALTH, THE DISTRIBUTION OF THOSE RESOURCES WILL TILT.
THE MORE INCOME INEQUALITY, THE MORE CRITICISM OF THE RULING REGIME, WHICH WILL EVENTUALLY DEVELOP INTO ACTION.
ARE YOU SAYING THAT YOU AGREE WITH THEIR ACCUSATIONS, CAPTAIN GLORIA?
DID I?

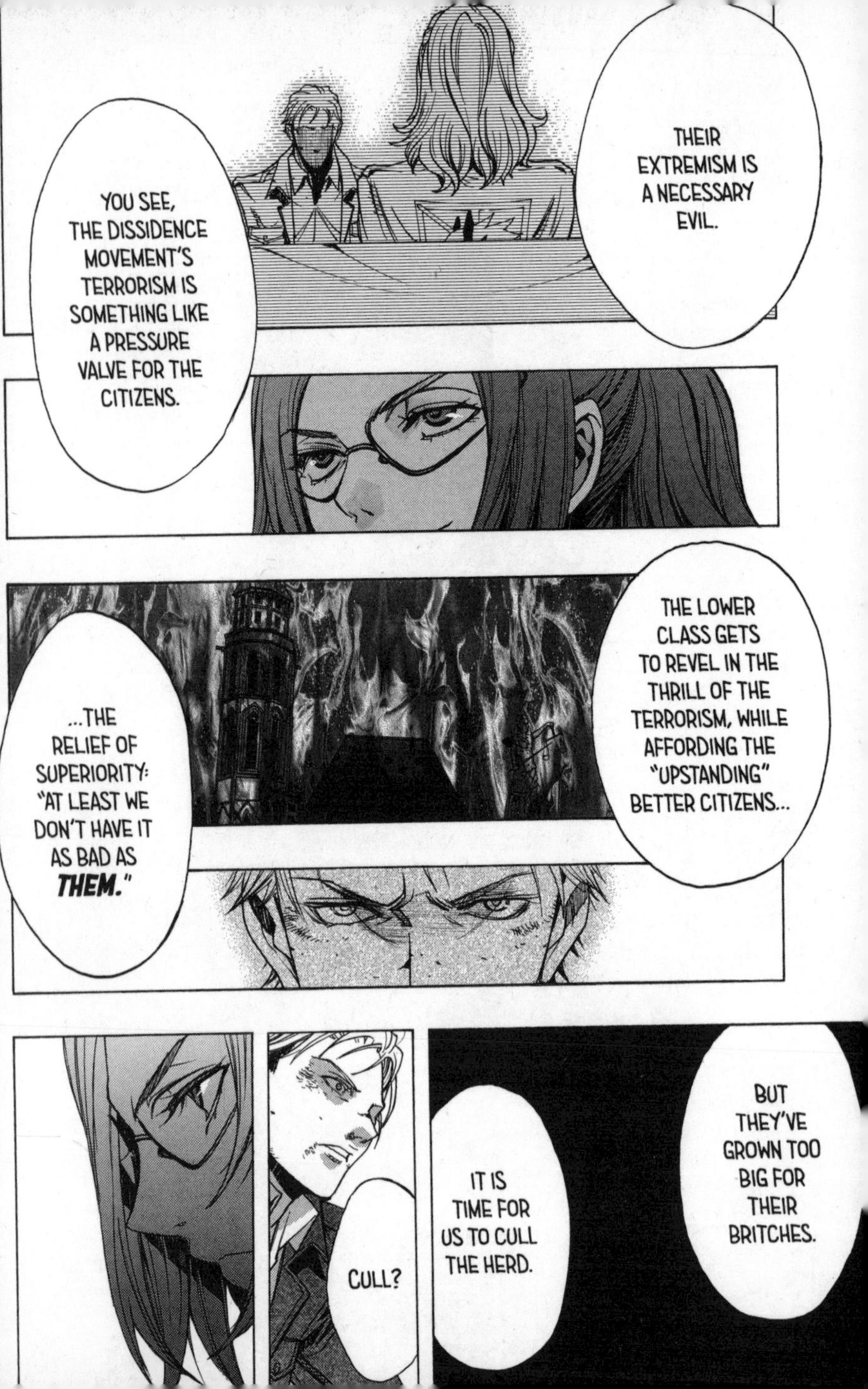
THEIR EXTREMISM IS A NECESSARY EVIL.
YOU SEE, THE DISSIDENCE MOVEMENT'S TERRORISM IS SOMETHING LIKE A PRESSURE VALVE FOR THE CITIZENS.
THE LOWER CLASS GETS TO REVEL IN THE THRILL OF THE TERRORISM, WHILE AFFORDING THE "UPSTANDING" BETTER CITIZENS...
...THE RELIEF OF SUPERIORITY: "AT LEAST WE DON'T HAVE IT AS BAD AS ***THEM.***"
BUT THEY'VE GROWN TOO BIG FOR THEIR BRITCHES.
IT IS TIME FOR US TO CULL THE HERD.
CULL?

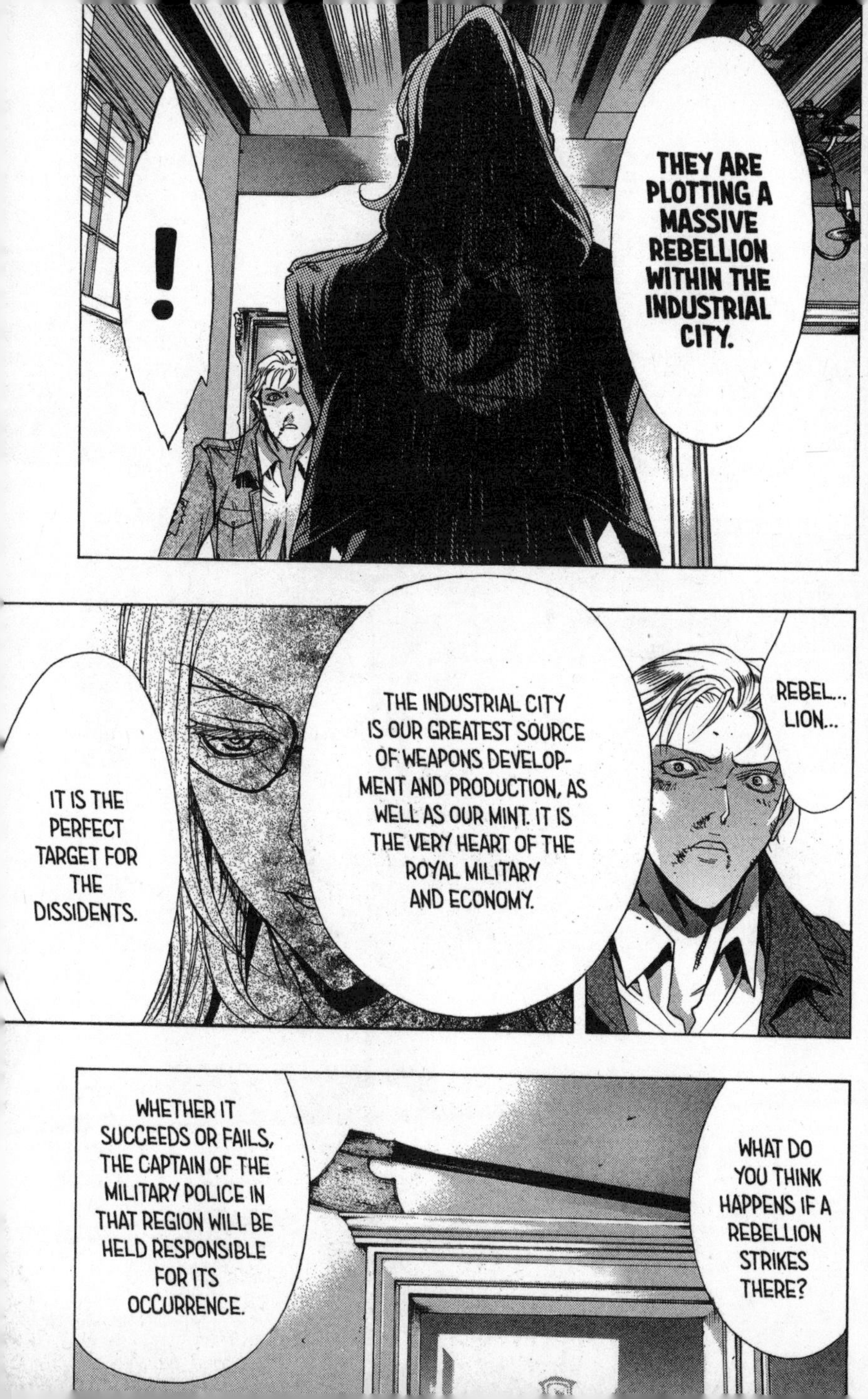
THEY ARE PLOTTING A MASSIVE REBELLION WITHIN THE INDUSTRIAL CITY.
!
REBEL... LION...
THE INDUSTRIAL CITY IS OUR GREATEST SOURCE OF WEAPONS DEVELOP-MENT AND PRODUCTION, AS WELL AS OUR MINT. IT IS THE VERY HEART OF THE ROYAL MILITARY AND ECONOMY.
IT IS THE PERFECT TARGET FOR THE DISSIDENTS.
WHAT DO YOU THINK HAPPENS IF A REBELLION STRIKES THERE?
WHETHER IT SUCCEEDS OR FAILS, THE CAPTAIN OF THE MILITARY POLICE IN THAT REGION WILL BE HELD RESPONSIBLE FOR ITS OCCURRENCE.

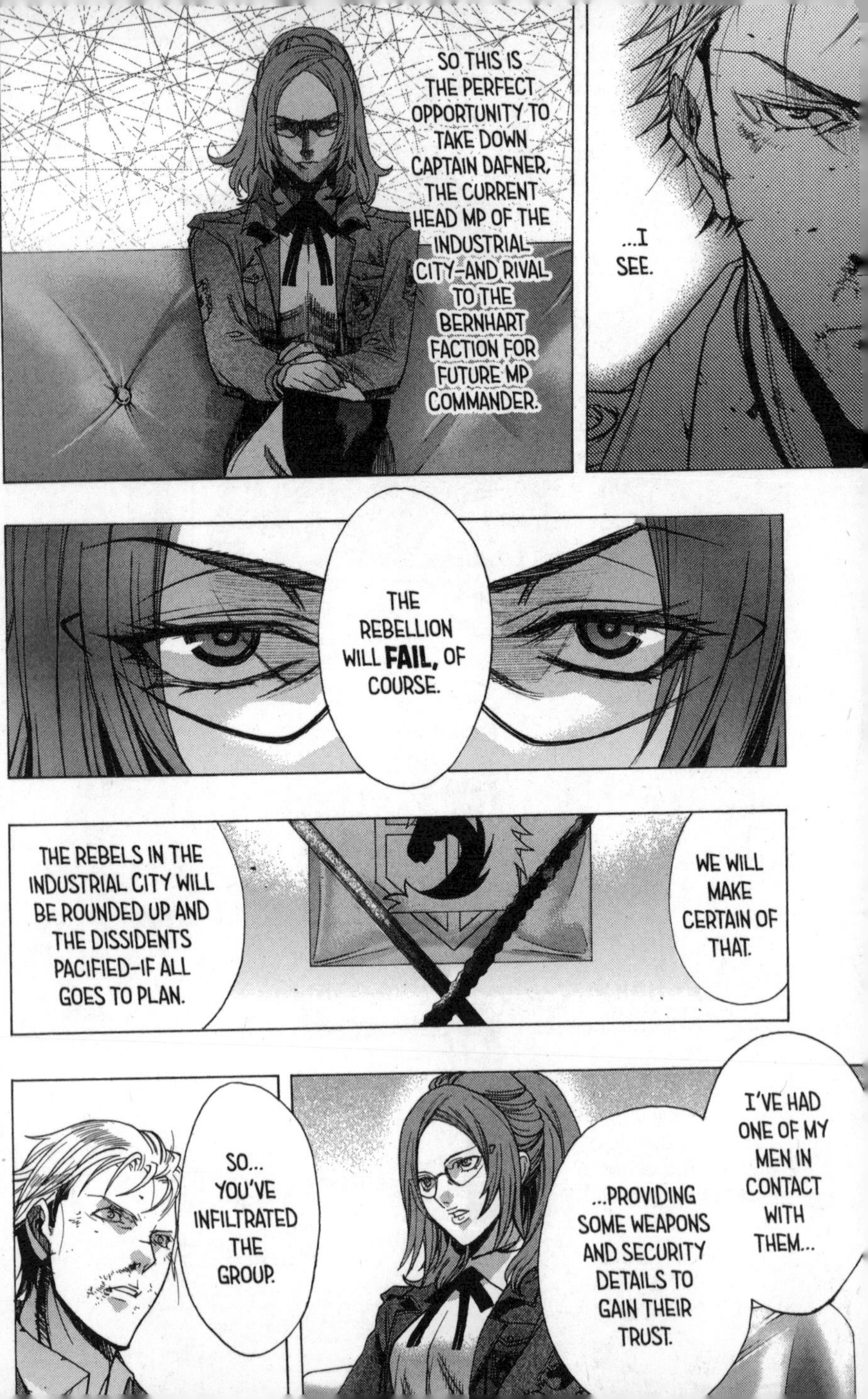
...I SEE.
SO THIS IS THE PERFECT OPPORTUNITY TO TAKE DOWN CAPTAIN DAFNER, THE CURRENT HEAD MP OF THE INDUSTRIAL CITY–AND RIVAL TO THE BERNHART FACTION FOR FUTURE MP COMMANDER.
THE REBELLION WILL **FAIL,** OF COURSE.
WE WILL MAKE CERTAIN OF THAT.
THE REBELS IN THE INDUSTRIAL CITY WILL BE ROUNDED UP AND THE DISSIDENTS PACIFIED–IF ALL GOES TO PLAN.
I'VE HAD ONE OF MY MEN IN CONTACT WITH THEM...
...PROVIDING SOME WEAPONS AND SECURITY DETAILS TO GAIN THEIR TRUST.
SO... YOU'VE INFILTRATED THE GROUP.

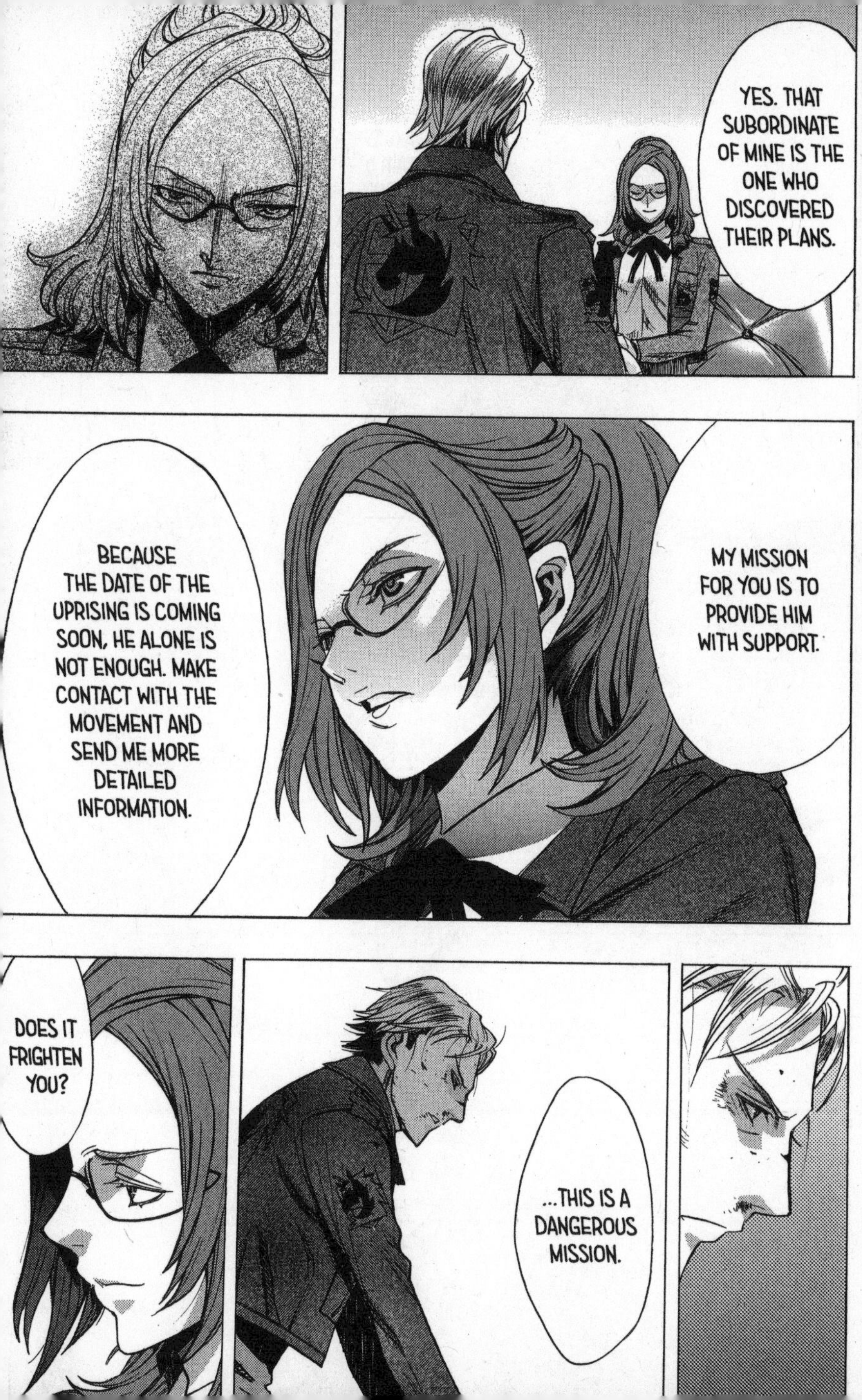
YES. THAT SUBORDINATE OF MINE IS THE ONE WHO DISCOVERED THEIR PLANS.
MY MISSION FOR YOU IS TO PROVIDE HIM WITH SUPPORT.
BECAUSE THE DATE OF THE UPRISING IS COMING SOON, HE ALONE IS NOT ENOUGH. MAKE CONTACT WITH THE MOVEMENT AND SEND ME MORE DETAILED INFORMATION.
...THIS IS A DANGEROUS MISSION.
DOES IT FRIGHTEN YOU?

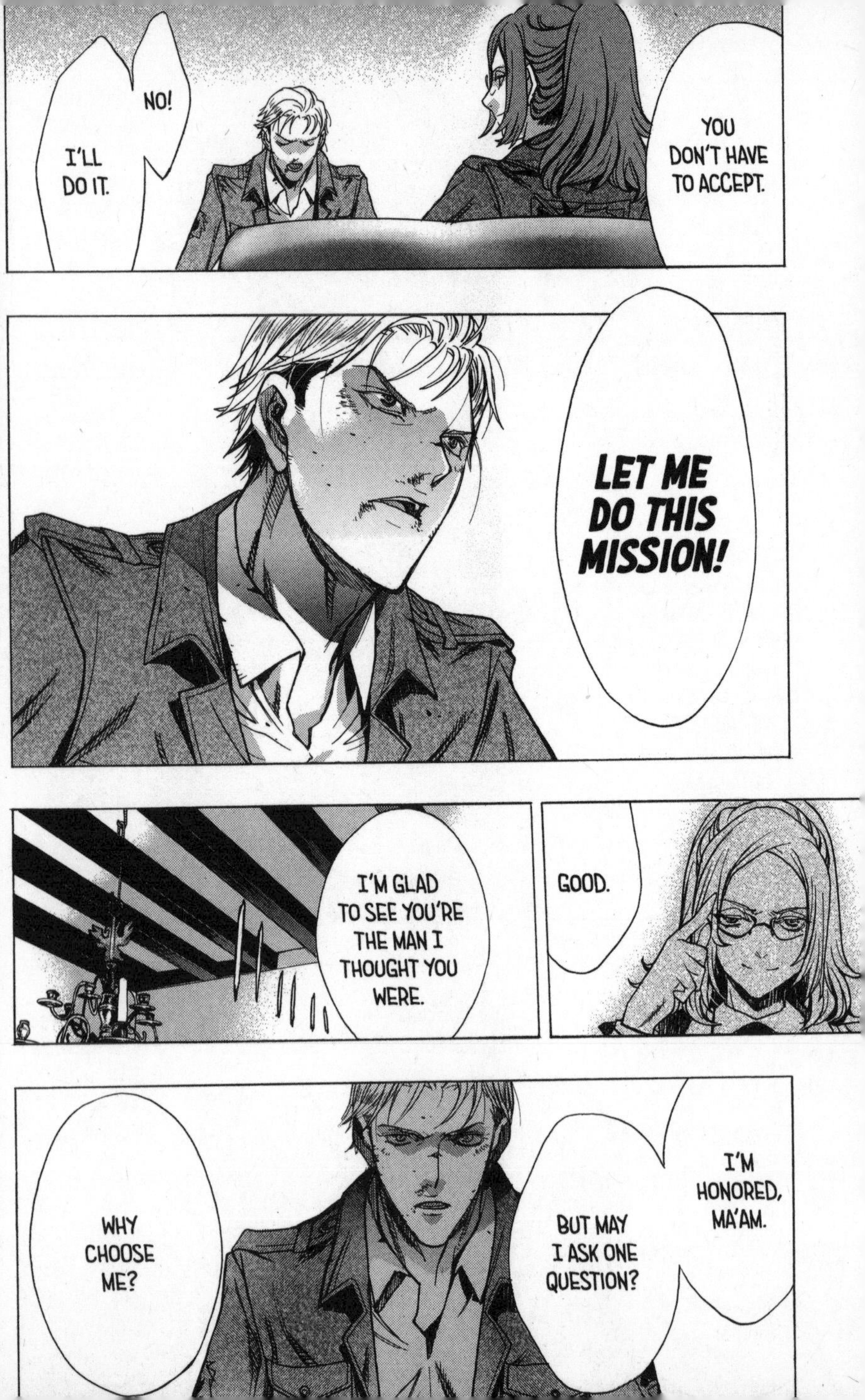
YOU DON'T HAVE TO ACCEPT.
NO!
I'LL DO IT.
LET ME DO THIS MISSION!
GOOD.
I'M GLAD TO SEE YOU'RE THE MAN I THOUGHT YOU WERE.
I'M HONORED, MA'AM.
BUT MAY I ASK ONE QUESTION?
WHY CHOOSE ME?

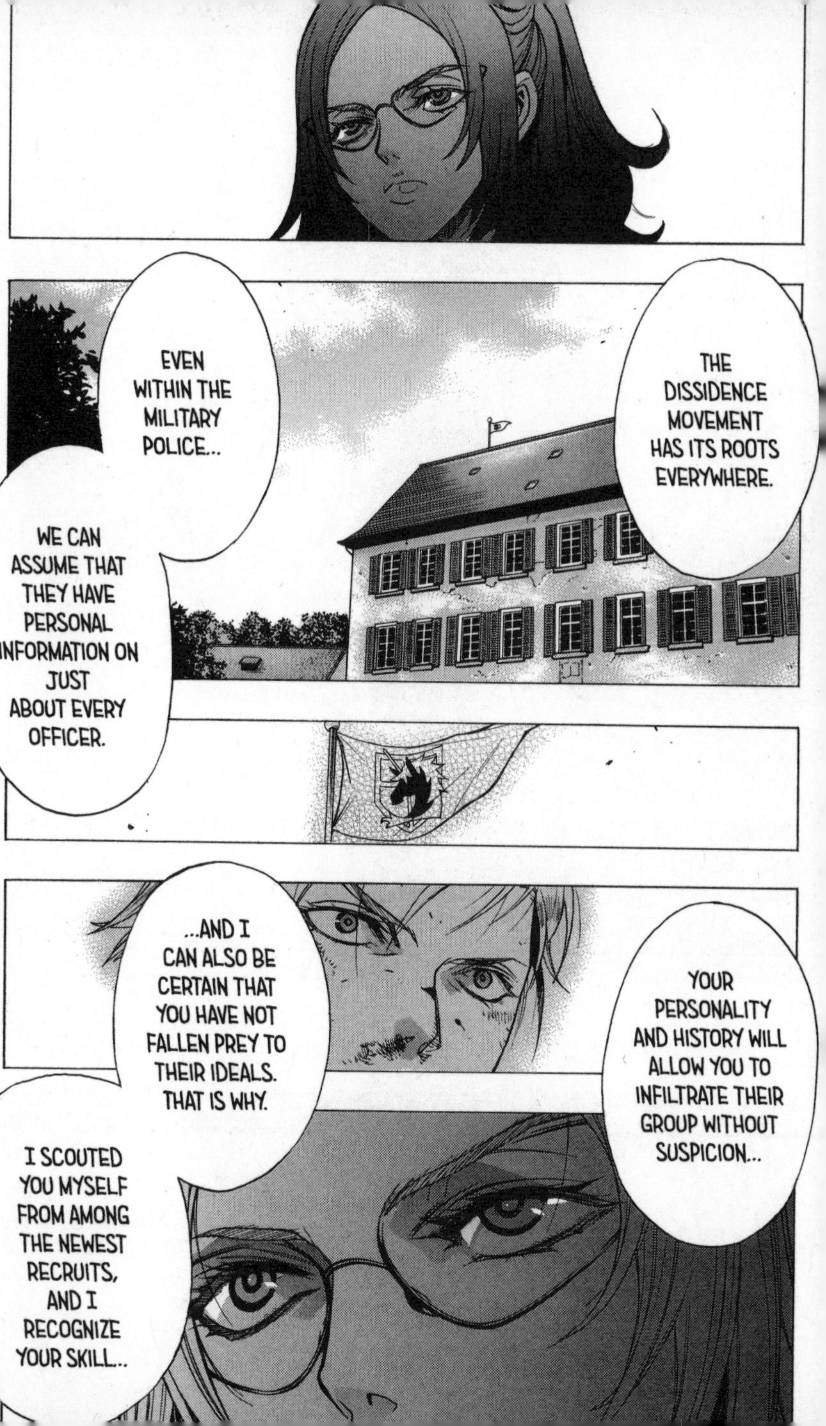
THE DISSIDENCE MOVEMENT HAS ITS ROOTS EVERYWHERE.
EVEN WITHIN THE MILITARY POLICE...
WE CAN ASSUME THAT THEY HAVE PERSONAL INFORMATION ON JUST ABOUT EVERY OFFICER.
YOUR PERSONALITY AND HISTORY WILL ALLOW YOU TO INFILTRATE THEIR GROUP WITHOUT SUSPICION...
...AND I CAN ALSO BE CERTAIN THAT YOU HAVE NOT FALLEN PREY TO THEIR IDEALS. THAT IS WHY.
I SCOUTED YOU MYSELF FROM AMONG THE NEWEST RECRUITS, AND I RECOGNIZE YOUR SKILL...

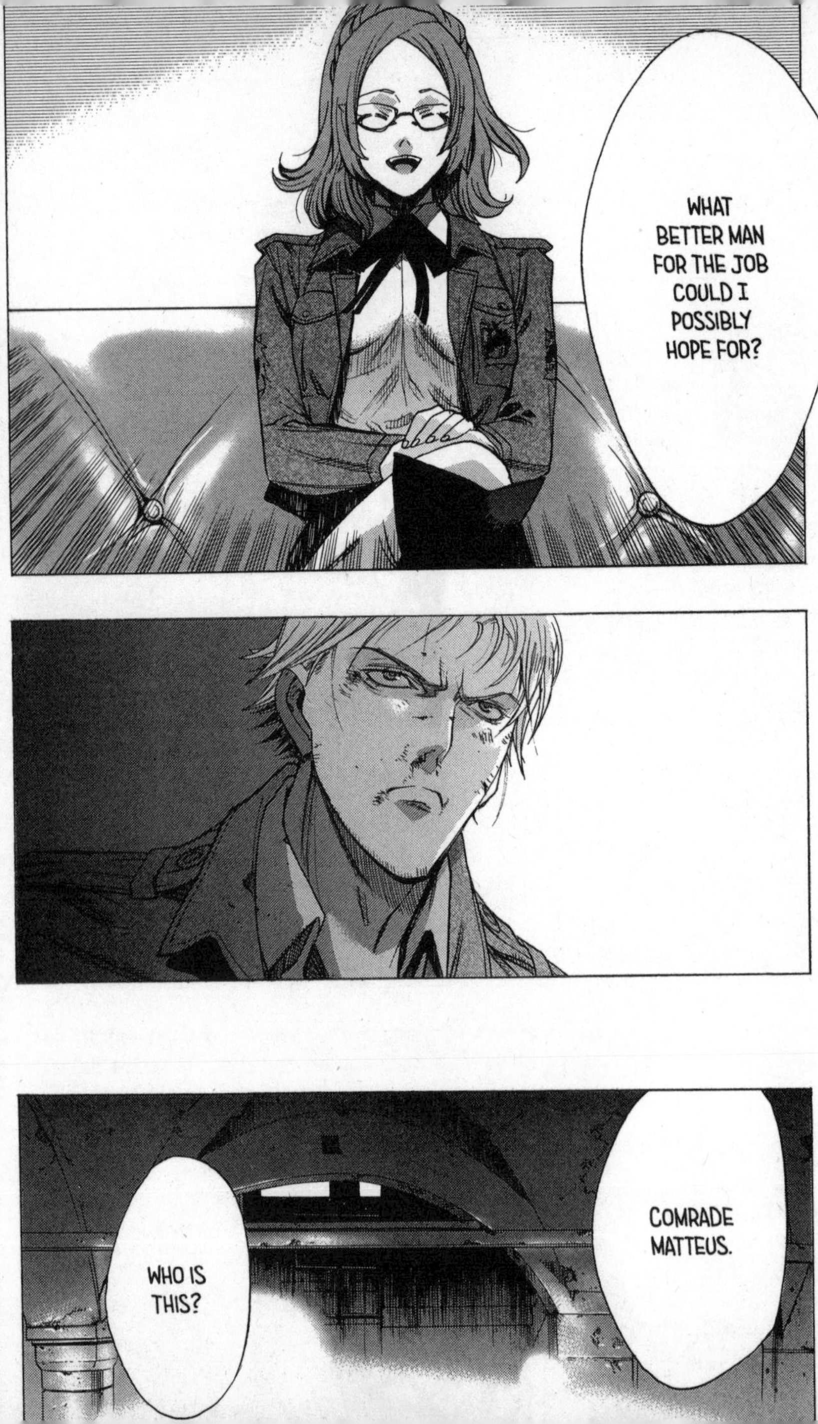
WHAT BETTER MAN FOR THE JOB COULD I POSSIBLY HOPE FOR?
COMRADE MATTEUS.
WHO IS THIS?

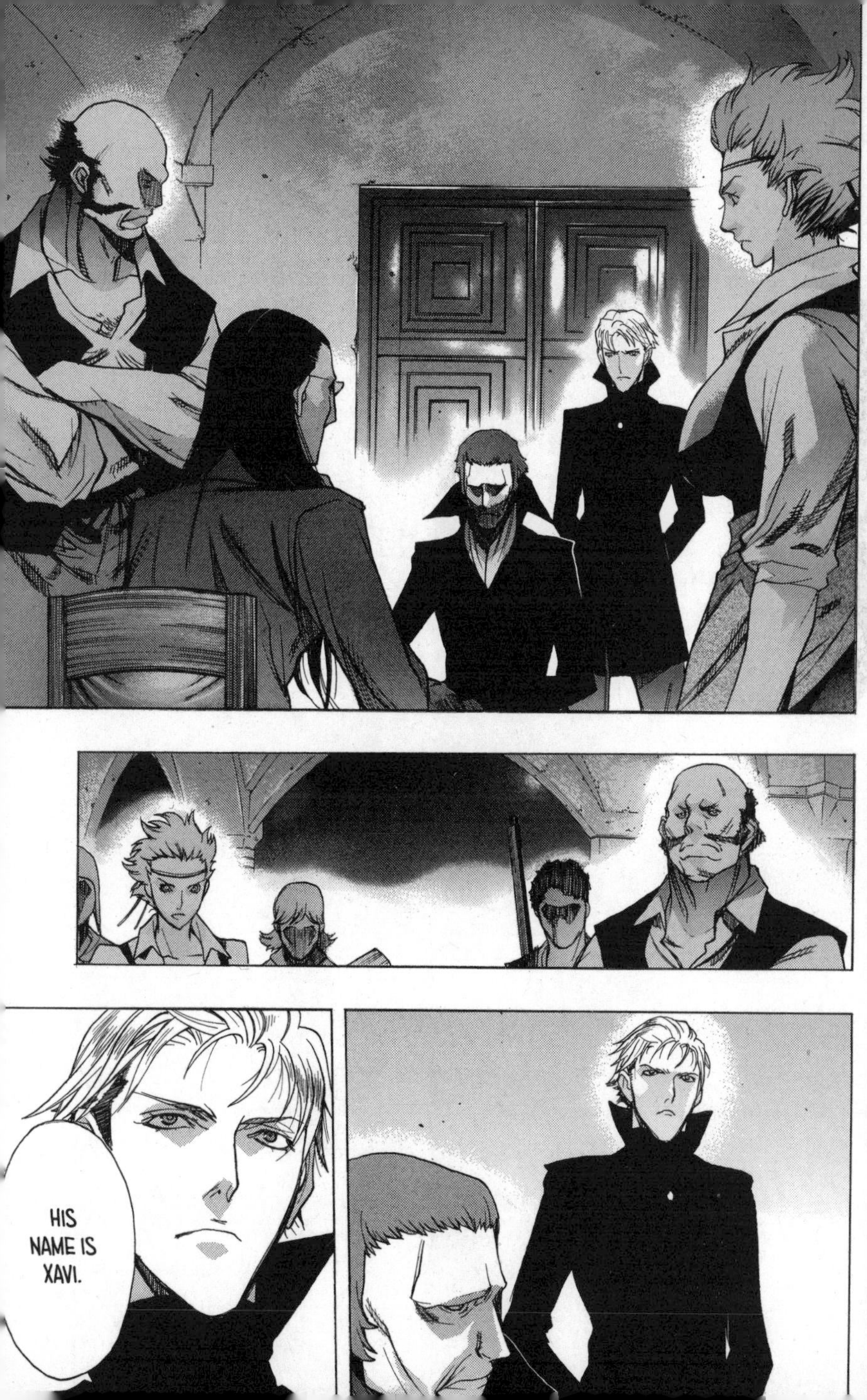
HIS NAME IS XAVI.

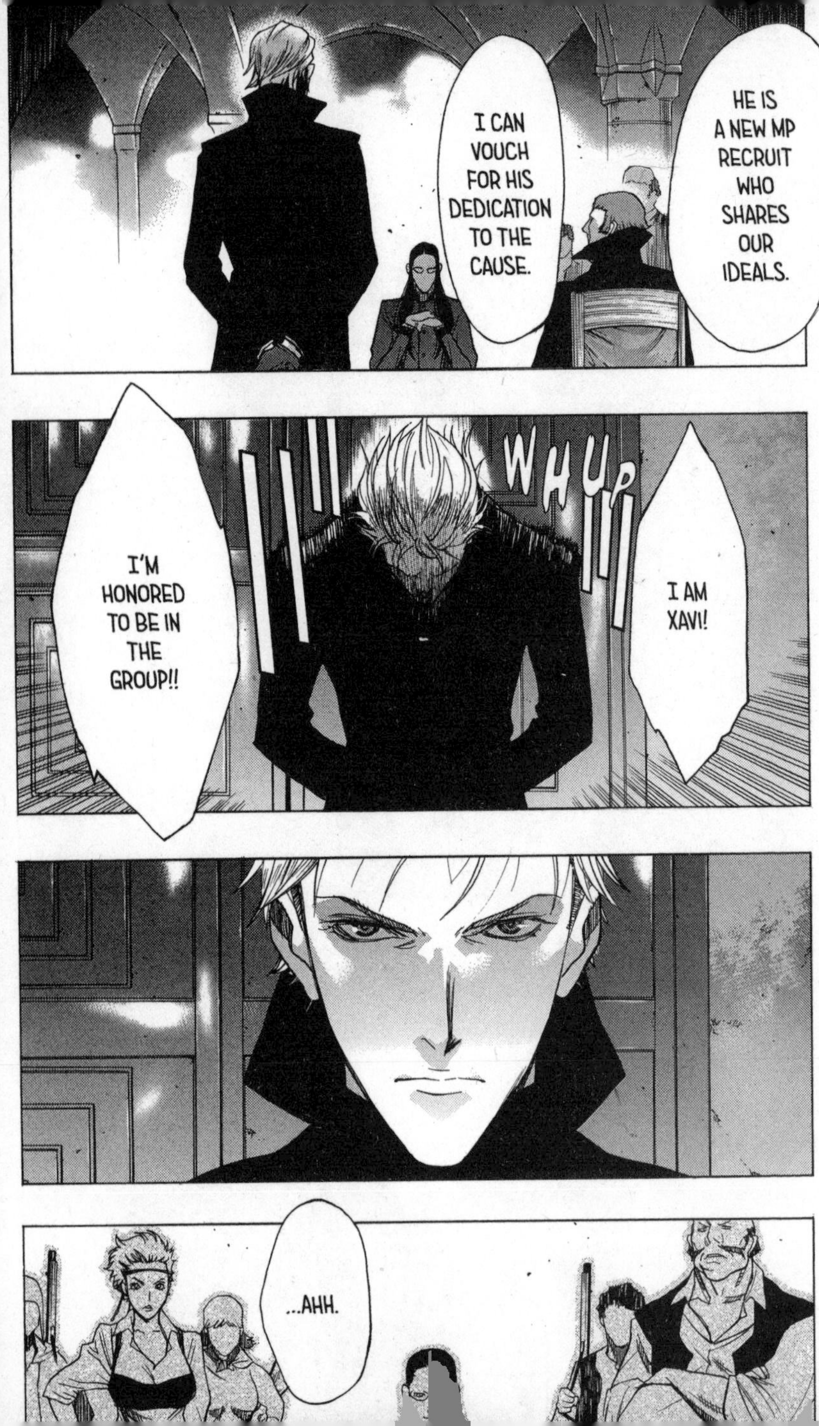
HE IS A NEW MP RECRUIT WHO SHARES OUR IDEALS.
I CAN VOUCH FOR HIS DEDICATION TO THE CAUSE.
I AM XAVI!
WHUP
I'M HONORED TO BE IN THE GROUP!!
...AHH.

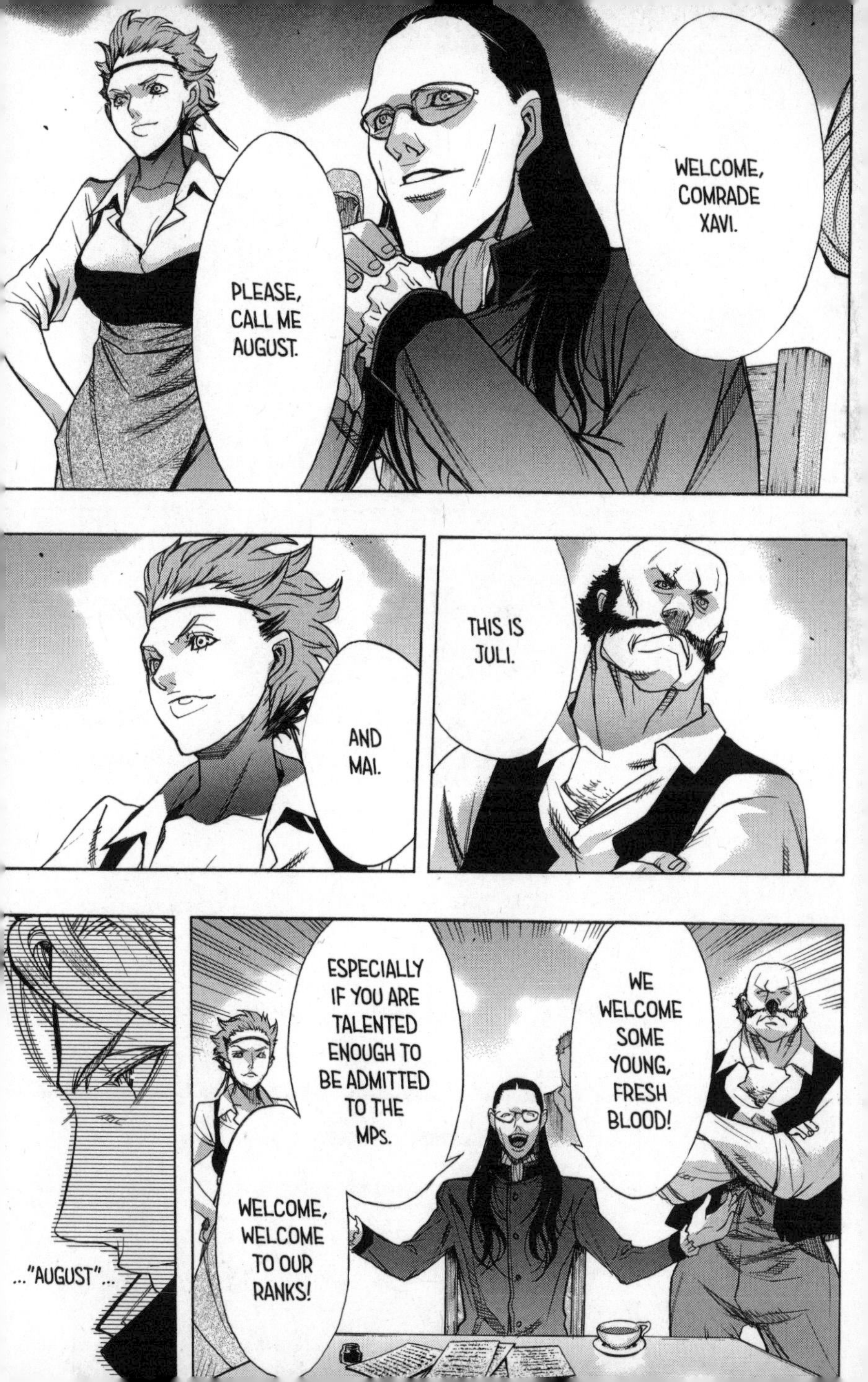
WELCOME, COMRADE XAVI.
PLEASE, CALL ME AUGUST.
THIS IS JULI.
AND MAI.
WE WELCOME SOME YOUNG, FRESH BLOOD!
ESPECIALLY IF YOU ARE TALENTED ENOUGH TO BE ADMITTED TO THE MPs.
WELCOME, WELCOME TO OUR RANKS!
..."AUGUST"...

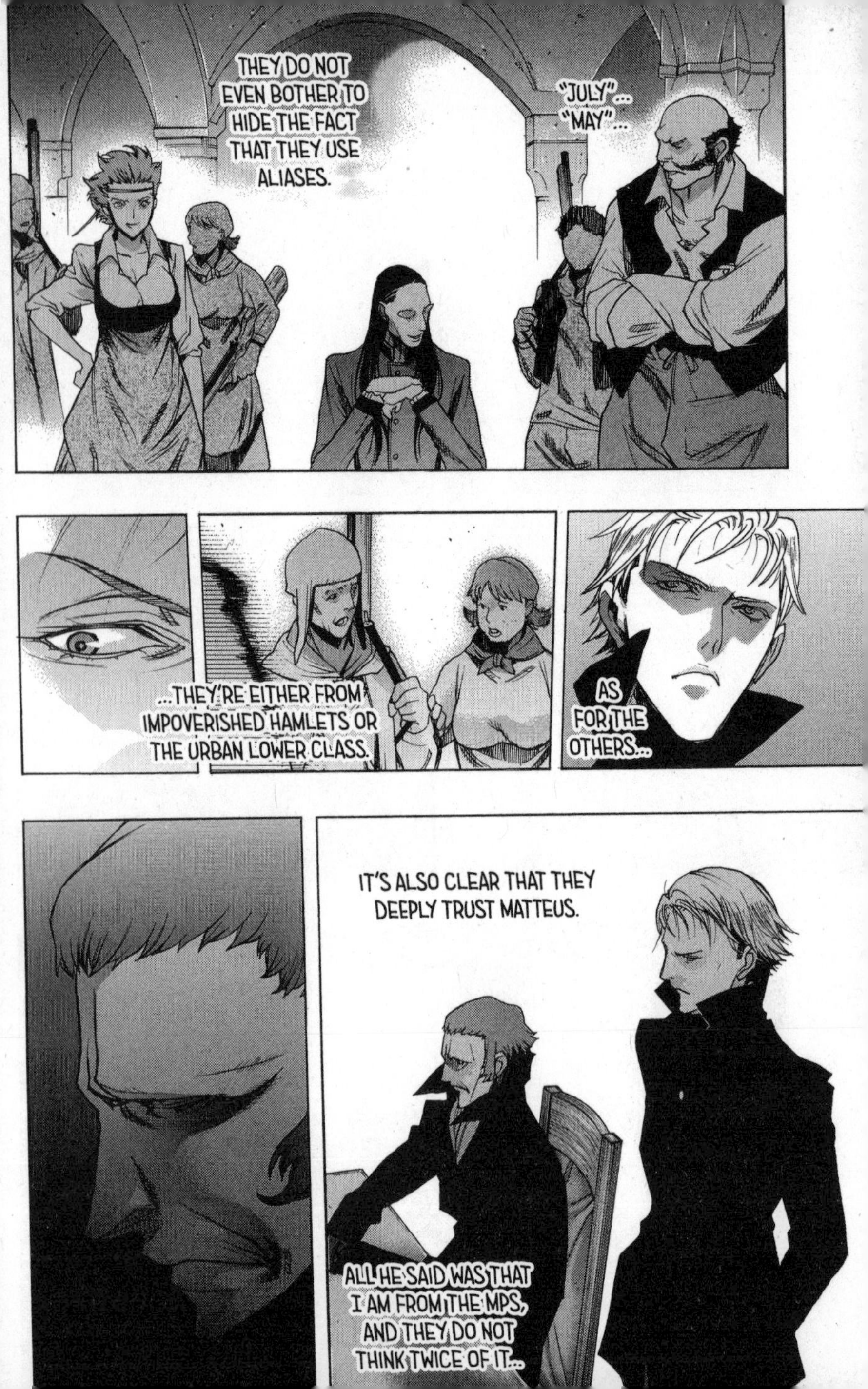
"JULY"... "MAY"...
THEY DO NOT EVEN BOTHER TO HIDE THE FACT THAT THEY USE ALIASES.
AS FOR THE OTHERS...
...THEY'RE EITHER FROM IMPOVERISHED HAMLETS OR THE URBAN LOWER CLASS.
IT'S ALSO CLEAR THAT THEY DEEPLY TRUST MATTEUS.
ALL HE SAID WAS THAT I AM FROM THE MPS, AND THEY DO NOT THINK TWICE OF IT...

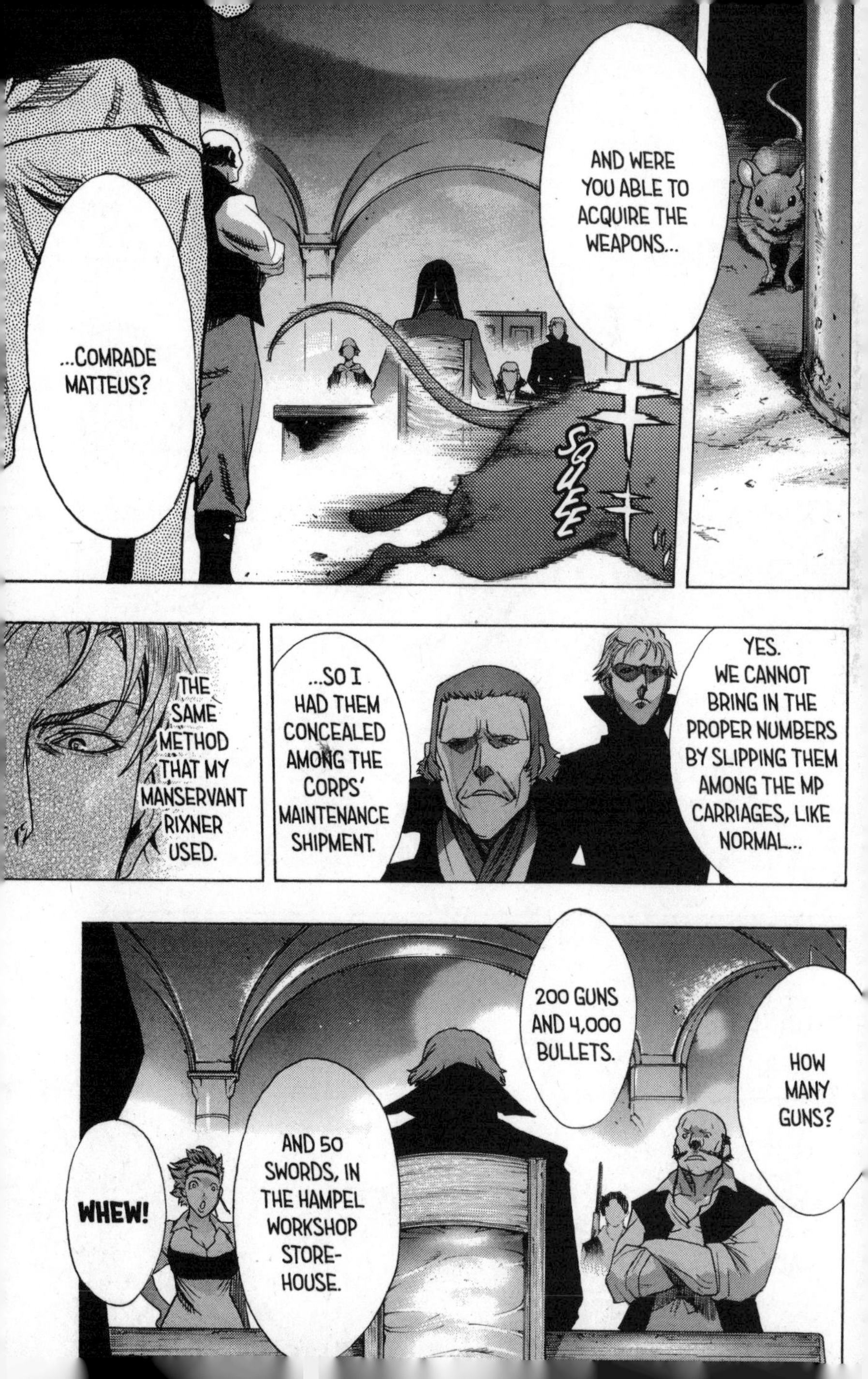
AND WERE YOU ABLE TO ACQUIRE THE WEAPONS...
...COMRADE MATTEUS?
SQUEE
YES. WE CANNOT BRING IN THE PROPER NUMBERS BY SLIPPING THEM AMONG THE MP CARRIAGES, LIKE NORMAL...
...SO I HAD THEM CONCEALED AMONG THE CORPS' MAINTENANCE SHIPMENT.
THE SAME METHOD THAT MY MANSERVANT RIXNER USED.
HOW MANY GUNS?
200 GUNS AND 4,000 BULLETS.
AND 50 SWORDS, IN THE HAMPEL WORKSHOP STORE-HOUSE.
WHEW!

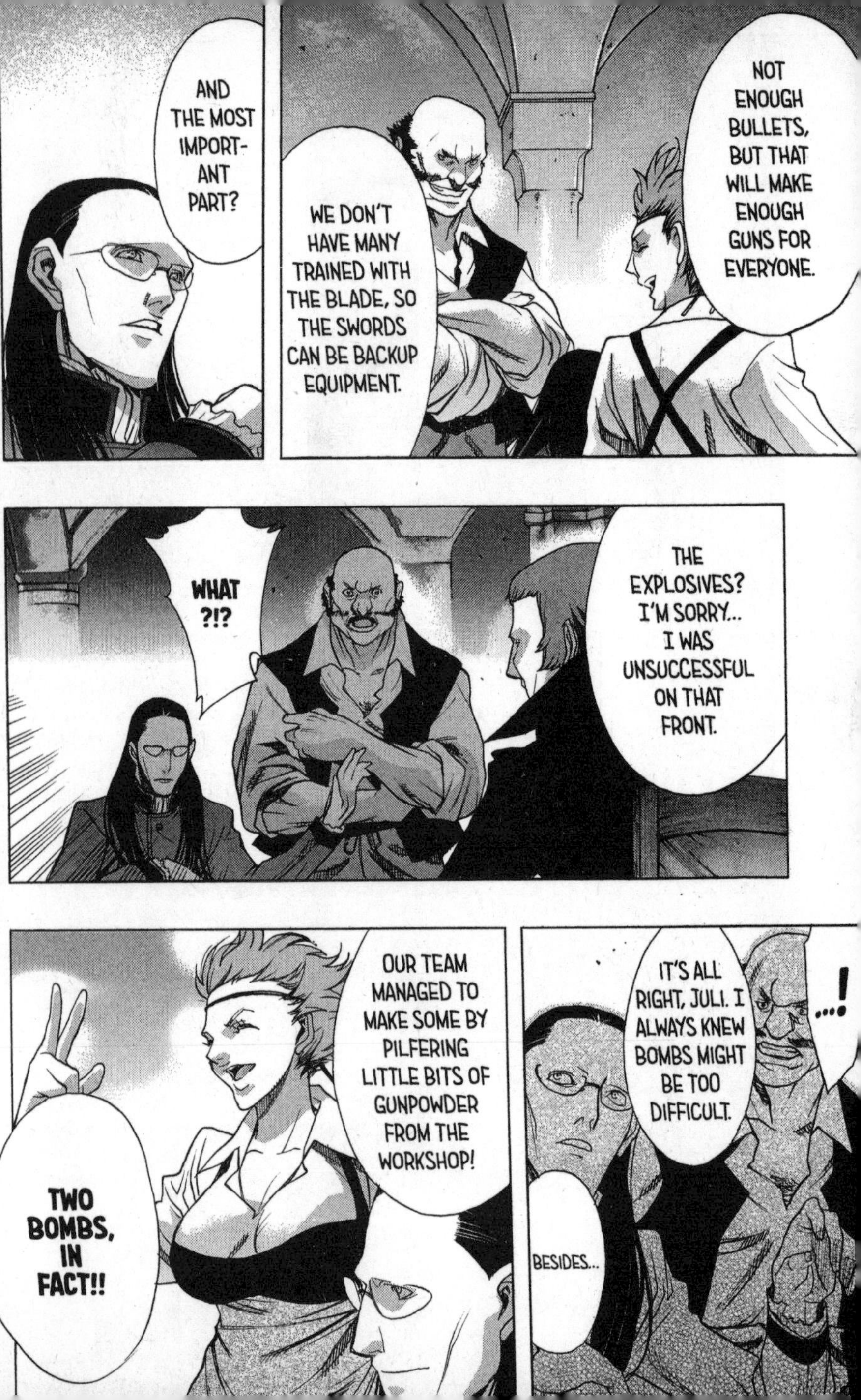
NOT ENOUGH BULLETS, BUT THAT WILL MAKE ENOUGH GUNS FOR EVERYONE.
WE DON'T HAVE MANY TRAINED WITH THE BLADE, SO THE SWORDS CAN BE BACKUP EQUIPMENT.
AND THE MOST IMPORT-ANT PART?
THE EXPLOSIVES? I'M SORRY... I WAS UNSUCCESSFUL ON THAT FRONT.
WHAT?!?
IT'S ALL RIGHT, JULI. I ALWAYS KNEW BOMBS MIGHT BE TOO DIFFICULT.
...!
BESIDES...
OUR TEAM MANAGED TO MAKE SOME BY PILFERING LITTLE BITS OF GUNPOWDER FROM THE WORKSHOP!
TWO BOMBS, IN FACT!!

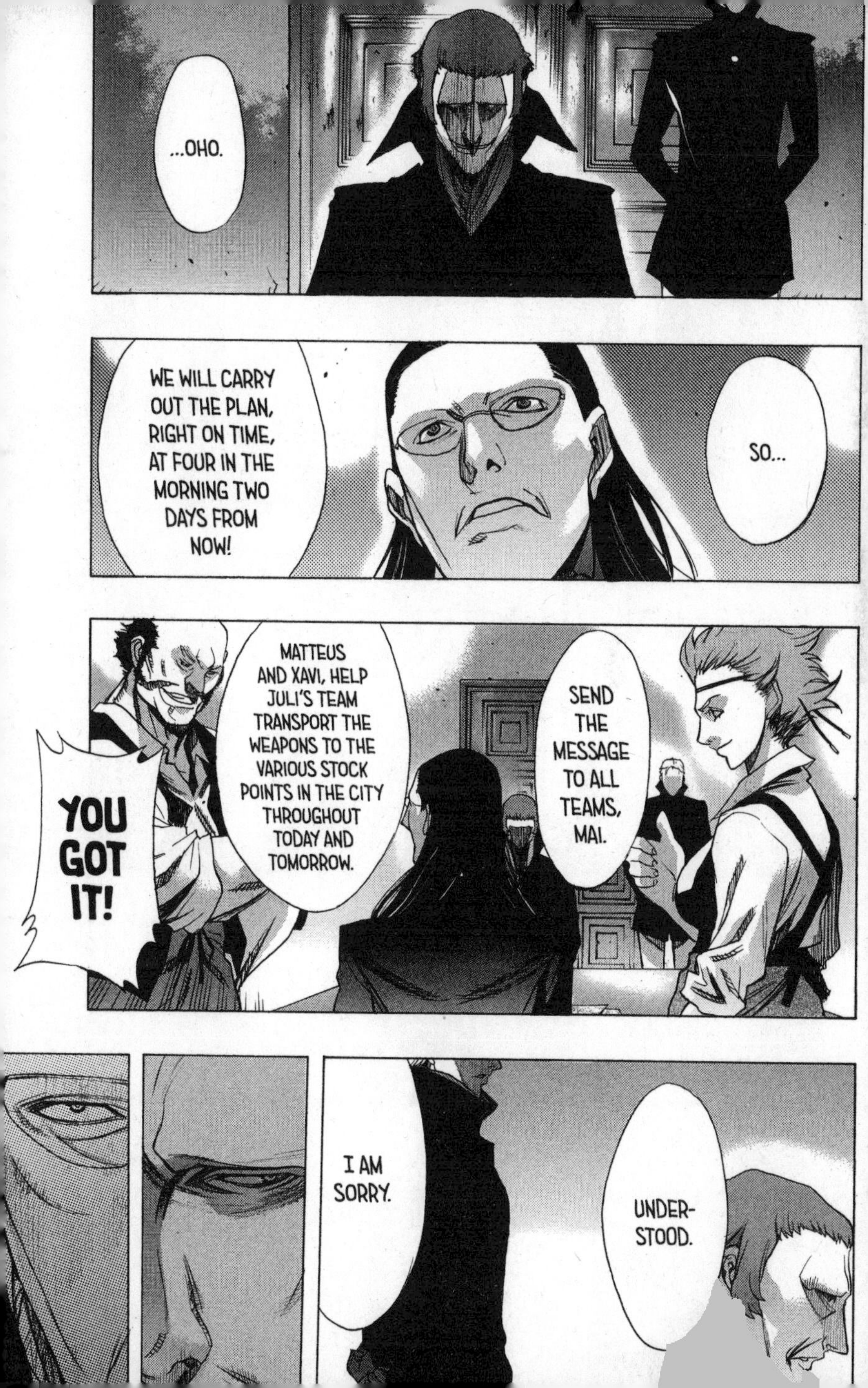
...OHO.
SO...
WE WILL CARRY OUT THE PLAN, RIGHT ON TIME, AT FOUR IN THE MORNING TWO DAYS FROM NOW!
SEND THE MESSAGE TO ALL TEAMS, MAI.
MATTEUS AND XAVI, HELP JULI'S TEAM TRANSPORT THE WEAPONS TO THE VARIOUS STOCK POINTS IN THE CITY THROUGHOUT TODAY AND TOMORROW.
YOU GOT IT!
UNDER-STOOD.
I AM SORRY.

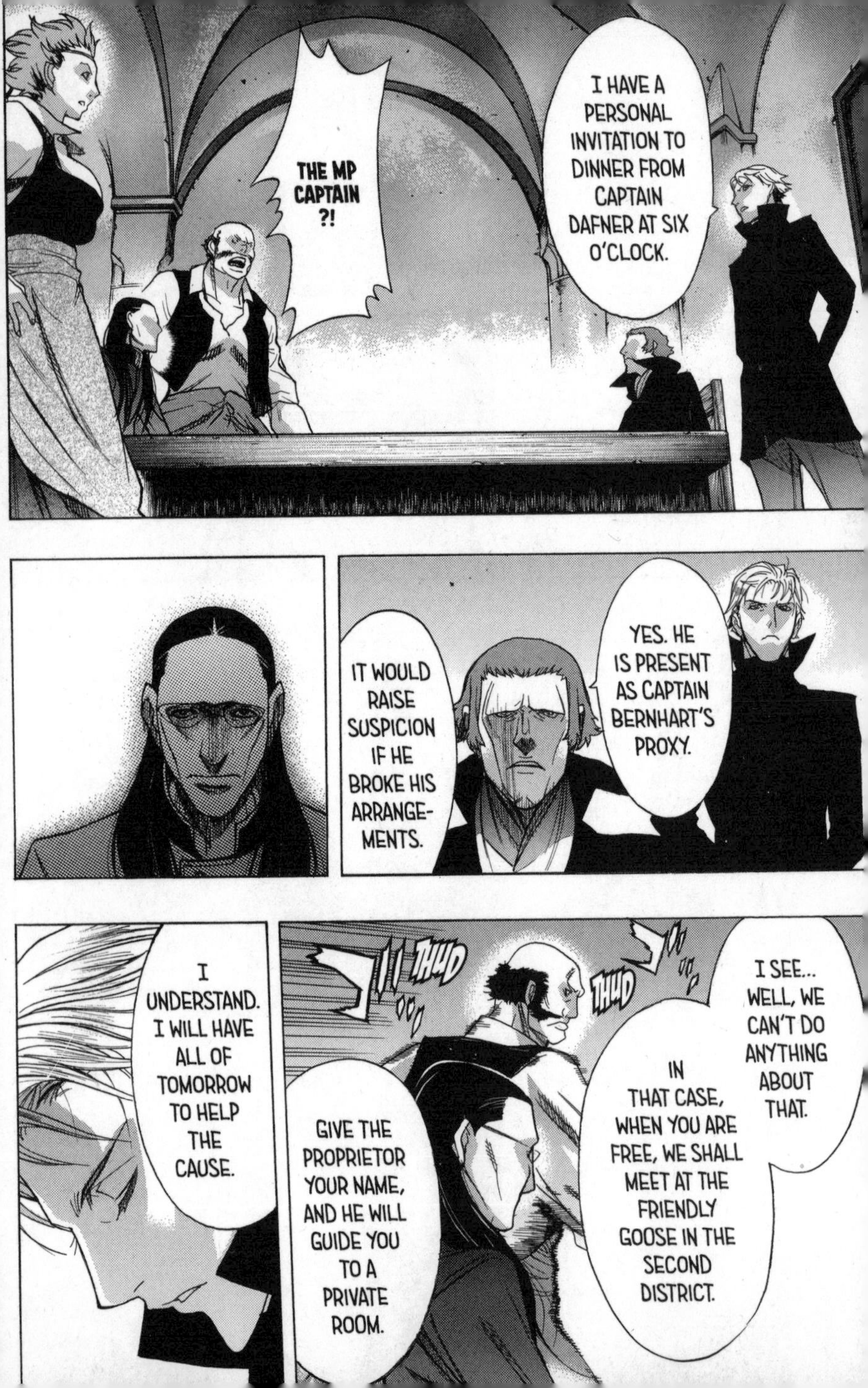
I HAVE A PERSONAL INVITATION TO DINNER FROM CAPTAIN DAFNER AT SIX O'CLOCK.
THE MP CAPTAIN ?!
YES. HE IS PRESENT AS CAPTAIN BERNHART'S PROXY.
IT WOULD RAISE SUSPICION IF HE BROKE HIS ARRANGE-MENTS.
I SEE... WELL, WE CAN'T DO ANYTHING ABOUT THAT.
THUD
THUD
IN THAT CASE, WHEN YOU ARE FREE, WE SHALL MEET AT THE FRIENDLY GOOSE IN THE SECOND DISTRICT.
GIVE THE PROPRIETOR YOUR NAME, AND HE WILL GUIDE YOU TO A PRIVATE ROOM.
I UNDERSTAND. I WILL HAVE ALL OF TOMORROW TO HELP THE CAUSE.

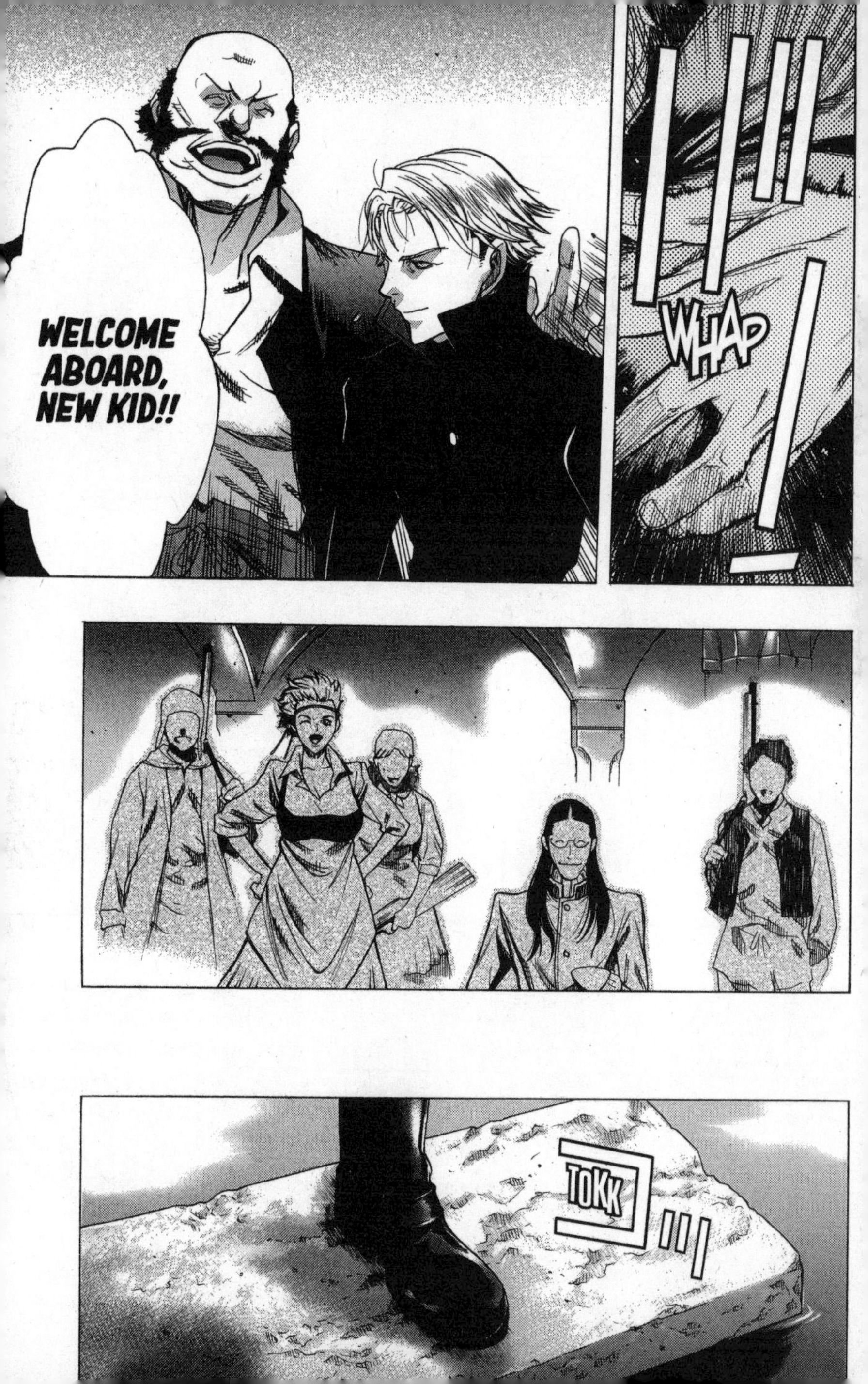
WHAP
WELCOME ABOARD, NEW KID!!
TOKK

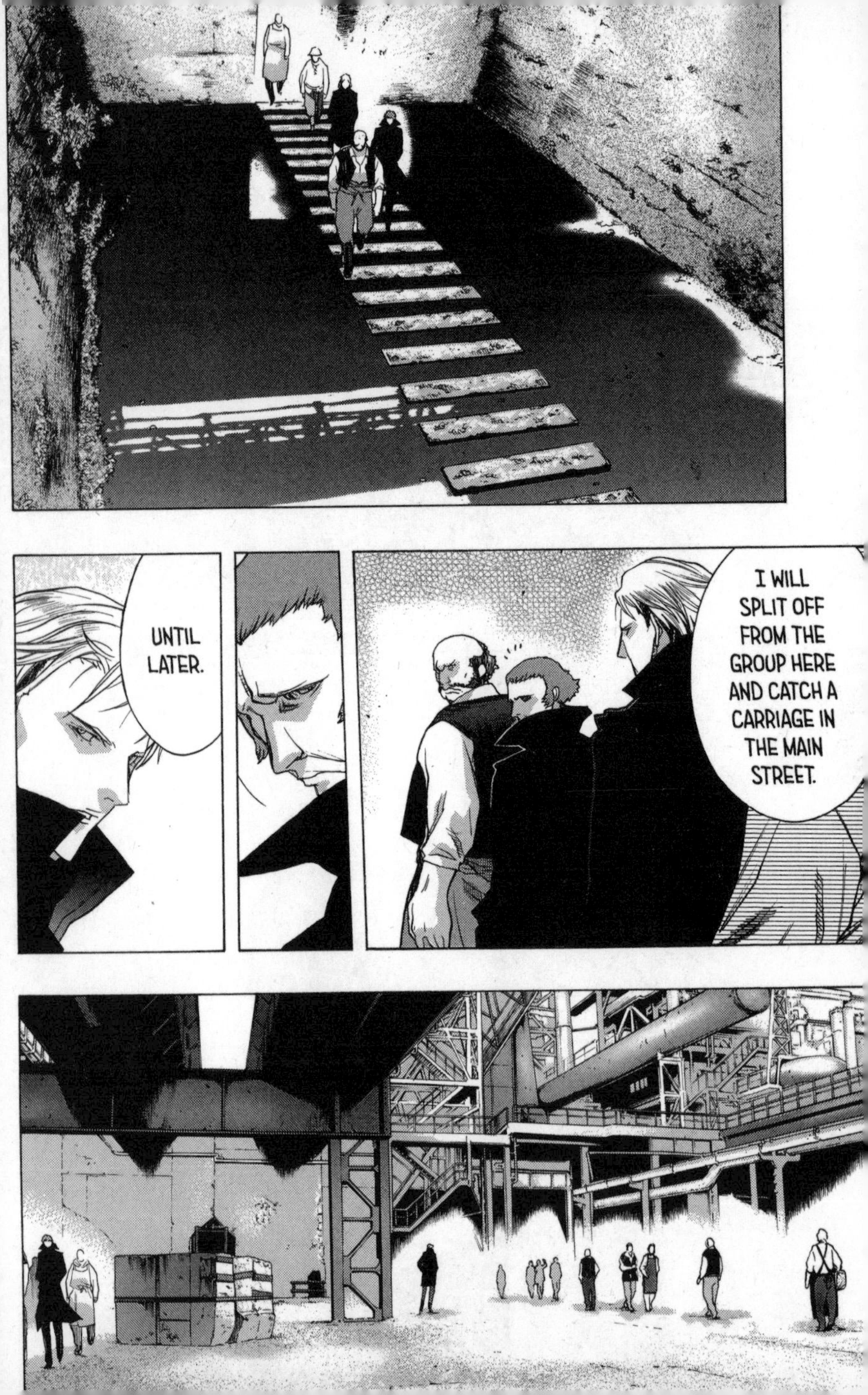
I WILL SPLIT OFF FROM THE GROUP HERE AND CATCH A CARRIAGE IN THE MAIN STREET.
UNTIL LATER.

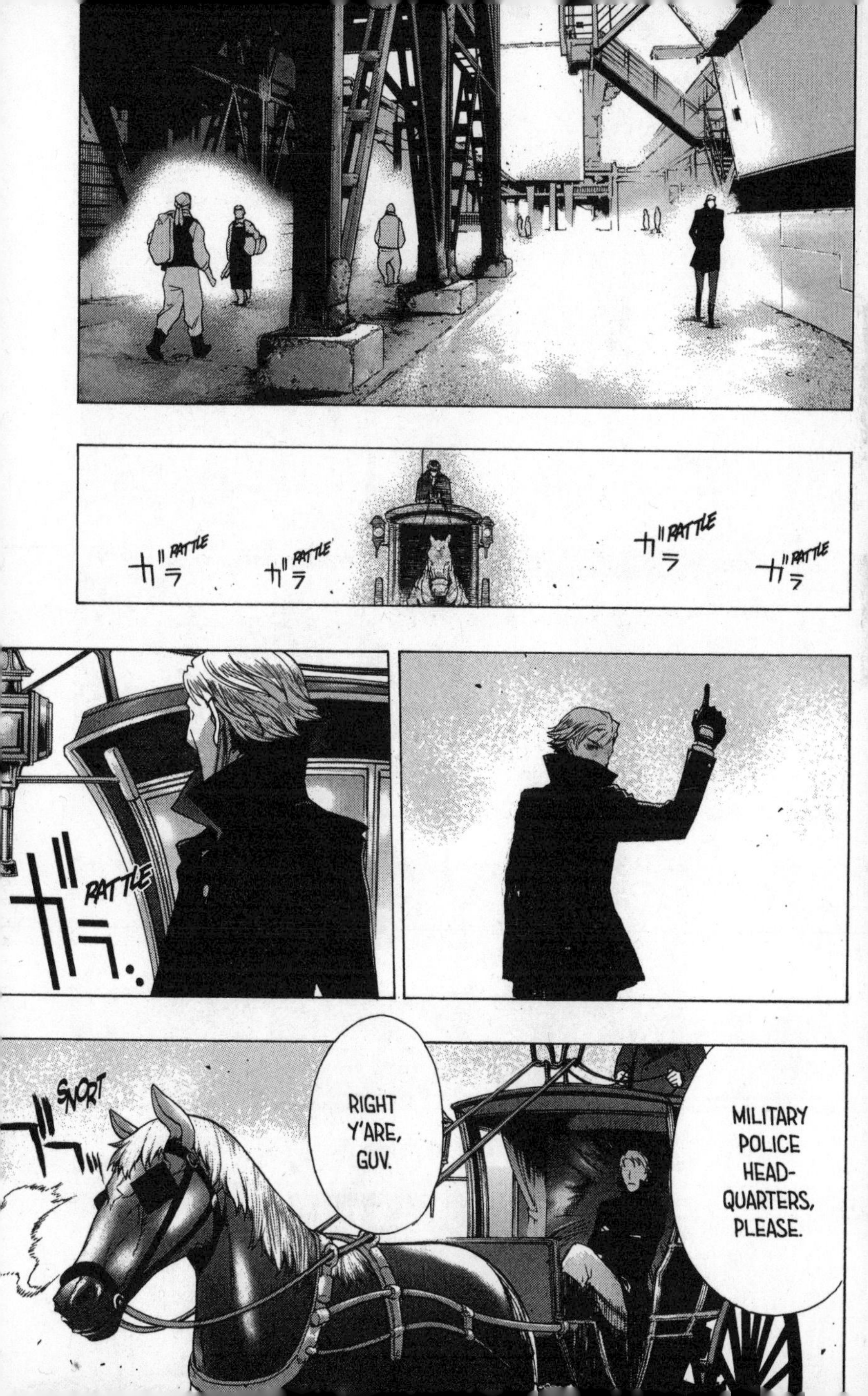

ガラ RATTLE
ガラ RATTLE
ガラ RATTLE
ガラ RATTLE
ガラ.. RATTLE
MILITARY POLICE HEAD-QUARTERS, PLEASE.
RIGHT Y'ARE, GUV.
SNORT

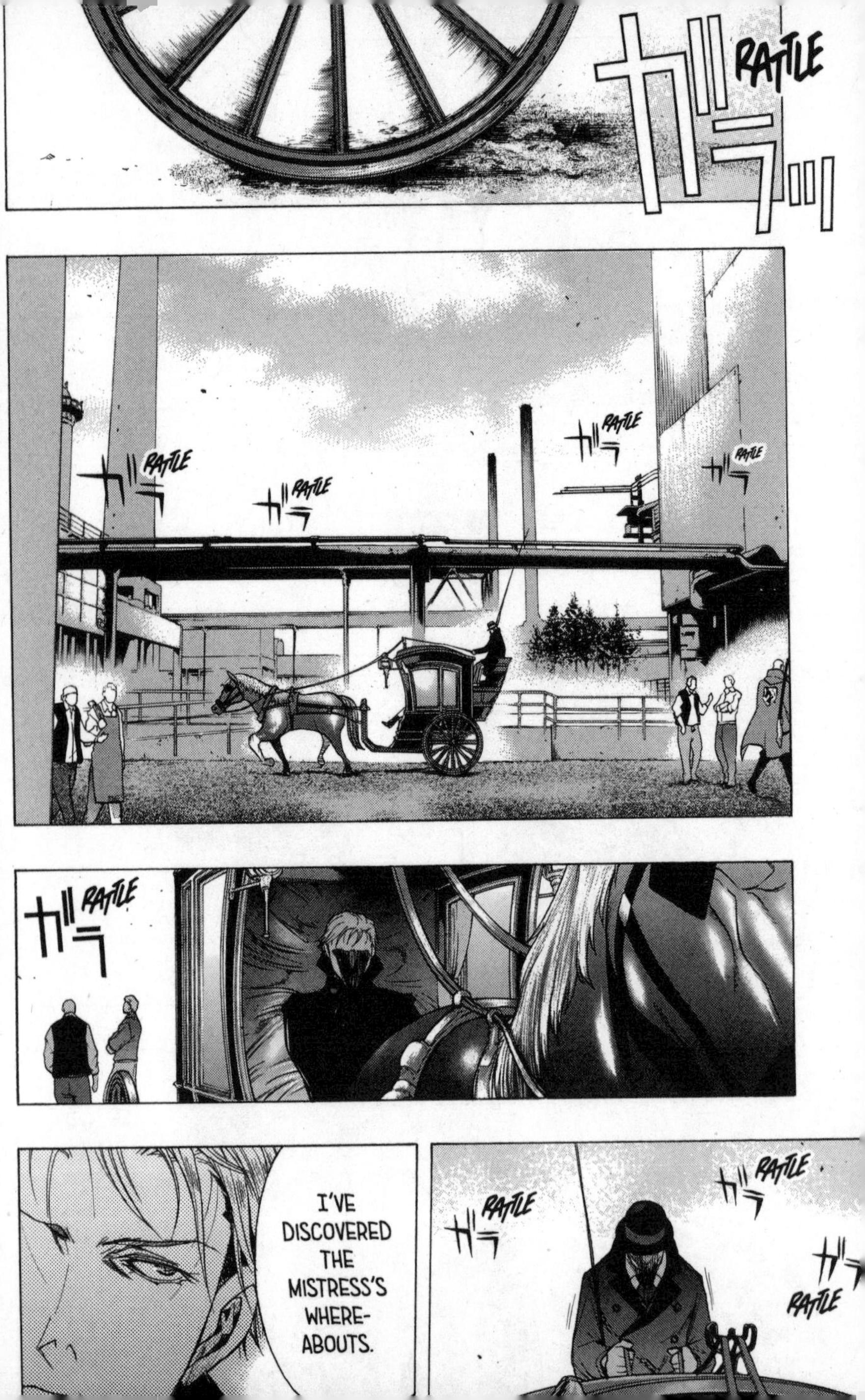
ガラッ
RATTLE
ガラ
RATTLE
ガラ
RATTLE
ガラ
RATTLE
ガラ
RATTLE
ガラ
RATTLE
ガラ
RATTLE
ガラ
RATTLE
RATTLE
I'VE DISCOVERED THE MISTRESS'S WHERE-ABOUTS.

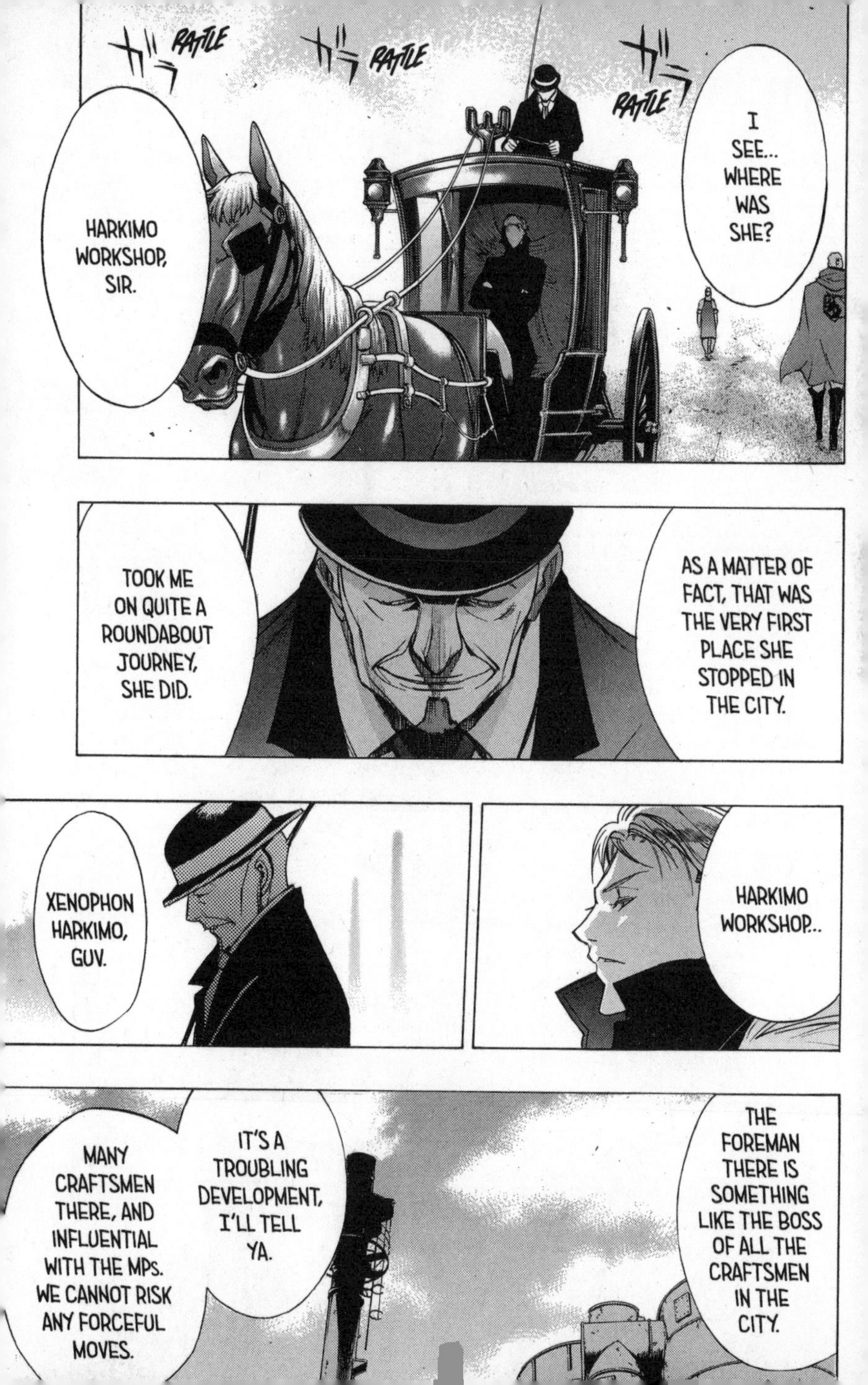
ガラ RATTLE
ガラ RATTLE
ガラ RATTLE
I SEE... WHERE WAS SHE?
HARKIMO WORKSHOP, SIR.
AS A MATTER OF FACT, THAT WAS THE VERY FIRST PLACE SHE STOPPED IN THE CITY.
TOOK ME ON QUITE A ROUNDABOUT JOURNEY, SHE DID.
HARKIMO WORKSHOP...
XENOPHON HARKIMO, GUV.
THE FOREMAN THERE IS SOMETHING LIKE THE BOSS OF ALL THE CRAFTSMEN IN THE CITY.
IT'S A TROUBLING DEVELOPMENT, I'LL TELL YA.
MANY CRAFTSMEN THERE, AND INFLUENTIAL WITH THE MPs. WE CANNOT RISK ANY FORCEFUL MOVES.

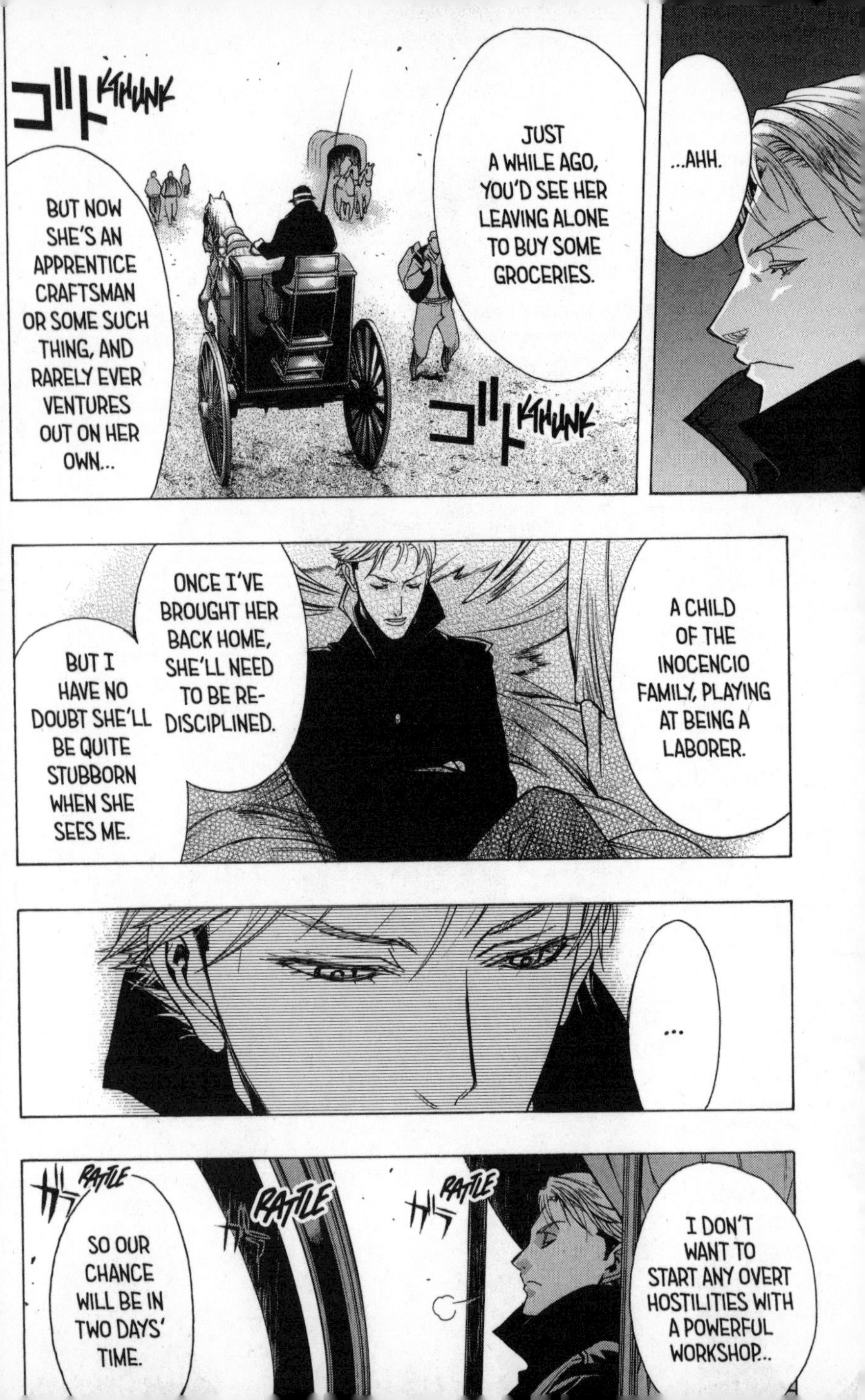
...AHH.
JUST A WHILE AGO, YOU'D SEE HER LEAVING ALONE TO BUY SOME GROCERIES.
ゴト KTHUNK
BUT NOW SHE'S AN APPRENTICE CRAFTSMAN OR SOME SUCH THING, AND RARELY EVER VENTURES OUT ON HER OWN...
ゴト KTHUNK
A CHILD OF THE INOCENCIO FAMILY, PLAYING AT BEING A LABORER.
ONCE I'VE BROUGHT HER BACK HOME, SHE'LL NEED TO BE RE-DISCIPLINED.
BUT I HAVE NO DOUBT SHE'LL BE QUITE STUBBORN WHEN SHE SEES ME.
...
I DON'T WANT TO START ANY OVERT HOSTILITIES WITH A POWERFUL WORKSHOP...
RATTLE
RATTLE
RATTLE
SO OUR CHANCE WILL BE IN TWO DAYS' TIME.

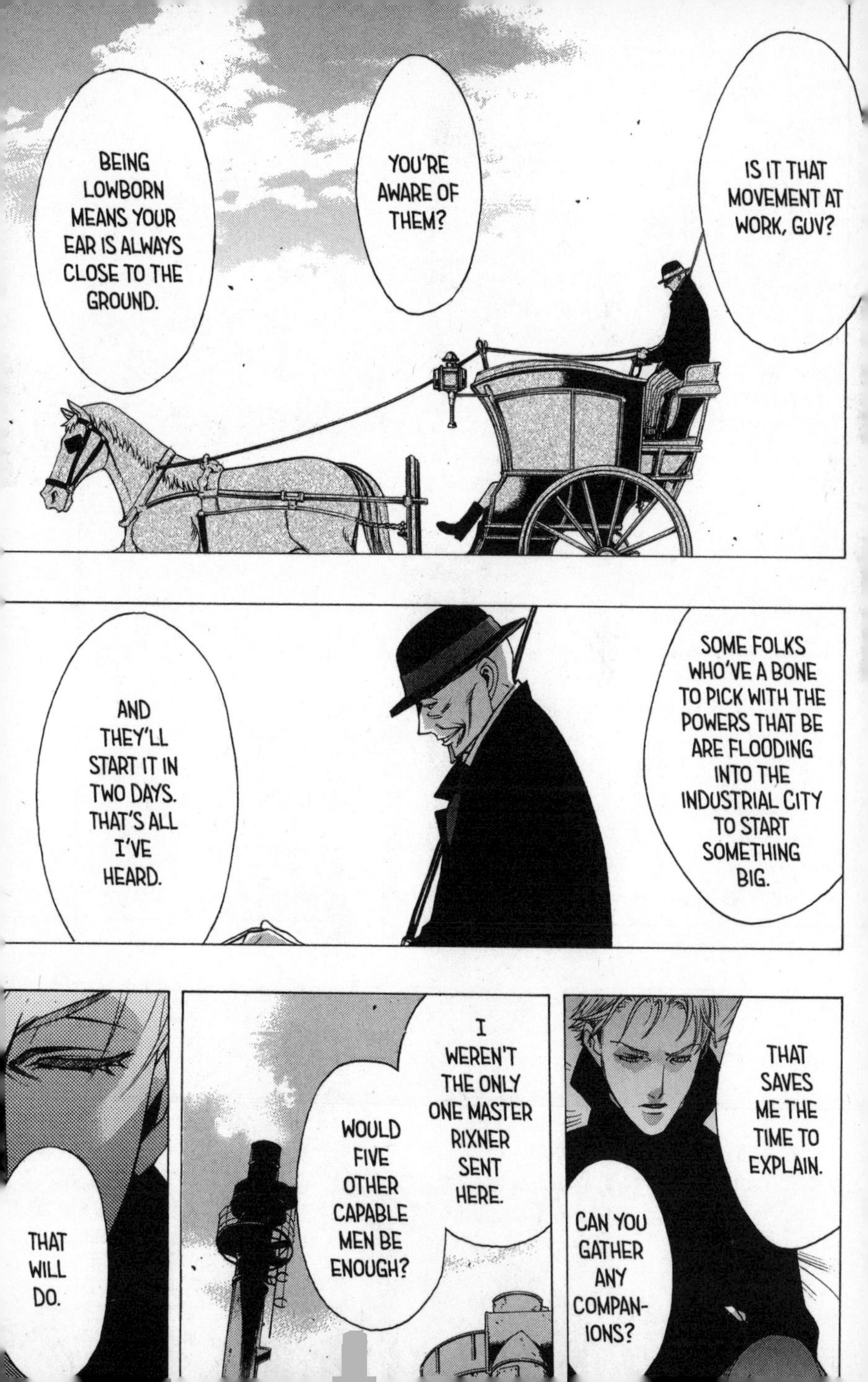
IS IT THAT MOVEMENT AT WORK, GUV?
YOU'RE AWARE OF THEM?
BEING LOWBORN MEANS YOUR EAR IS ALWAYS CLOSE TO THE GROUND.
SOME FOLKS WHO'VE A BONE TO PICK WITH THE POWERS THAT BE ARE FLOODING INTO THE INDUSTRIAL CITY TO START SOMETHING BIG.
AND THEY'LL START IT IN TWO DAYS. THAT'S ALL I'VE HEARD.
THAT SAVES ME THE TIME TO EXPLAIN.
CAN YOU GATHER ANY COMPAN-IONS?
I WEREN'T THE ONLY ONE MASTER RIXNER SENT HERE.
WOULD FIVE OTHER CAPABLE MEN BE ENOUGH?
THAT WILL DO.

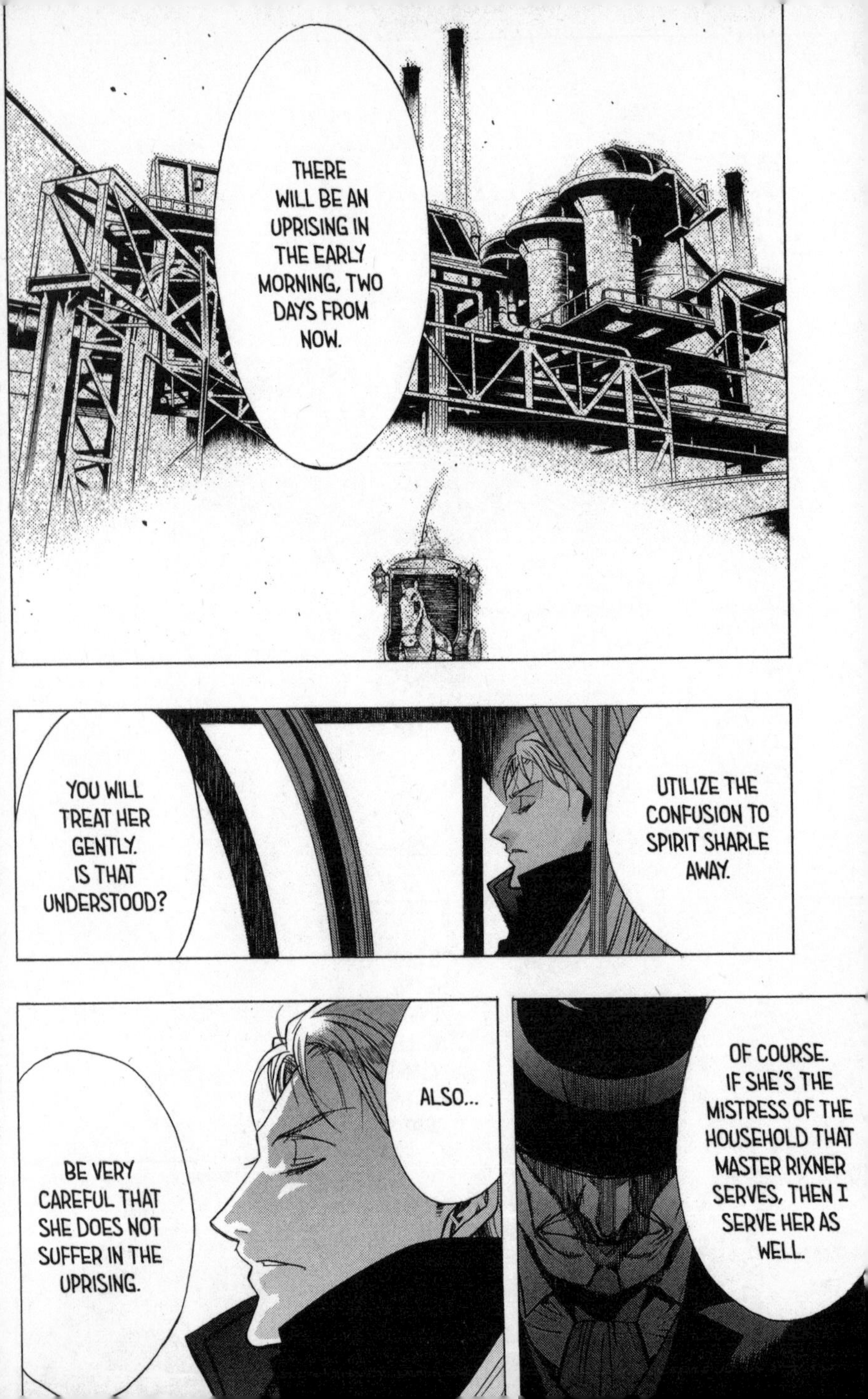
THERE WILL BE AN UPRISING IN THE EARLY MORNING, TWO DAYS FROM NOW.
UTILIZE THE CONFUSION TO SPIRIT SHARLE AWAY.
YOU WILL TREAT HER GENTLY. IS THAT UNDERSTOOD?
OF COURSE. IF SHE'S THE MISTRESS OF THE HOUSEHOLD THAT MASTER RIXNER SERVES, THEN I SERVE HER AS WELL.
ALSO...
BE VERY CAREFUL THAT SHE DOES NOT SUFFER IN THE UPRISING.

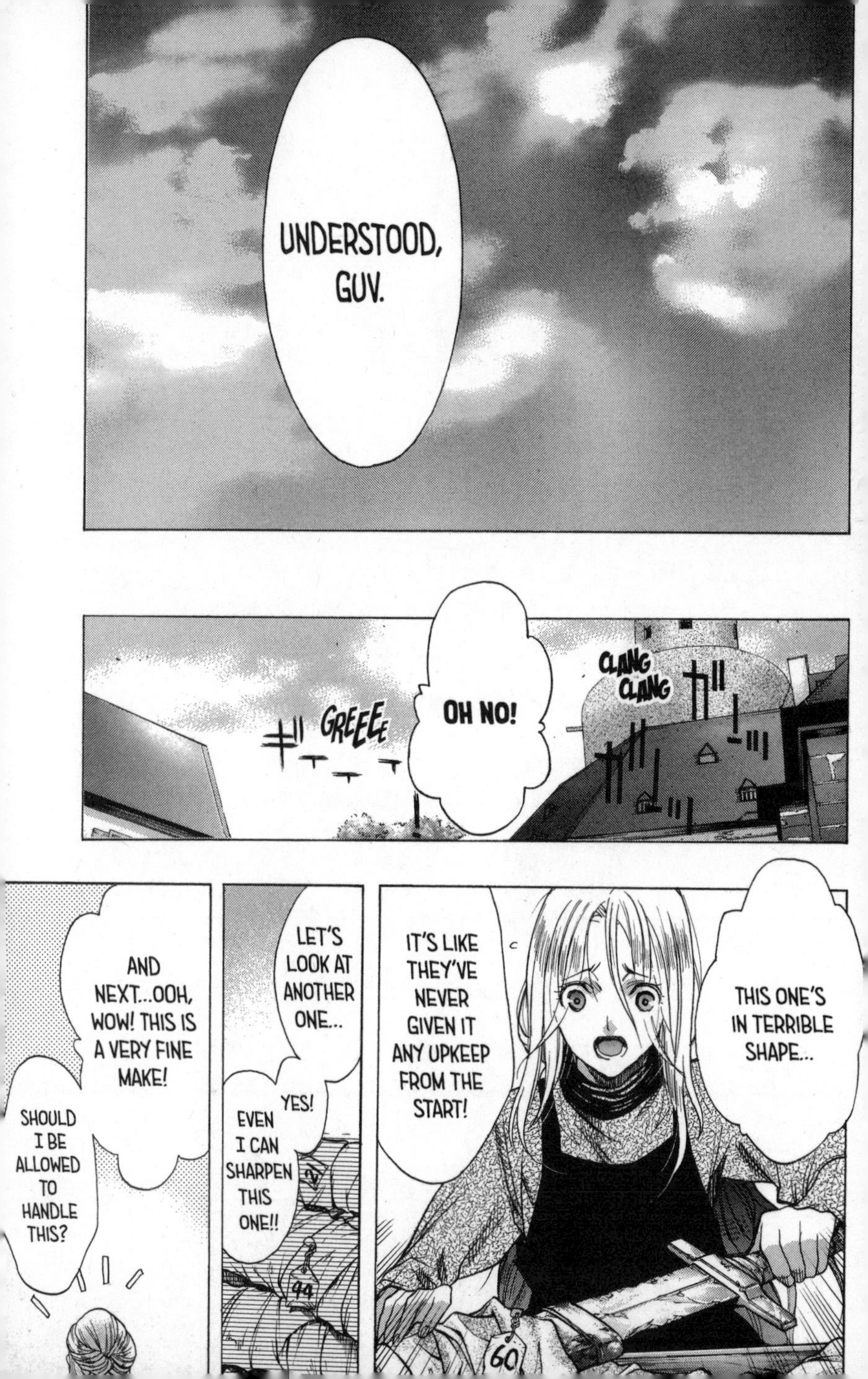
UNDERSTOOD, GUV.
CLANG CLANG
OH NO!
GREEEE
THIS ONE'S IN TERRIBLE SHAPE...
IT'S LIKE THEY'VE NEVER GIVEN IT ANY UPKEEP FROM THE START!
LET'S LOOK AT ANOTHER ONE...
YES!
EVEN I CAN SHARPEN THIS ONE!!
AND NEXT...OOH, WOW! THIS IS A VERY FINE MAKE!
SHOULD I BE ALLOWED TO HANDLE THIS?

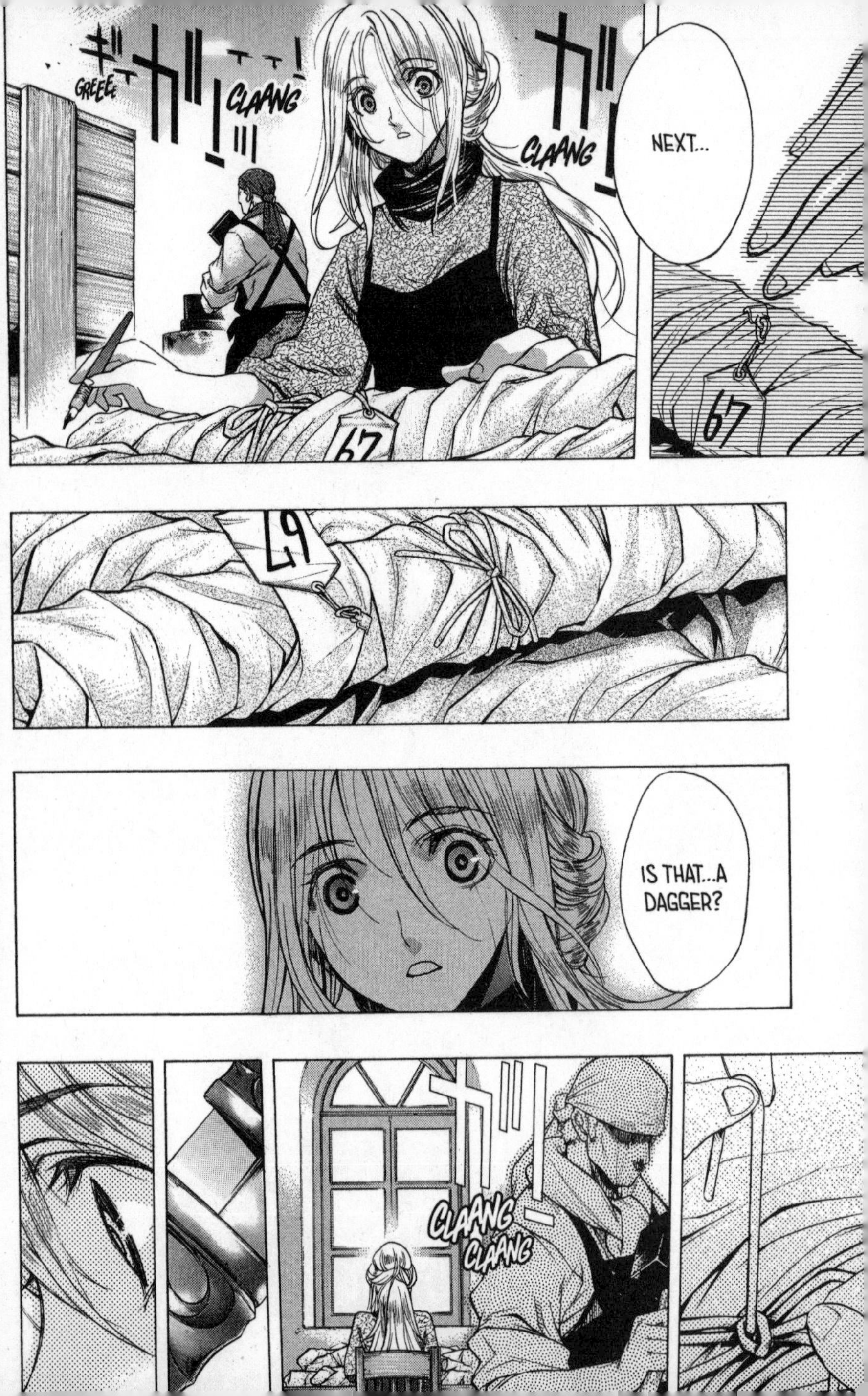
NEXT...
CLAANG
CLAANG
GREEE
IS THAT...A DAGGER?
CLAANG
CLAANG

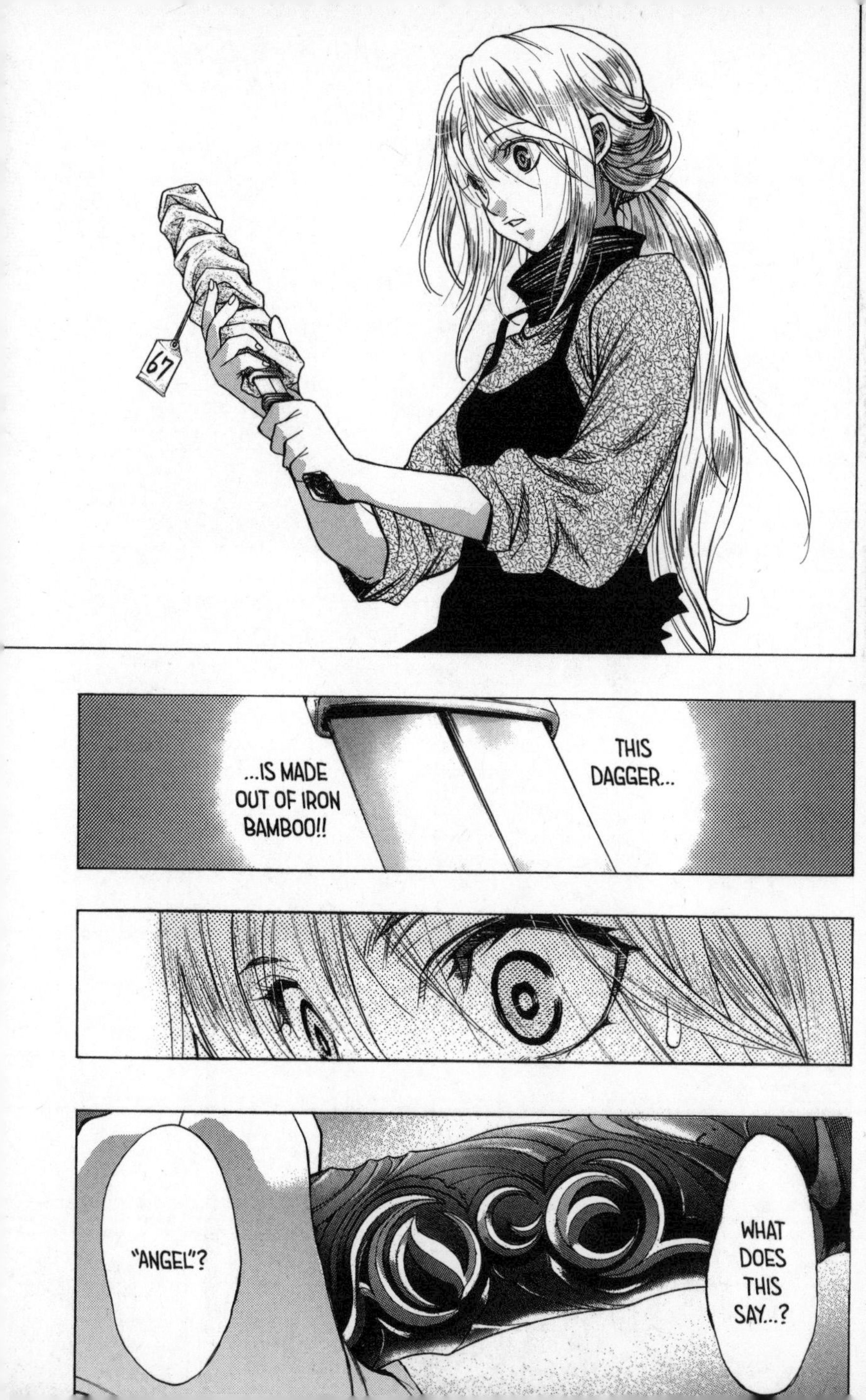
67
THIS DAGGER...
...IS MADE OUT OF IRON BAMBOO!!
WHAT DOES THIS SAY...?
"ANGEL"?

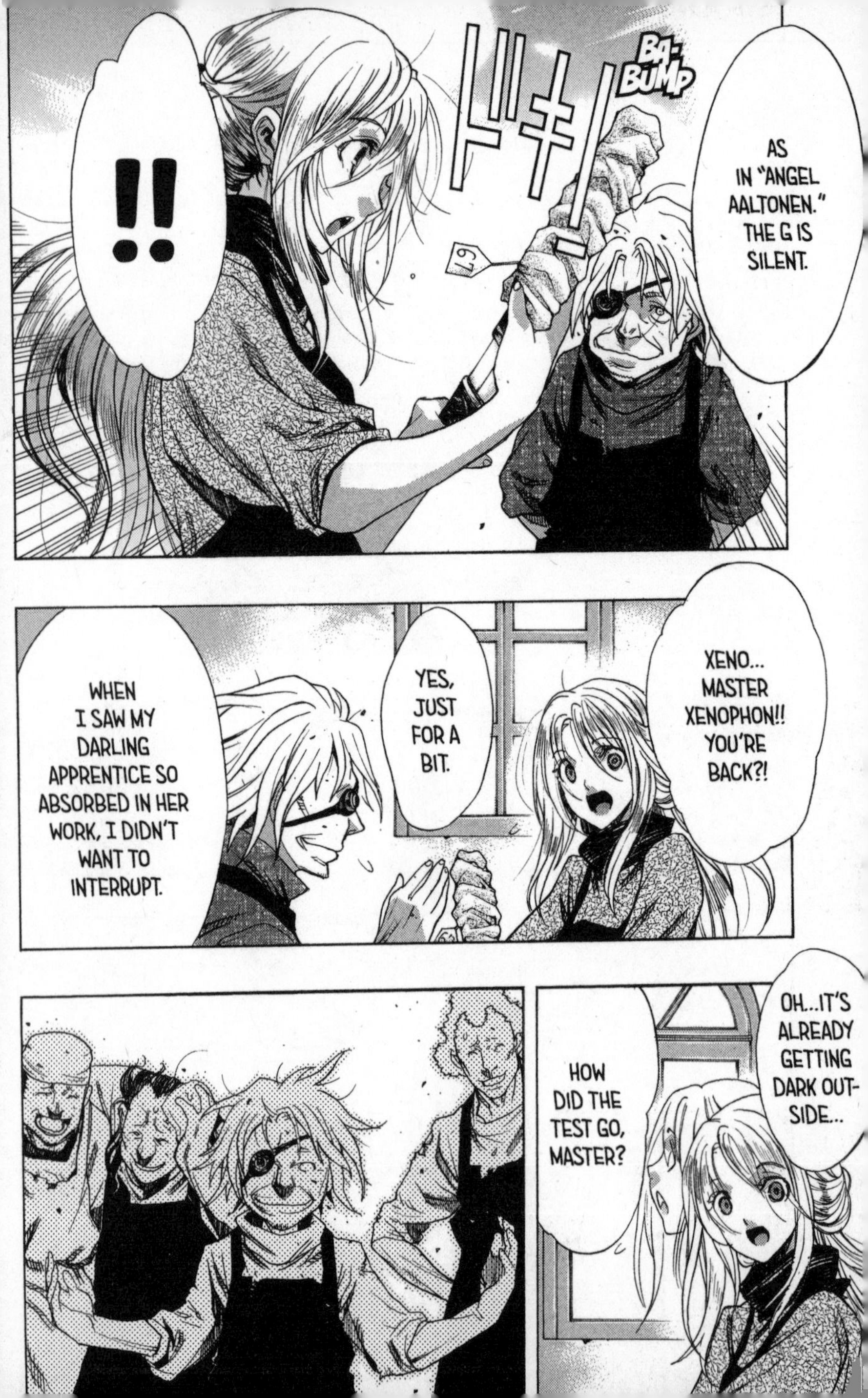
AS IN "ANGEL AALTONEN." THE G IS SILENT.
BA-BUMP
ドキ!
!!
XENO... MASTER XENOPHON!! YOU'RE BACK?!
YES, JUST FOR A BIT.
WHEN I SAW MY DARLING APPRENTICE SO ABSORBED IN HER WORK, I DIDN'T WANT TO INTERRUPT.
OH...IT'S ALREADY GETTING DARK OUT-SIDE...
HOW DID THE TEST GO, MASTER?

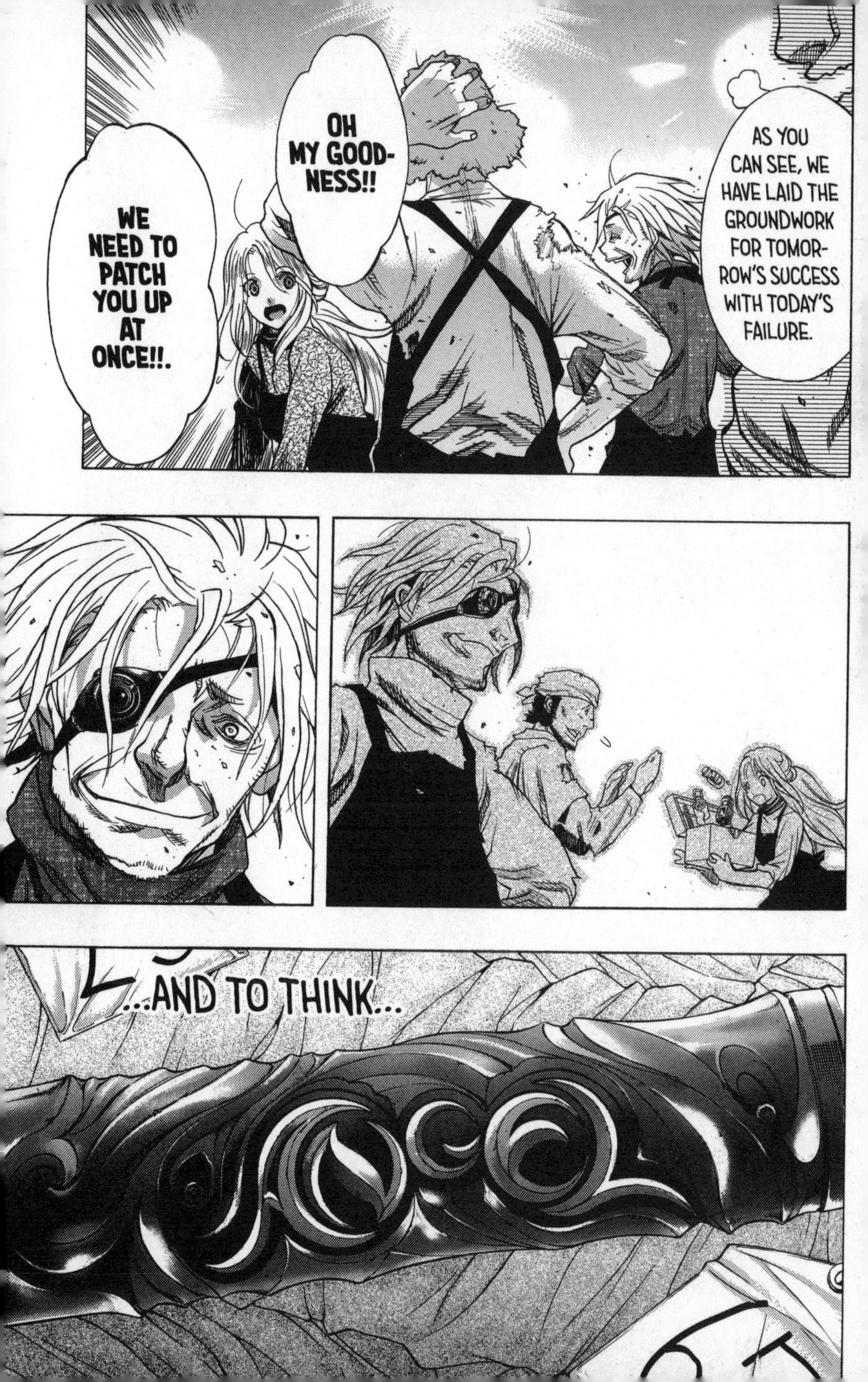
AS YOU CAN SEE, WE HAVE LAID THE GROUNDWORK FOR TOMOR-ROW'S SUCCESS WITH TODAY'S FAILURE.
OH MY GOOD-NESS!!
WE NEED TO PATCH YOU UP AT ONCE!!.
...AND TO THINK...

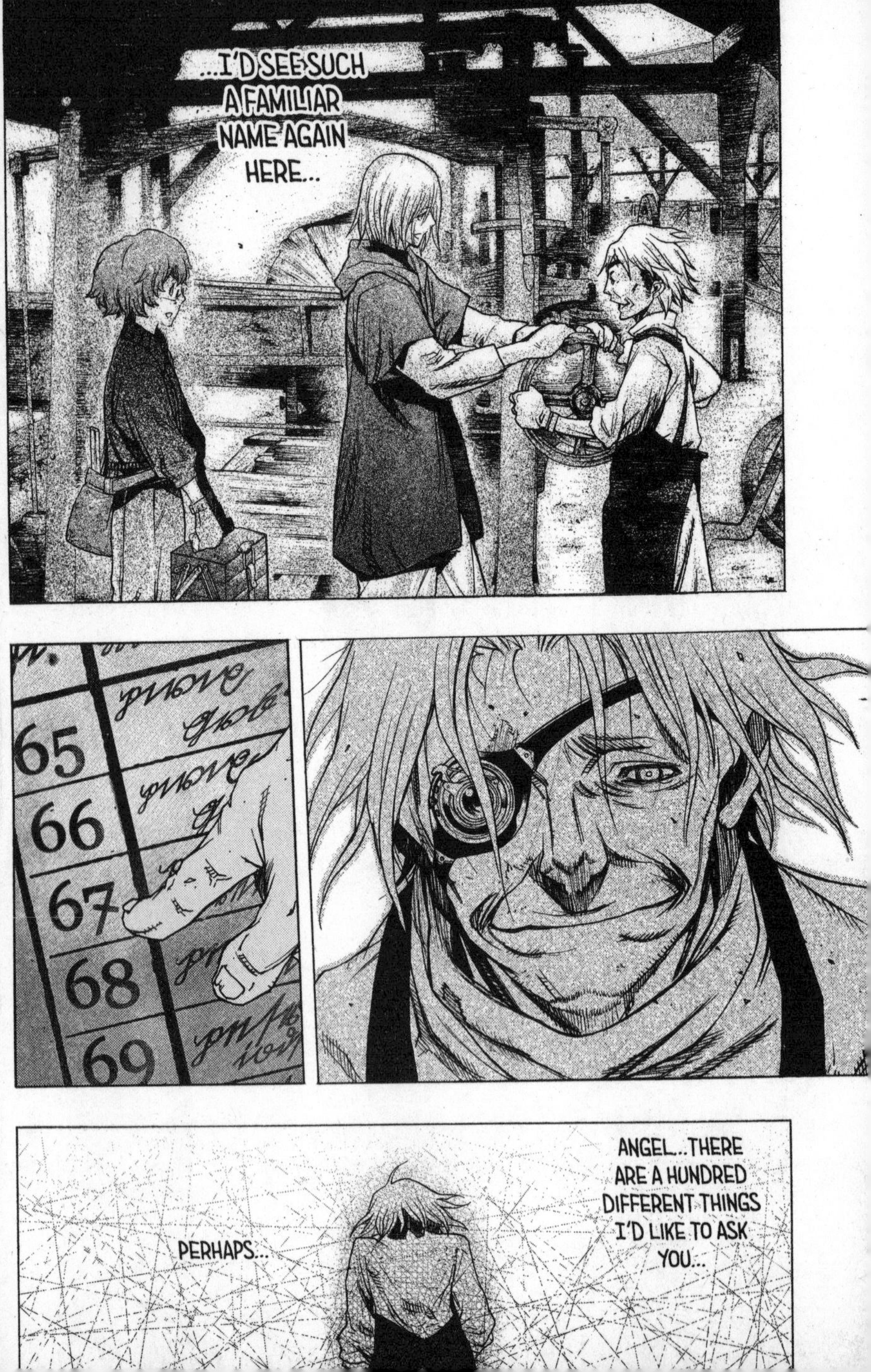
...I'D SEE SUCH A FAMILIAR NAME AGAIN HERE...
65
66
67
68
69
ANGEL...THERE ARE A HUNDRED DIFFERENT THINGS I'D LIKE TO ASK YOU...
PERHAPS...

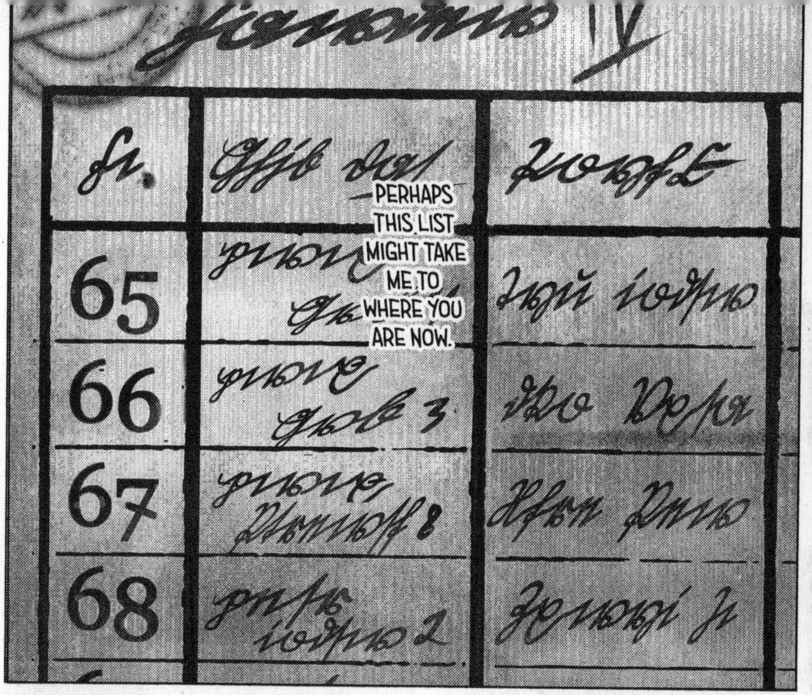
65
66
67
68
PERHAPS THIS LIST MIGHT TAKE ME TO WHERE YOU ARE NOW.

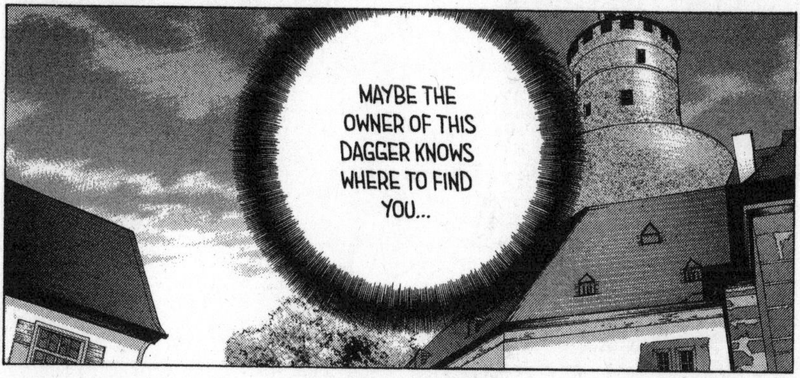
MAYBE THE OWNER OF THIS DAGGER KNOWS WHERE TO FIND YOU...

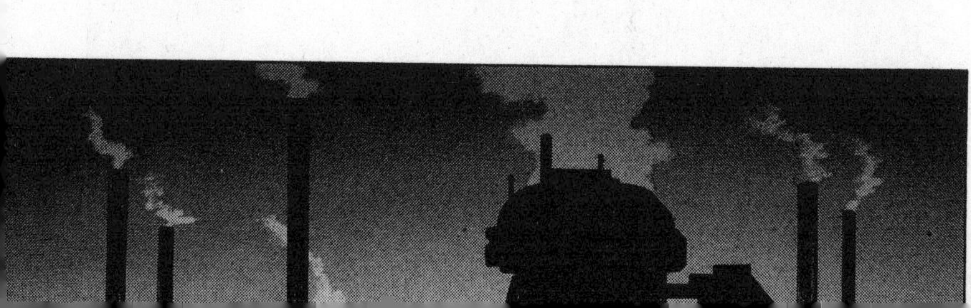

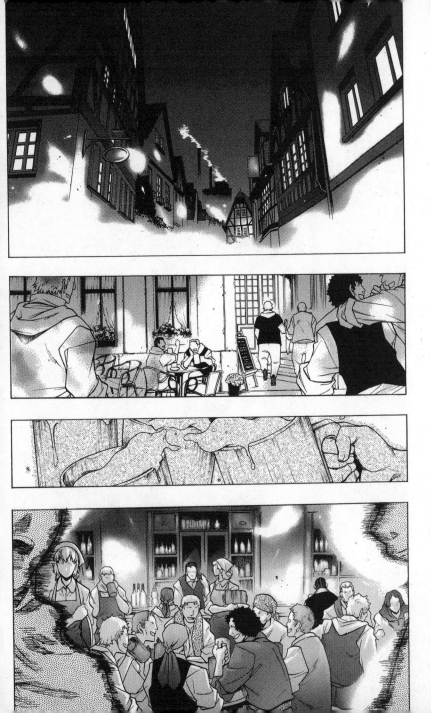

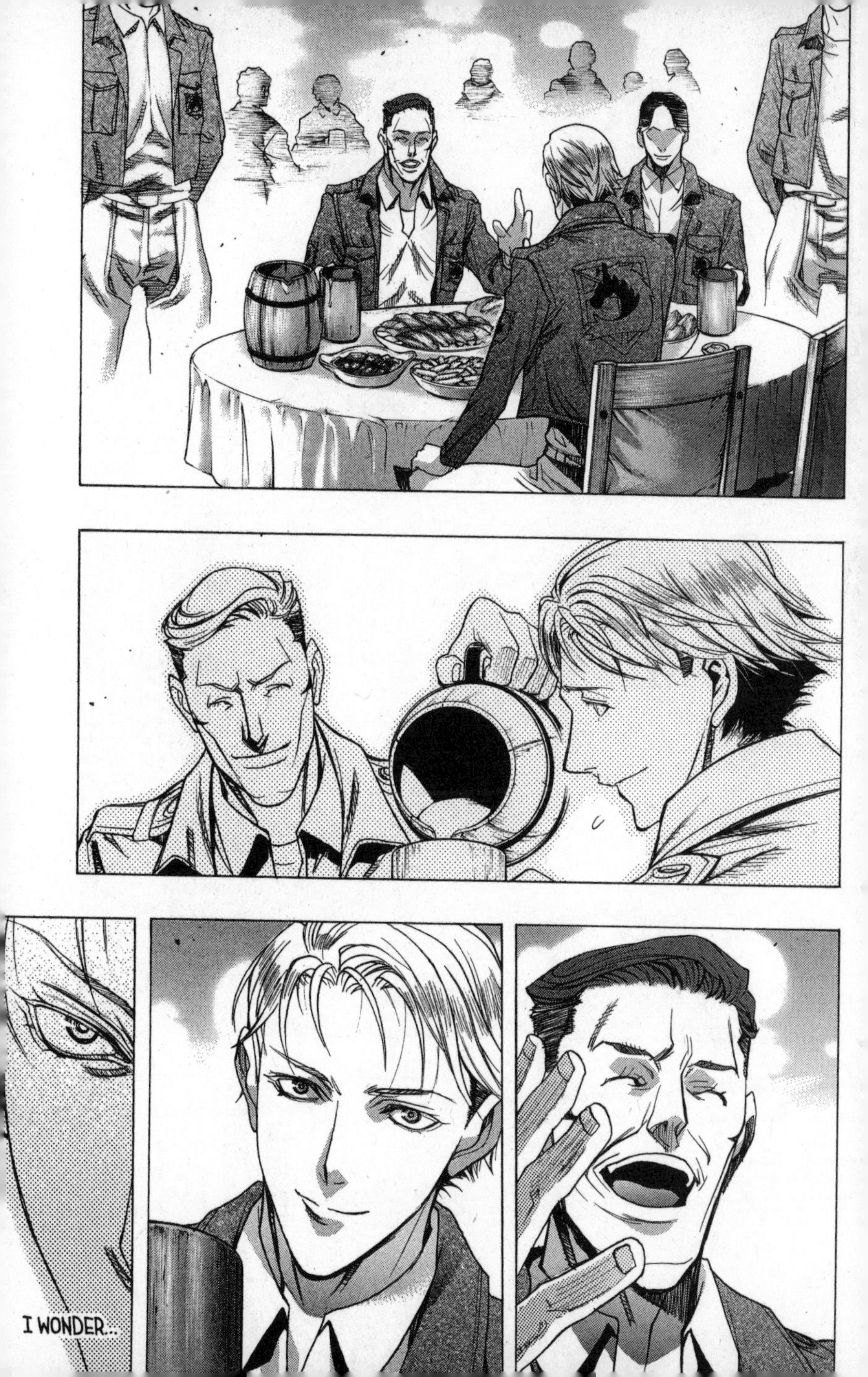
I WONDER...

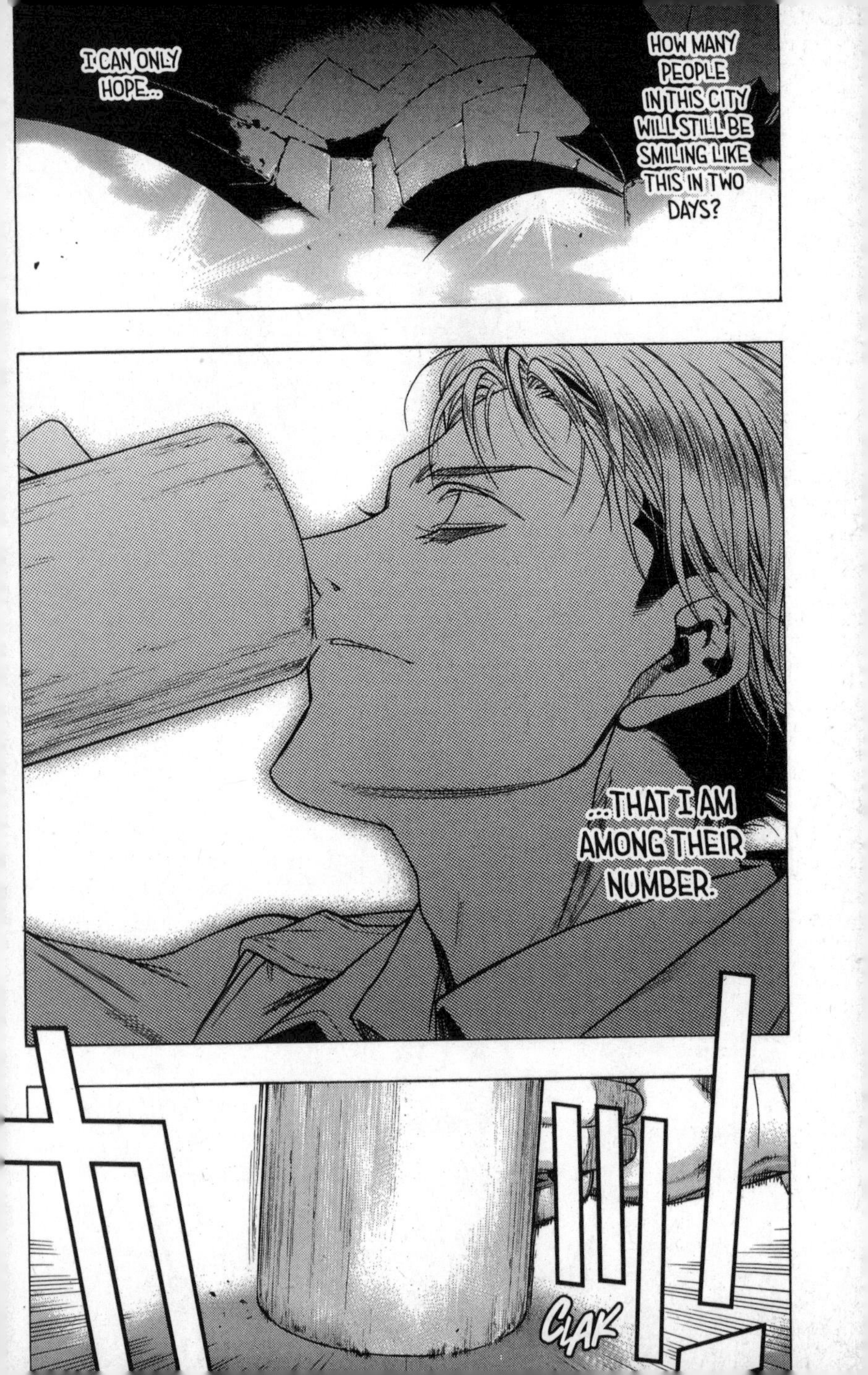
HOW MANY PEOPLE IN THIS CITY WILL STILL BE SMILING LIKE THIS IN TWO DAYS?
I CAN ONLY HOPE...
...THAT I AM AMONG THEIR NUMBER.
CLAK

Chapter 25: Before the Storm · End

ATTACK on TITAN

BEFORE THE FALL

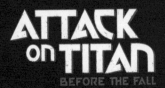

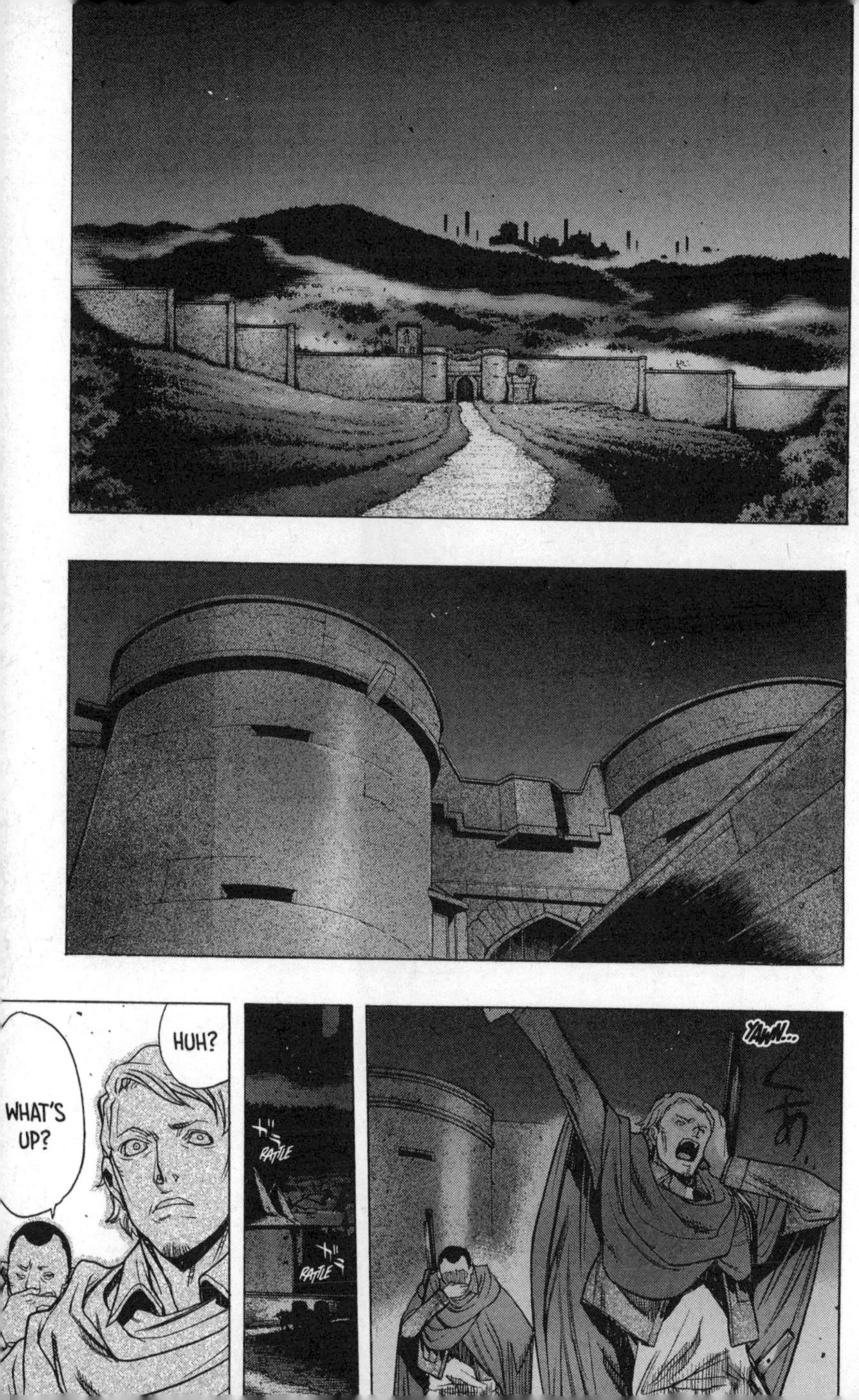
YAWN...
RATTLE
RATTLE
HUH?
WHAT'S UP?

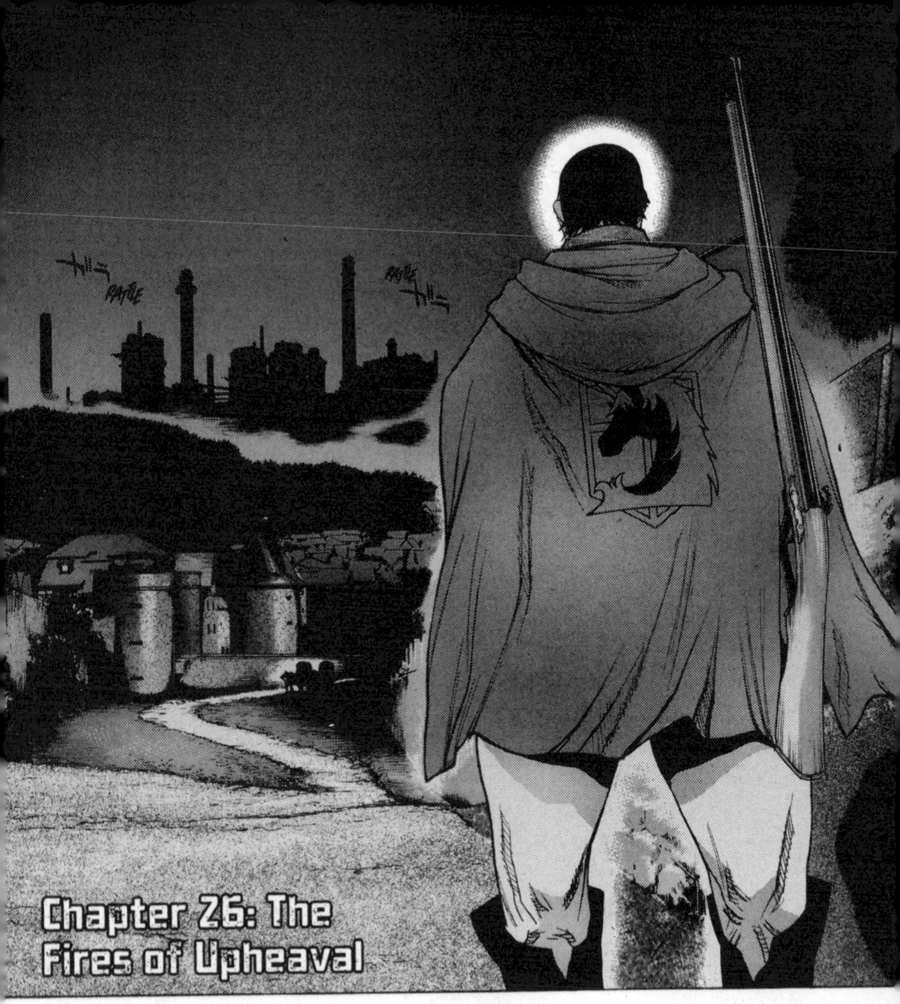
RATTLE
RATTLE
Chapter 26: The Fires of Upheaval

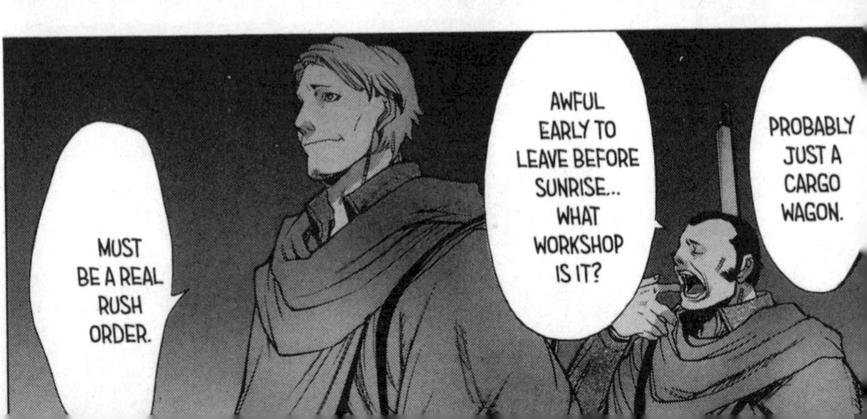
PROBABLY JUST A CARGO WAGON.
AWFUL EARLY TO LEAVE BEFORE SUNRISE... WHAT WORKSHOP IS IT?
MUST BE A REAL RUSH ORDER.

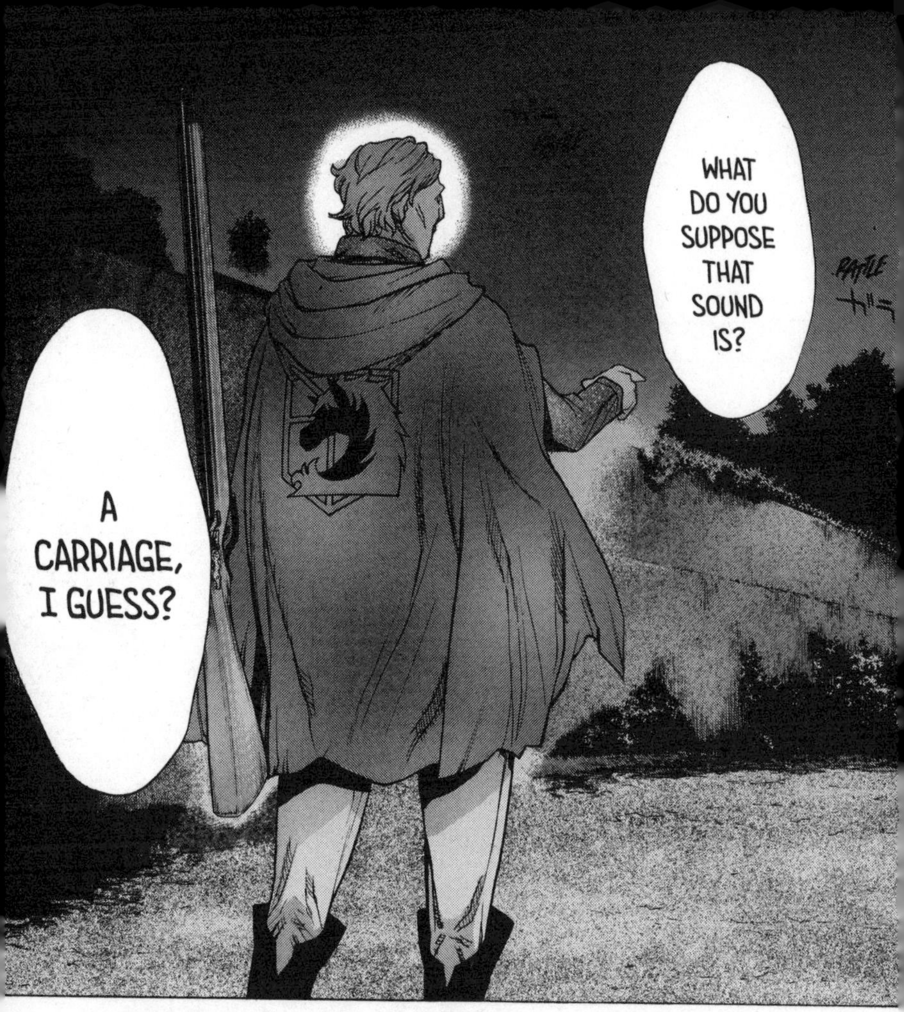
WHAT DO YOU SUPPOSE THAT SOUND IS?
RATTLE
A CARRIAGE, I GUESS?
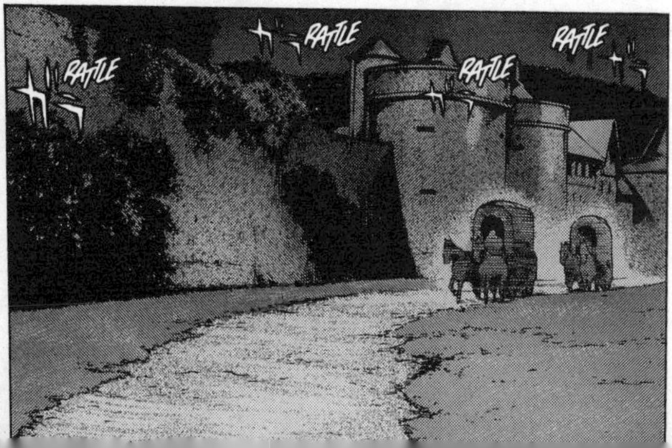
RATTLE
RATTLE
RATTLE
RATTLE
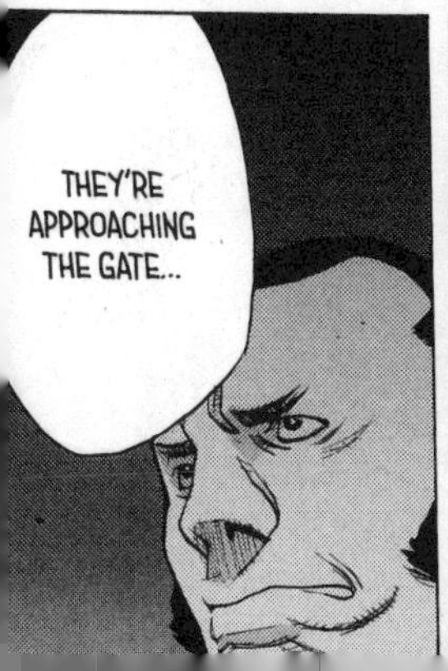
THEY'RE APPROACHING THE GATE...

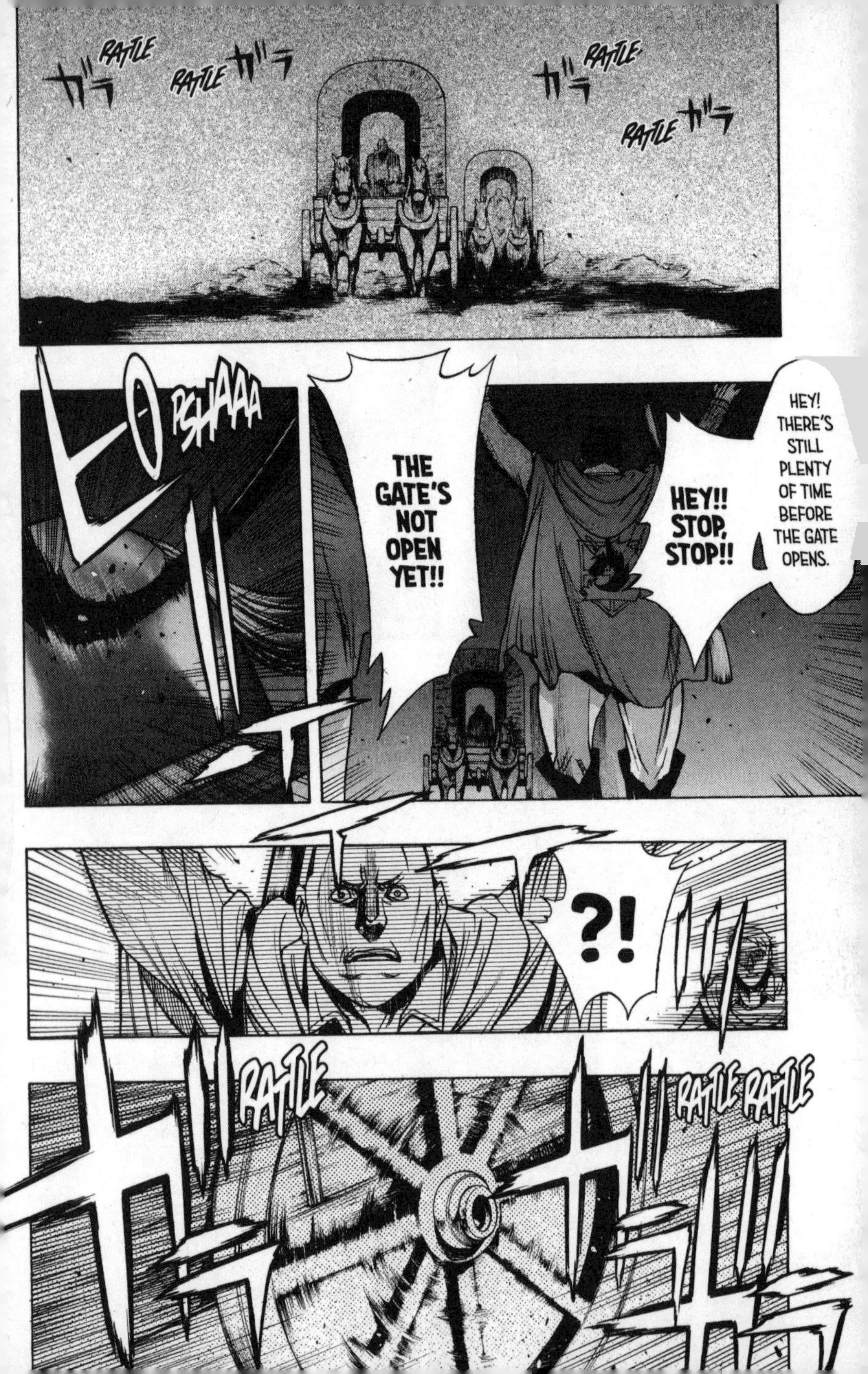

RATTLE ガラ
RATTLE ガラ
RATTLE ガラ
RATTLE ガラ
HEY! THERE'S STILL PLENTY OF TIME BEFORE THE GATE OPENS.
HEY!! STOP, STOP!!
THE GATE'S NOT OPEN YET!!
PSHAAA
?!
RATTLE RATTLE
RATTLE

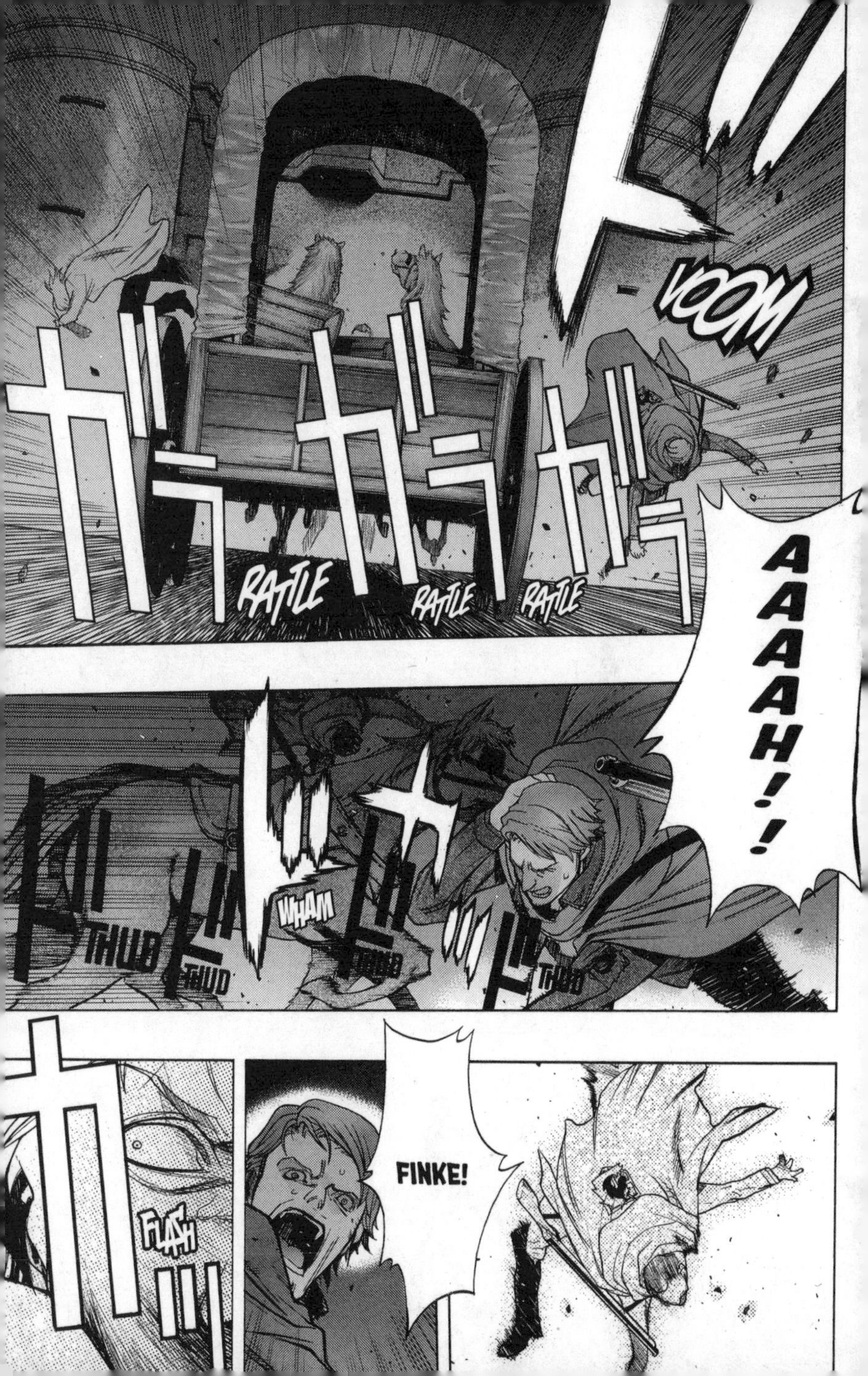
VOOM
RATTLE
RATTLE
RATTLE
AAAAH!!
WHAM
THUD
THUD
THUD
THUD
FINKE!
FLASH

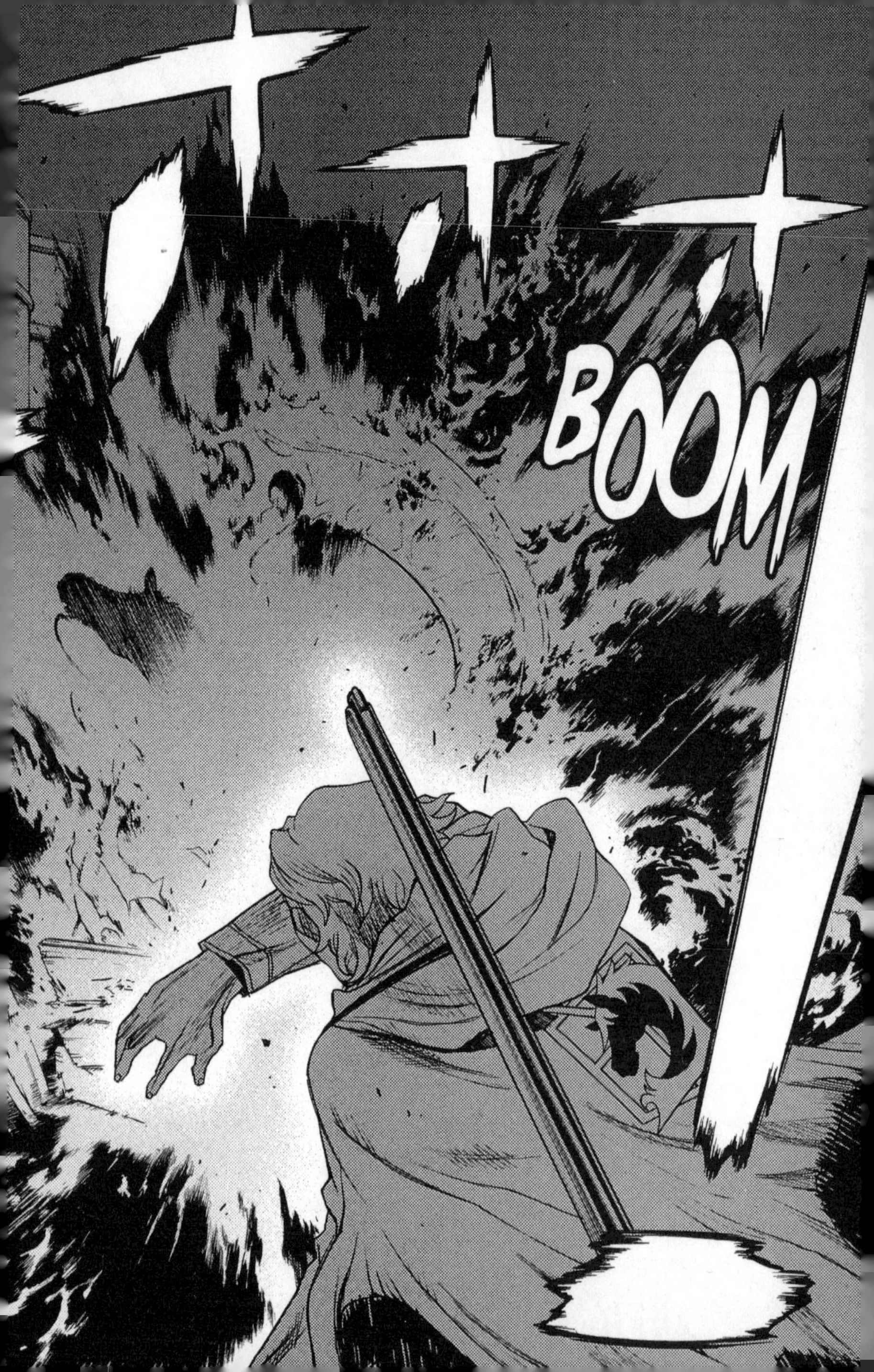
BOOM

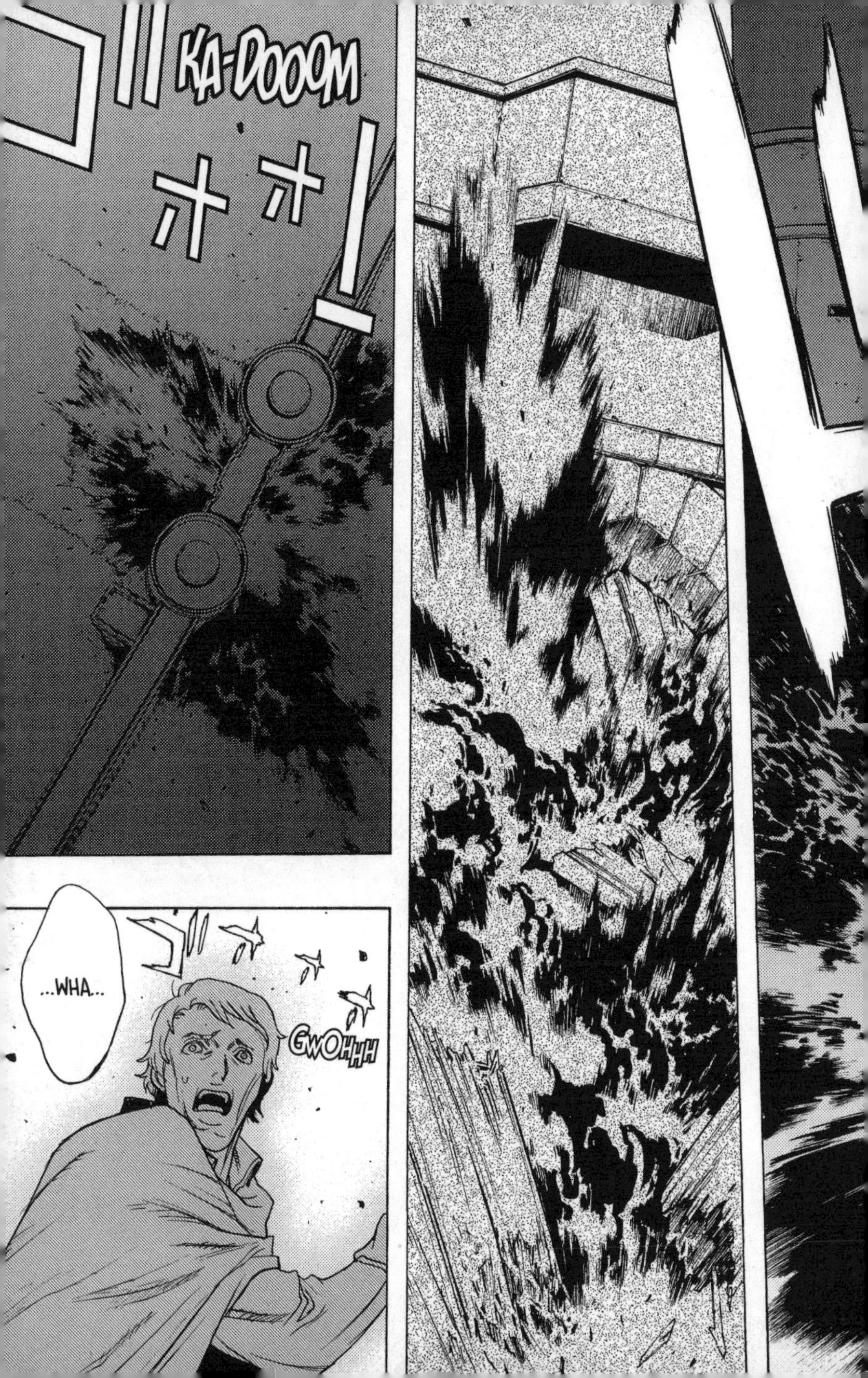
KA-DOOOM
...WHA...
GWOHHH

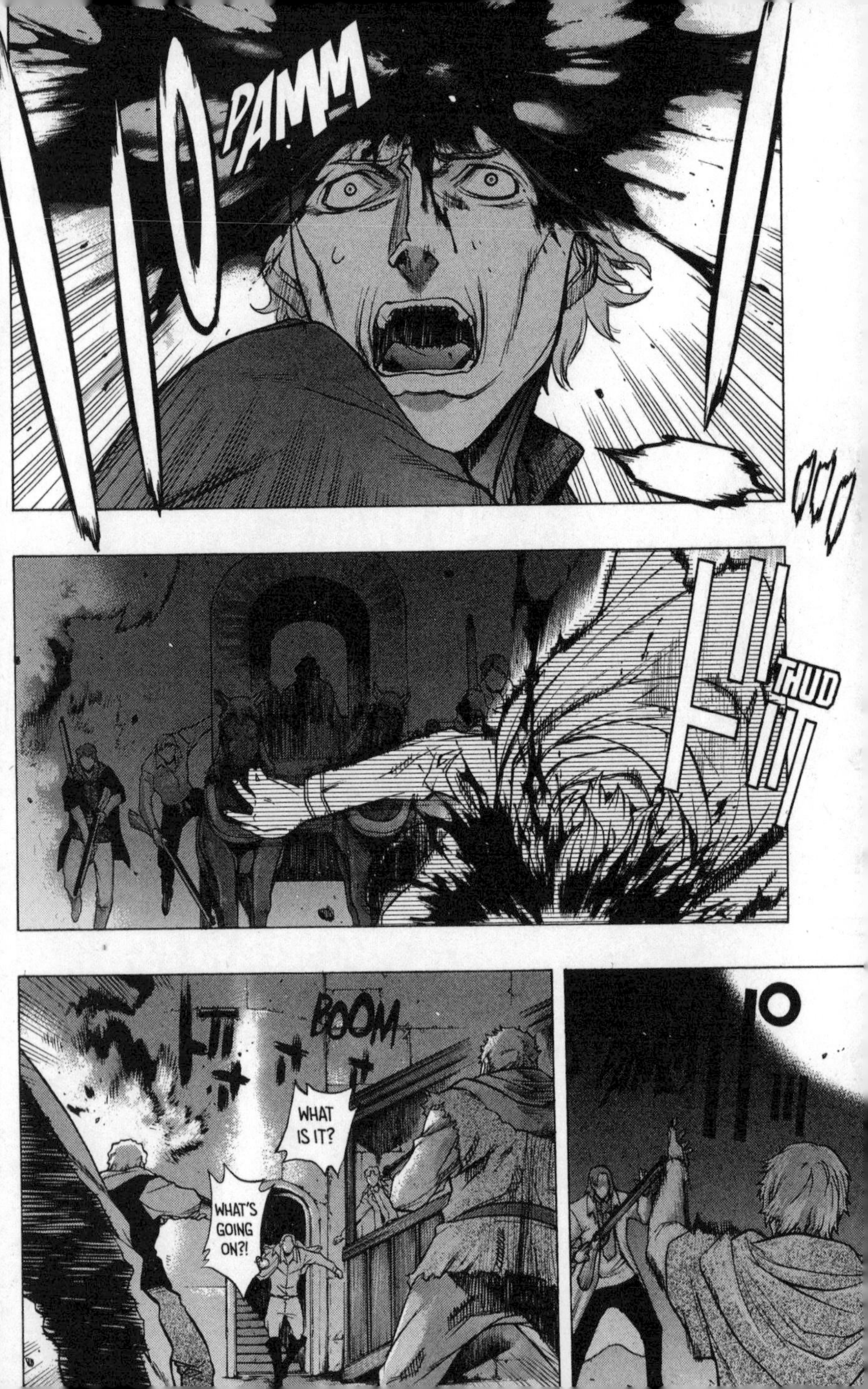
PAMM
THUD
BOOM
WHAT IS IT?
WHAT'S GOING ON?!

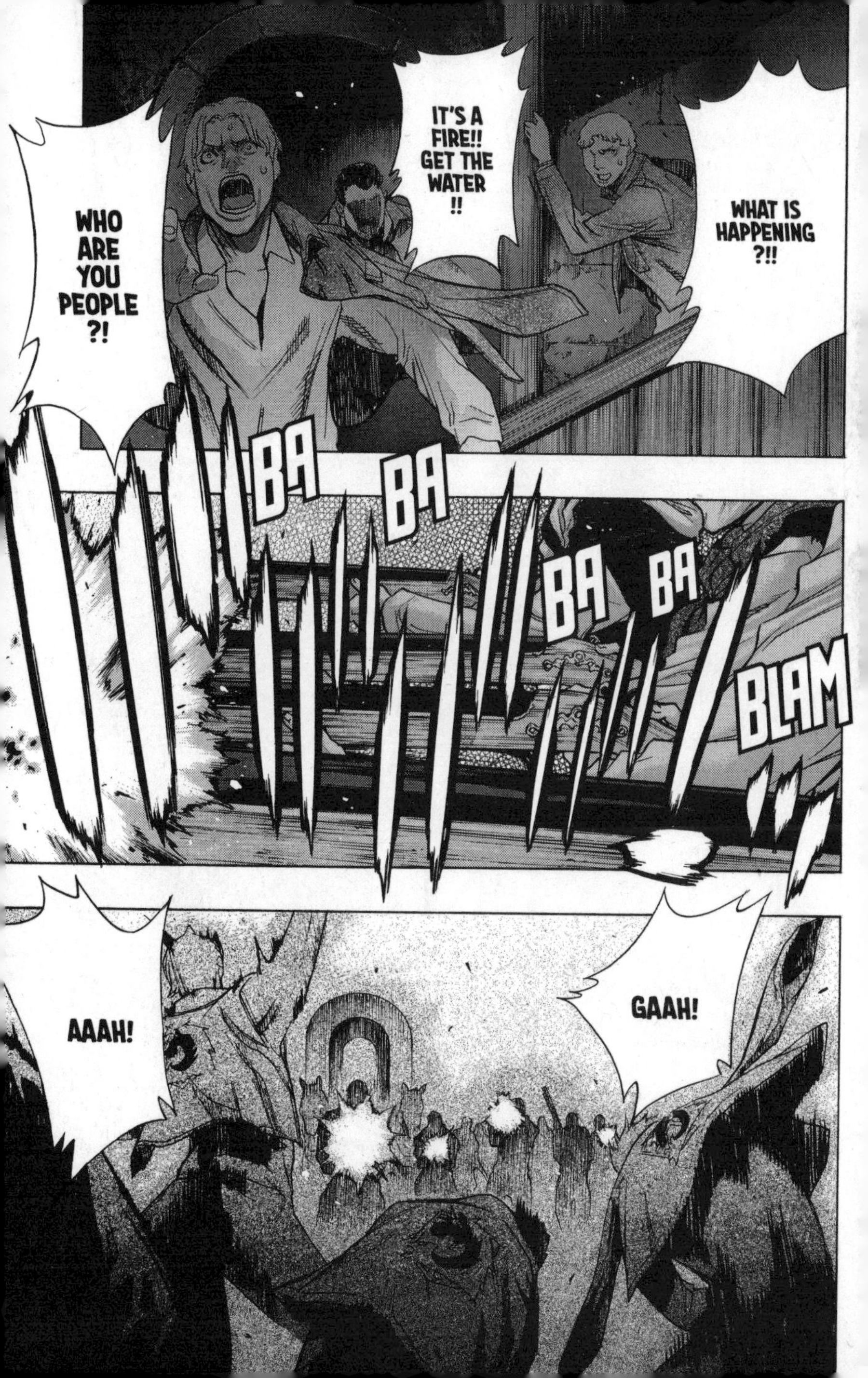
WHAT IS HAPPENING ?!!
IT'S A FIRE!! GET THE WATER !!
WHO ARE YOU PEOPLE ?!
BA
BA
BA
BA
BLAM
GAAH!
AAAH!

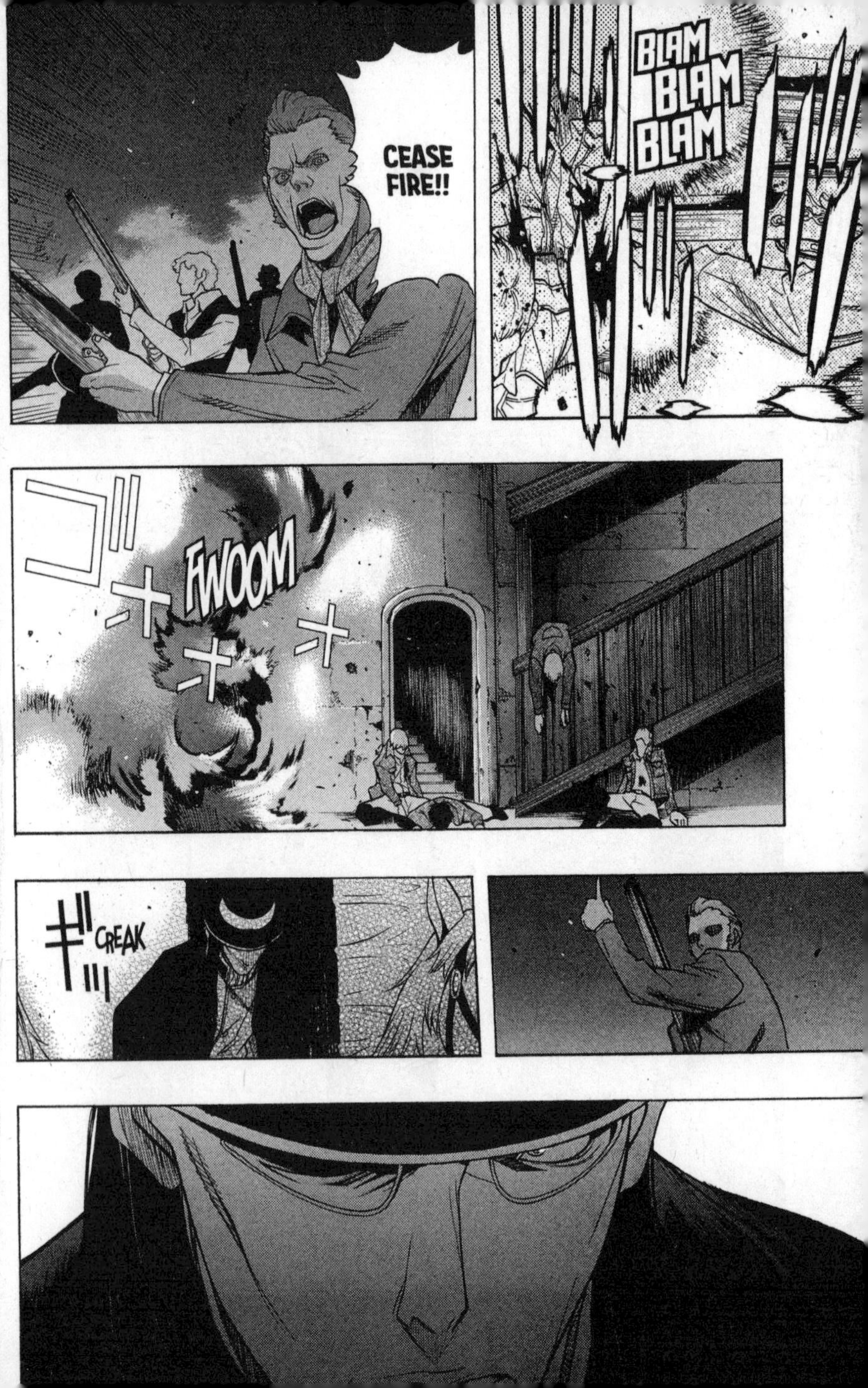
BLAM BLAM BLAM
CEASE FIRE!!
FWOOM
CREAK

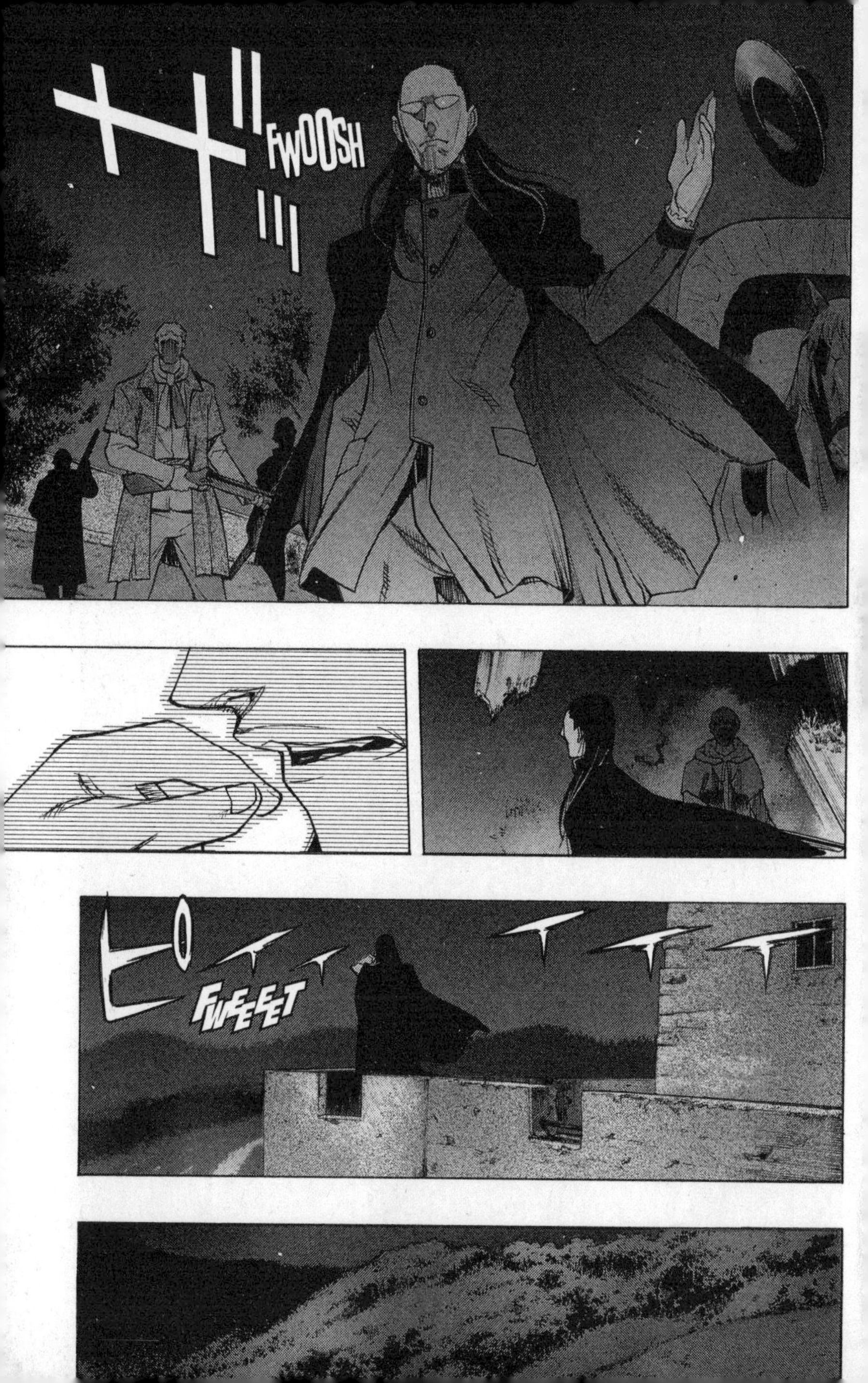
FWOOSH
FWEEEET

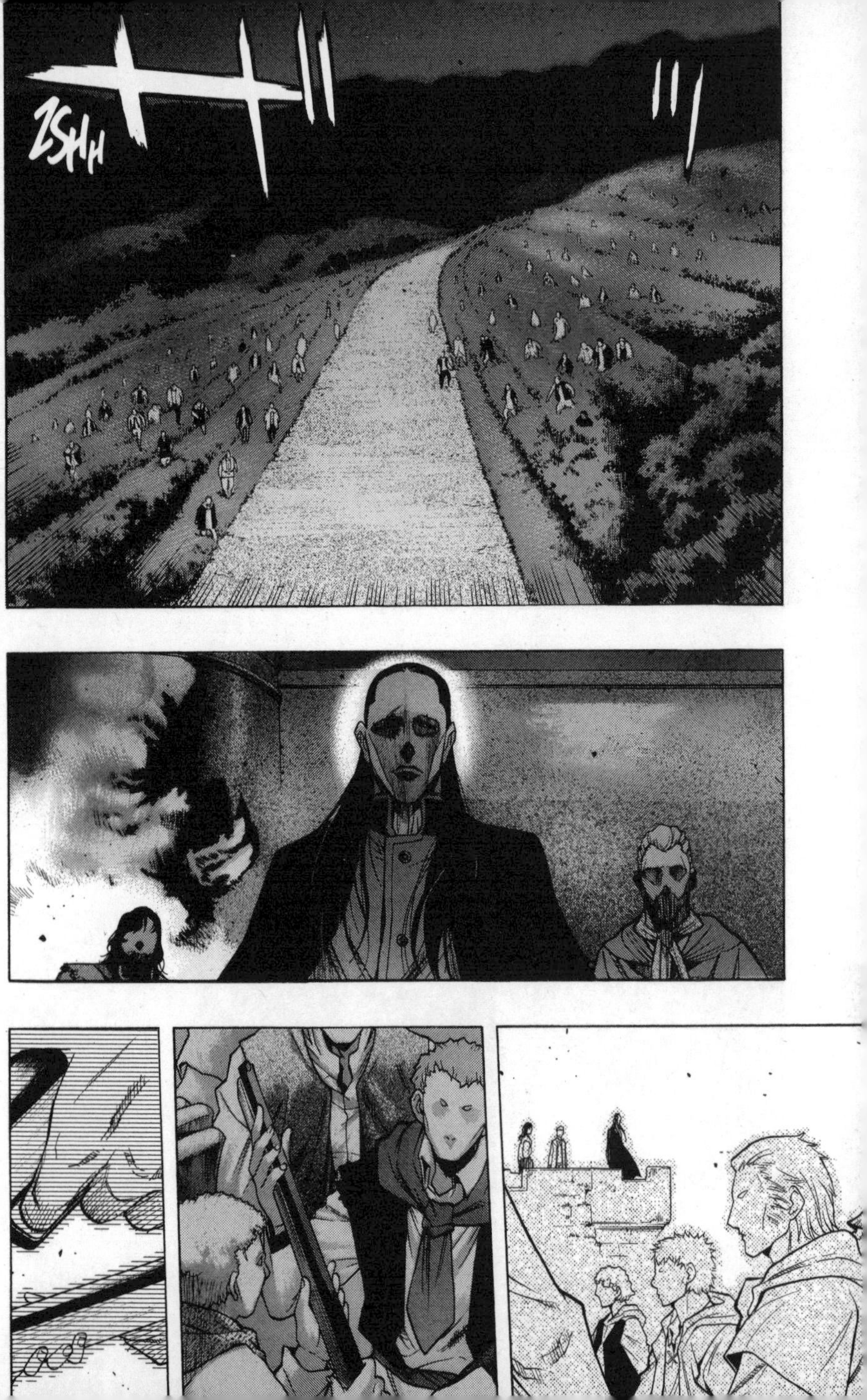
ZSHH

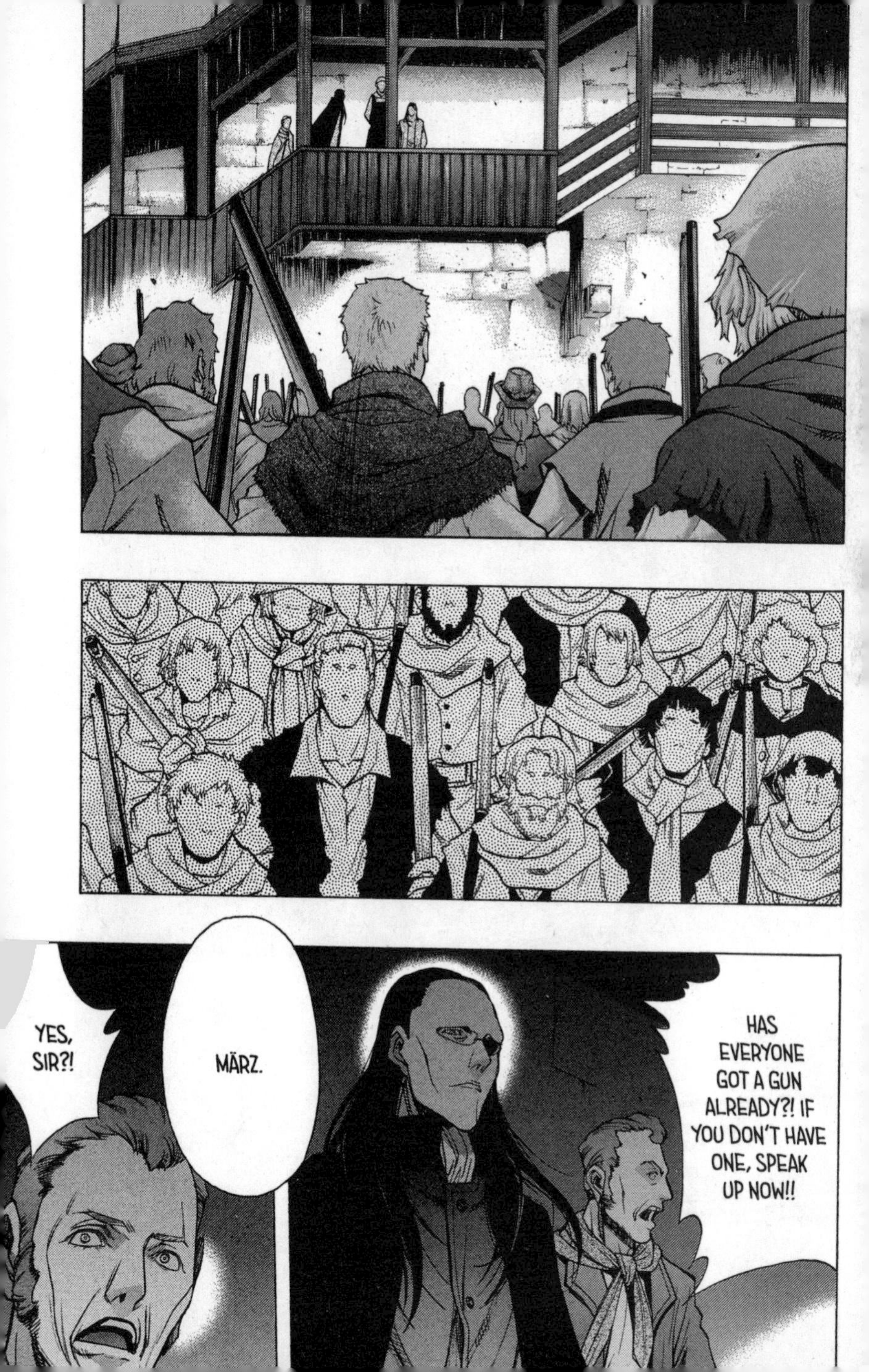
HAS EVERYONE GOT A GUN ALREADY?! IF YOU DON'T HAVE ONE, SPEAK UP NOW!!
MÄRZ.
YES, SIR?!

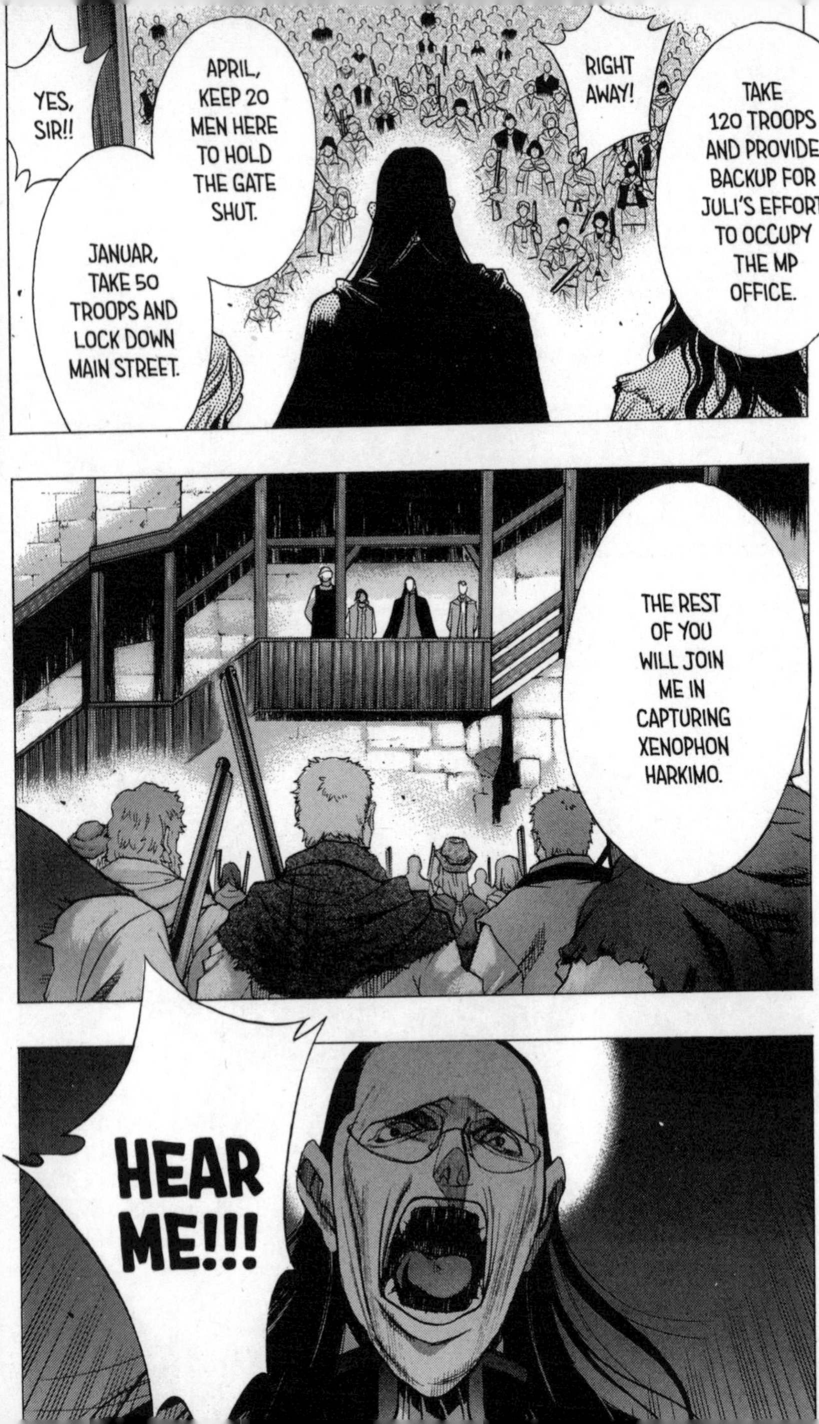
TAKE 120 TROOPS AND PROVIDE BACKUP FOR JULI'S EFFORT TO OCCUPY THE MP OFFICE.
RIGHT AWAY!
APRIL, KEEP 20 MEN HERE TO HOLD THE GATE SHUT.
YES, SIR!!
JANUAR, TAKE 50 TROOPS AND LOCK DOWN MAIN STREET.
THE REST OF YOU WILL JOIN ME IN CAPTURING XENOPHON HARKIMO.
HEAR ME!!!

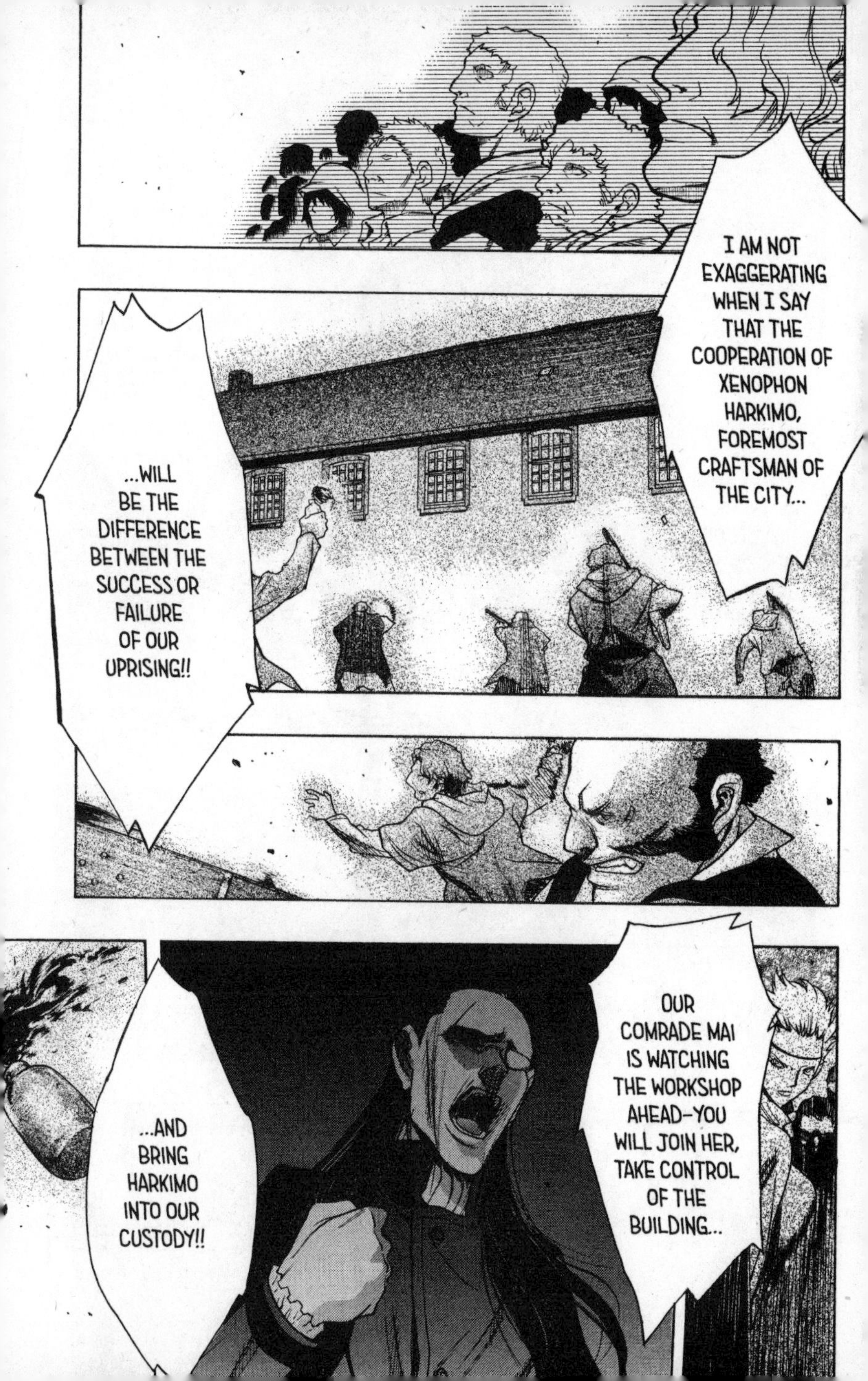
I AM NOT EXAGGERATING WHEN I SAY THAT THE COOPERATION OF XENOPHON HARKIMO, FOREMOST CRAFTSMAN OF THE CITY...
...WILL BE THE DIFFERENCE BETWEEN THE SUCCESS OR FAILURE OF OUR UPRISING!!
OUR COMRADE MAI IS WATCHING THE WORKSHOP AHEAD—YOU WILL JOIN HER, TAKE CONTROL OF THE BUILDING...
...AND BRING HARKIMO INTO OUR CUSTODY!!

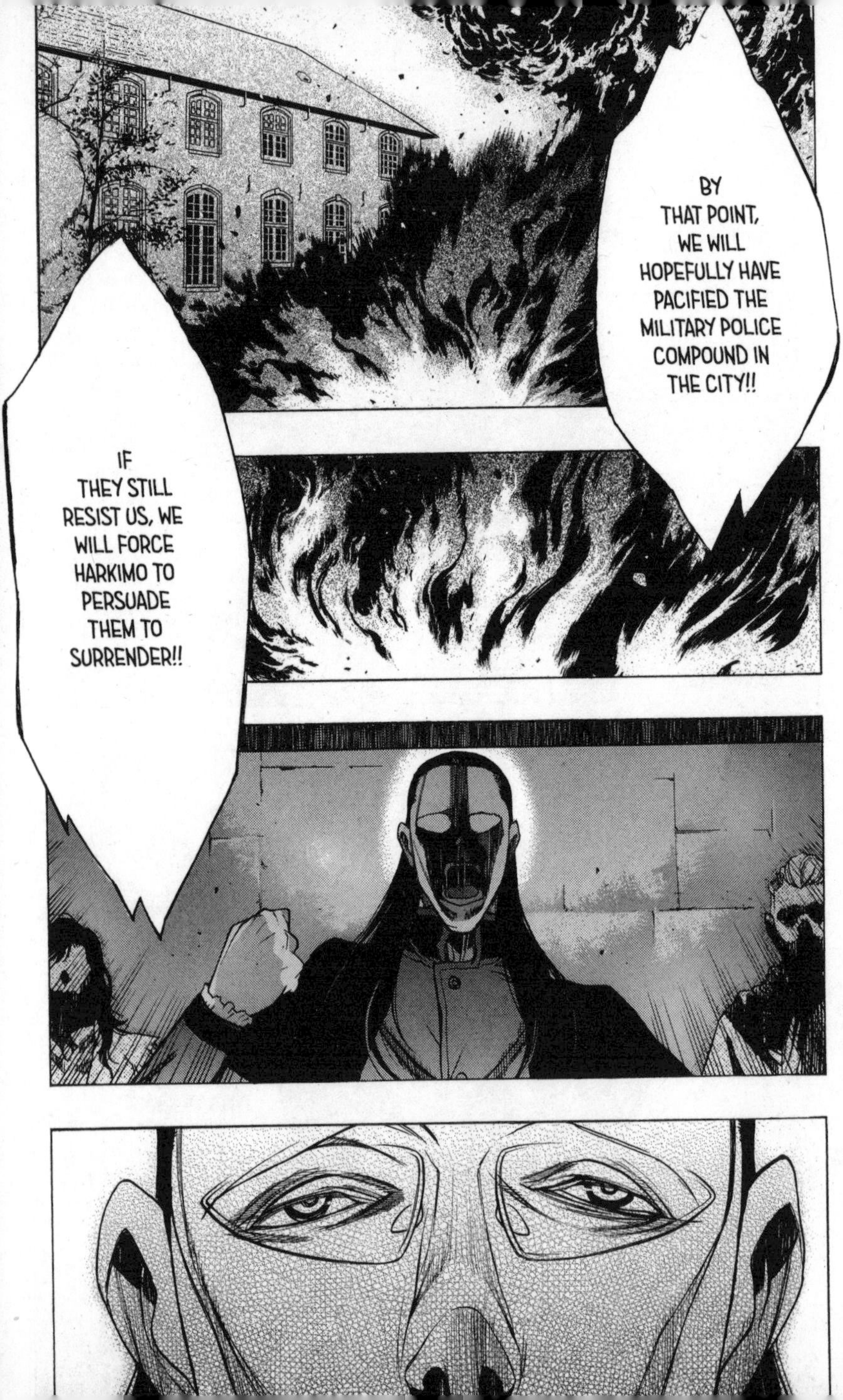
BY THAT POINT, WE WILL HOPEFULLY HAVE PACIFIED THE MILITARY POLICE COMPOUND IN THE CITY!!
IF THEY STILL RESIST US, WE WILL FORCE HARKIMO TO PERSUADE THEM TO SURRENDER!!

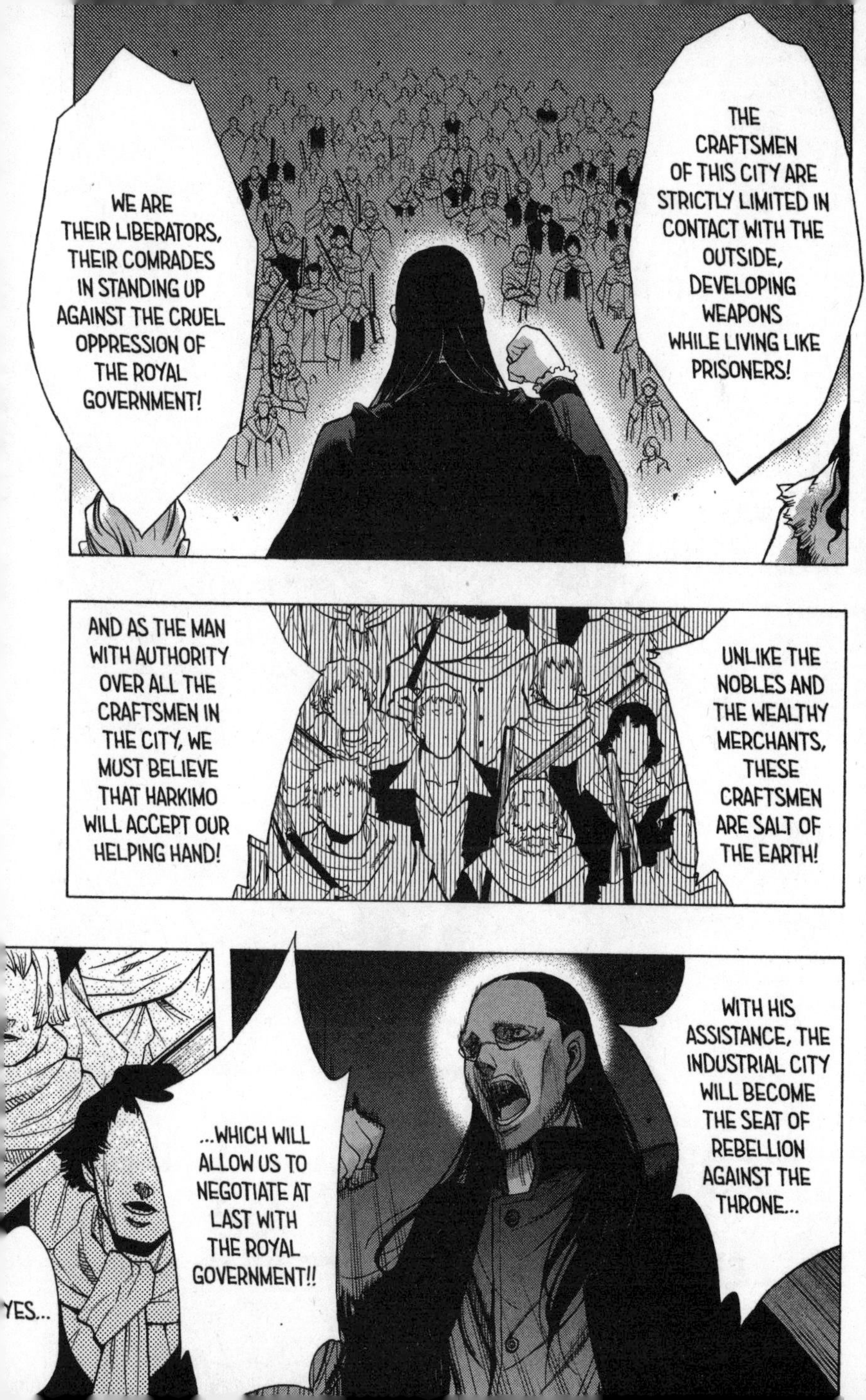
THE CRAFTSMEN OF THIS CITY ARE STRICTLY LIMITED IN CONTACT WITH THE OUTSIDE, DEVELOPING WEAPONS WHILE LIVING LIKE PRISONERS!
WE ARE THEIR LIBERATORS, THEIR COMRADES IN STANDING UP AGAINST THE CRUEL OPPRESSION OF THE ROYAL GOVERNMENT!
UNLIKE THE NOBLES AND THE WEALTHY MERCHANTS, THESE CRAFTSMEN ARE SALT OF THE EARTH!
AND AS THE MAN WITH AUTHORITY OVER ALL THE CRAFTSMEN IN THE CITY, WE MUST BELIEVE THAT HARKIMO WILL ACCEPT OUR HELPING HAND!
WITH HIS ASSISTANCE, THE INDUSTRIAL CITY WILL BECOME THE SEAT OF REBELLION AGAINST THE THRONE...
...WHICH WILL ALLOW US TO NEGOTIATE AT LAST WITH THE ROYAL GOVERNMENT!!
YES...

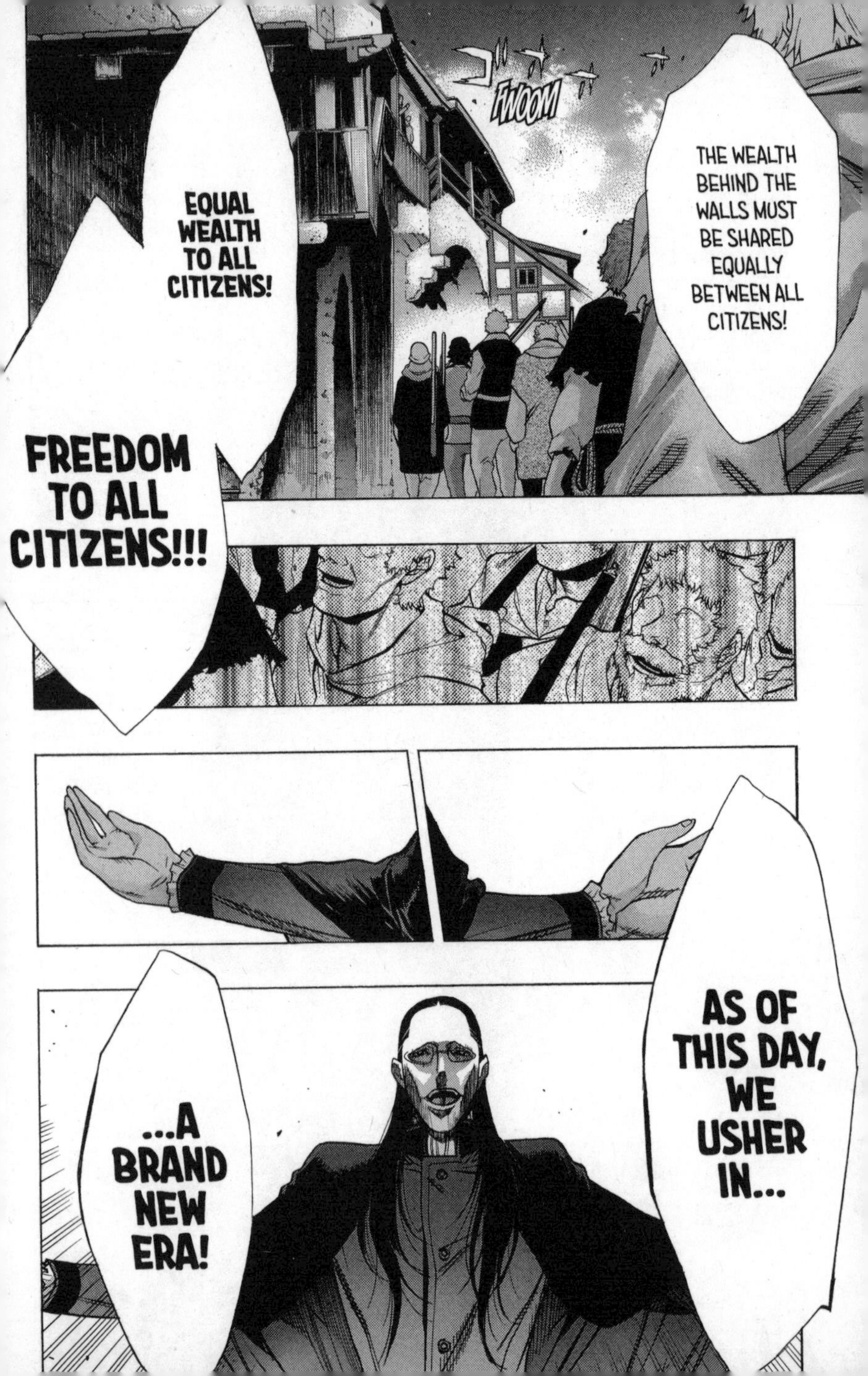
FWOOM
THE WEALTH BEHIND THE WALLS MUST BE SHARED EQUALLY BETWEEN ALL CITIZENS!
EQUAL WEALTH TO ALL CITIZENS!
FREEDOM TO ALL CITIZENS!!!
AS OF THIS DAY, WE USHER IN...
...A BRAND NEW ERA!

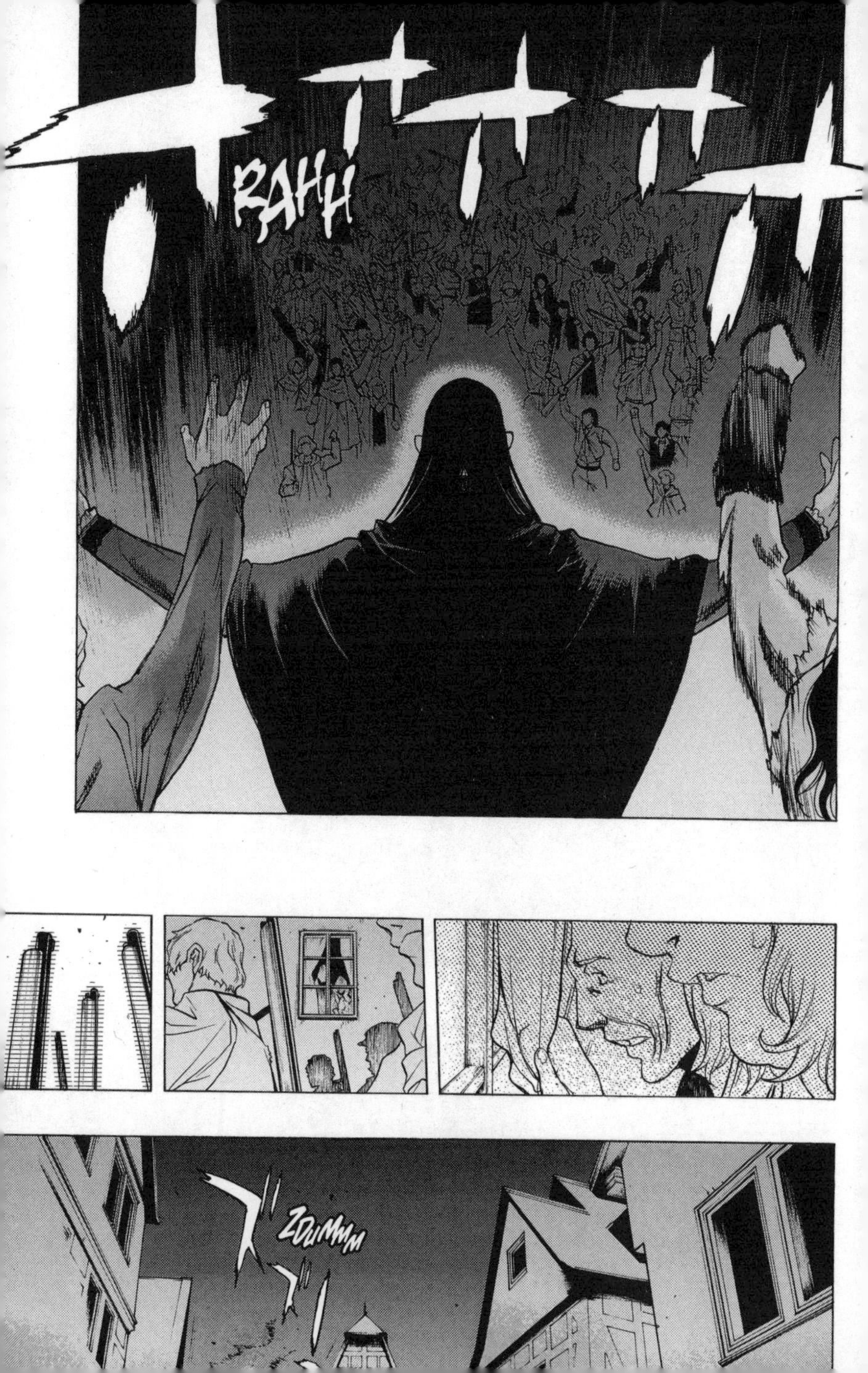
RAHH
ZDUMMM

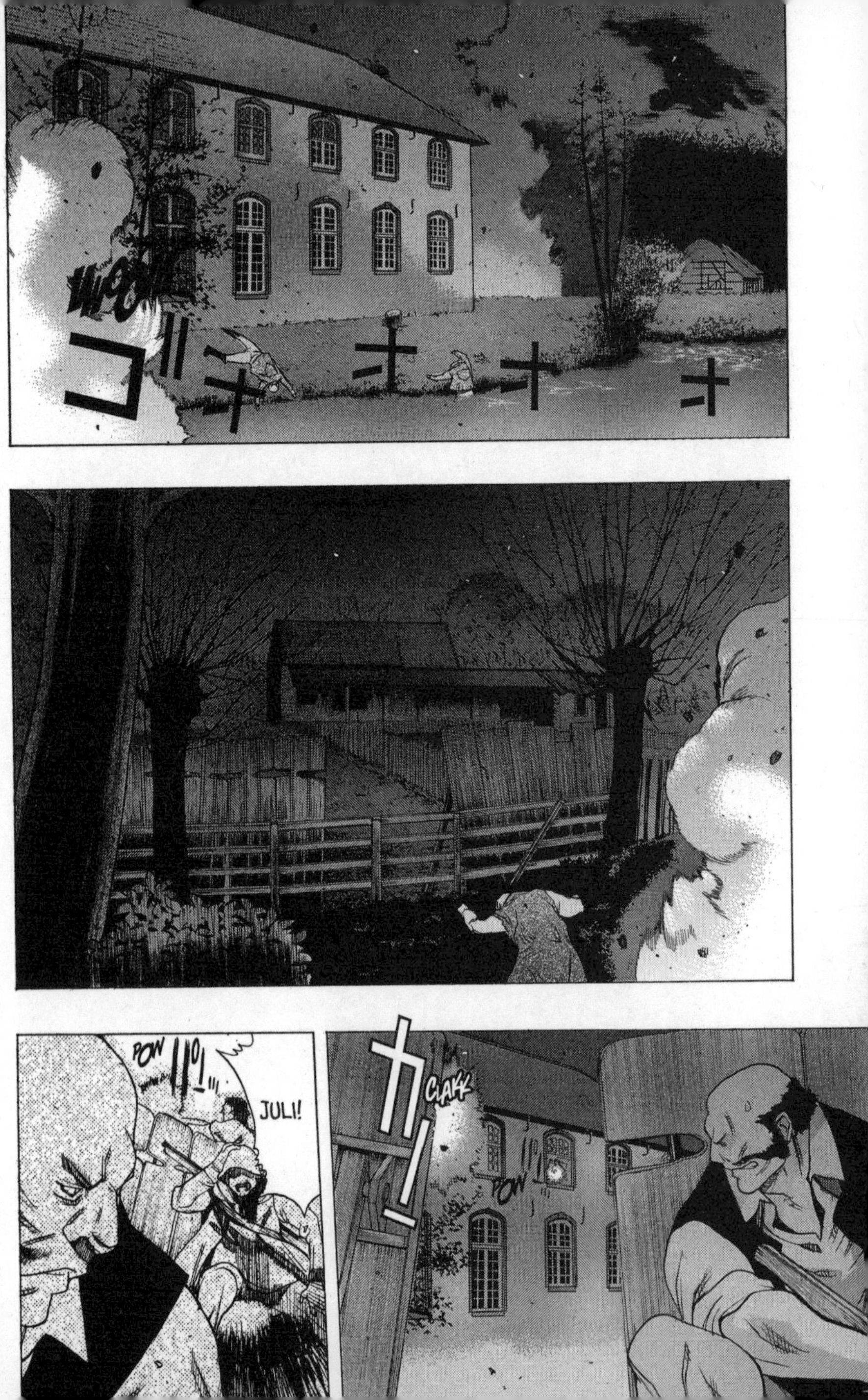
ゴォォォ
カー
CLAKK
POW
POW
パン
JULI!

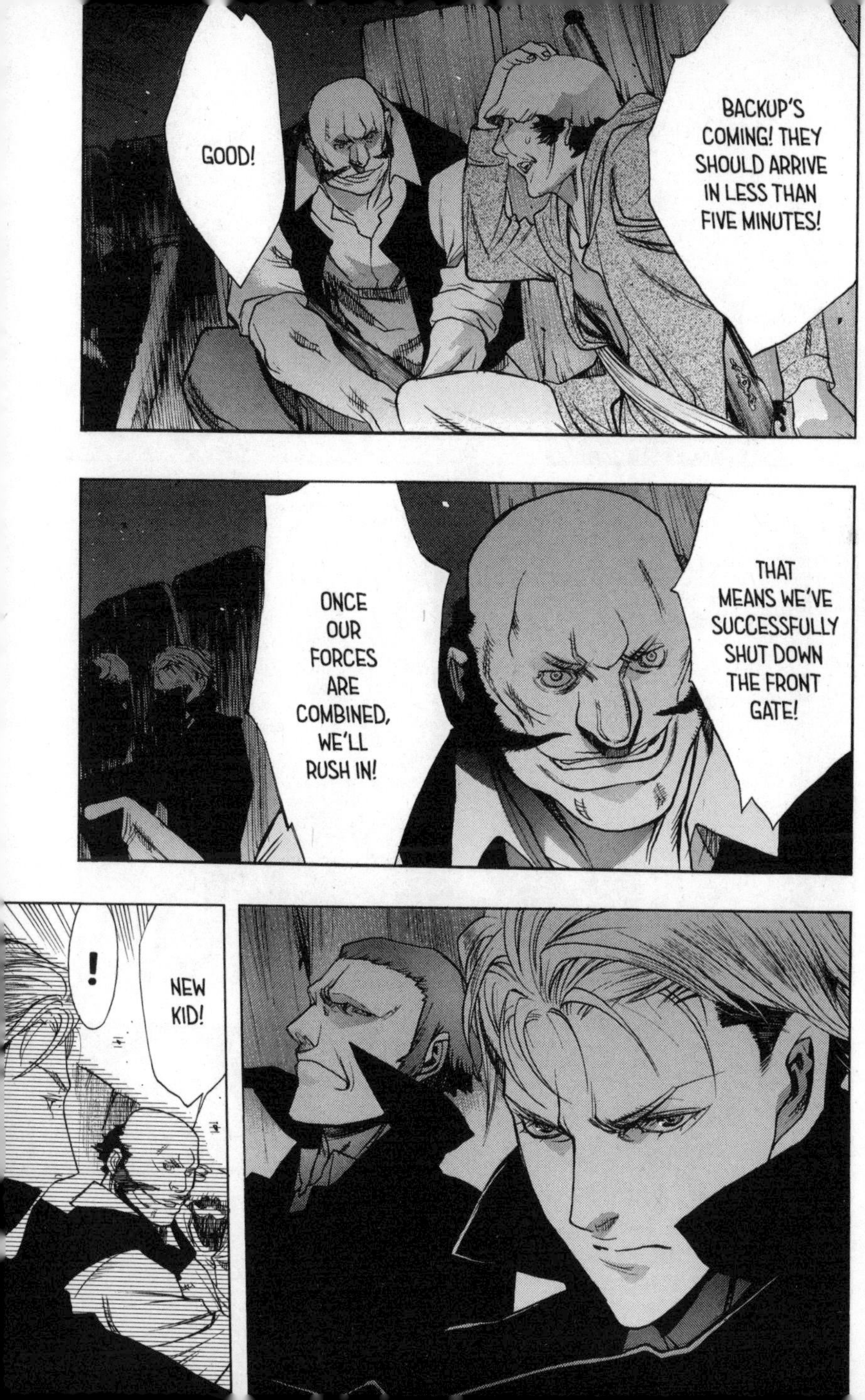
BACKUP'S COMING! THEY SHOULD ARRIVE IN LESS THAN FIVE MINUTES!
GOOD!
THAT MEANS WE'VE SUCCESSFULLY SHUT DOWN THE FRONT GATE!
ONCE OUR FORCES ARE COMBINED, WE'LL RUSH IN!
NEW KID!
!

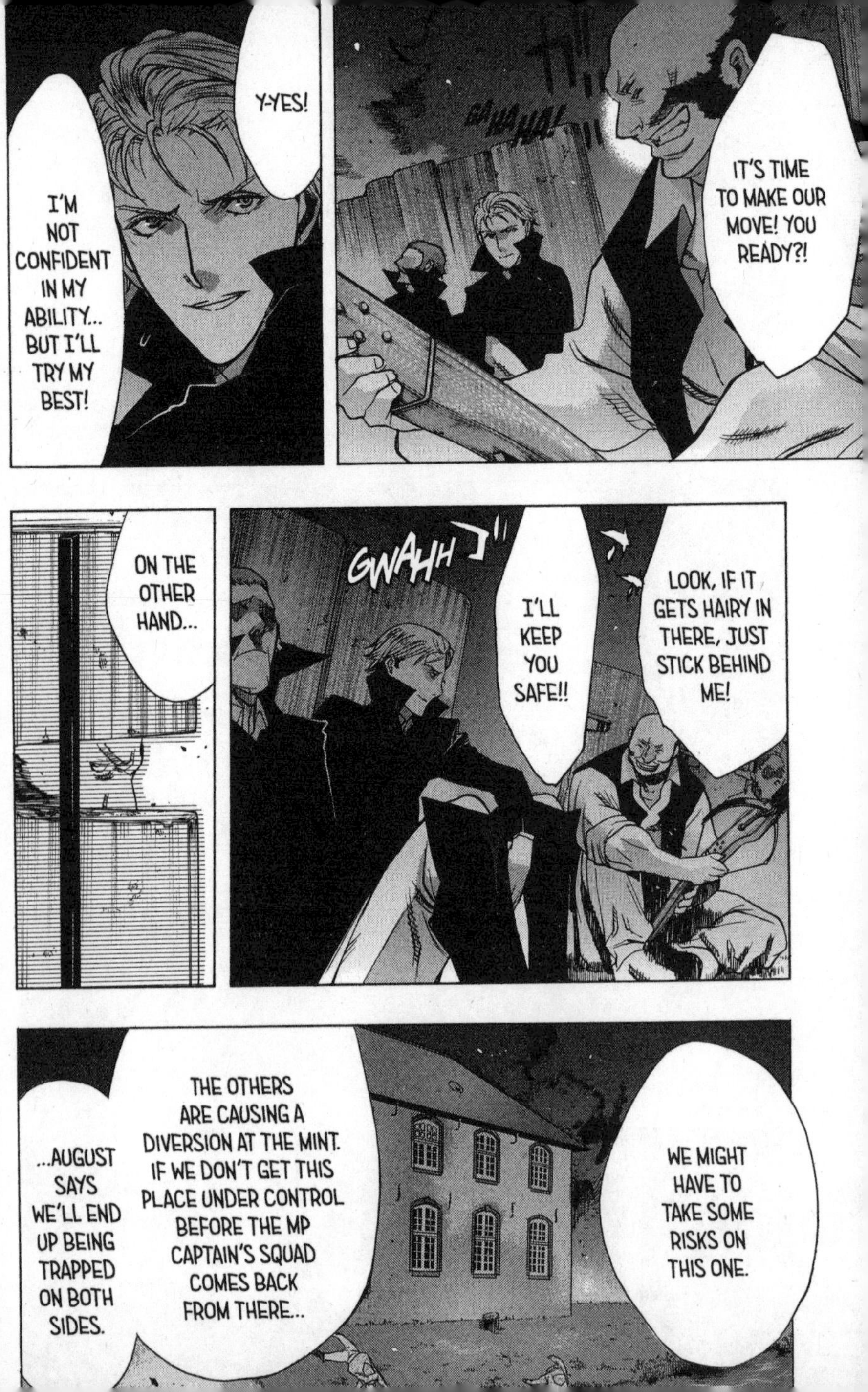
GA HA HA!
IT'S TIME TO MAKE OUR MOVE! YOU READY?!
Y-YES!
I'M NOT CONFIDENT IN MY ABILITY... BUT I'LL TRY MY BEST!
LOOK, IF IT GETS HAIRY IN THERE, JUST STICK BEHIND ME!
I'LL KEEP YOU SAFE!!
GWAHH
ON THE OTHER HAND...
WE MIGHT HAVE TO TAKE SOME RISKS ON THIS ONE.
THE OTHERS ARE CAUSING A DIVERSION AT THE MINT. IF WE DON'T GET THIS PLACE UNDER CONTROL BEFORE THE MP CAPTAIN'S SQUAD COMES BACK FROM THERE...
...AUGUST SAYS WE'LL END UP BEING TRAPPED ON BOTH SIDES.

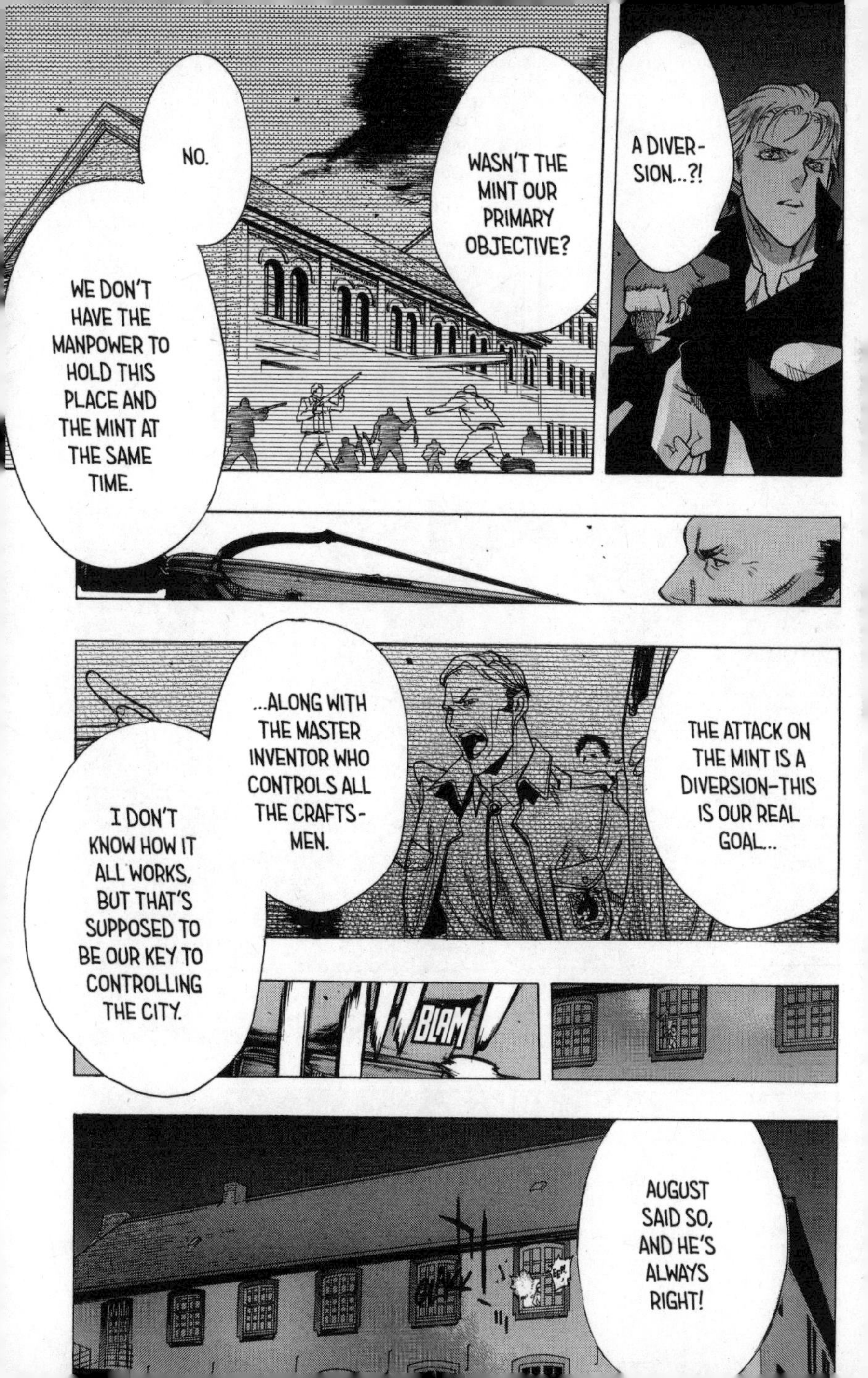
A DIVER-SION...?!
WASN'T THE MINT OUR PRIMARY OBJECTIVE?
NO.
WE DON'T HAVE THE MANPOWER TO HOLD THIS PLACE AND THE MINT AT THE SAME TIME.
THE ATTACK ON THE MINT IS A DIVERSION—THIS IS OUR REAL GOAL...
...ALONG WITH THE MASTER INVENTOR WHO CONTROLS ALL THE CRAFTS-MEN.
I DON'T KNOW HOW IT ALL WORKS, BUT THAT'S SUPPOSED TO BE OUR KEY TO CONTROLLING THE CITY.
BLAM
AUGUST SAID SO, AND HE'S ALWAYS RIGHT!

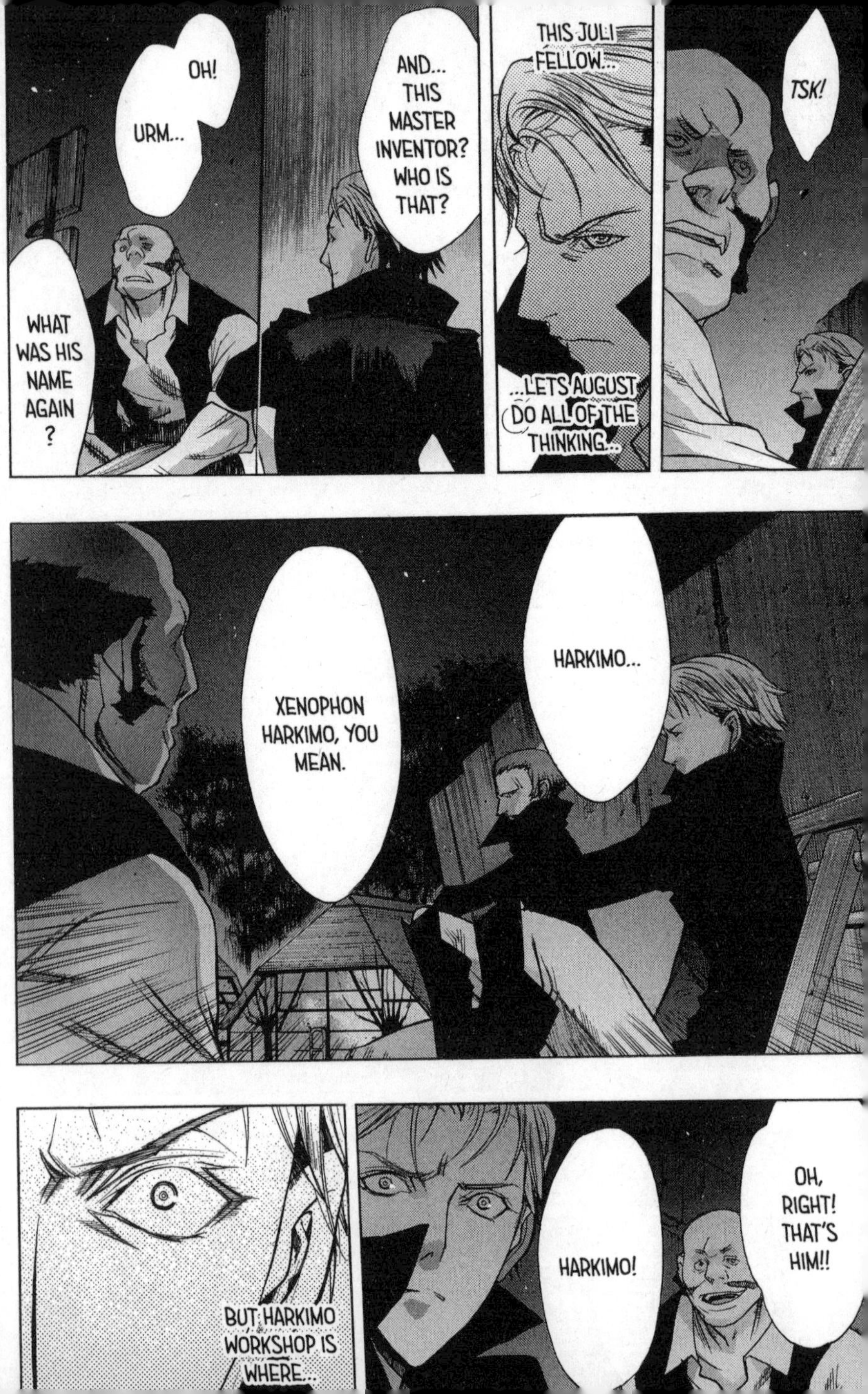
TSK!
THIS JULI FELLOW...
...LETS AUGUST DO ALL OF THE THINKING...
AND... THIS MASTER INVENTOR? WHO IS THAT?
OH!
URM...
WHAT WAS HIS NAME AGAIN ?
HARKIMO...
XENOPHON HARKIMO, YOU MEAN.
OH, RIGHT! THAT'S HIM!!
HARKIMO!
BUT HARKIMO WORKSHOP IS WHERE...

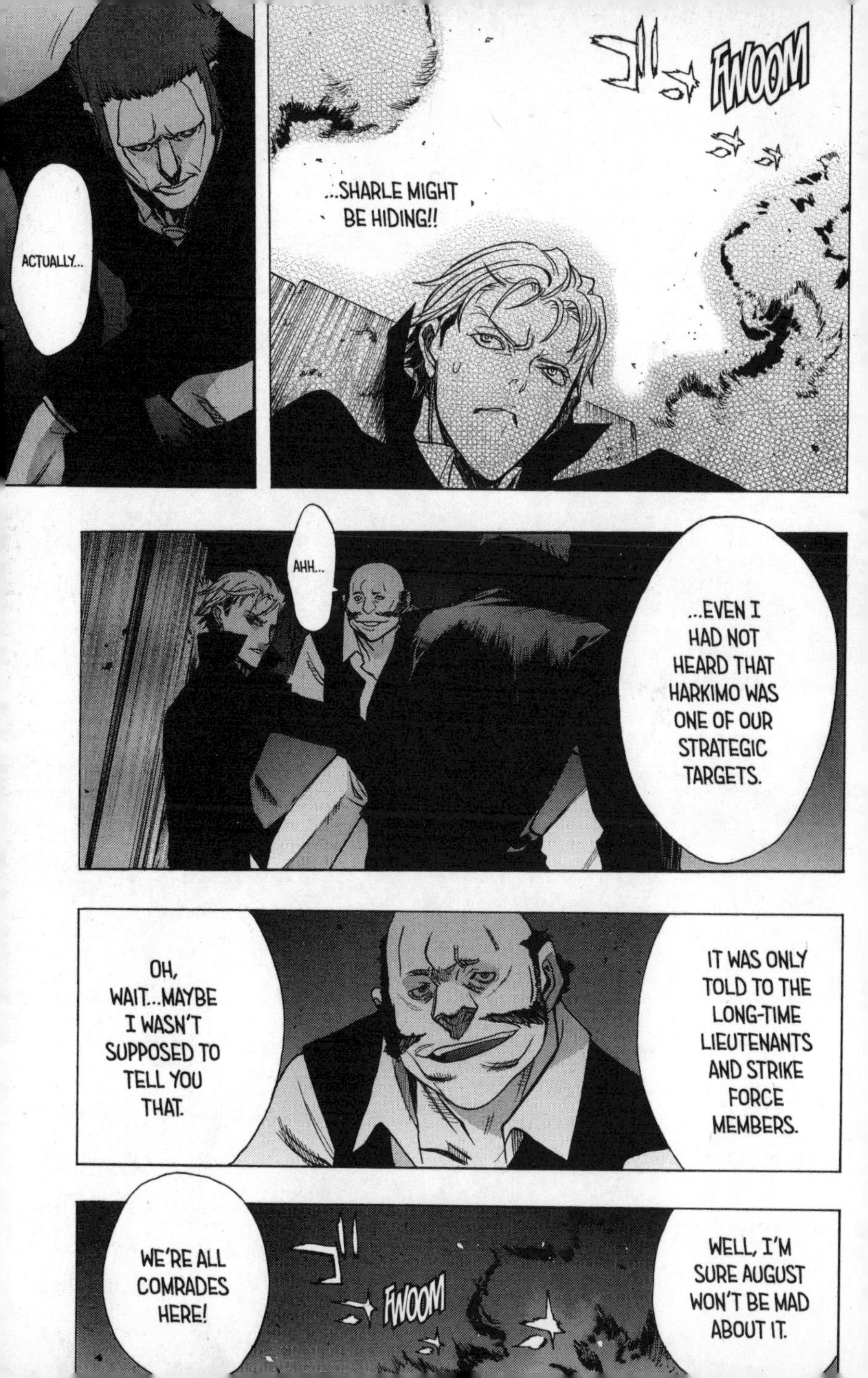
FWOOM
...SHARLE MIGHT BE HIDING!!
ACTUALLY...
...EVEN I HAD NOT HEARD THAT HARKIMO WAS ONE OF OUR STRATEGIC TARGETS.
AHH...
IT WAS ONLY TOLD TO THE LONG-TIME LIEUTENANTS AND STRIKE FORCE MEMBERS.
OH, WAIT...MAYBE I WASN'T SUPPOSED TO TELL YOU THAT.
WELL, I'M SURE AUGUST WON'T BE MAD ABOUT IT.
FWOOM
WE'RE ALL COMRADES HERE!

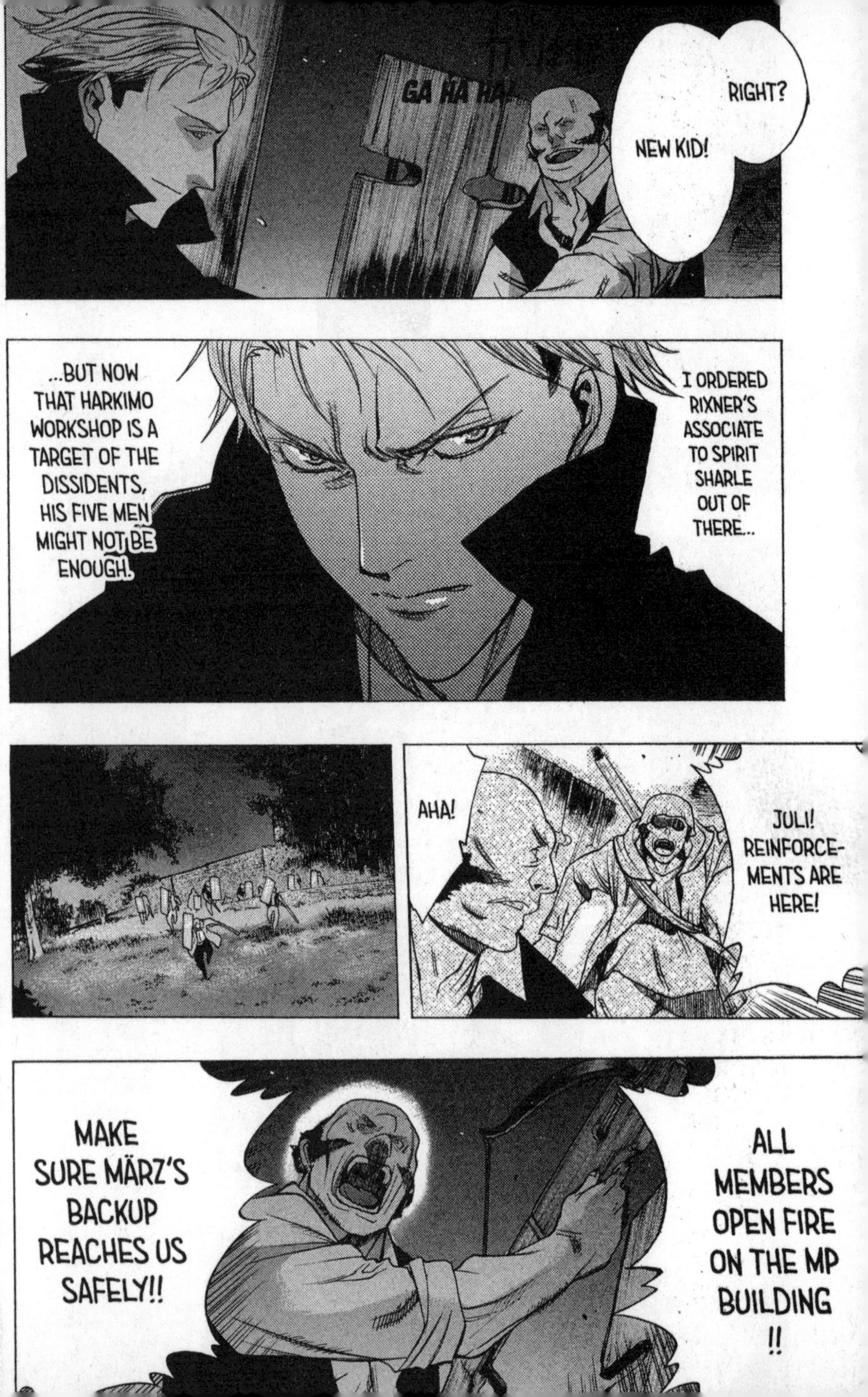
RIGHT?
NEW KID!
GA HA HA
I ORDERED RIXNER'S ASSOCIATE TO SPIRIT SHARLE OUT OF THERE...
...BUT NOW THAT HARKIMO WORKSHOP IS A TARGET OF THE DISSIDENTS, HIS FIVE MEN MIGHT NOT BE ENOUGH.
JULI! REINFORCE-MENTS ARE HERE!
AHA!
ALL MEMBERS OPEN FIRE ON THE MP BUILDING !!
MAKE SURE MÄRZ'S BACKUP REACHES US SAFELY!!

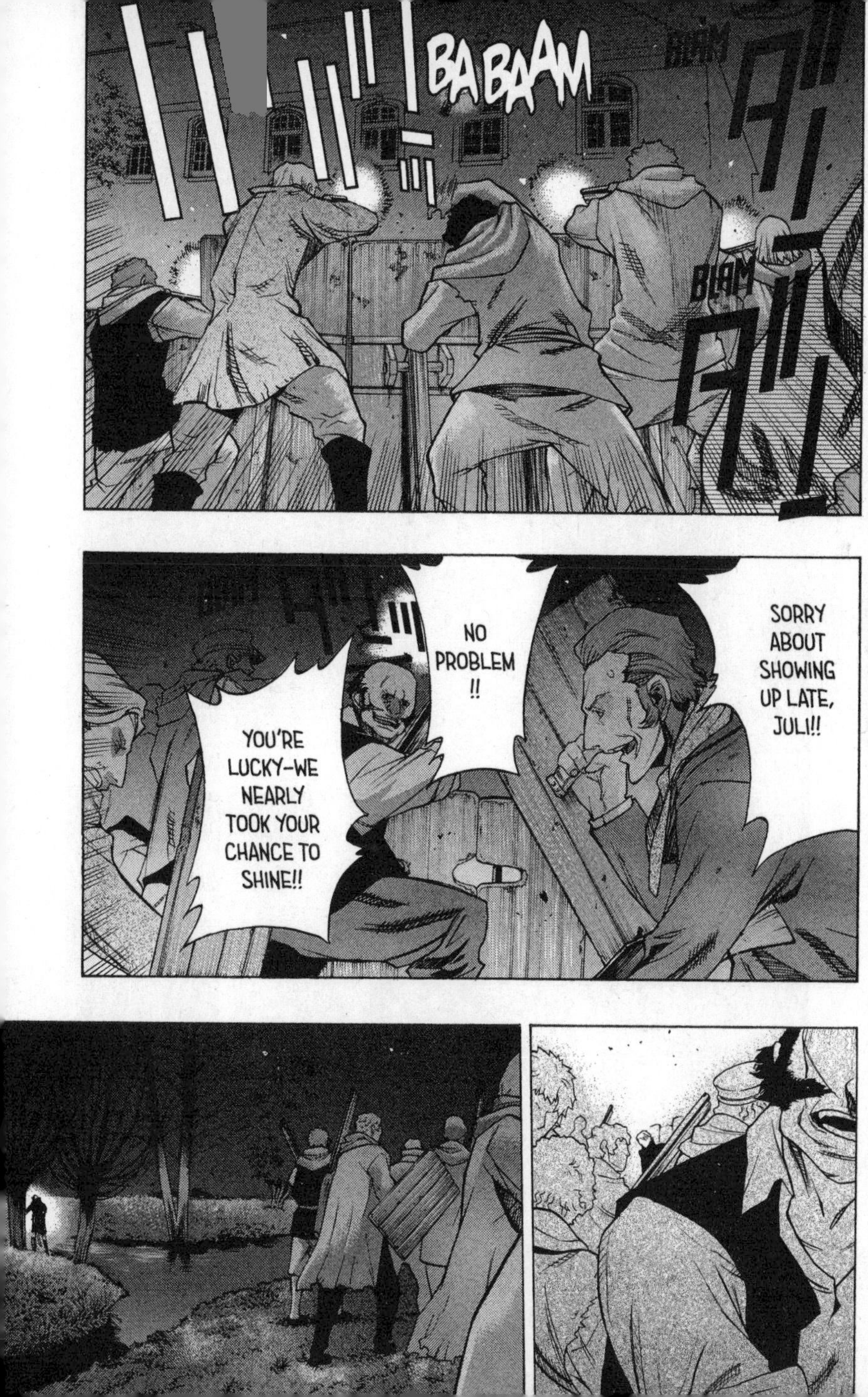
BLAM
BA BAAM
BLAM
SORRY ABOUT SHOWING UP LATE, JULI!!
NO PROBLEM !!
YOU'RE LUCKY–WE NEARLY TOOK YOUR CHANCE TO SHINE!!

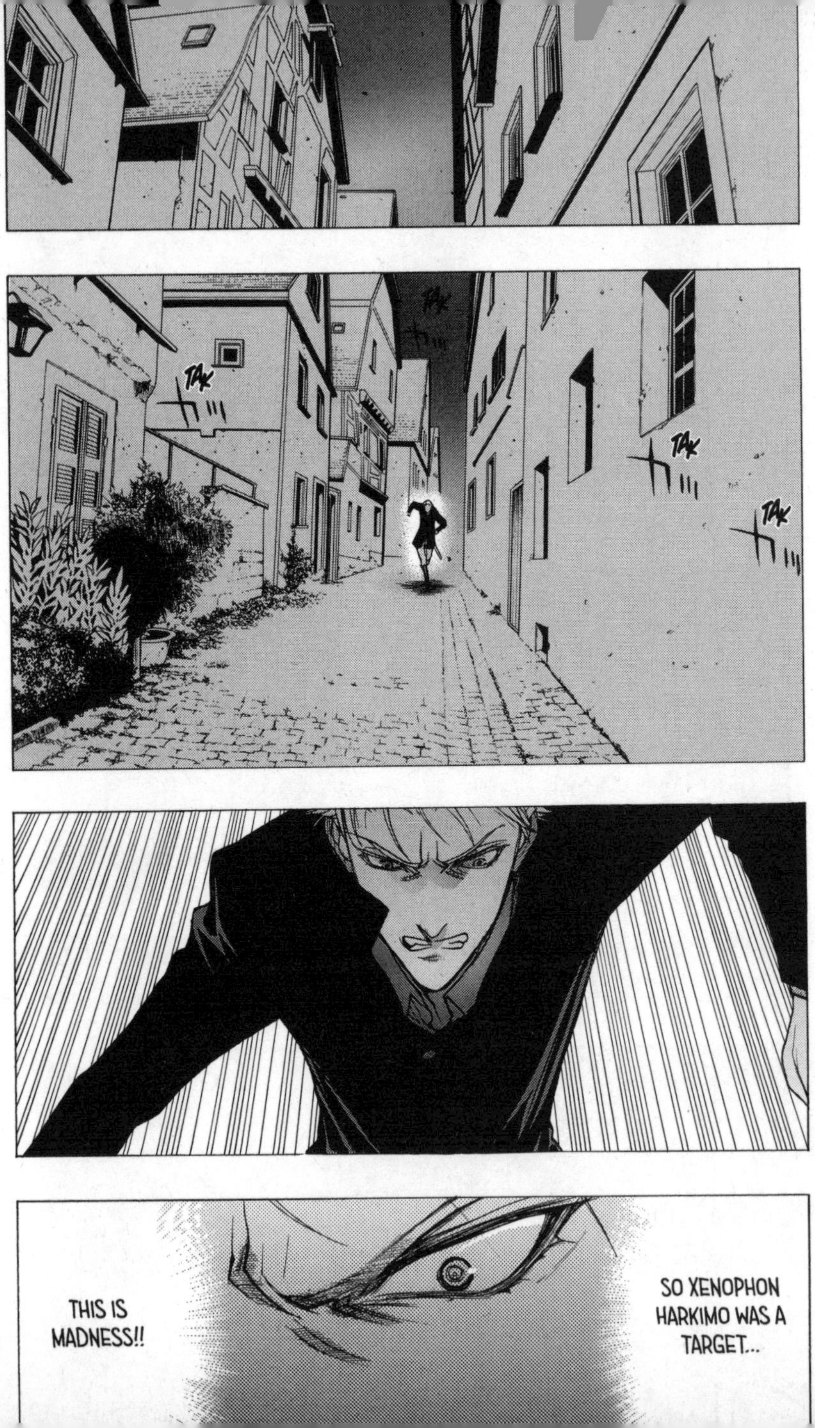
TAK
TAK
TAK
TAK
SO XENOPHON HARKIMO WAS A TARGET...
THIS IS MADNESS!!

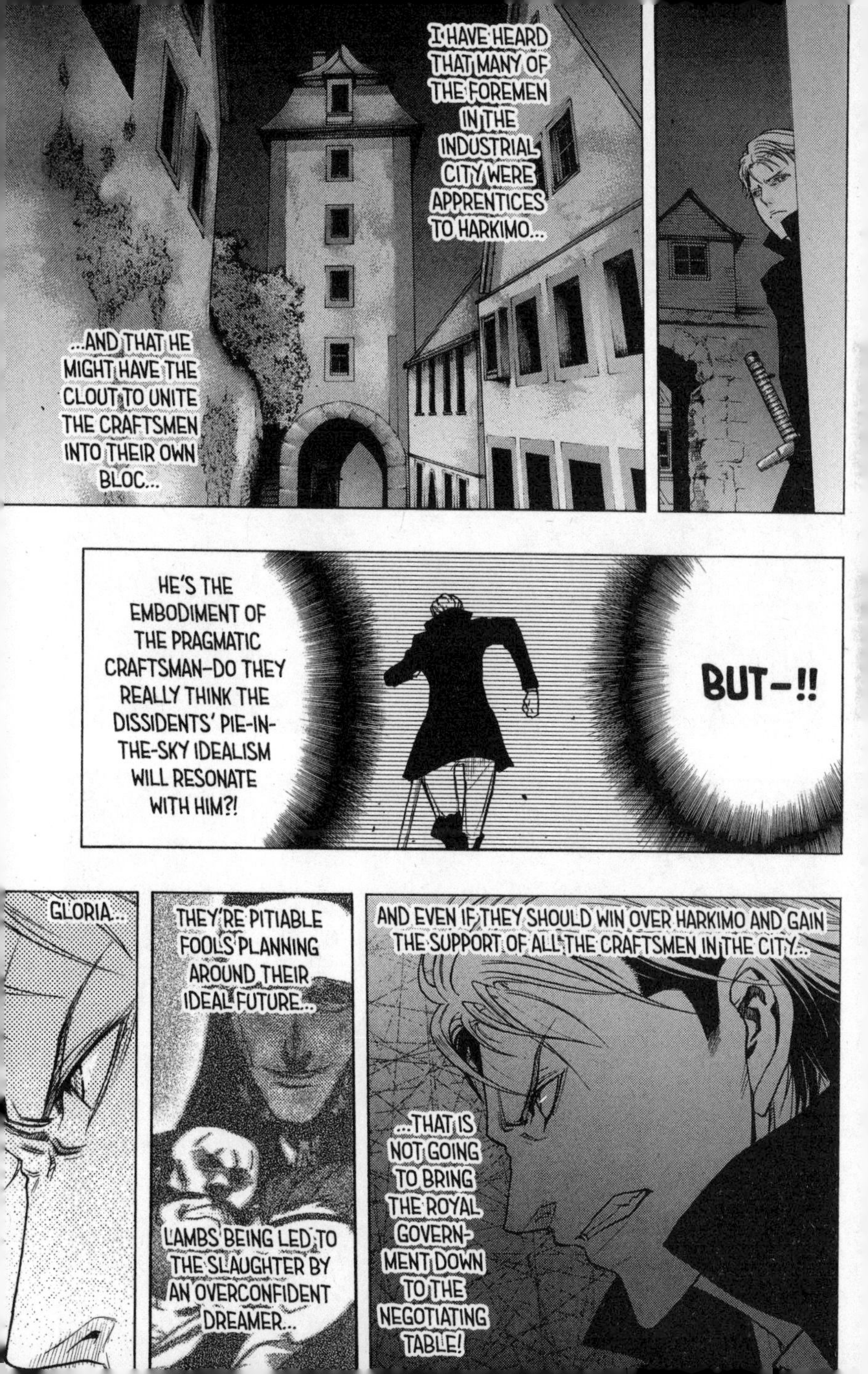
I HAVE HEARD THAT MANY OF THE FOREMEN IN THE INDUSTRIAL CITY WERE APPRENTICES TO HARKIMO...
...AND THAT HE MIGHT HAVE THE CLOUT TO UNITE THE CRAFTSMEN INTO THEIR OWN BLOC...
HE'S THE EMBODIMENT OF THE PRAGMATIC CRAFTSMAN—DO THEY REALLY THINK THE DISSIDENTS' PIE-IN-THE-SKY IDEALISM WILL RESONATE WITH HIM?!
BUT—!!
AND EVEN IF THEY SHOULD WIN OVER HARKIMO AND GAIN THE SUPPORT OF ALL THE CRAFTSMEN IN THE CITY...
...THAT IS NOT GOING TO BRING THE ROYAL GOVERN-MENT DOWN TO THE NEGOTIATING TABLE!
THEY'RE PITIABLE FOOLS PLANNING AROUND THEIR IDEAL FUTURE...
LAMBS BEING LED TO THE SLAUGHTER BY AN OVERCONFIDENT DREAMER...
GLORIA...

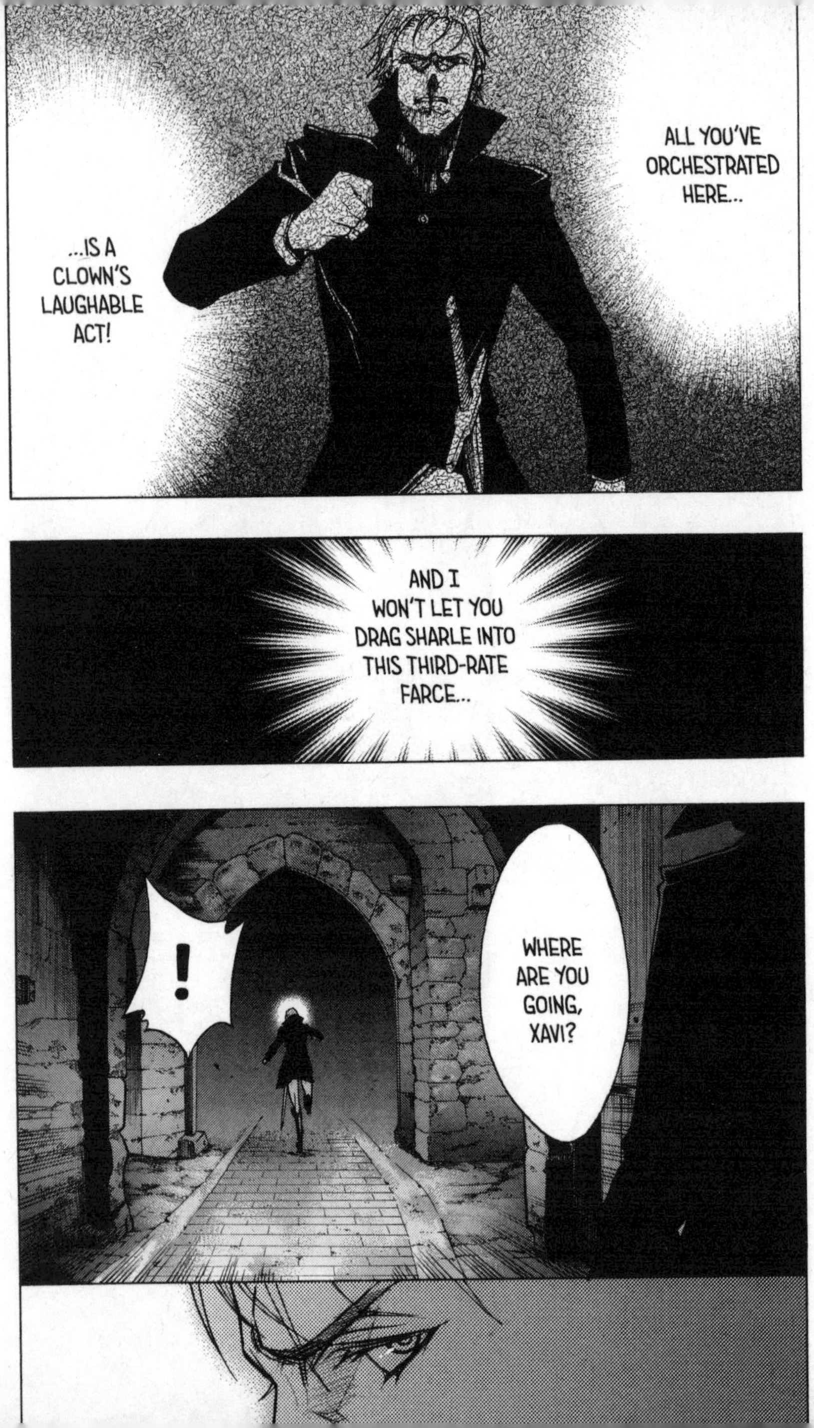
ALL YOU'VE ORCHESTRATED HERE...
...IS A CLOWN'S LAUGHABLE ACT!
AND I WON'T LET YOU DRAG SHARLE INTO THIS THIRD-RATE FARCE...
WHERE ARE YOU GOING, XAVI?
!

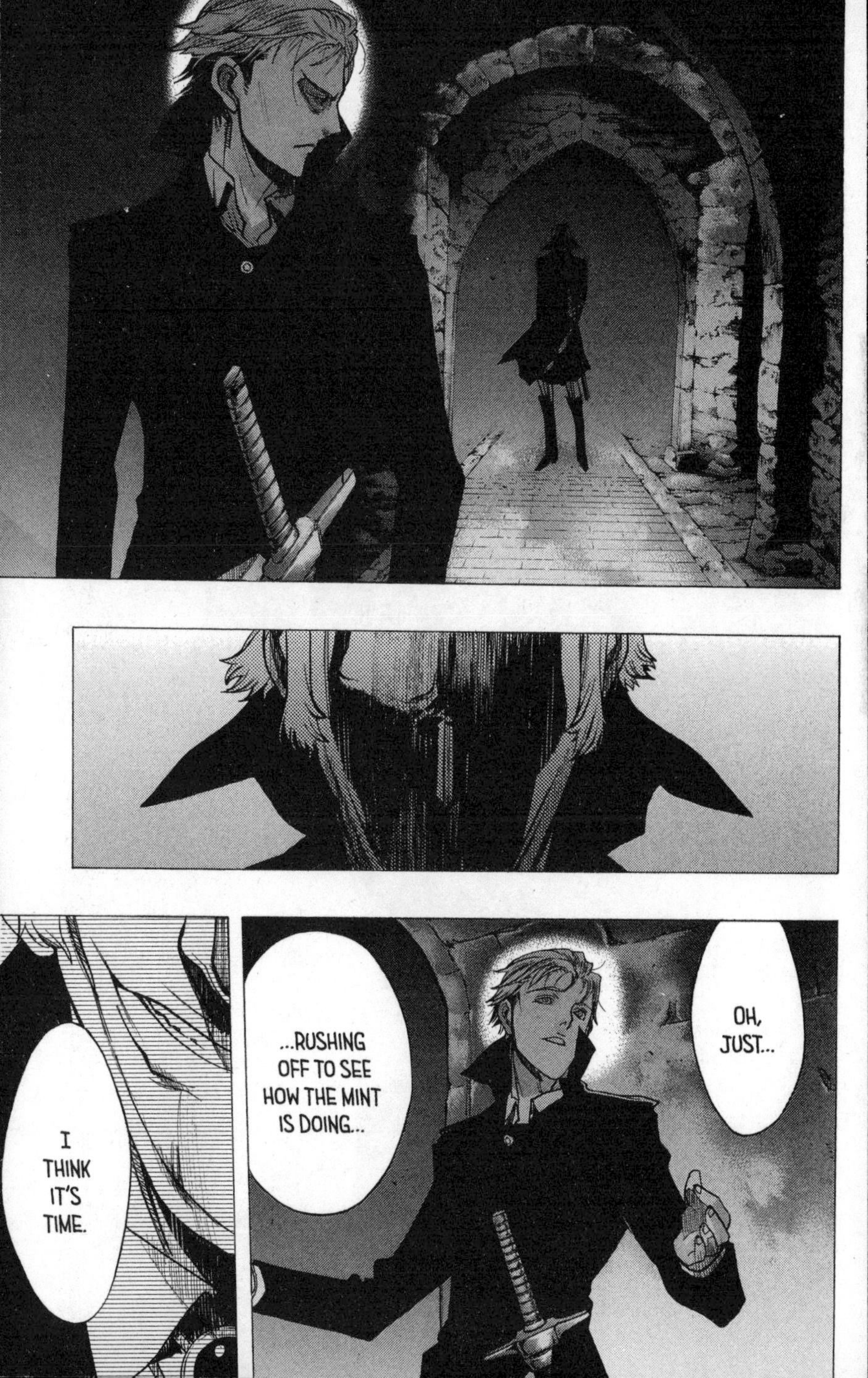
OH, JUST...
...RUSHING OFF TO SEE HOW THE MINT IS DOING...
I THINK IT'S TIME.

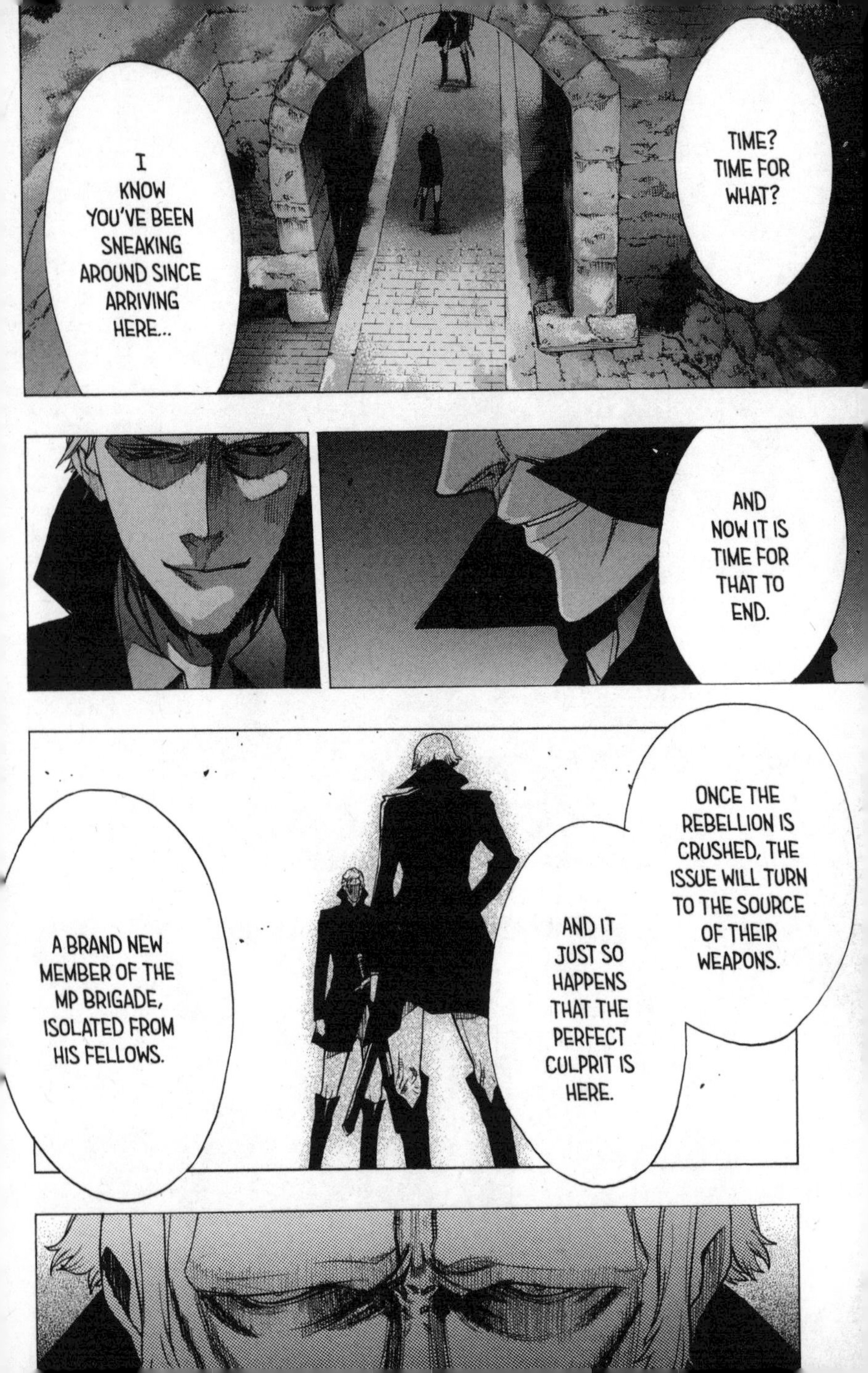
TIME? TIME FOR WHAT?
I KNOW YOU'VE BEEN SNEAKING AROUND SINCE ARRIVING HERE...
AND NOW IT IS TIME FOR THAT TO END.
ONCE THE REBELLION IS CRUSHED, THE ISSUE WILL TURN TO THE SOURCE OF THEIR WEAPONS.
AND IT JUST SO HAPPENS THAT THE PERFECT CULPRIT IS HERE.
A BRAND NEW MEMBER OF THE MP BRIGADE, ISOLATED FROM HIS FELLOWS.

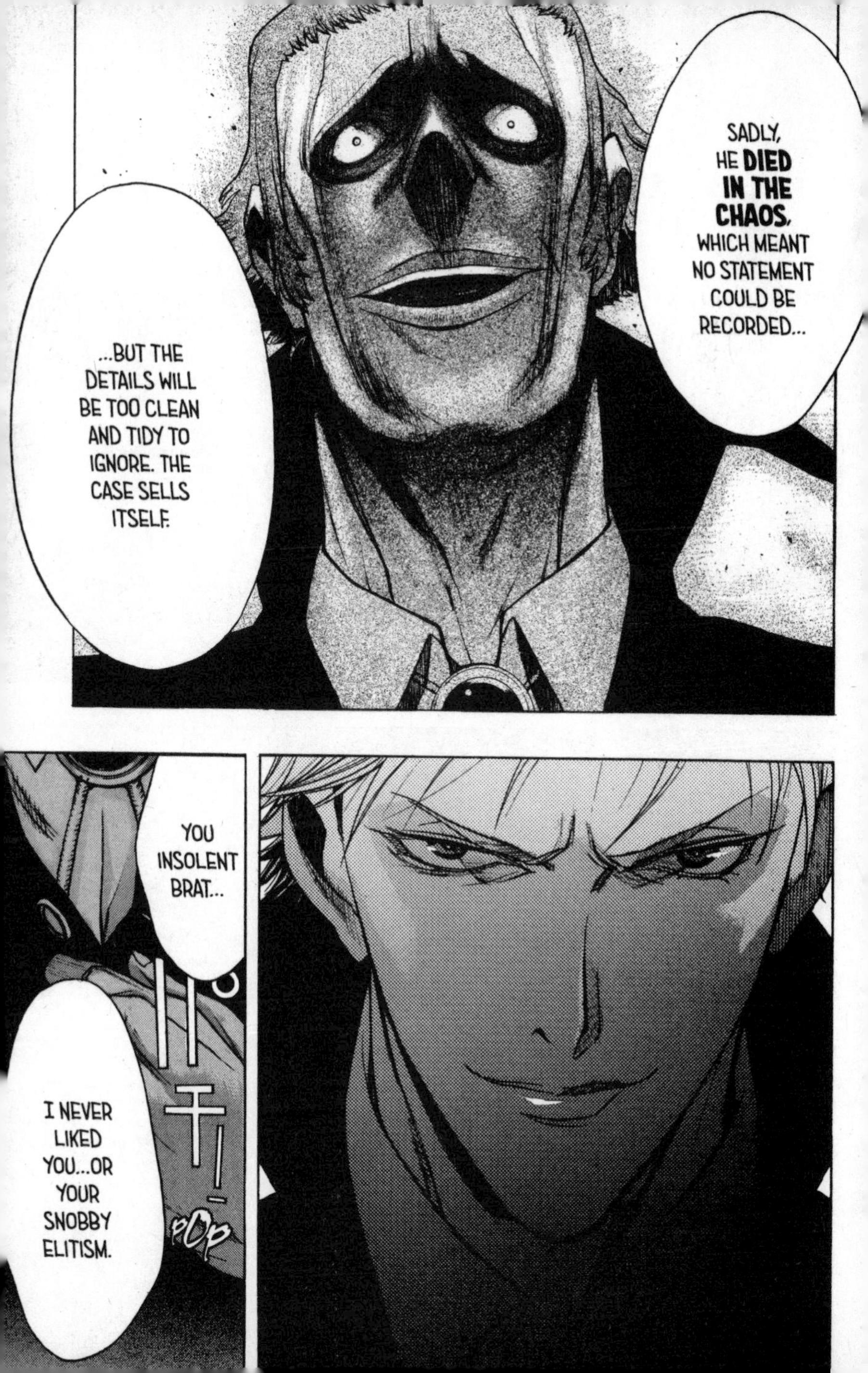
SADLY, HE **DIED IN THE CHAOS,** WHICH MEANT NO STATEMENT COULD BE RECORDED...
...BUT THE DETAILS WILL BE TOO CLEAN AND TIDY TO IGNORE. THE CASE SELLS ITSELF.
YOU INSOLENT BRAT...
POP
I NEVER LIKED YOU...OR YOUR SNOBBY ELITISM.

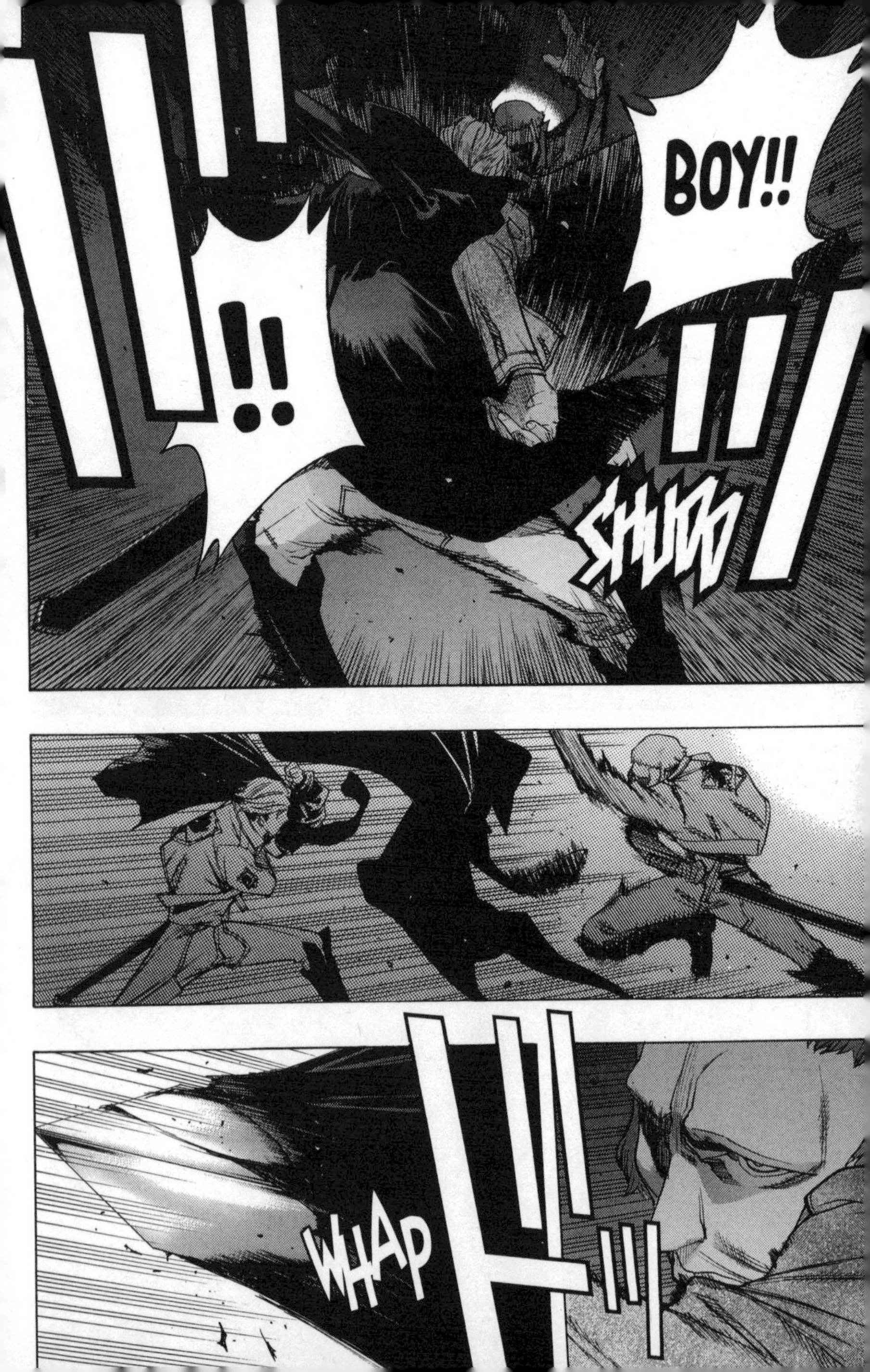
BOY!!
!!
SHUDD
WHAP

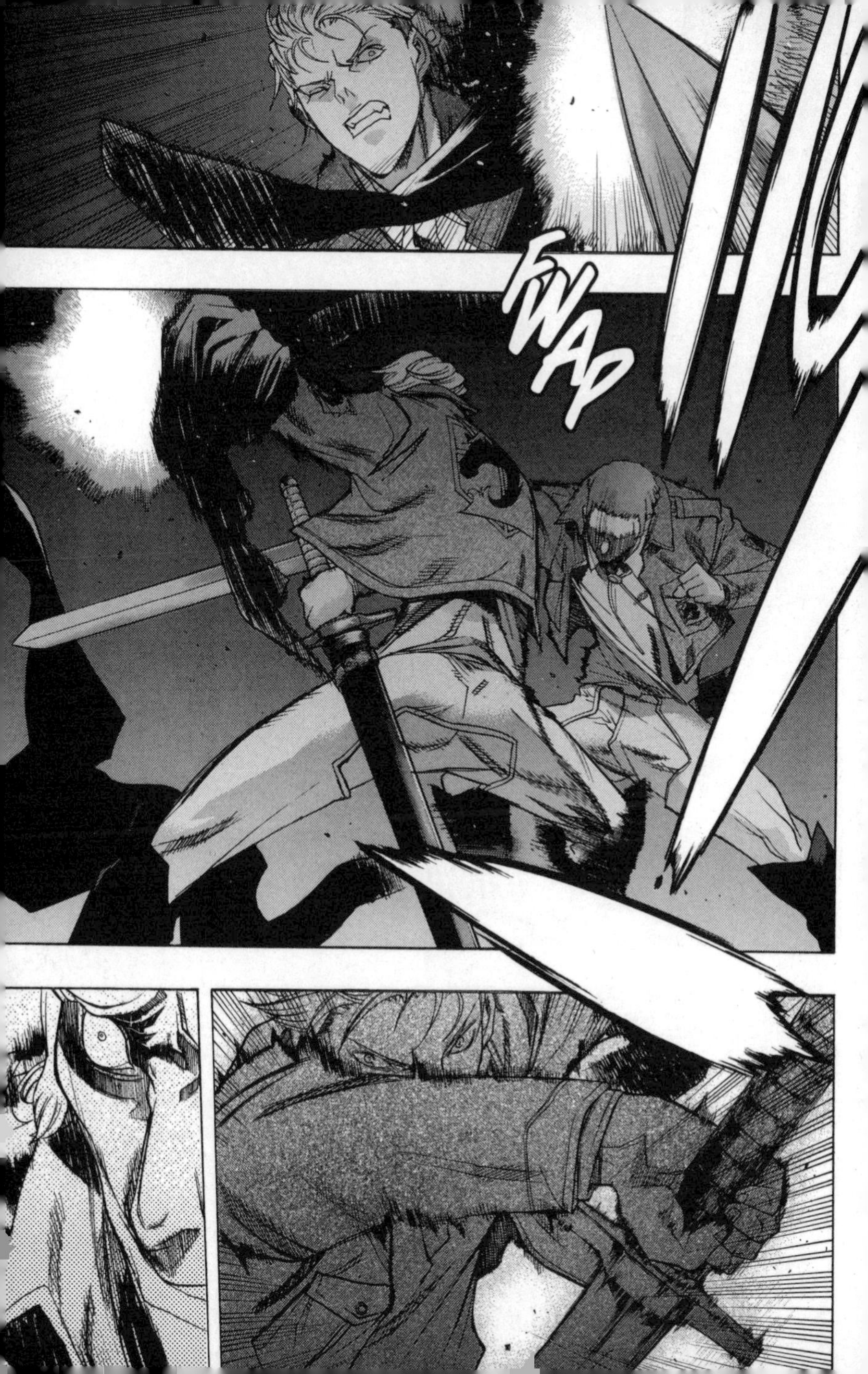
FWAP

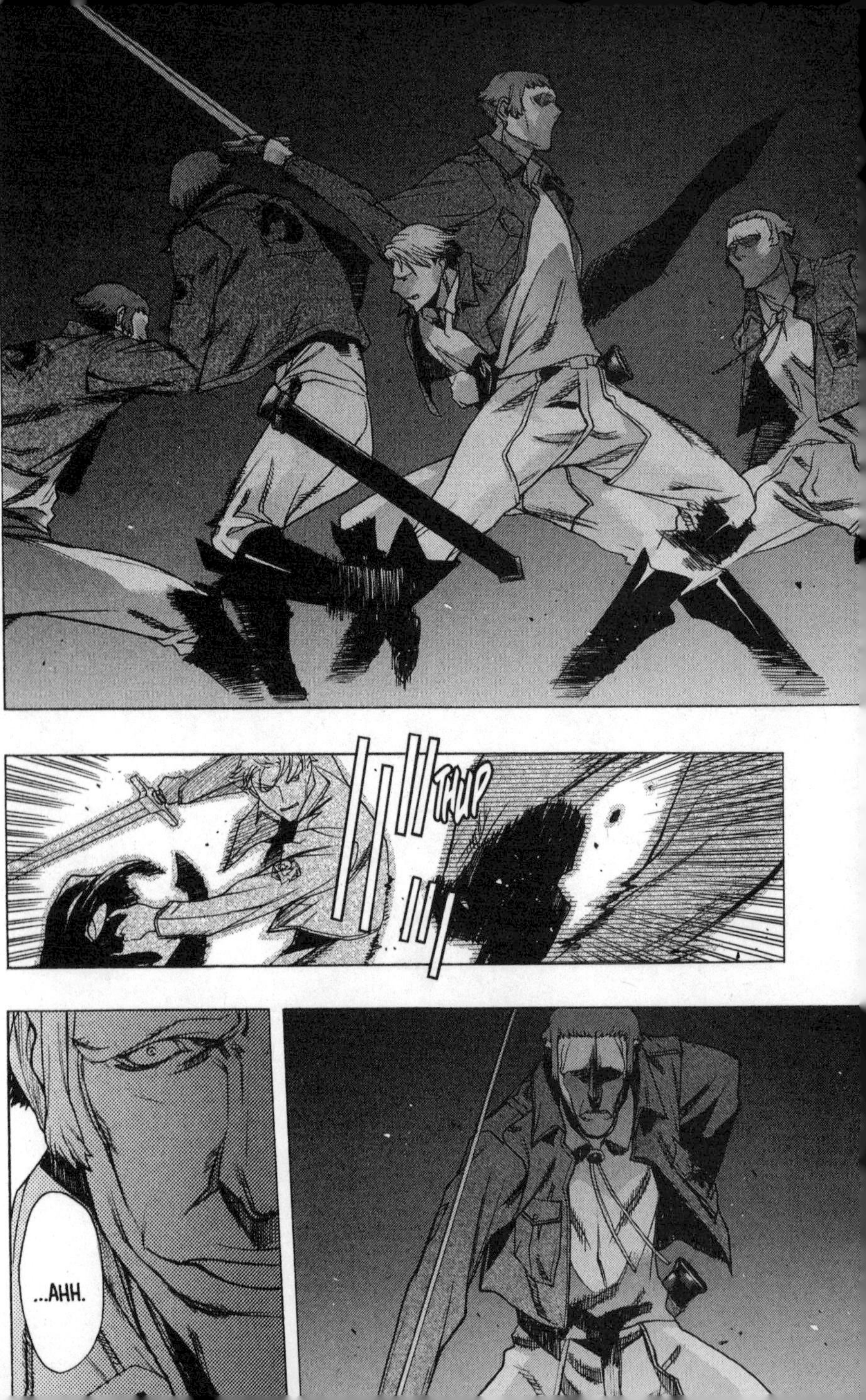
THUP
...AHH.

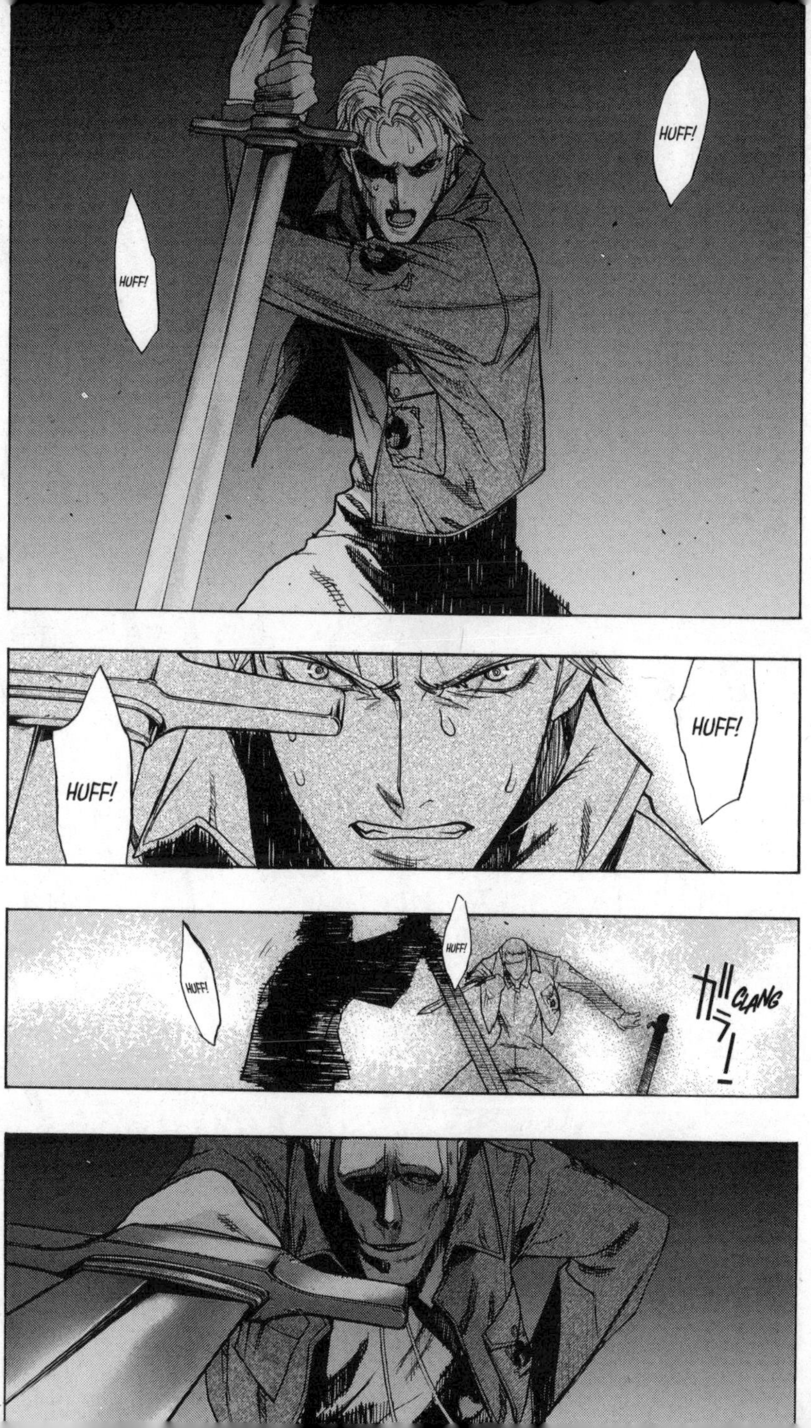
HUFF!
HUFF!
HUFF!
HUFF!
CLANG
HUFF!
HUFF!

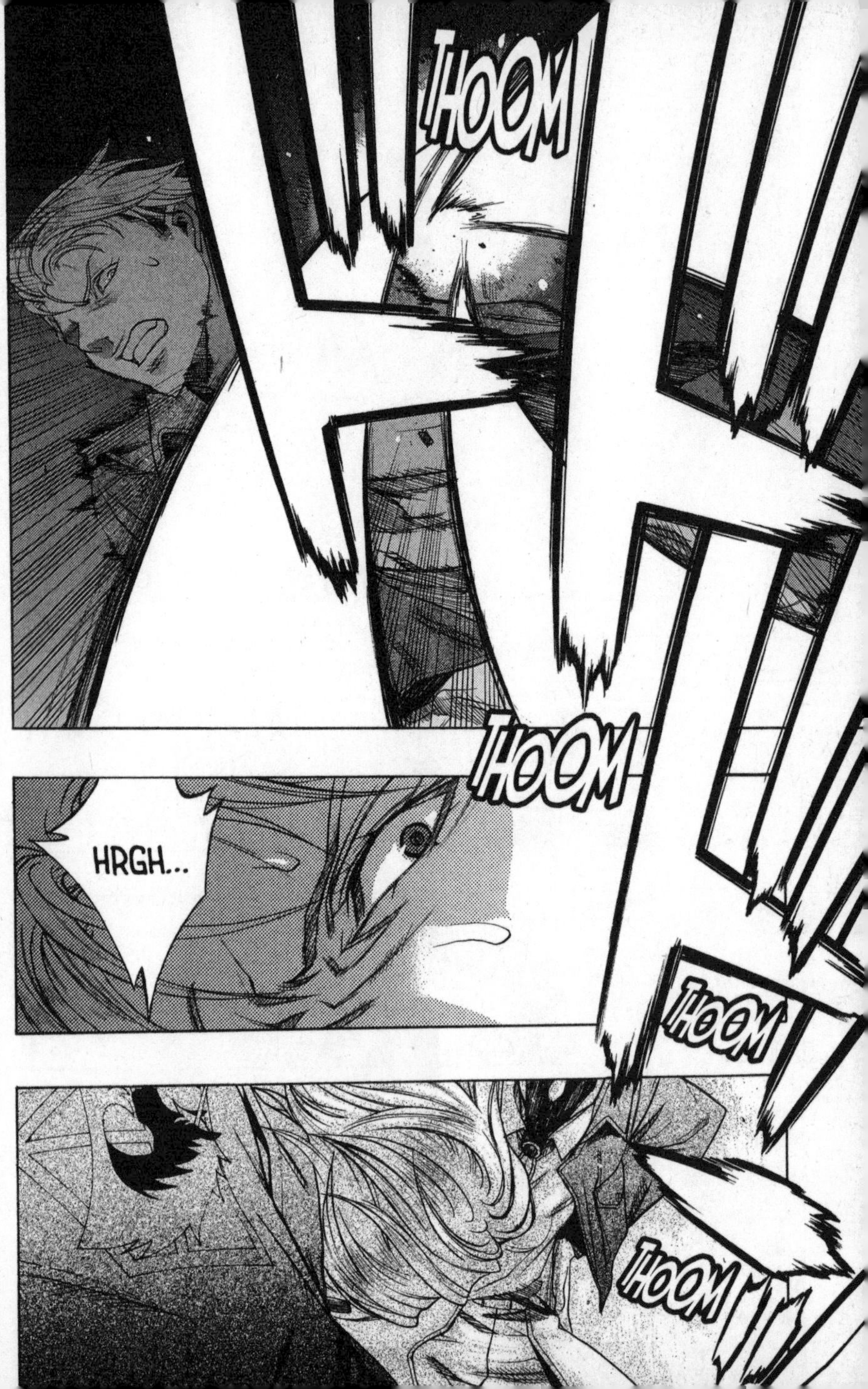
THOOM
THOOM
HRGH...
THOOM
THOOM

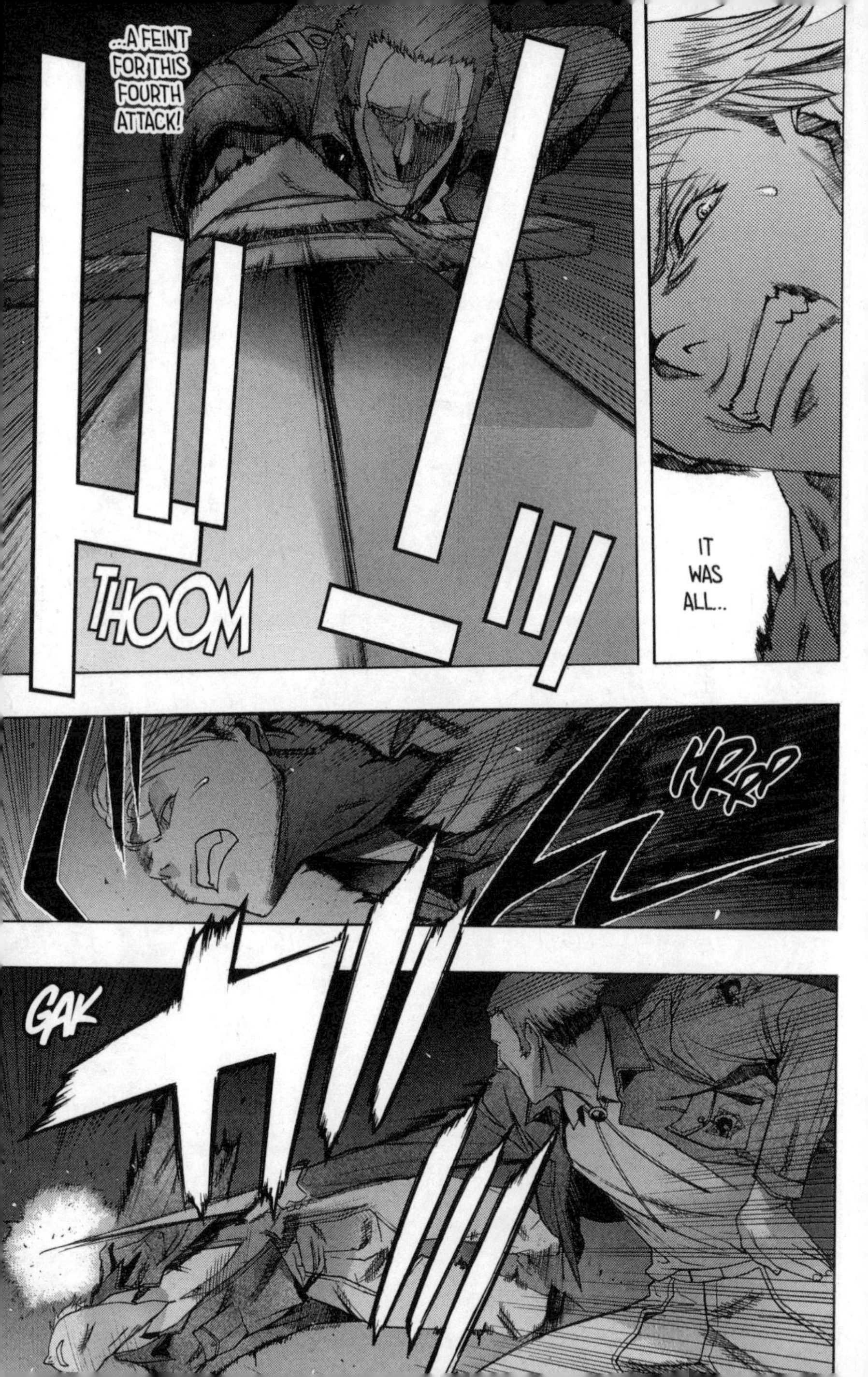
IT WAS ALL...
...A FEINT FOR THIS FOURTH ATTACK!
THOOM
HRAP
GAK

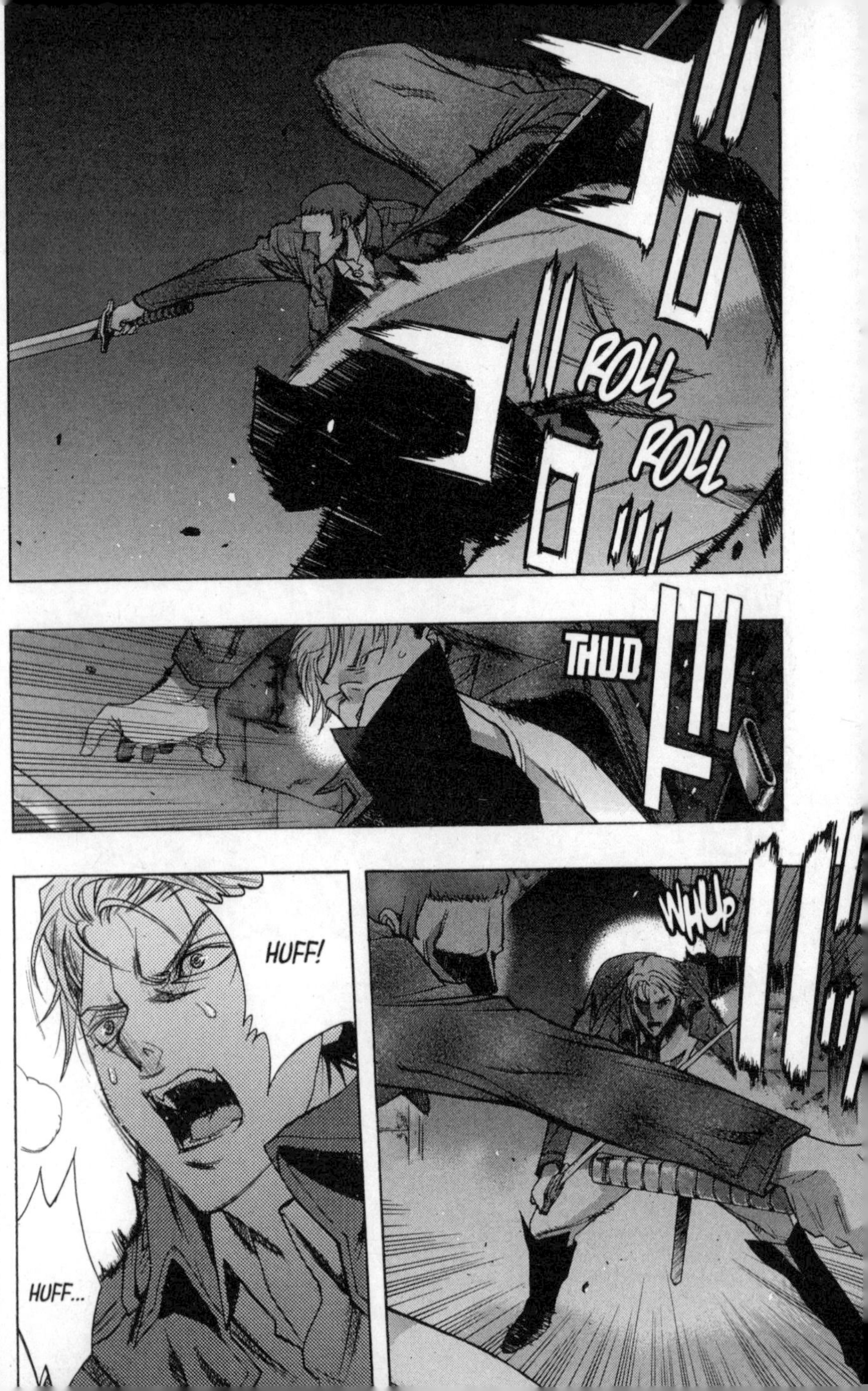
ROLL
ROLL
THUD
WHUP
HUFF!
HUFF...

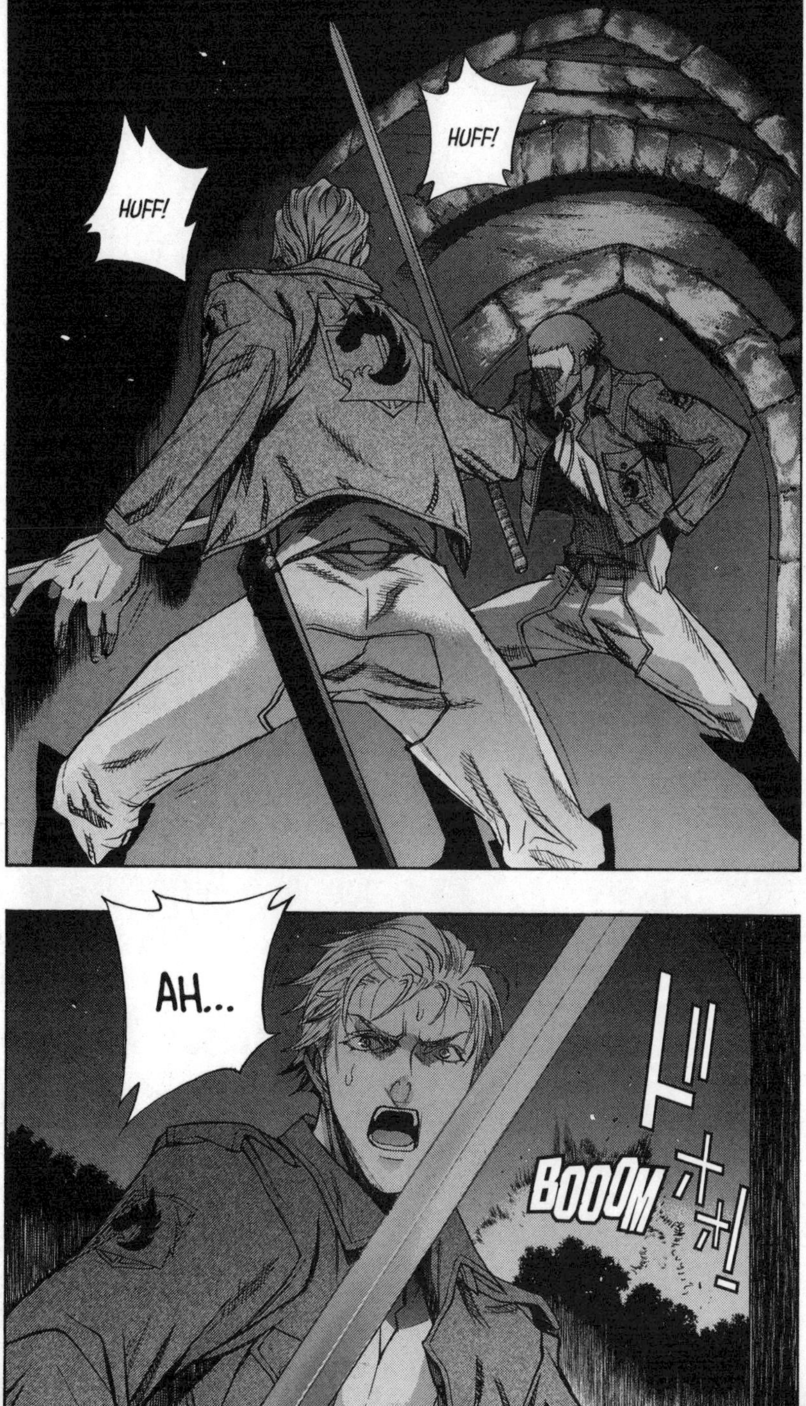
HUFF!
HUFF!
AH...
BOOOM

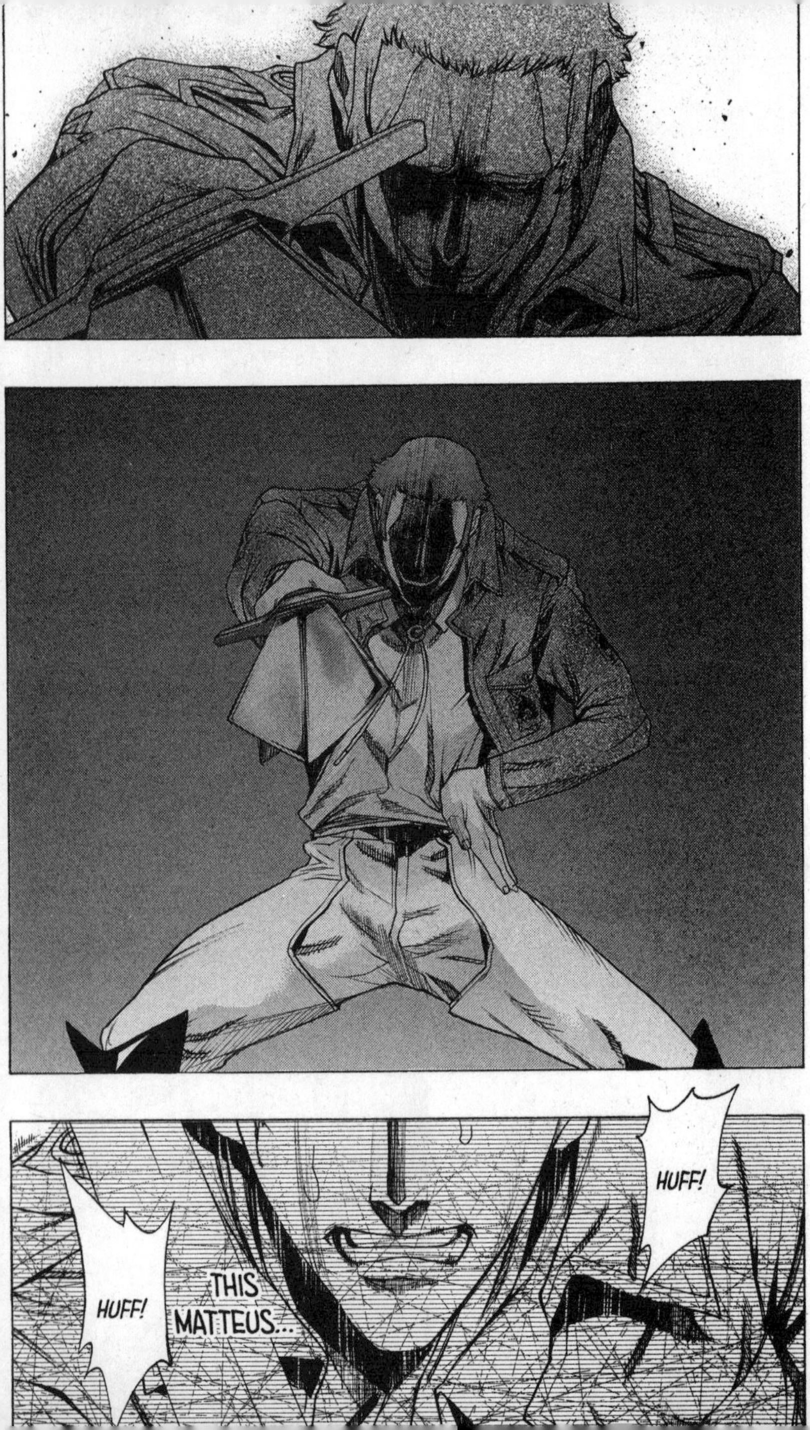
HUFF!
THIS MATTEUS...
HUFF!

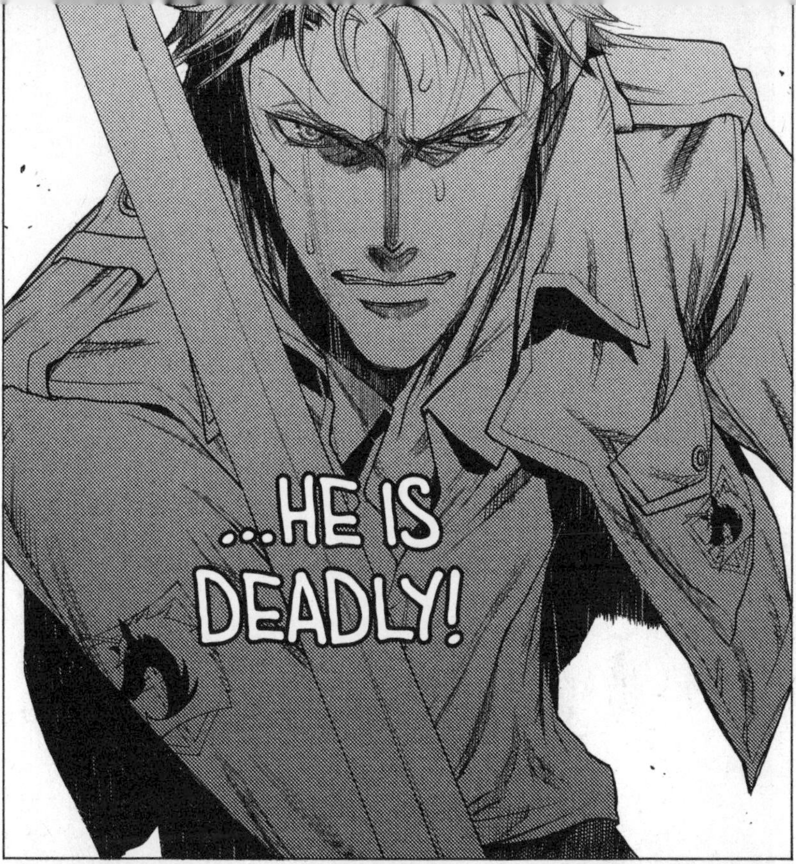
...HE IS DEADLY!
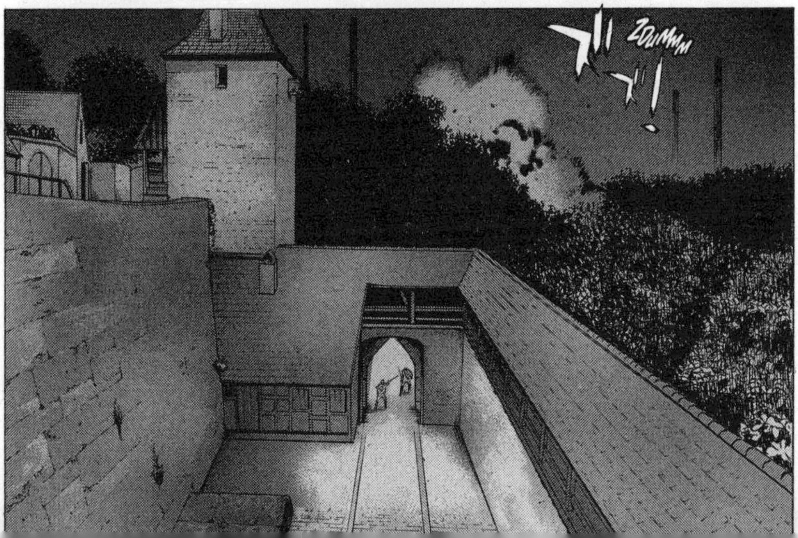
ZOUMMM

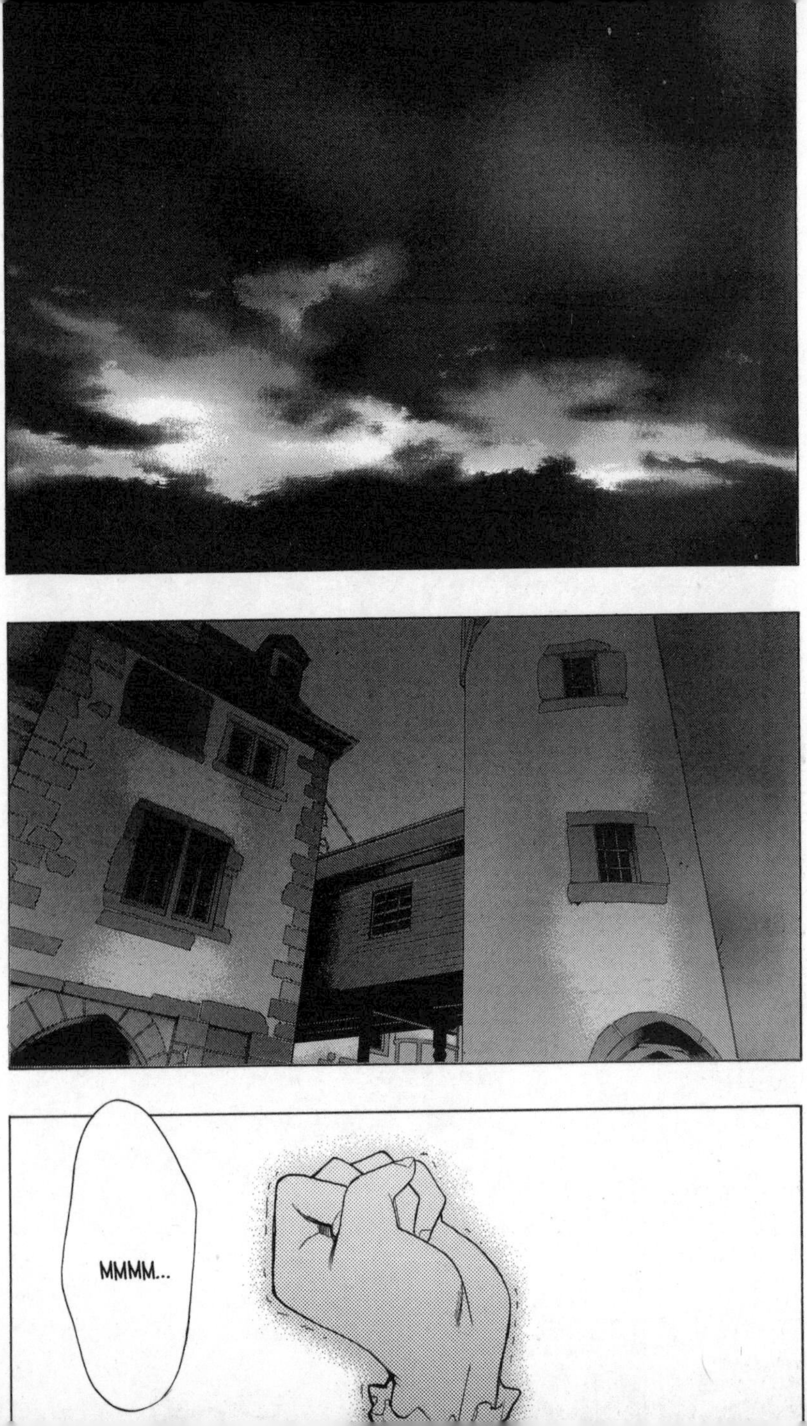
MMMM...

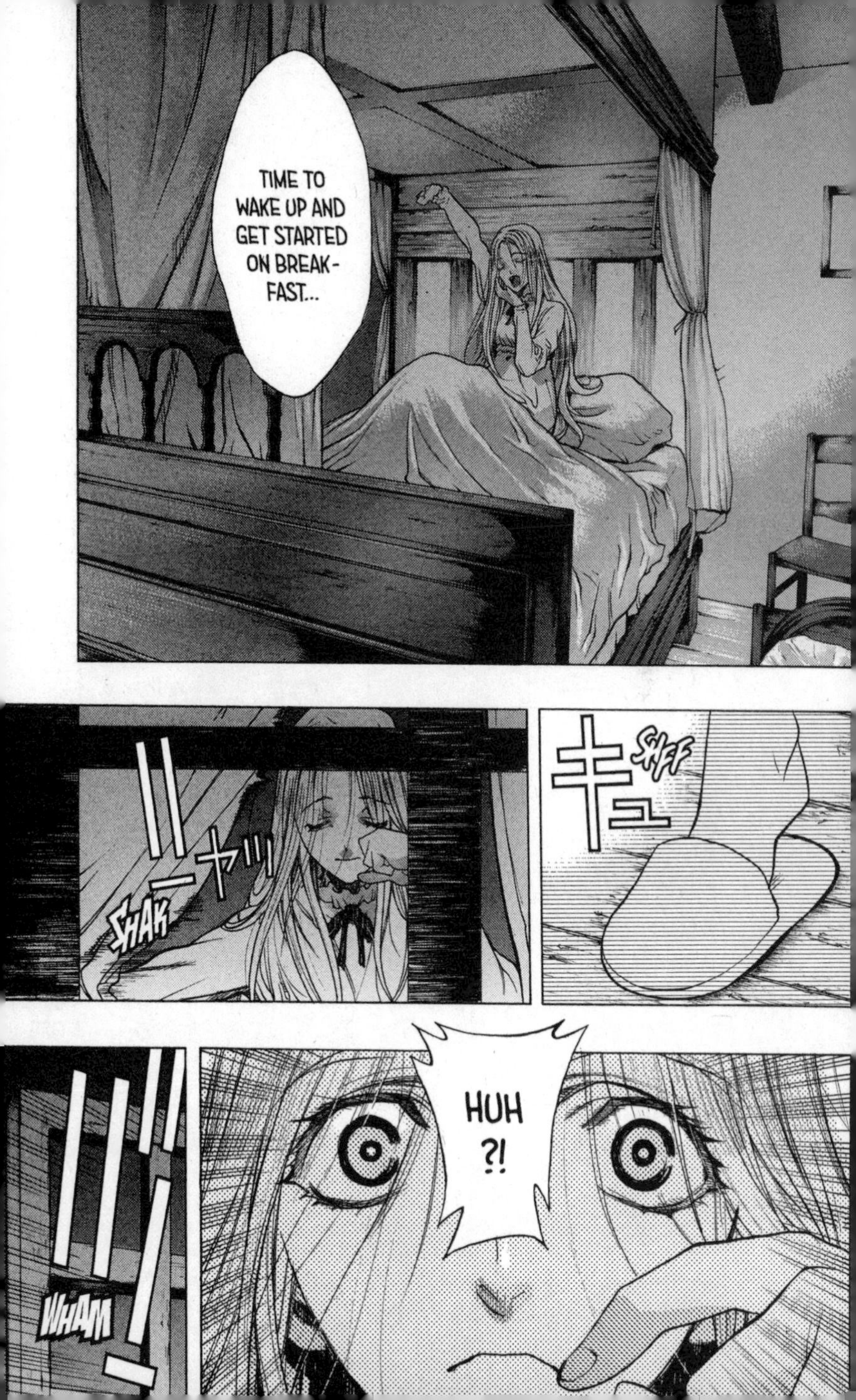
TIME TO WAKE UP AND GET STARTED ON BREAK-FAST...
SHFF
SHAK
HUH?!
WHAM

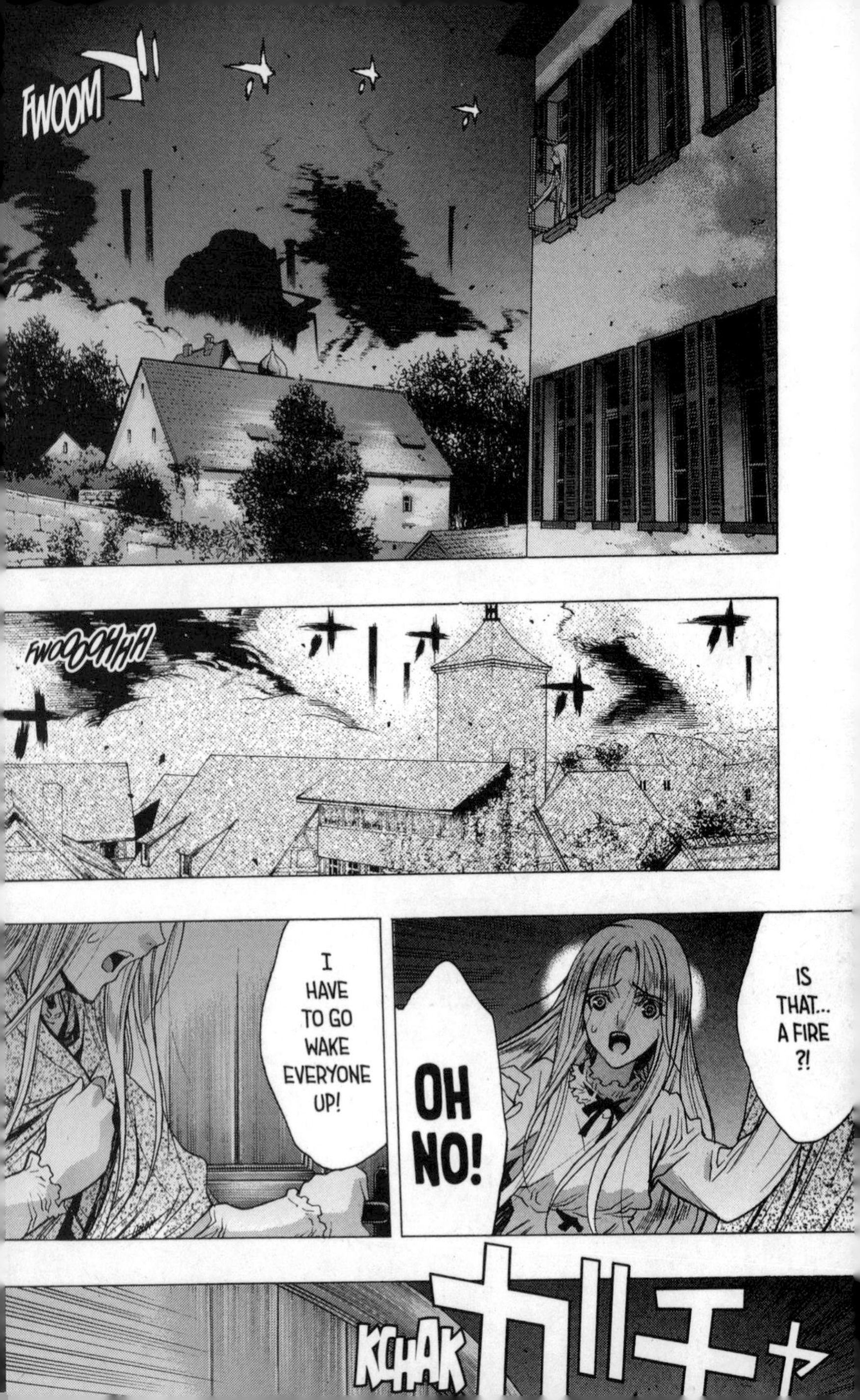
FWOOM ゴッ
FWOOOOHHH
IS THAT... A FIRE ?!
OH NO!
I HAVE TO GO WAKE EVERYONE UP!
KCHAK カチャ

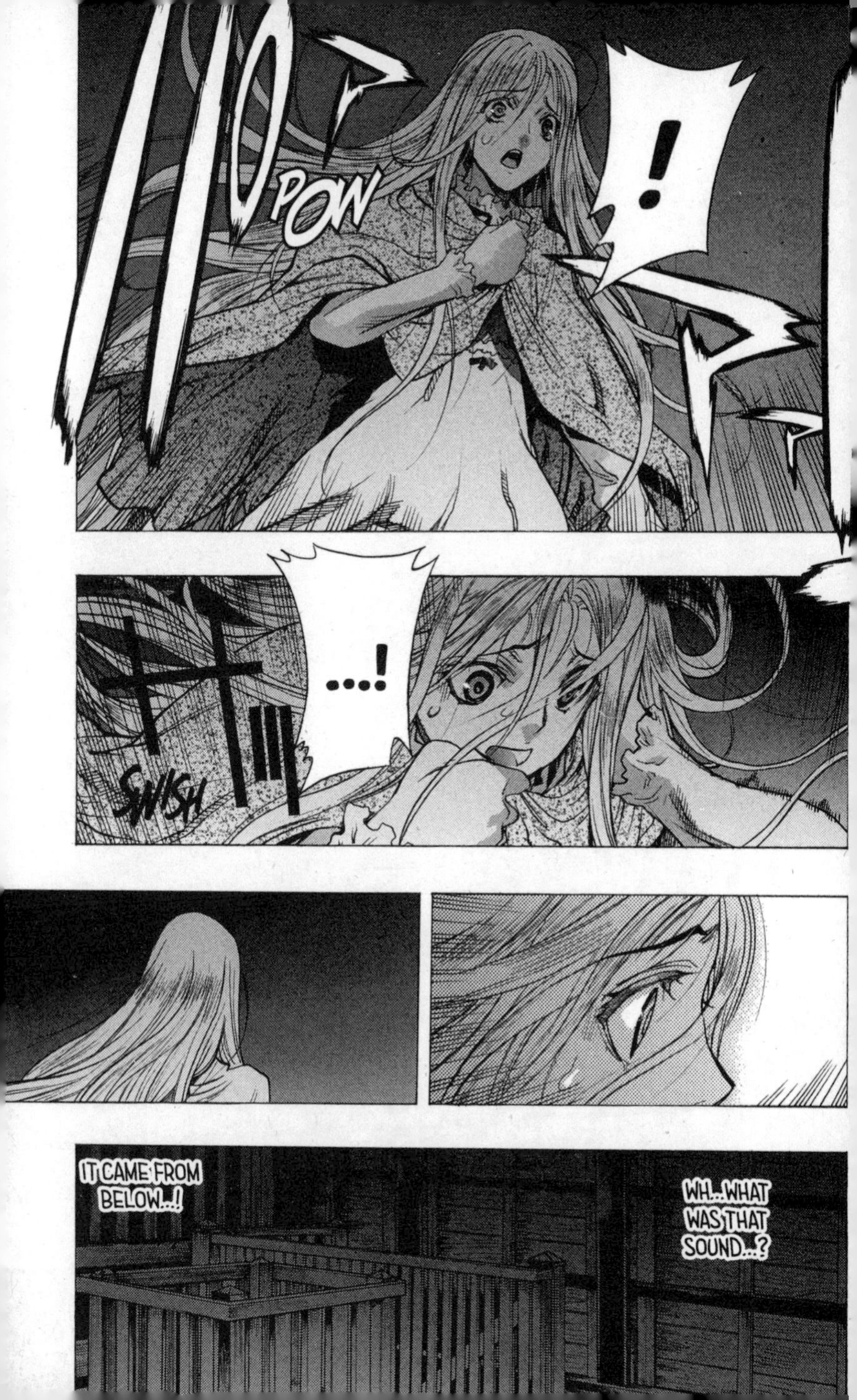
!
POW
...!
SWISH
WH...WHAT WAS THAT SOUND...?
IT CAME FROM BELOW...!

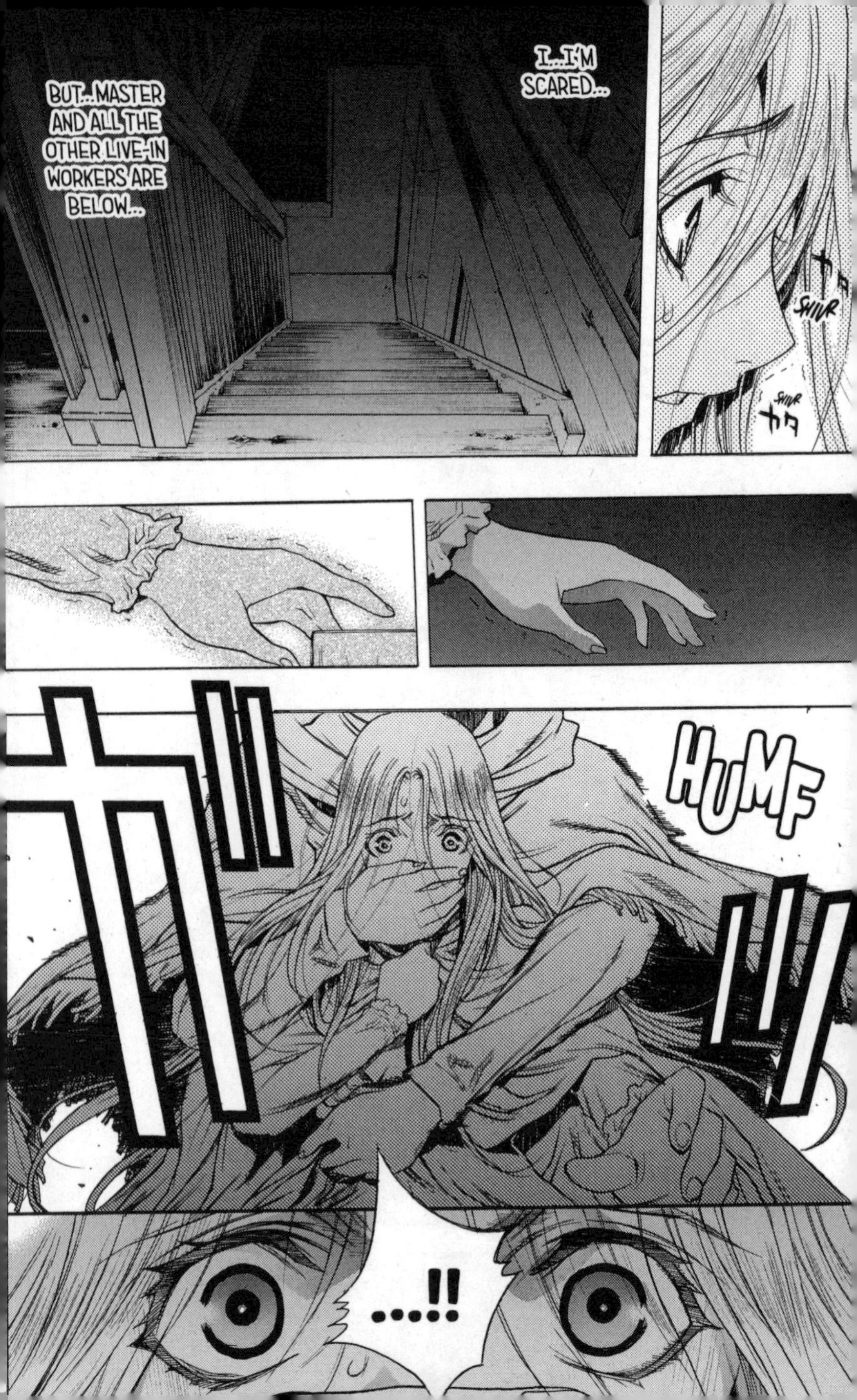
SHIVR
SHIVR
I...I'M SCARED...
BUT...MASTER AND ALL THE OTHER LIVE-IN WORKERS ARE BELOW...
HUMF
...!!

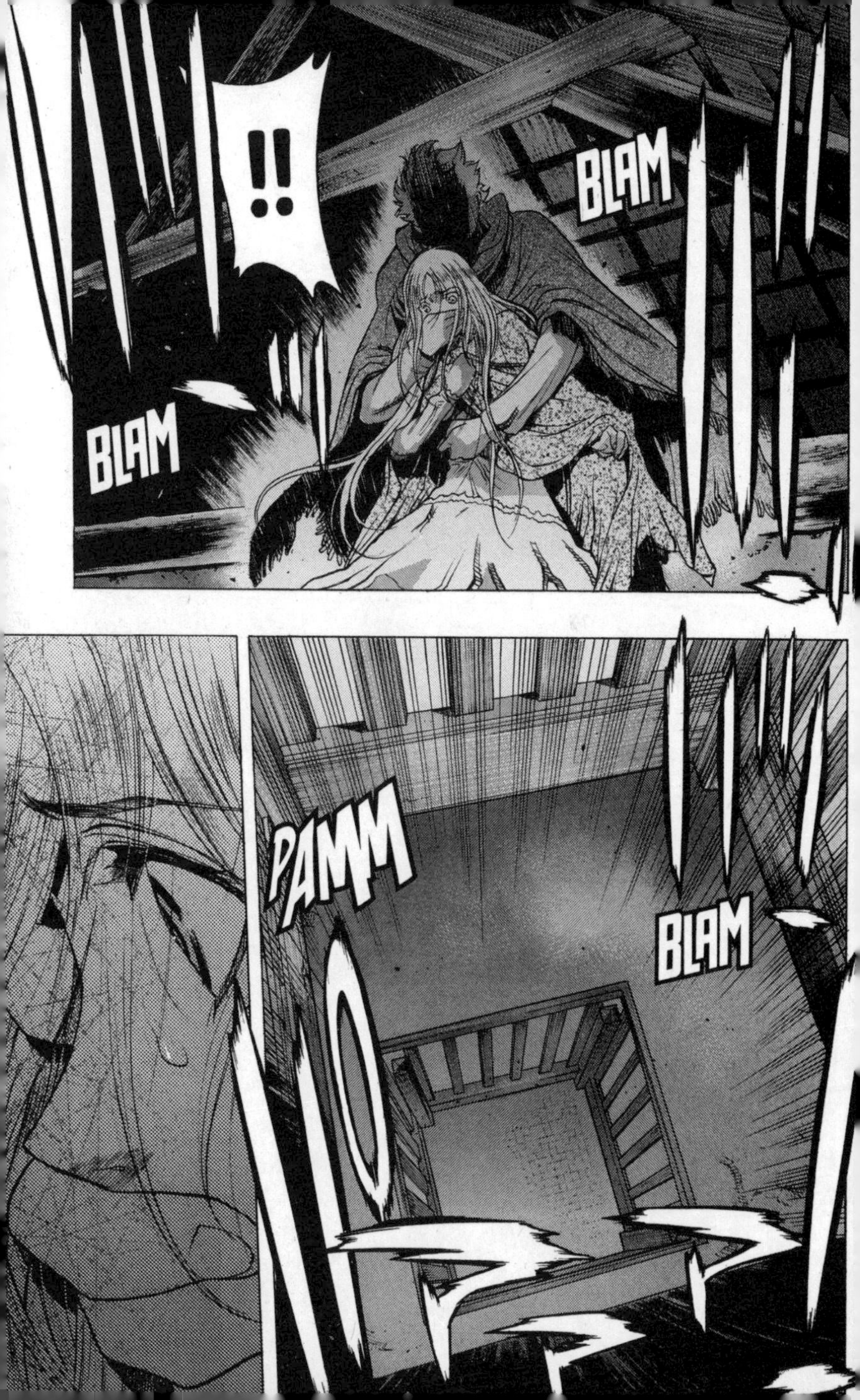
BLAM
!!
BLAM
PAMM
BLAM

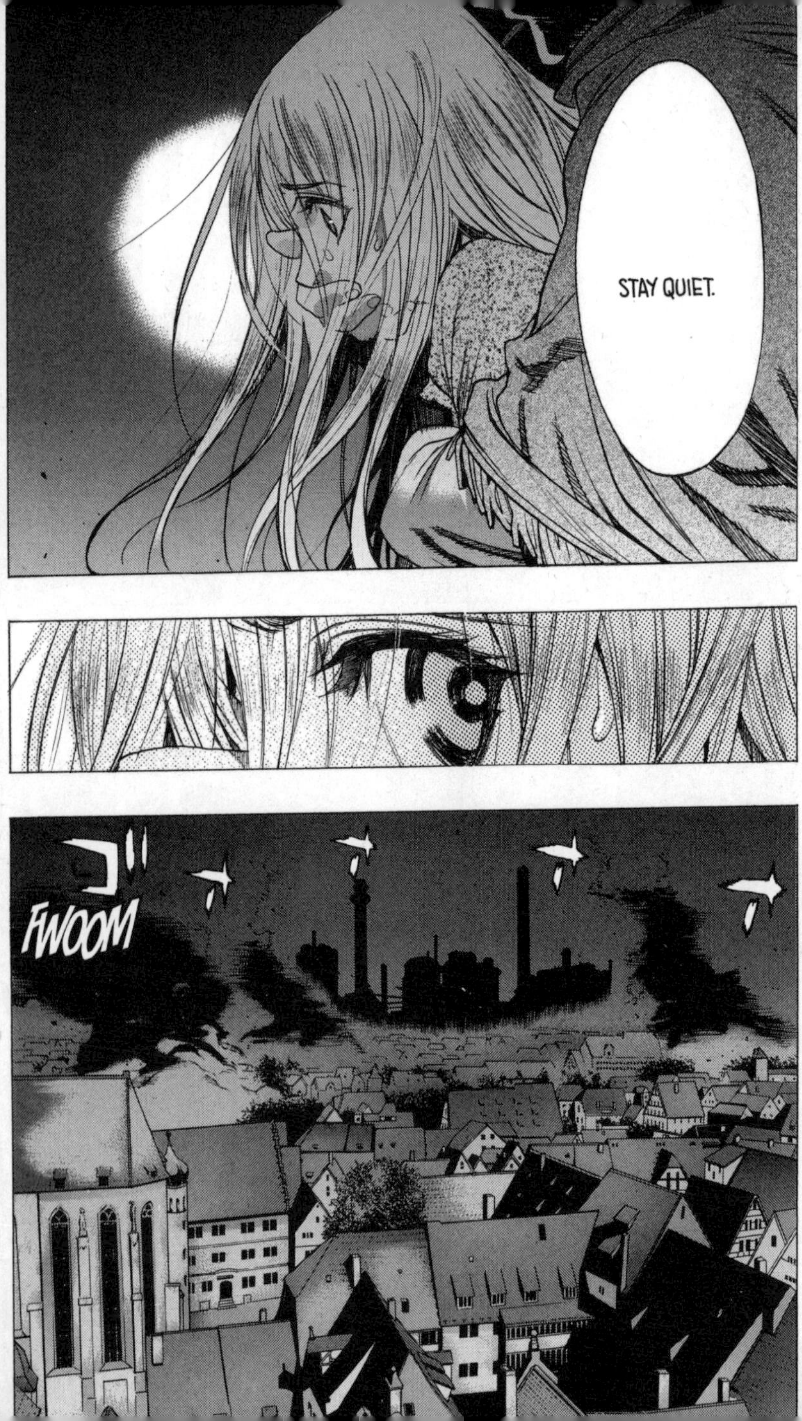
STAY QUIET.
FWOOM

Chapter 26: The Fires of Upheaval · End

ATTACK
on TITAN
BEFORE THE FALL

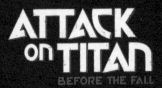

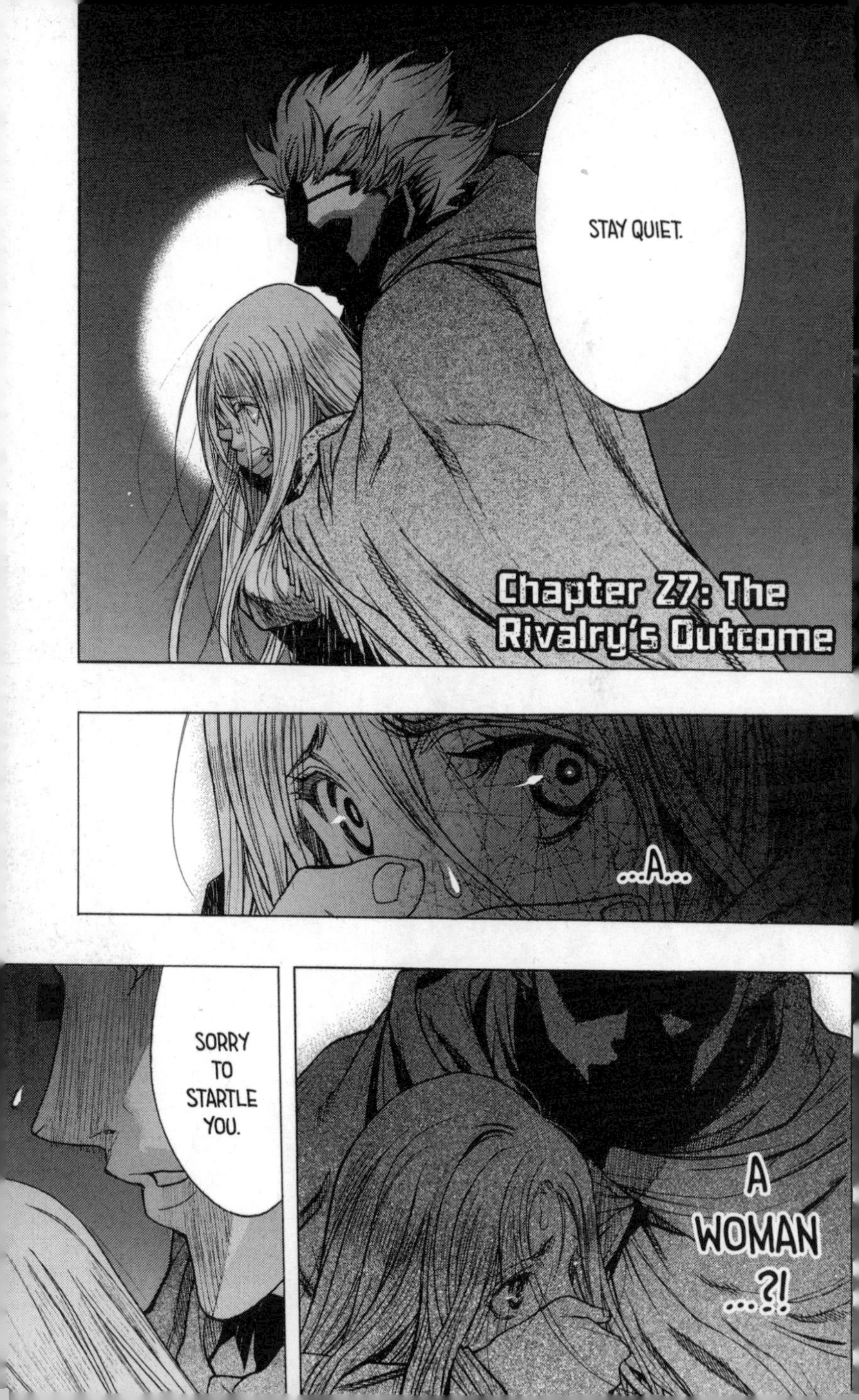
STAY QUIET.
Chapter 27: The Rivalry's Outcome
...A...
A WOMAN ...?!
SORRY TO STARTLE YOU.

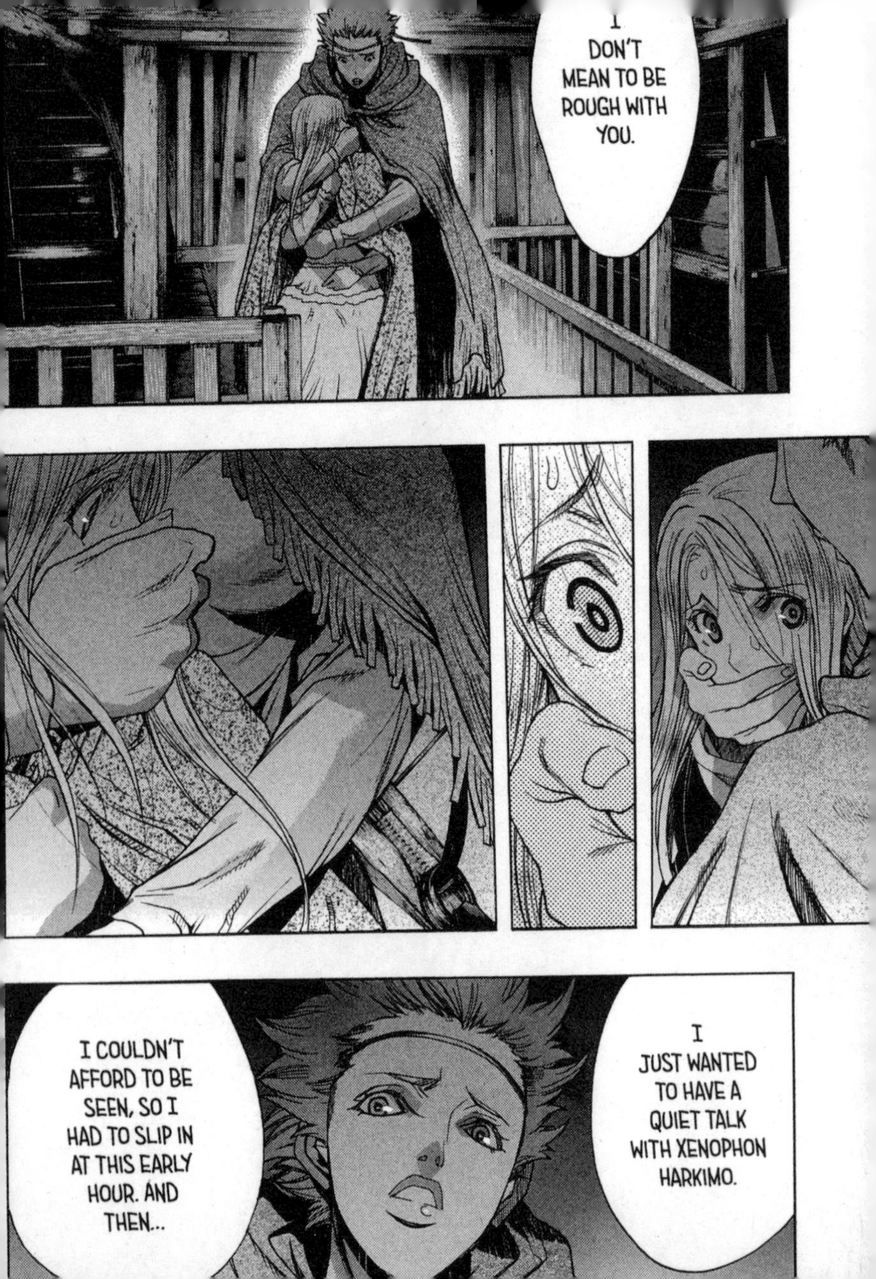
I DON'T MEAN TO BE ROUGH WITH YOU.
I JUST WANTED TO HAVE A QUIET TALK WITH XENOPHON HARKIMO.
I COULDN'T AFFORD TO BE SEEN, SO I HAD TO SLIP IN AT THIS EARLY HOUR. AND THEN...

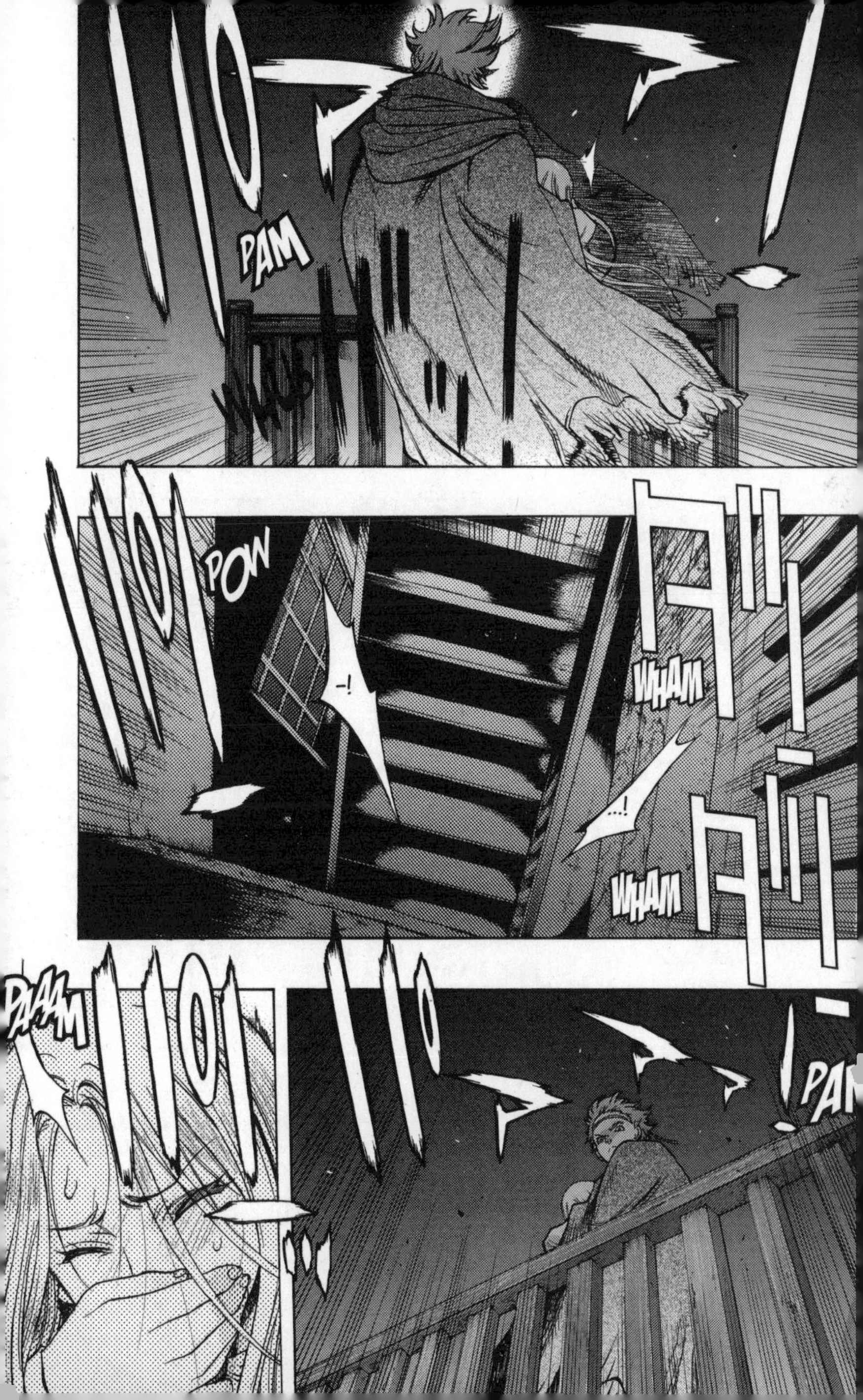
PAM
WHAM
...!
WHAM
–!
POW
PA
PAAAM

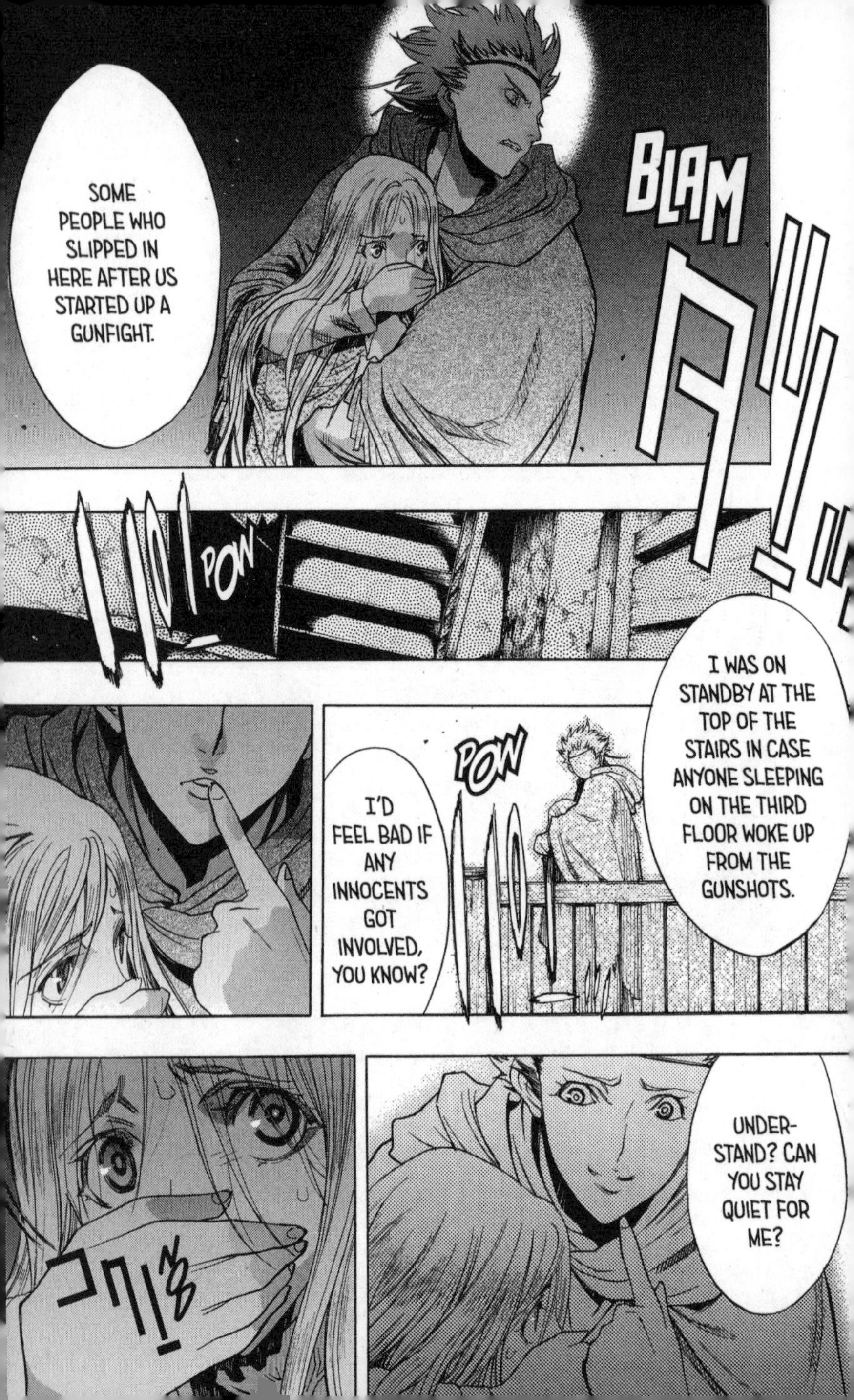
BLAM
SOME PEOPLE WHO SLIPPED IN HERE AFTER US STARTED UP A GUNFIGHT.
POW
POW
I WAS ON STANDBY AT THE TOP OF THE STAIRS IN CASE ANYONE SLEEPING ON THE THIRD FLOOR WOKE UP FROM THE GUNSHOTS.
I'D FEEL BAD IF ANY INNOCENTS GOT INVOLVED, YOU KNOW?
UNDER-STAND? CAN YOU STAY QUIET FOR ME?

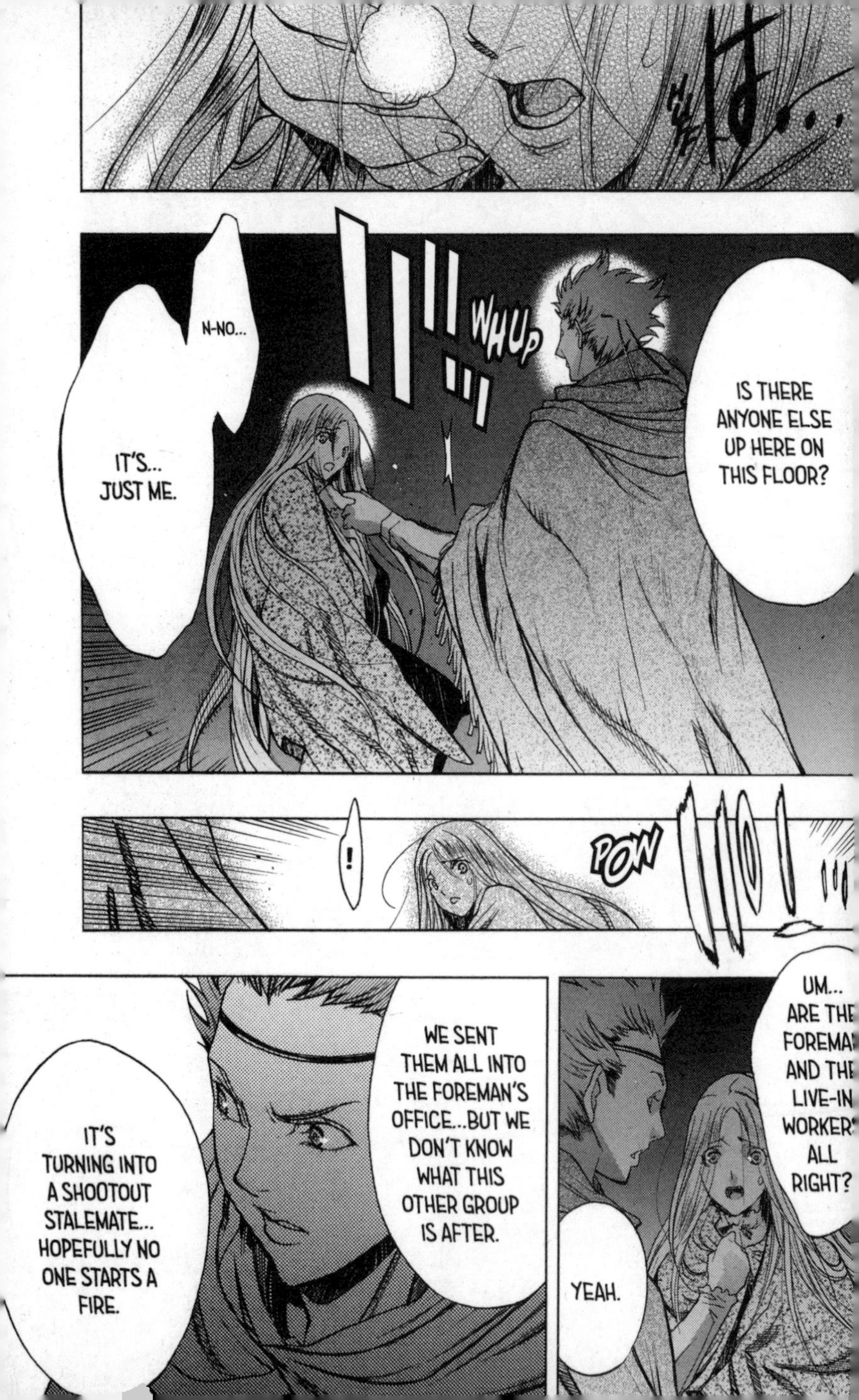
は…
IS THERE ANYONE ELSE UP HERE ON THIS FLOOR?
WHUP
N-NO...
IT'S... JUST ME.
POW
!
UM... ARE THE FOREMA AND THE LIVE-IN WORKER ALL RIGHT?
YEAH.
WE SENT THEM ALL INTO THE FOREMAN'S OFFICE...BUT WE DON'T KNOW WHAT THIS OTHER GROUP IS AFTER.
IT'S TURNING INTO A SHOOTOUT STALEMATE... HOPEFULLY NO ONE STARTS A FIRE.

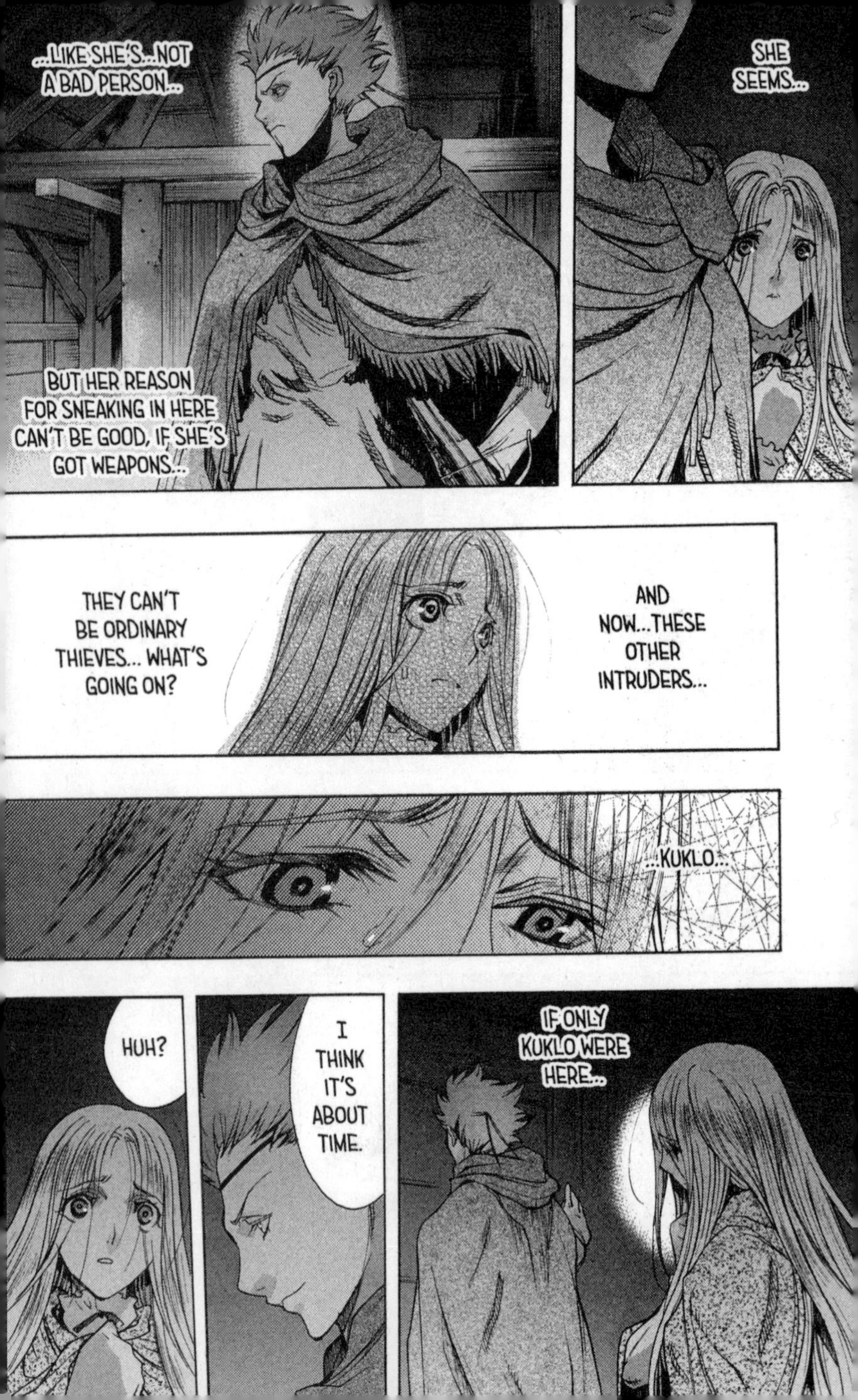
SHE SEEMS...
...LIKE SHE'S...NOT A BAD PERSON...
BUT HER REASON FOR SNEAKING IN HERE CAN'T BE GOOD, IF SHE'S GOT WEAPONS...
AND NOW...THESE OTHER INTRUDERS...
THEY CAN'T BE ORDINARY THIEVES... WHAT'S GOING ON?
...KUKLO...
IF ONLY KUKLO WERE HERE...
I THINK IT'S ABOUT TIME.
HUH?

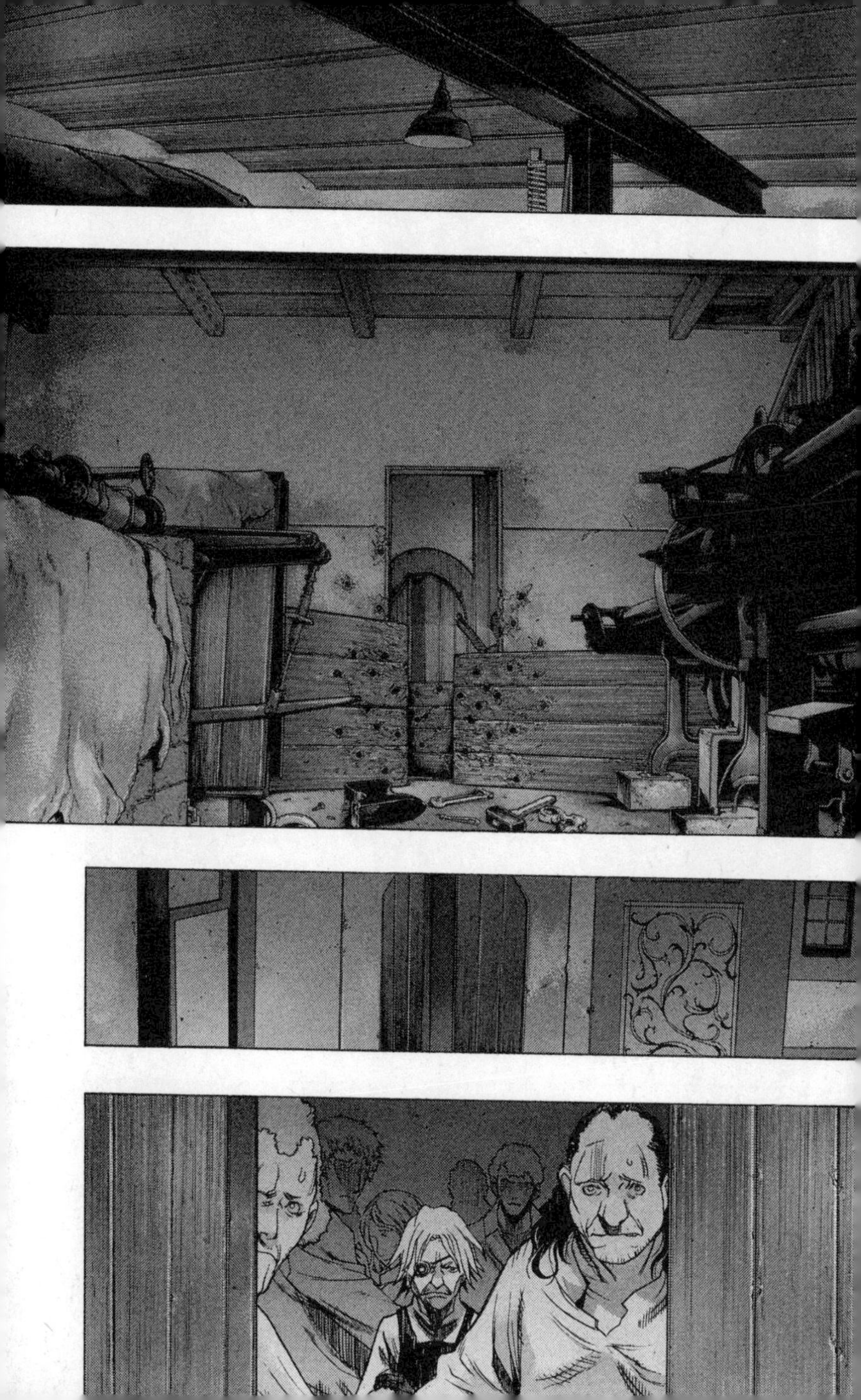

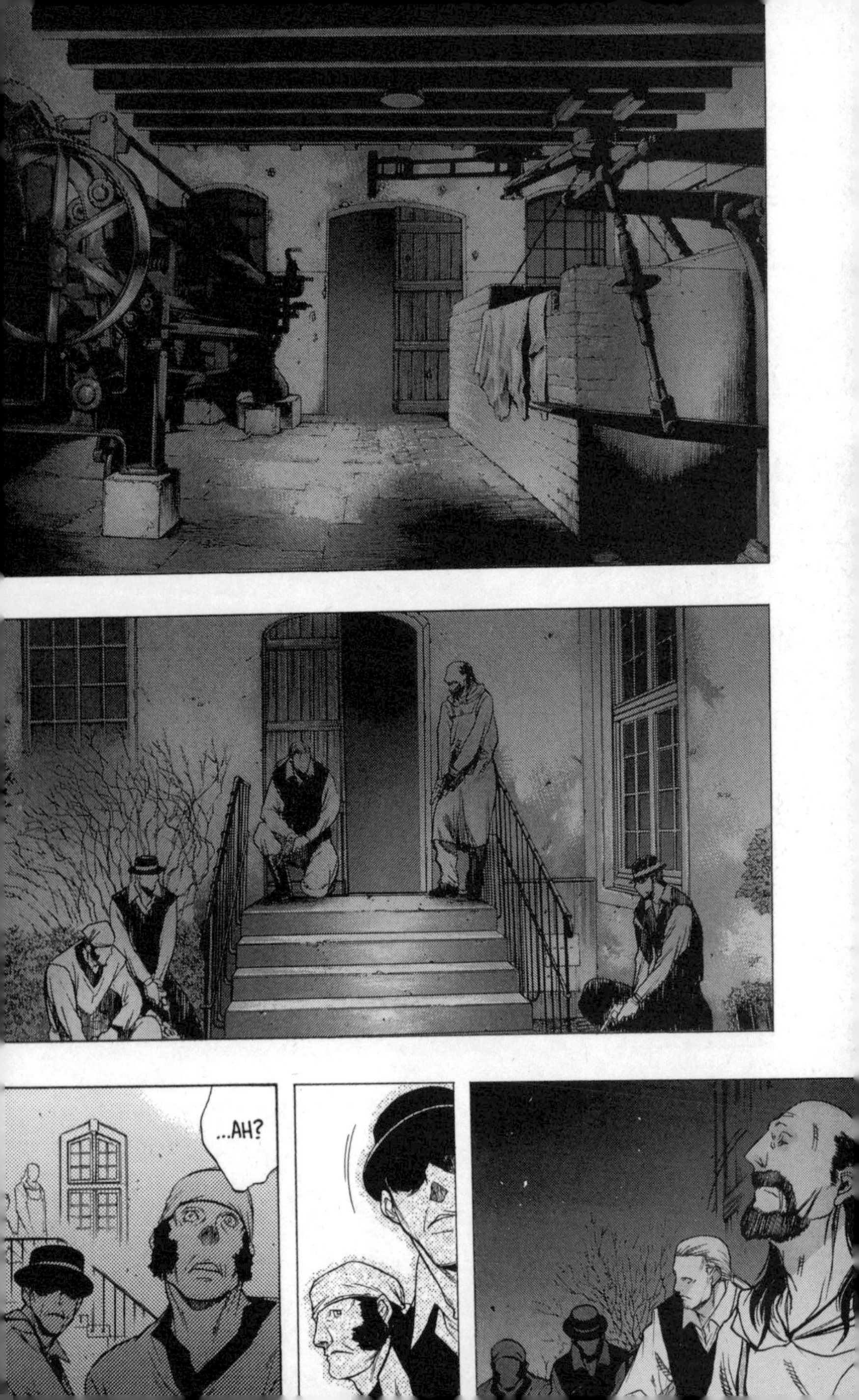
...AH?

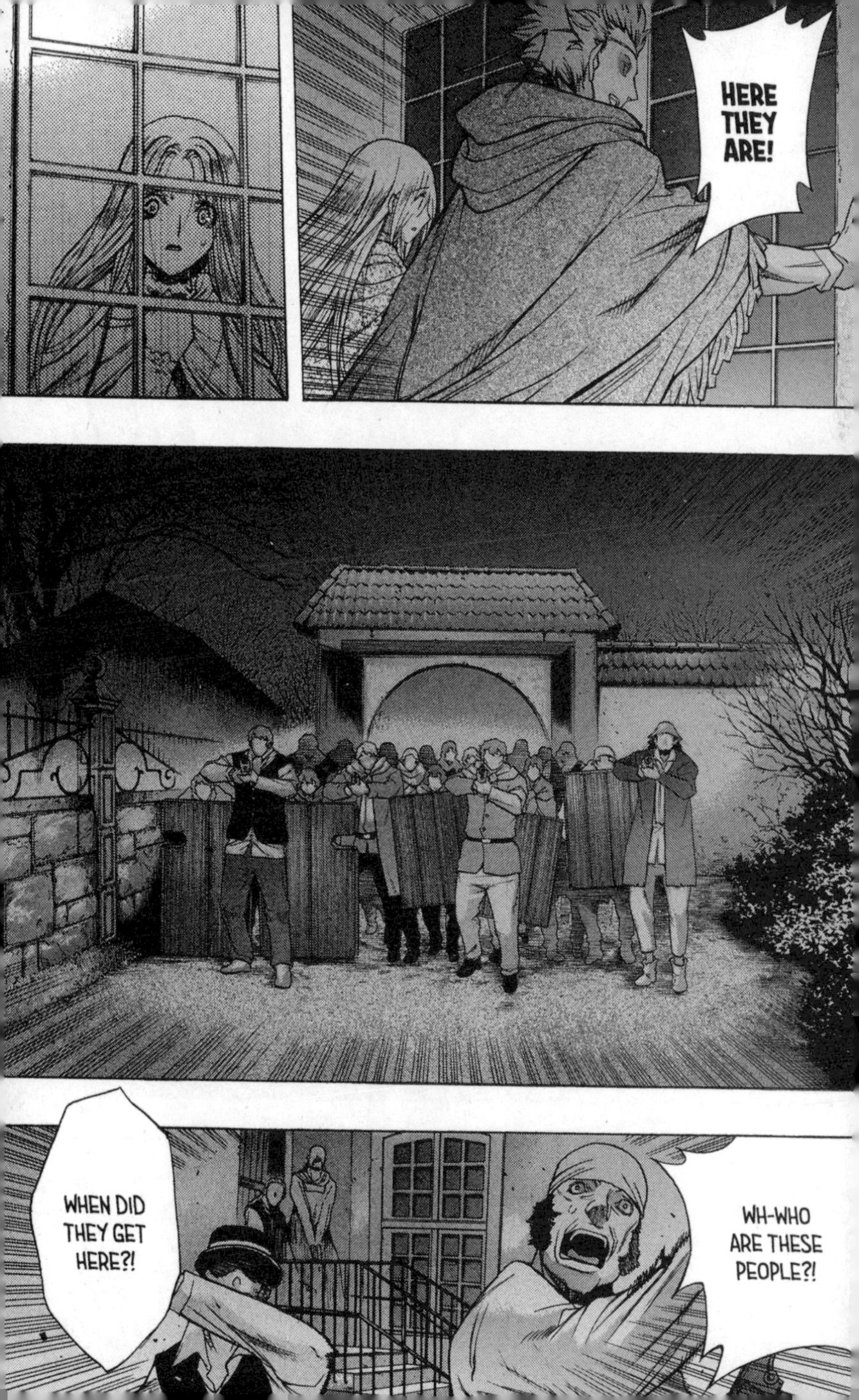
HERE THEY ARE!
WH-WHO ARE THESE PEOPLE?!
WHEN DID THEY GET HERE?!

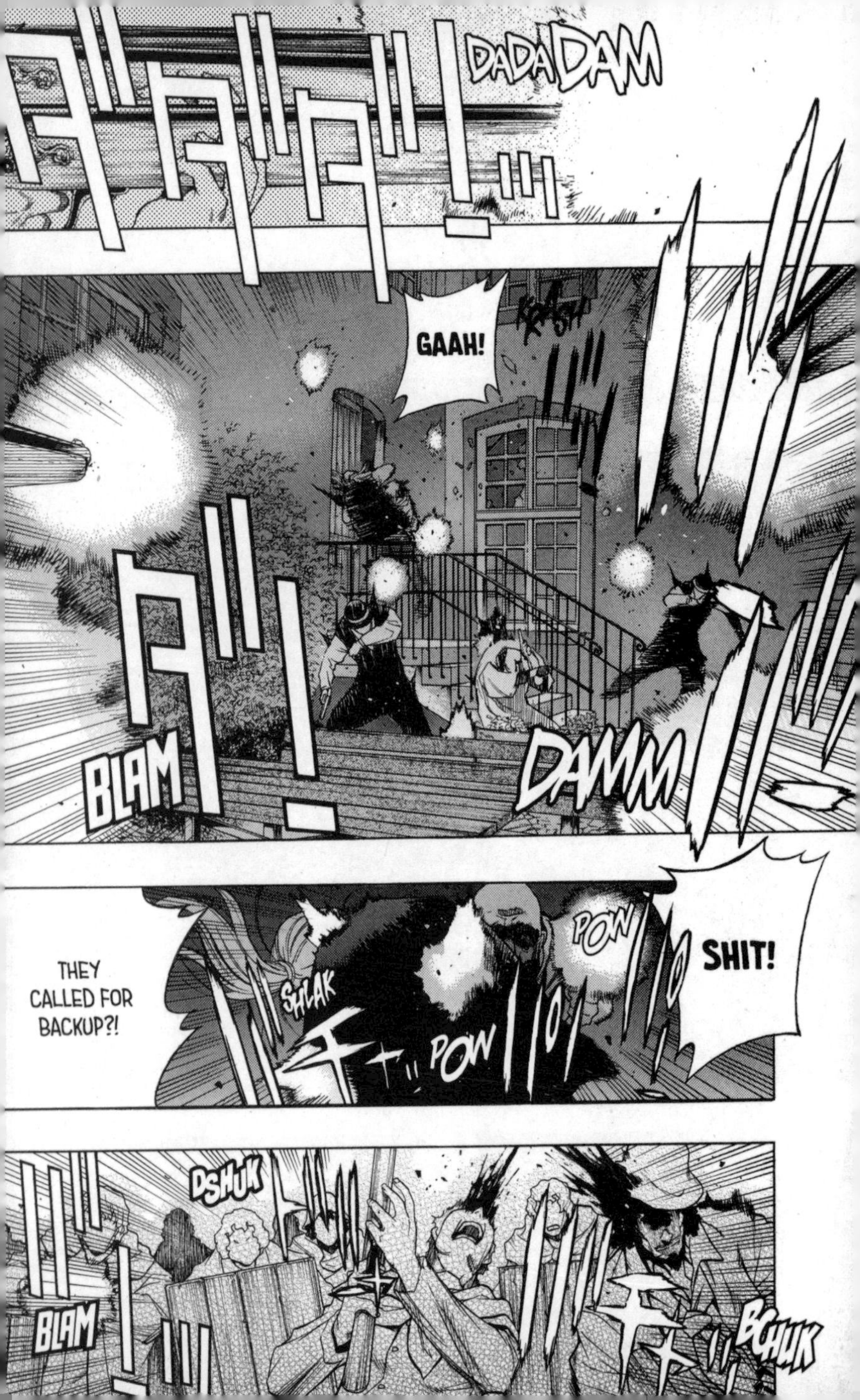
DADA DAM
GAAH!
KRASH
DAMM
BLAM
SHIT!
POW
THEY CALLED FOR BACKUP?!
SHLAK
POW
DSHUK
BCHUK
BLAM

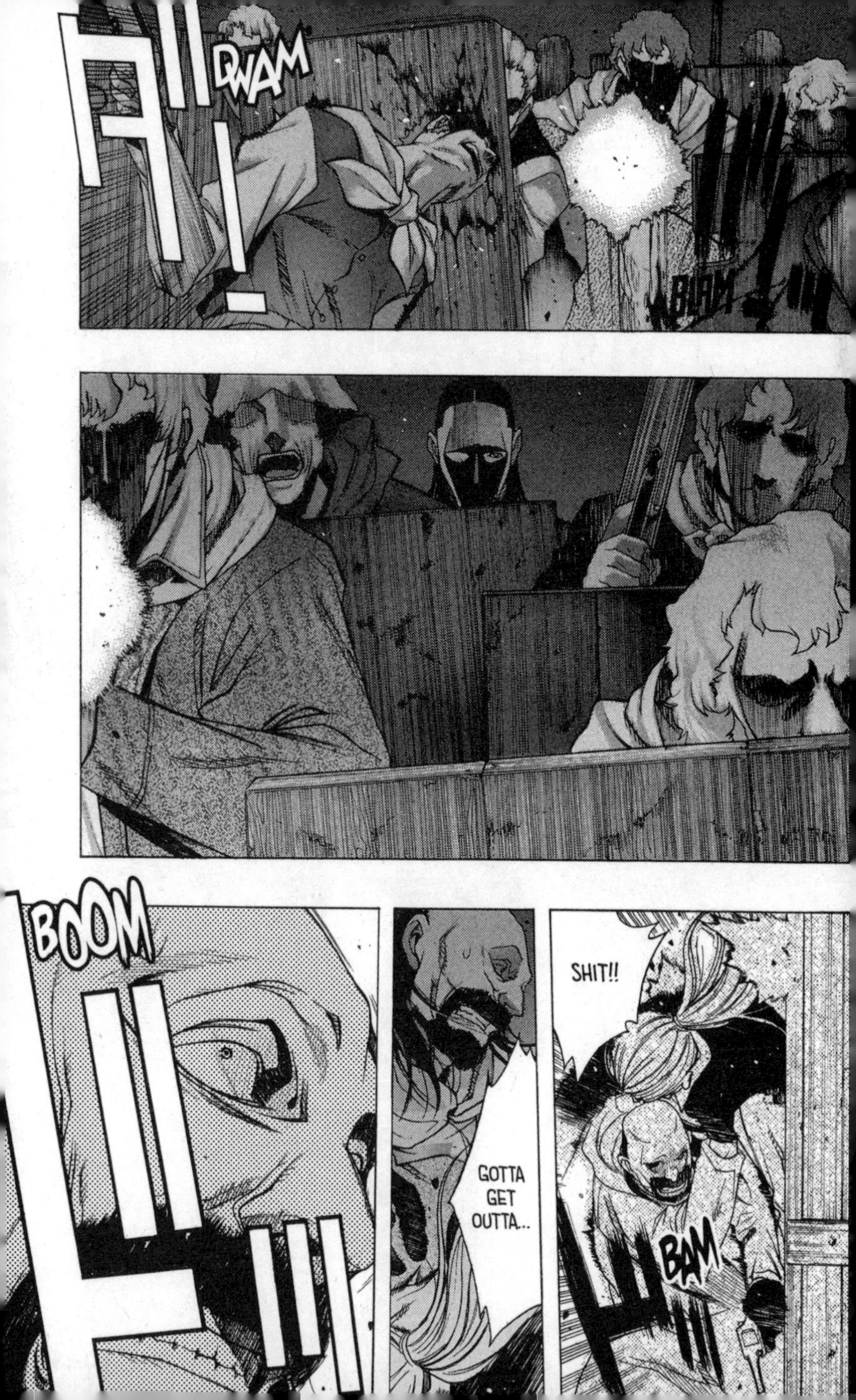
DWAM
BLAM
SHIT!!
BAM
GOTTA GET OUTTA..
BOOM

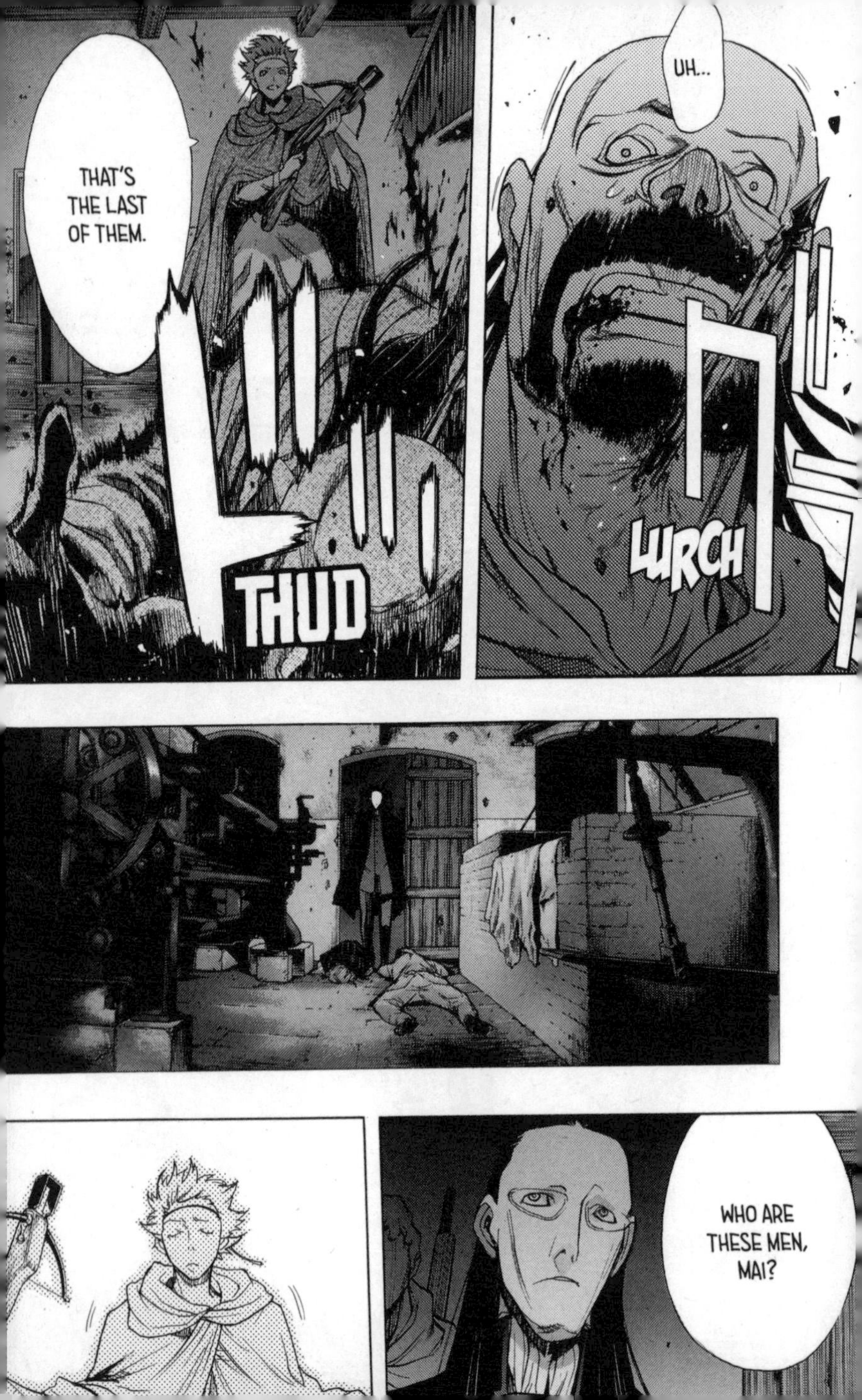
UH...
LURCH
THAT'S THE LAST OF THEM.
THUD
WHO ARE THESE MEN, MAI?

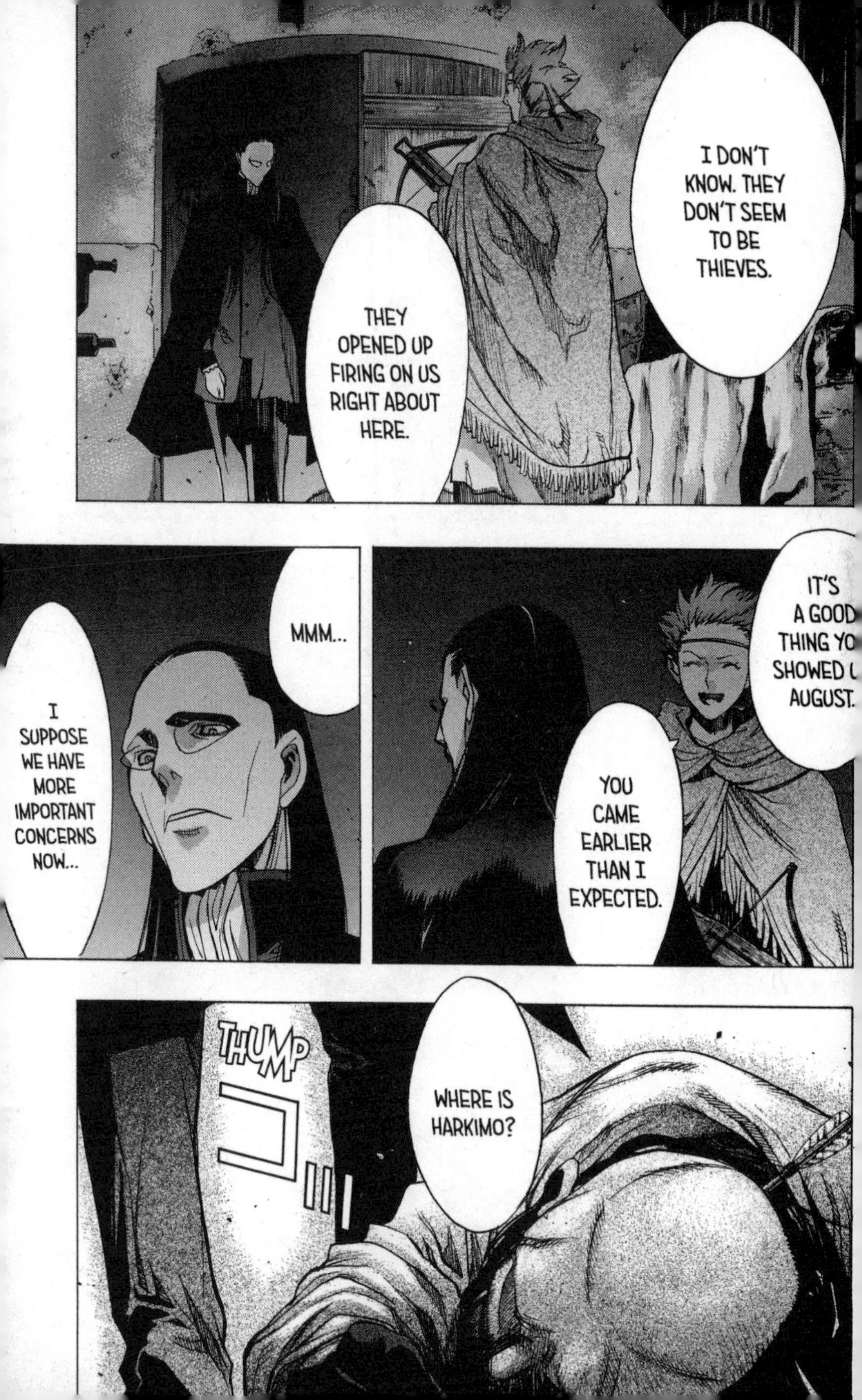
I DON'T KNOW. THEY DON'T SEEM TO BE THIEVES.
THEY OPENED UP FIRING ON US RIGHT ABOUT HERE.
IT'S A GOOD THING YO SHOWED AUGUST.
YOU CAME EARLIER THAN I EXPECTED.
MMM...
I SUPPOSE WE HAVE MORE IMPORTANT CONCERNS NOW...
WHERE IS HARKIMO?
THUMP

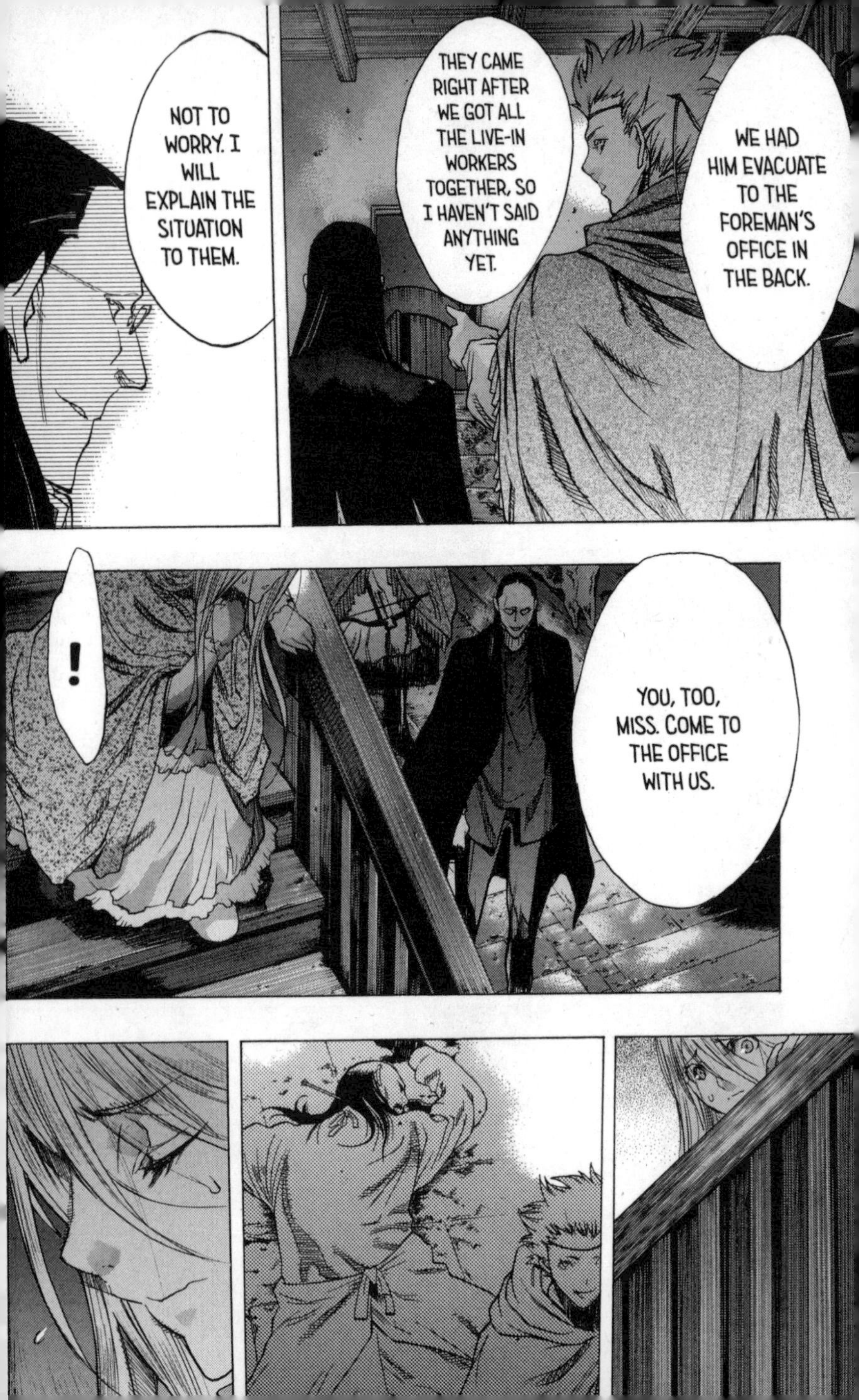
WE HAD HIM EVACUATE TO THE FOREMAN'S OFFICE IN THE BACK.
THEY CAME RIGHT AFTER WE GOT ALL THE LIVE-IN WORKERS TOGETHER, SO I HAVEN'T SAID ANYTHING YET.
NOT TO WORRY. I WILL EXPLAIN THE SITUATION TO THEM.
YOU, TOO, MISS. COME TO THE OFFICE WITH US.
!

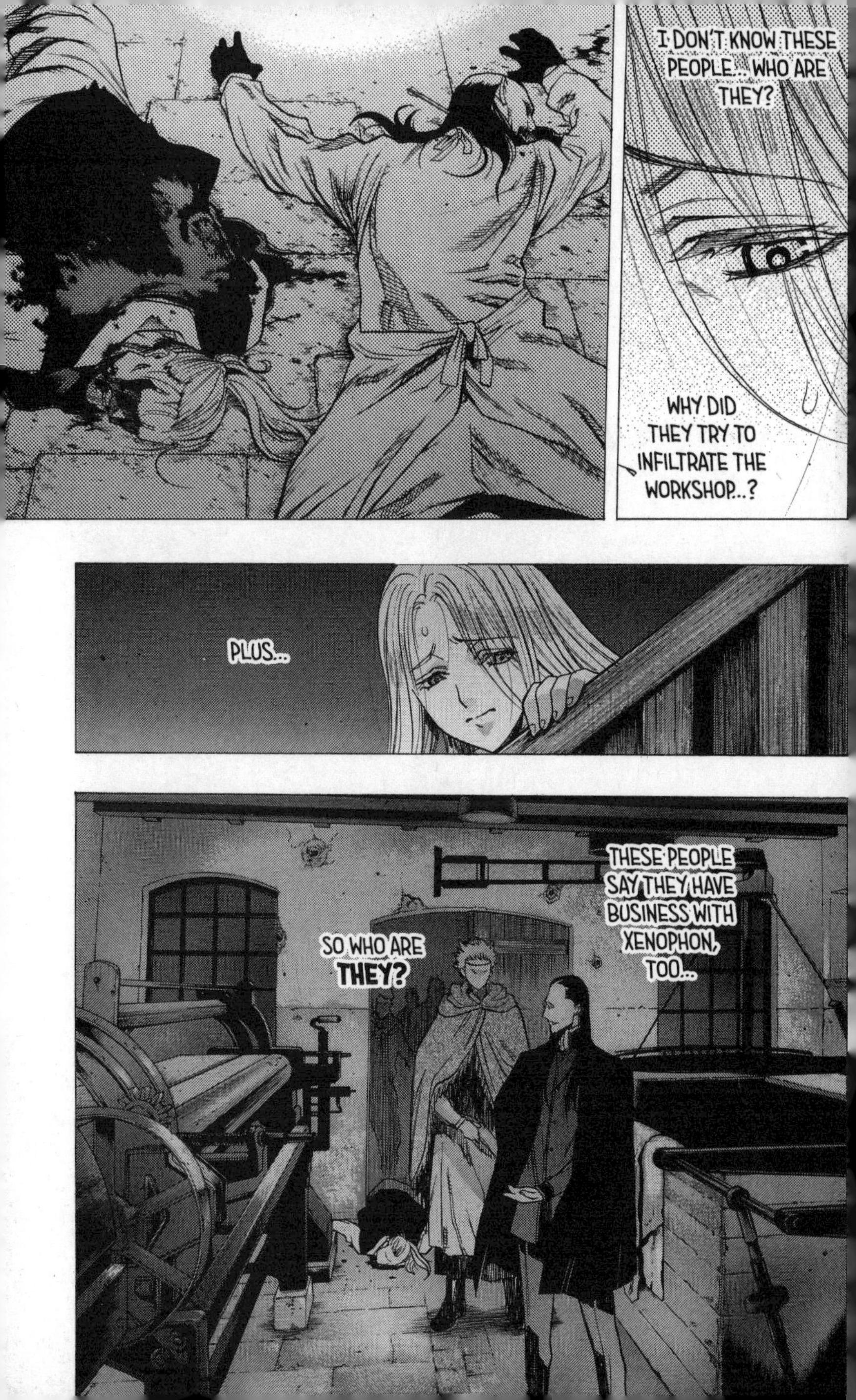
I DON'T KNOW THESE PEOPLE... WHO ARE THEY?
WHY DID THEY TRY TO INFILTRATE THE WORKSHOP...?
PLUS...
THESE PEOPLE SAY THEY HAVE BUSINESS WITH XENOPHON, TOO...
SO WHO ARE **THEY?**

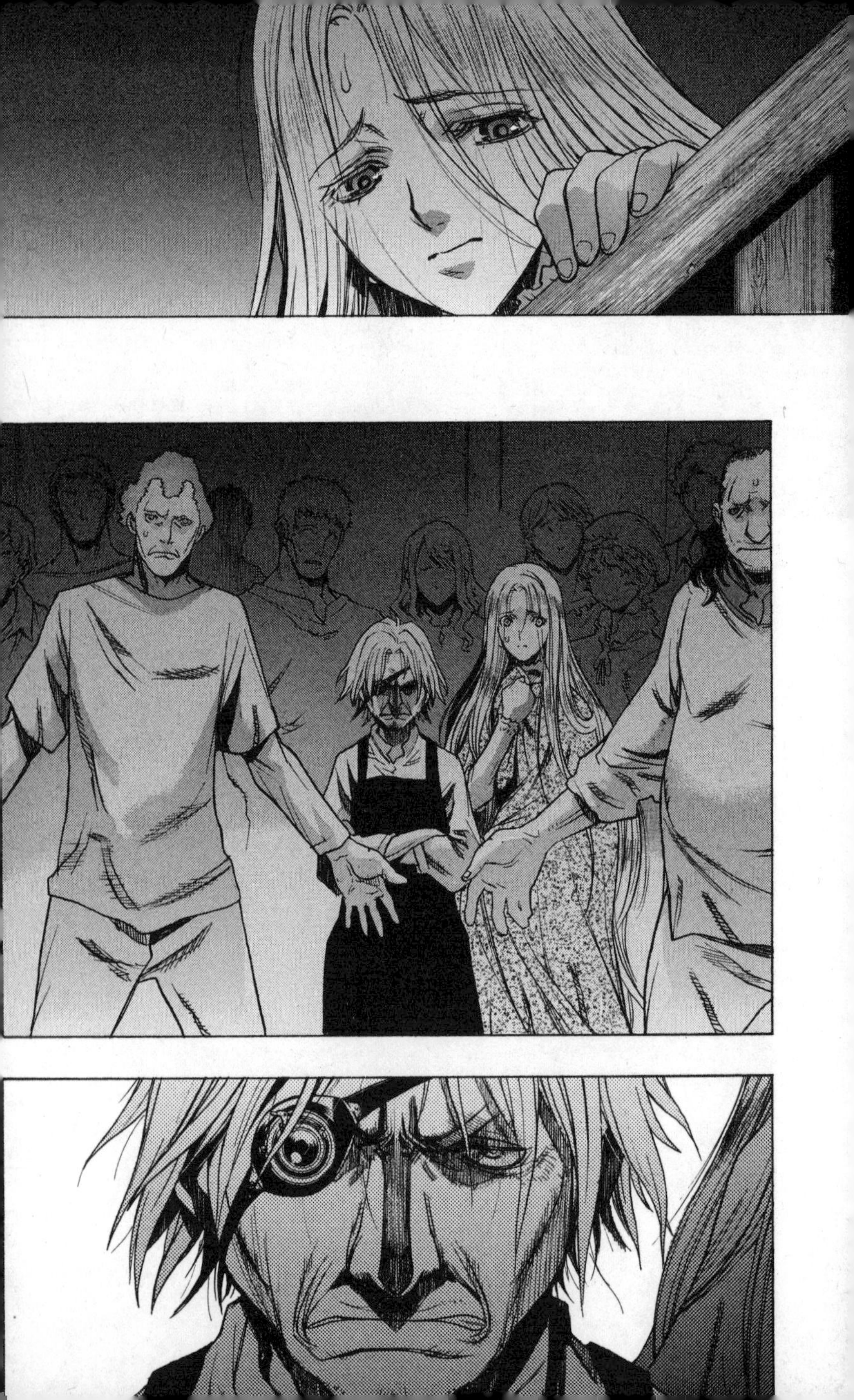

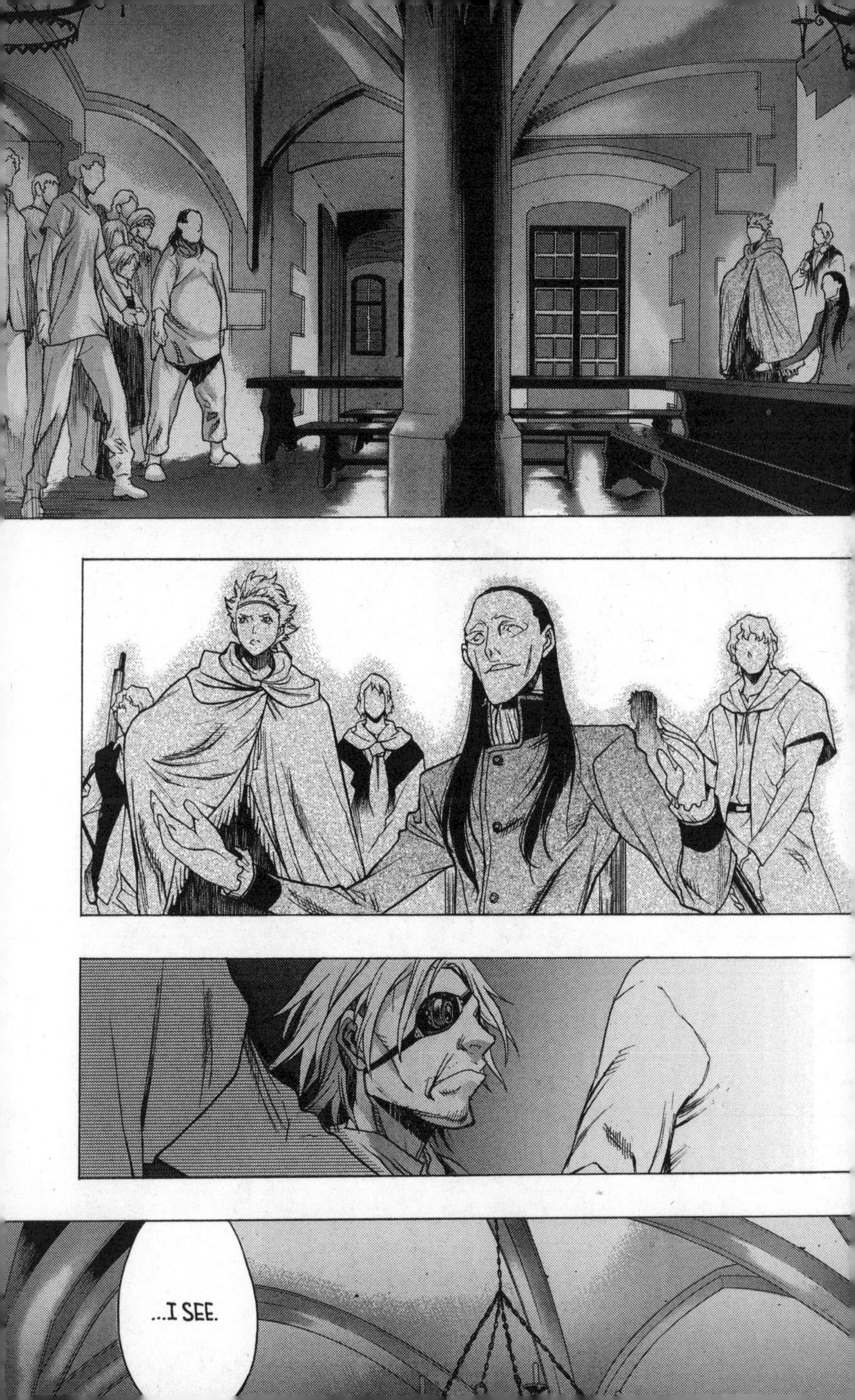
...I SEE.

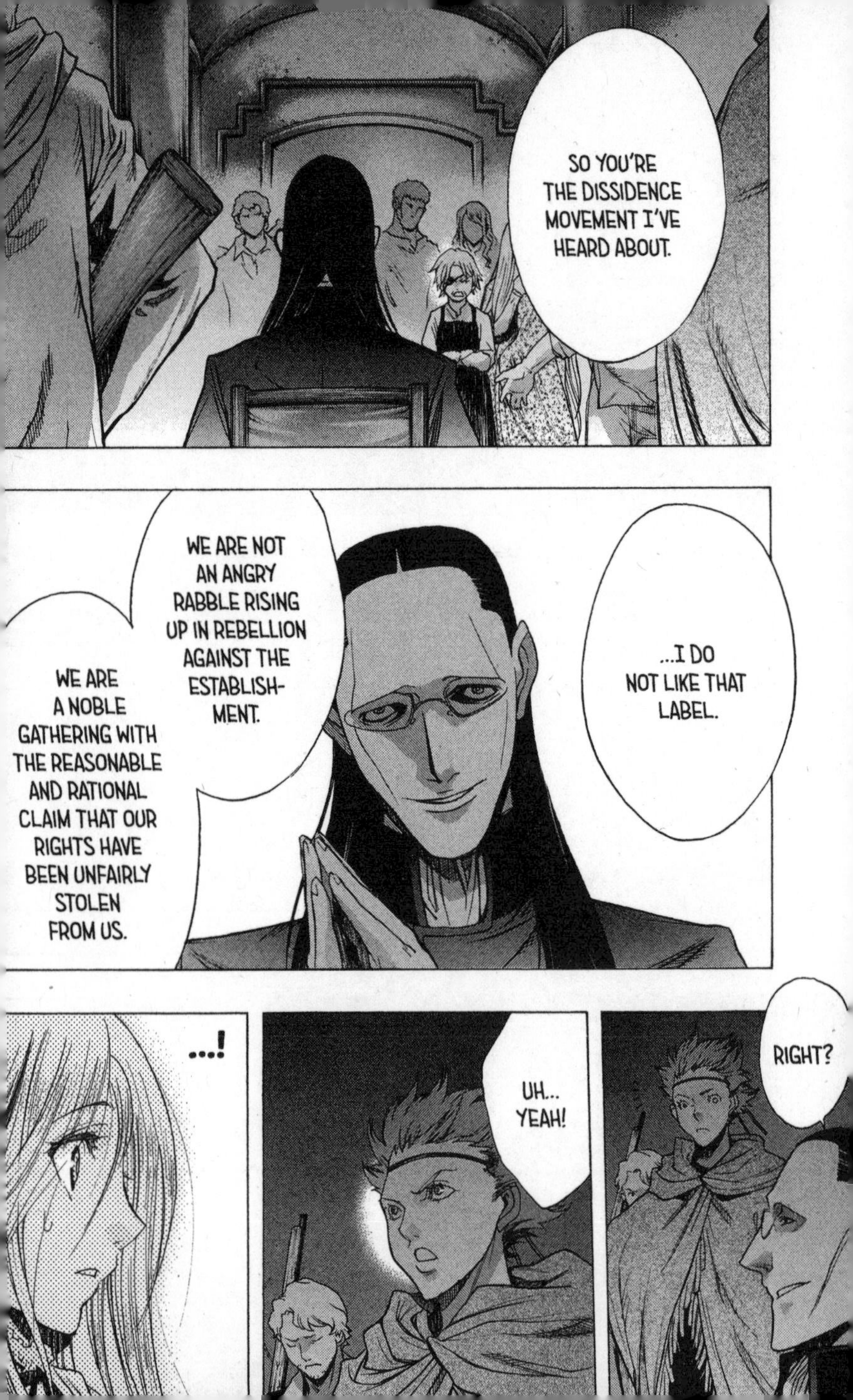

SO YOU'RE THE DISSIDENCE MOVEMENT I'VE HEARD ABOUT.
...I DO NOT LIKE THAT LABEL.
WE ARE NOT AN ANGRY RABBLE RISING UP IN REBELLION AGAINST THE ESTABLISH-MENT.
WE ARE A NOBLE GATHERING WITH THE REASONABLE AND RATIONAL CLAIM THAT OUR RIGHTS HAVE BEEN UNFAIRLY STOLEN FROM US.
RIGHT?
UH... YEAH!
...!

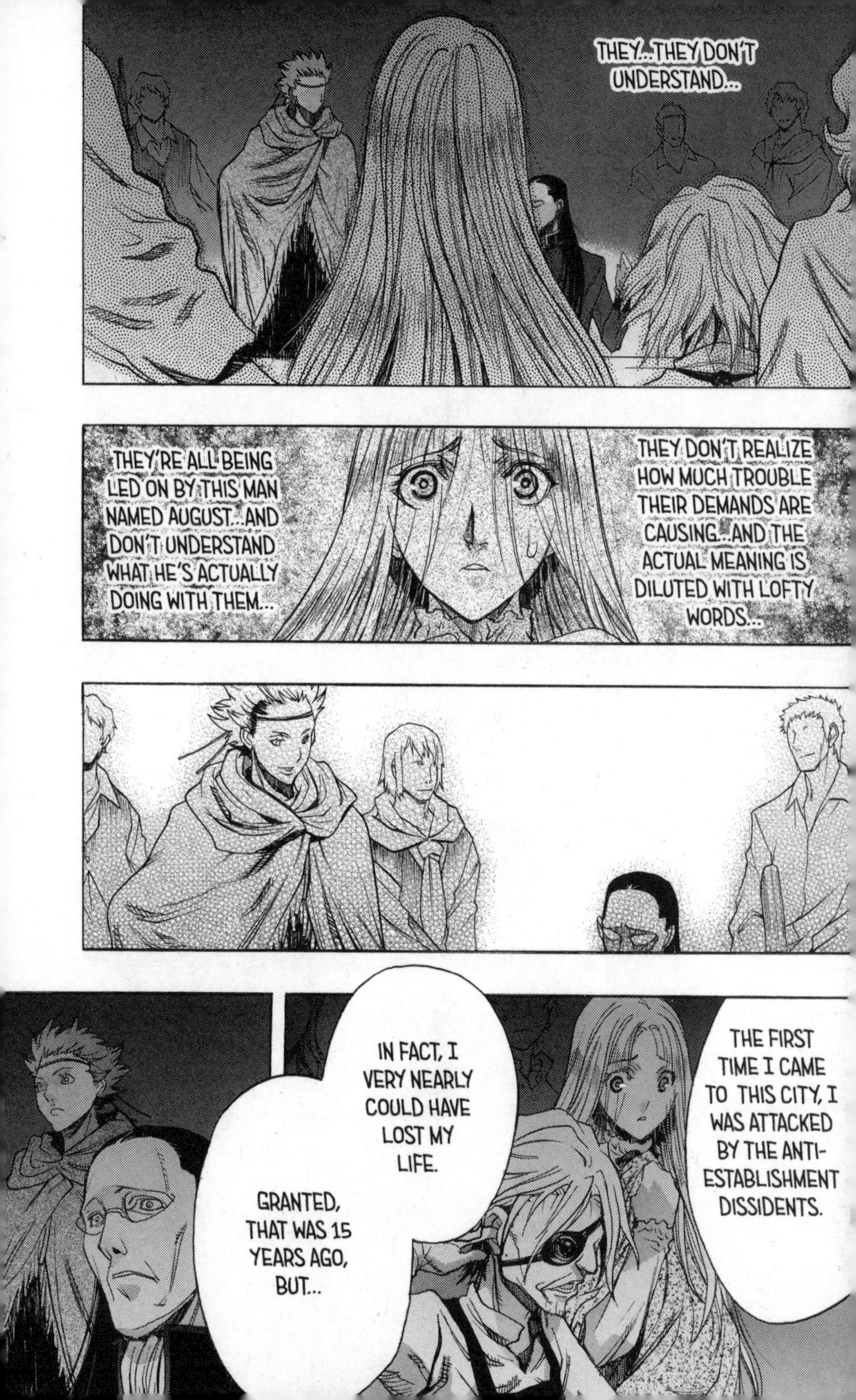
THEY... THEY DON'T UNDERSTAND...
THEY DON'T REALIZE HOW MUCH TROUBLE THEIR DEMANDS ARE CAUSING... AND THE ACTUAL MEANING IS DILUTED WITH LOFTY WORDS...
THEY'RE ALL BEING LED ON BY THIS MAN NAMED AUGUST... AND DON'T UNDERSTAND WHAT HE'S ACTUALLY DOING WITH THEM...
THE FIRST TIME I CAME TO THIS CITY, I WAS ATTACKED BY THE ANTI-ESTABLISHMENT DISSIDENTS.
IN FACT, I VERY NEARLY COULD HAVE LOST MY LIFE.
GRANTED, THAT WAS 15 YEARS AGO, BUT...

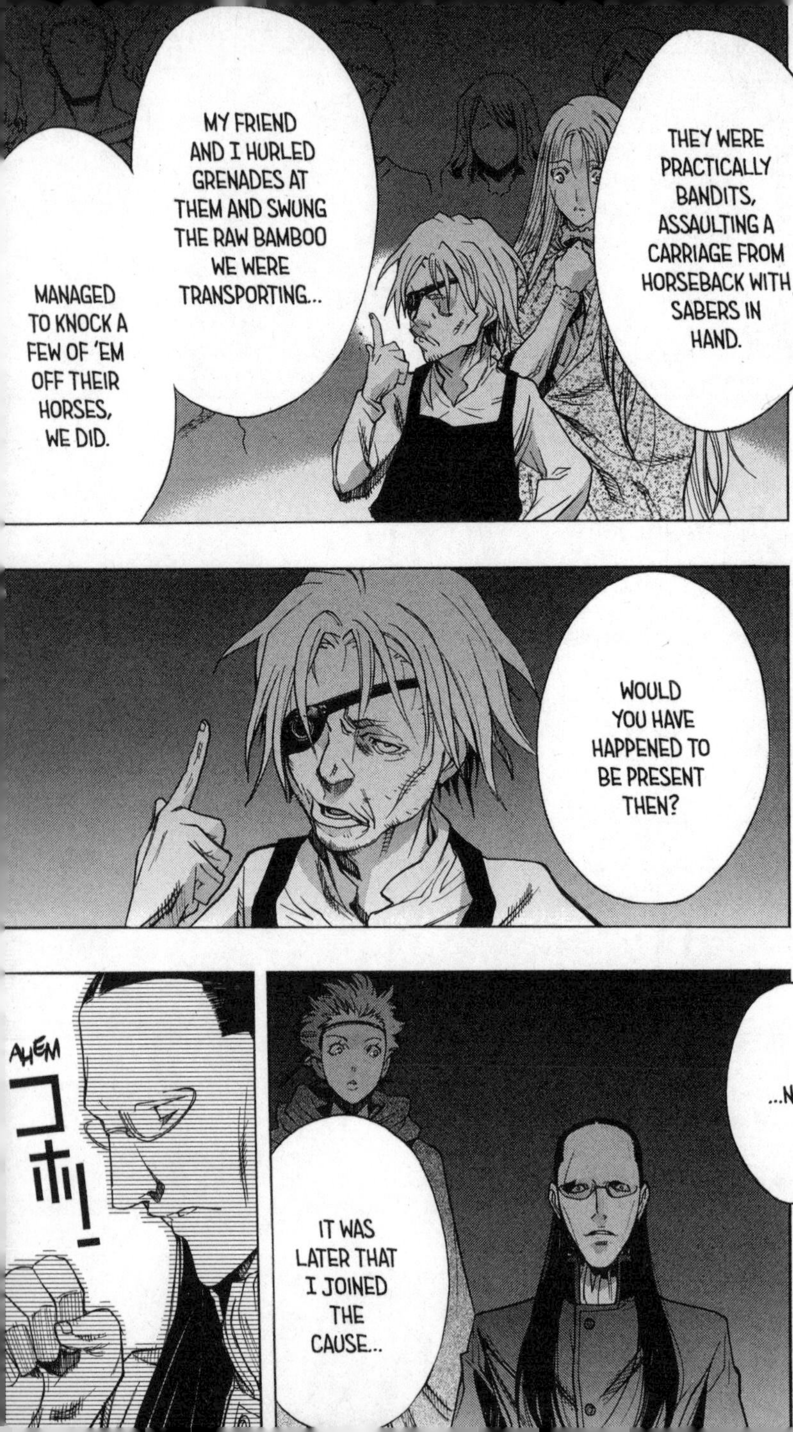
THEY WERE PRACTICALLY BANDITS, ASSAULTING A CARRIAGE FROM HORSEBACK WITH SABERS IN HAND.
MY FRIEND AND I HURLED GRENADES AT THEM AND SWUNG THE RAW BAMBOO WE WERE TRANSPORTING...
MANAGED TO KNOCK A FEW OF 'EM OFF THEIR HORSES, WE DID.
WOULD YOU HAVE HAPPENED TO BE PRESENT THEN?
...NO...
IT WAS LATER THAT I JOINED THE CAUSE...
AHEM
コホ!

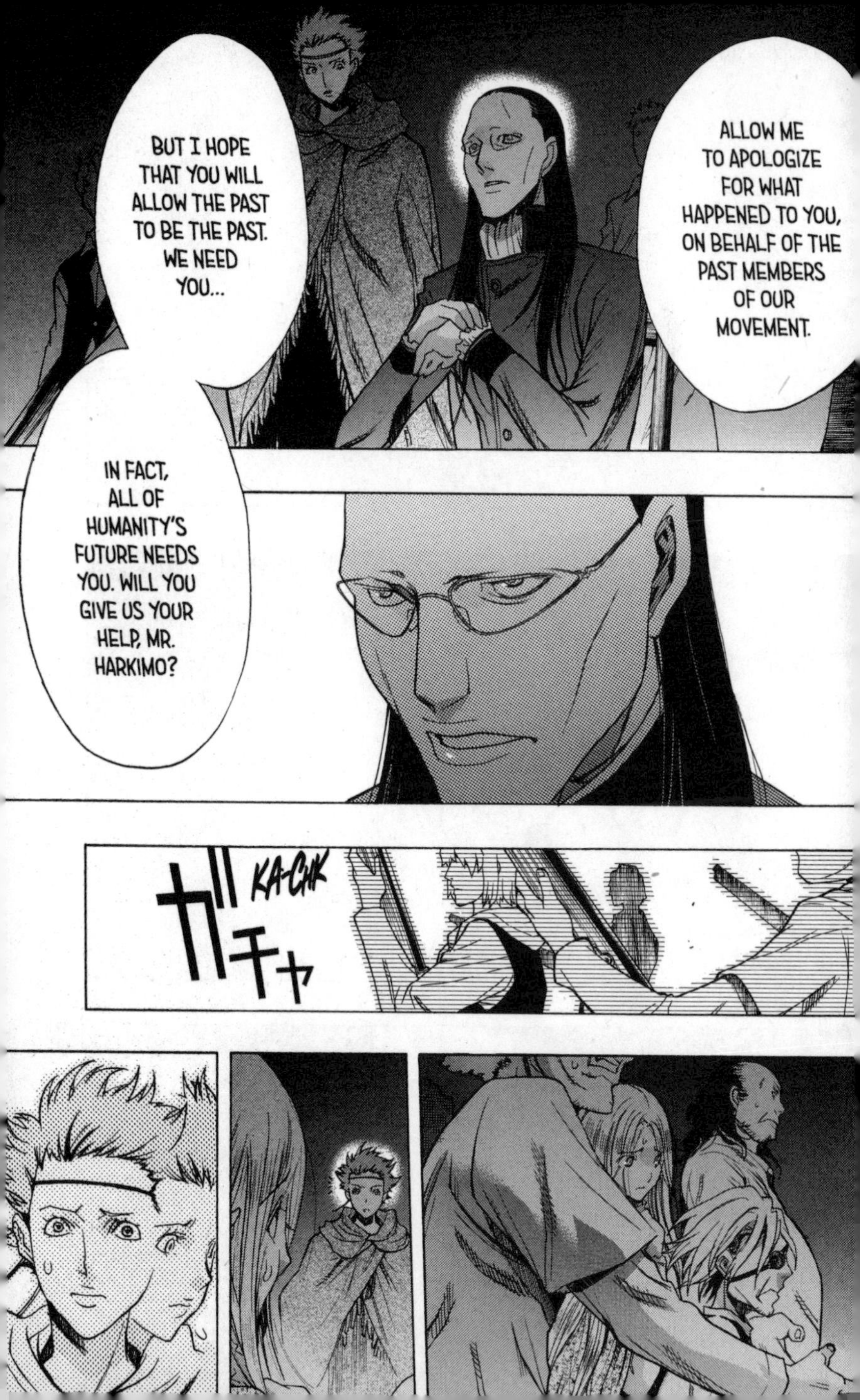
ALLOW ME TO APOLOGIZE FOR WHAT HAPPENED TO YOU, ON BEHALF OF THE PAST MEMBERS OF OUR MOVEMENT.
BUT I HOPE THAT YOU WILL ALLOW THE PAST TO BE THE PAST. WE NEED YOU...
IN FACT, ALL OF HUMANITY'S FUTURE NEEDS YOU. WILL YOU GIVE US YOUR HELP, MR. HARKIMO?
カチャ
KA-CHK

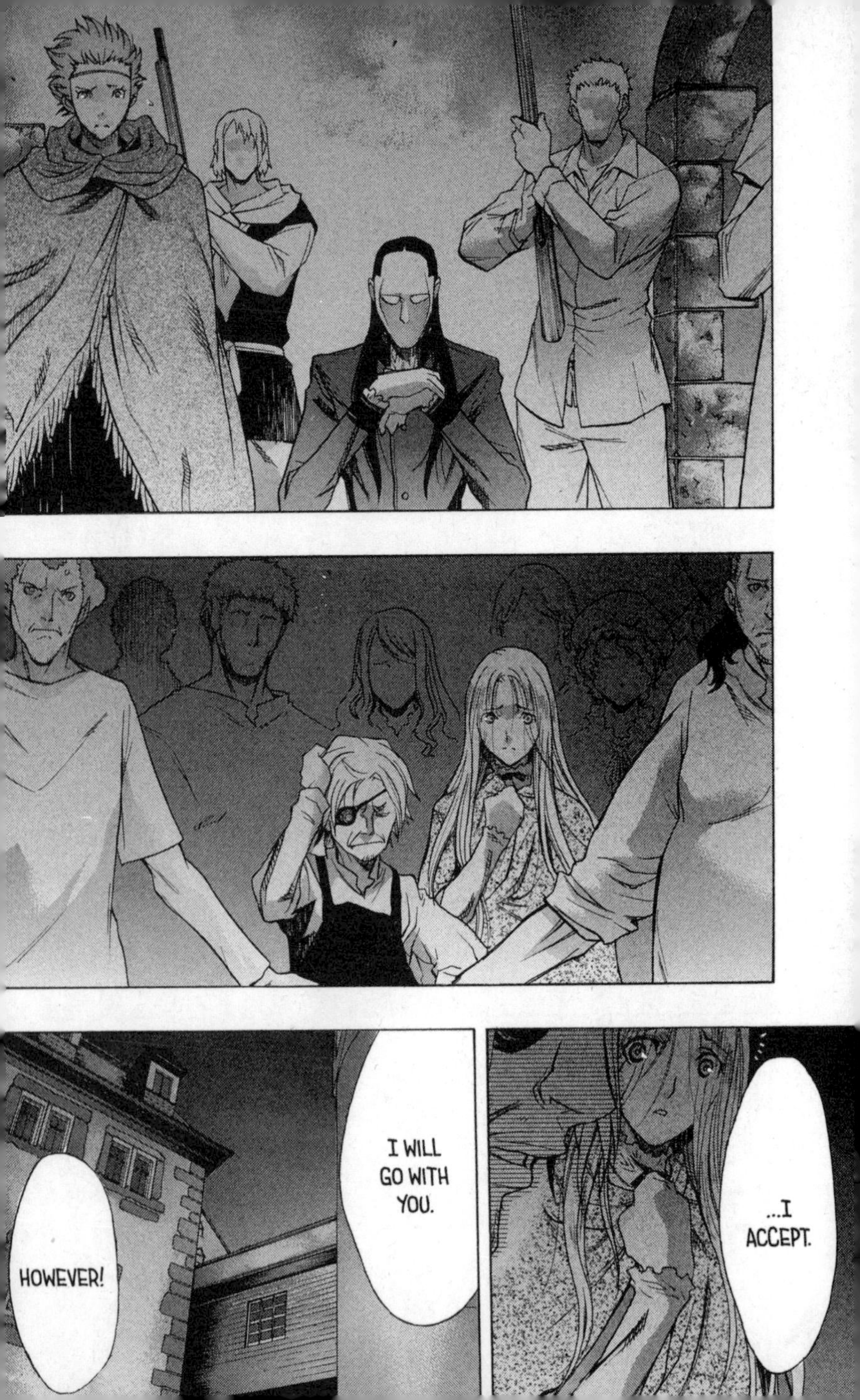
...I ACCEPT.
I WILL GO WITH YOU.
HOWEVER!

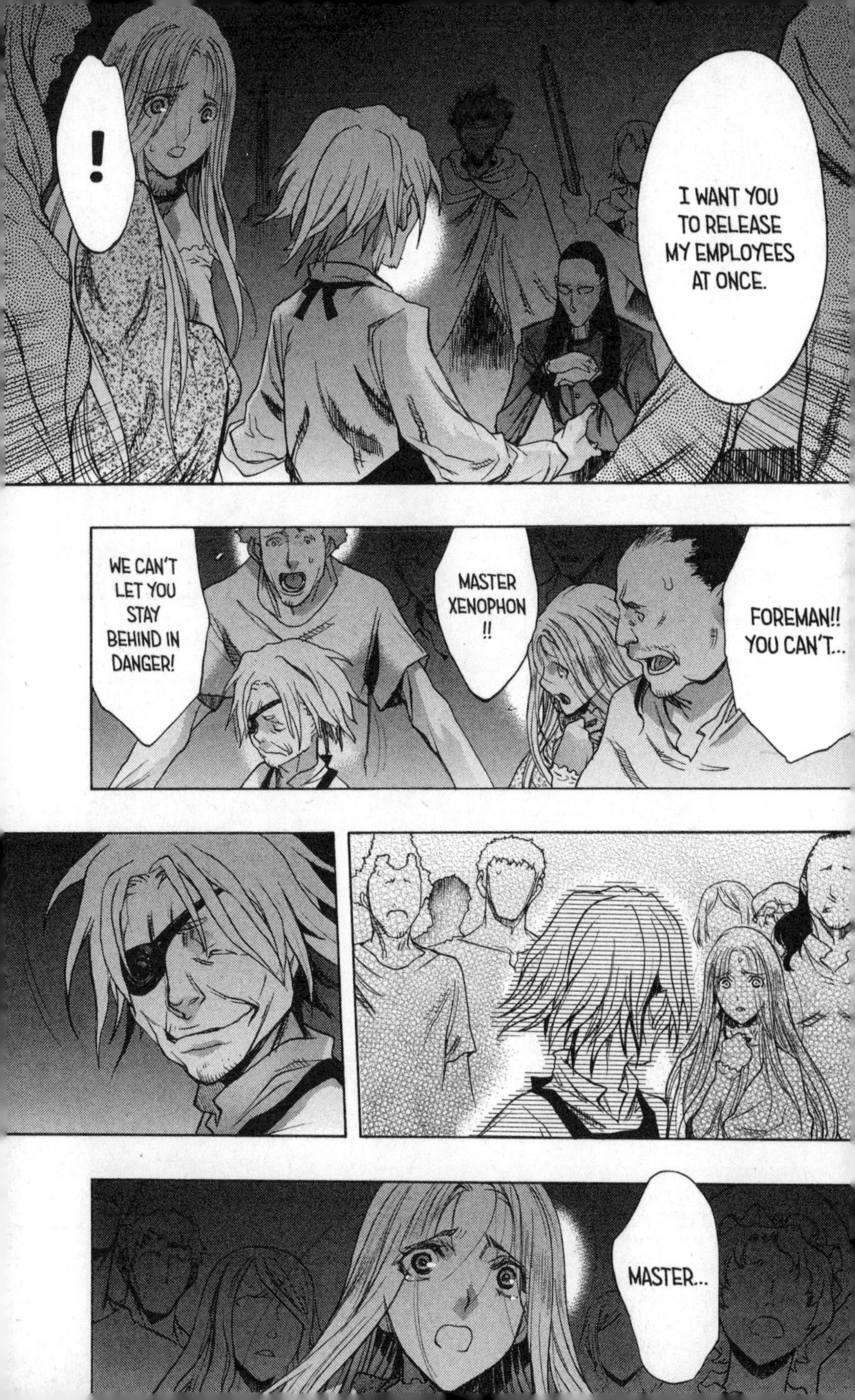
I WANT YOU TO RELEASE MY EMPLOYEES AT ONCE.
!
FOREMAN!! YOU CAN'T...
MASTER XENOPHON!!
WE CAN'T LET YOU STAY BEHIND IN DANGER!
MASTER...

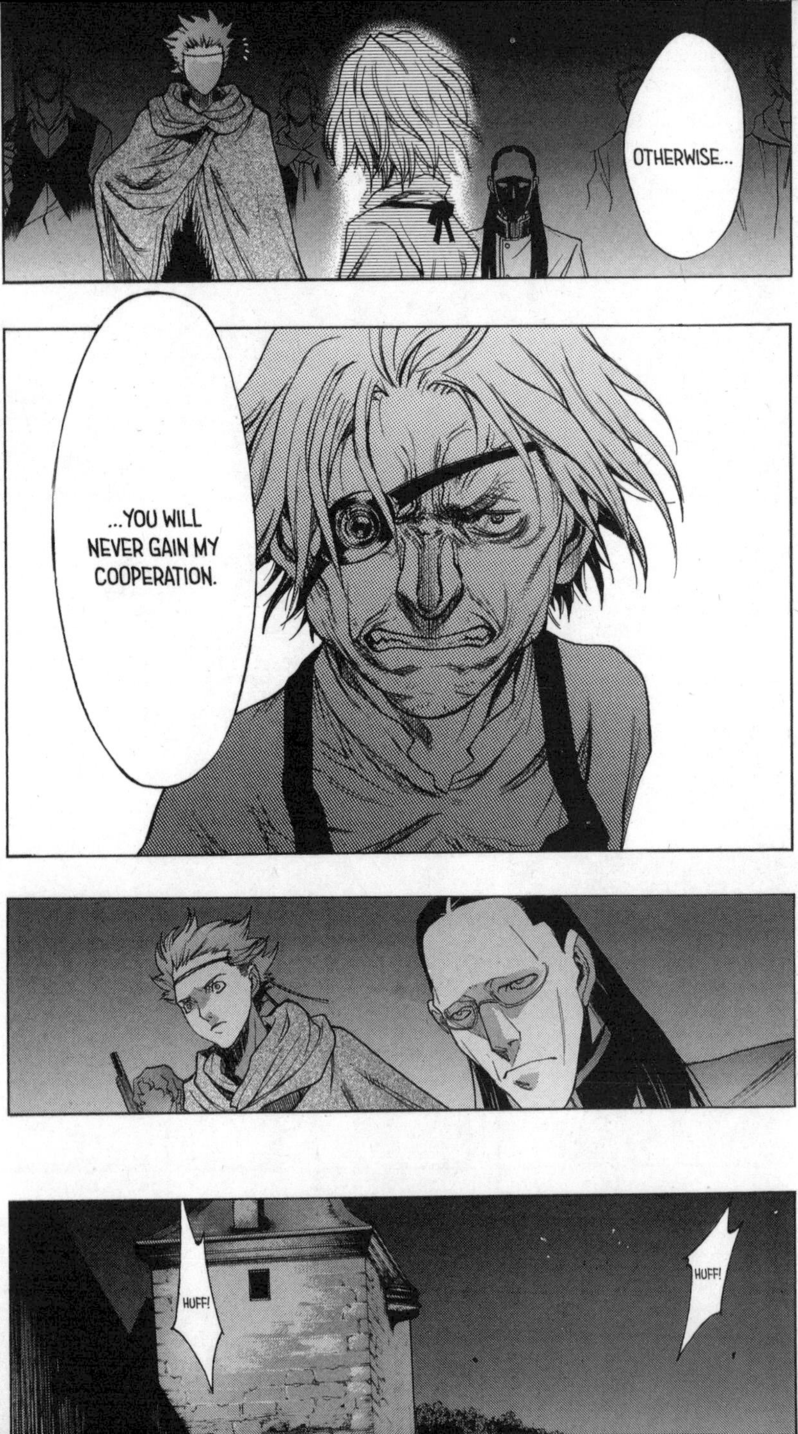
OTHERWISE...
...YOU WILL NEVER GAIN MY COOPERATION.
HUFF!
HUFF!

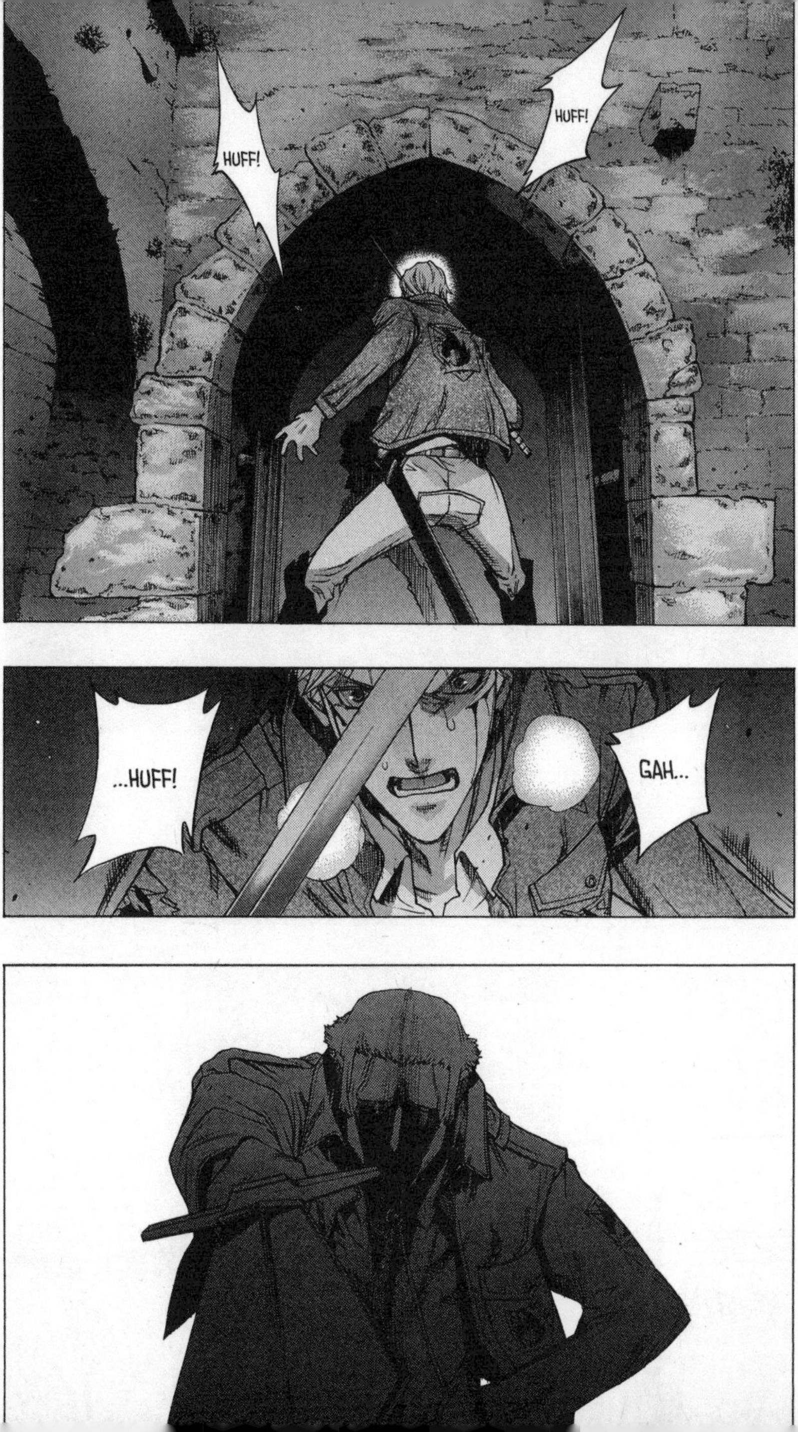
HUFF!
HUFF!
GAH...
...HUFF!

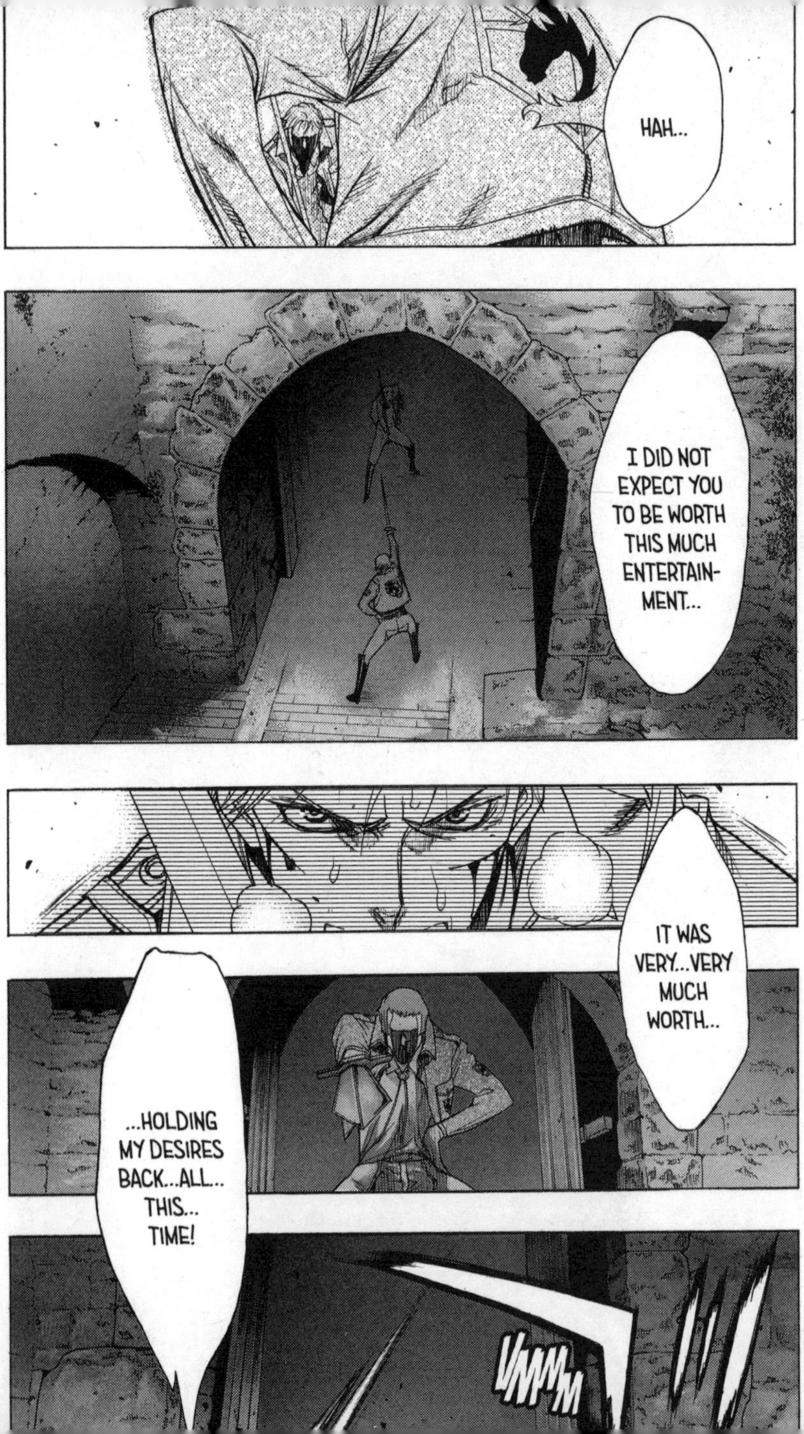
HAH...
I DID NOT EXPECT YOU TO BE WORTH THIS MUCH ENTERTAIN-MENT...
IT WAS VERY...VERY MUCH WORTH...
...HOLDING MY DESIRES BACK...ALL... THIS... TIME!

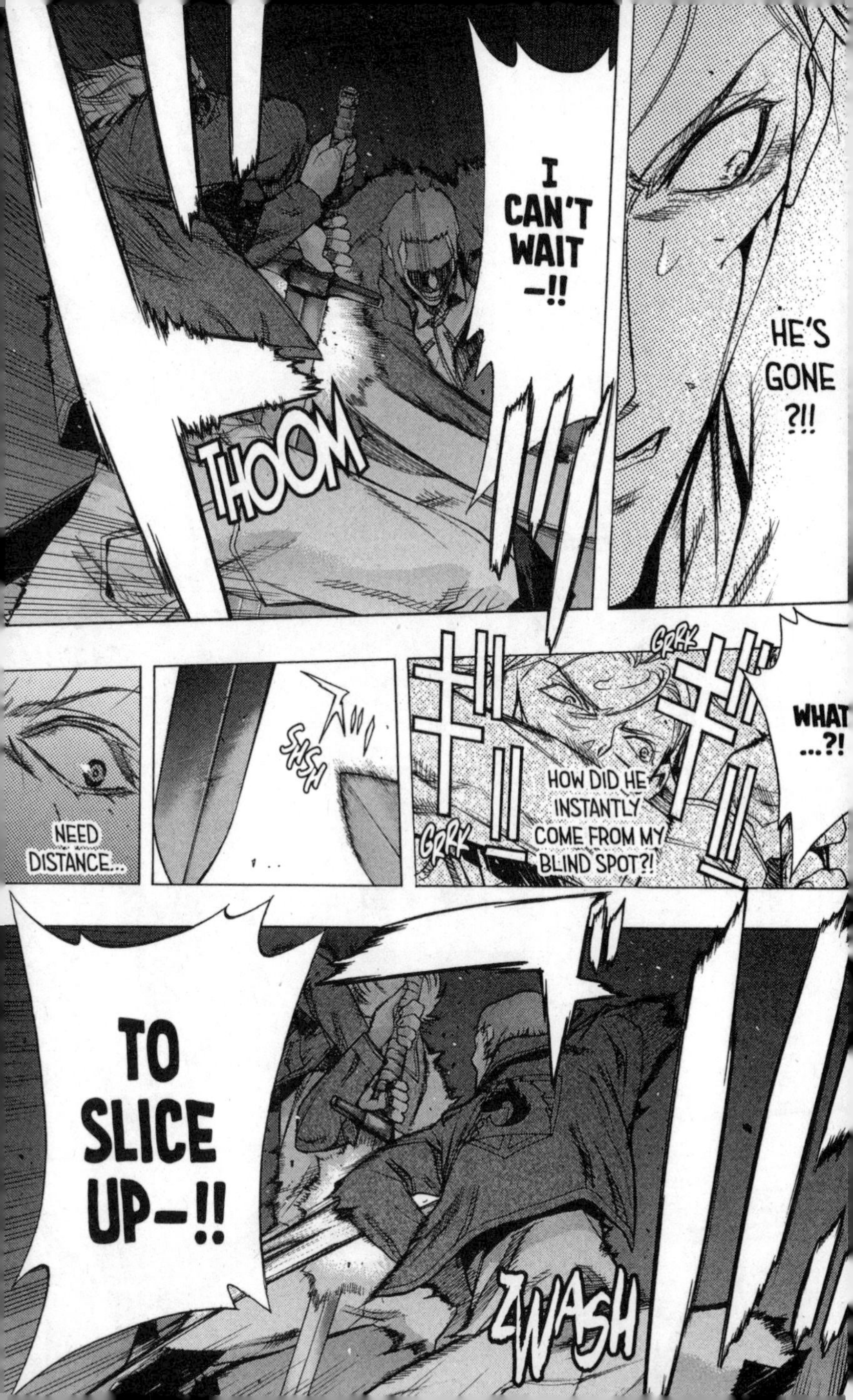
HE'S GONE ?!!
I CAN'T WAIT —!!
THOOM
WHAT ...?!
GRRK
HOW DID HE INSTANTLY COME FROM MY BLIND SPOT?!
GRRK
SHSH
NEED DISTANCE...
TO SLICE UP—!!
ZWASH

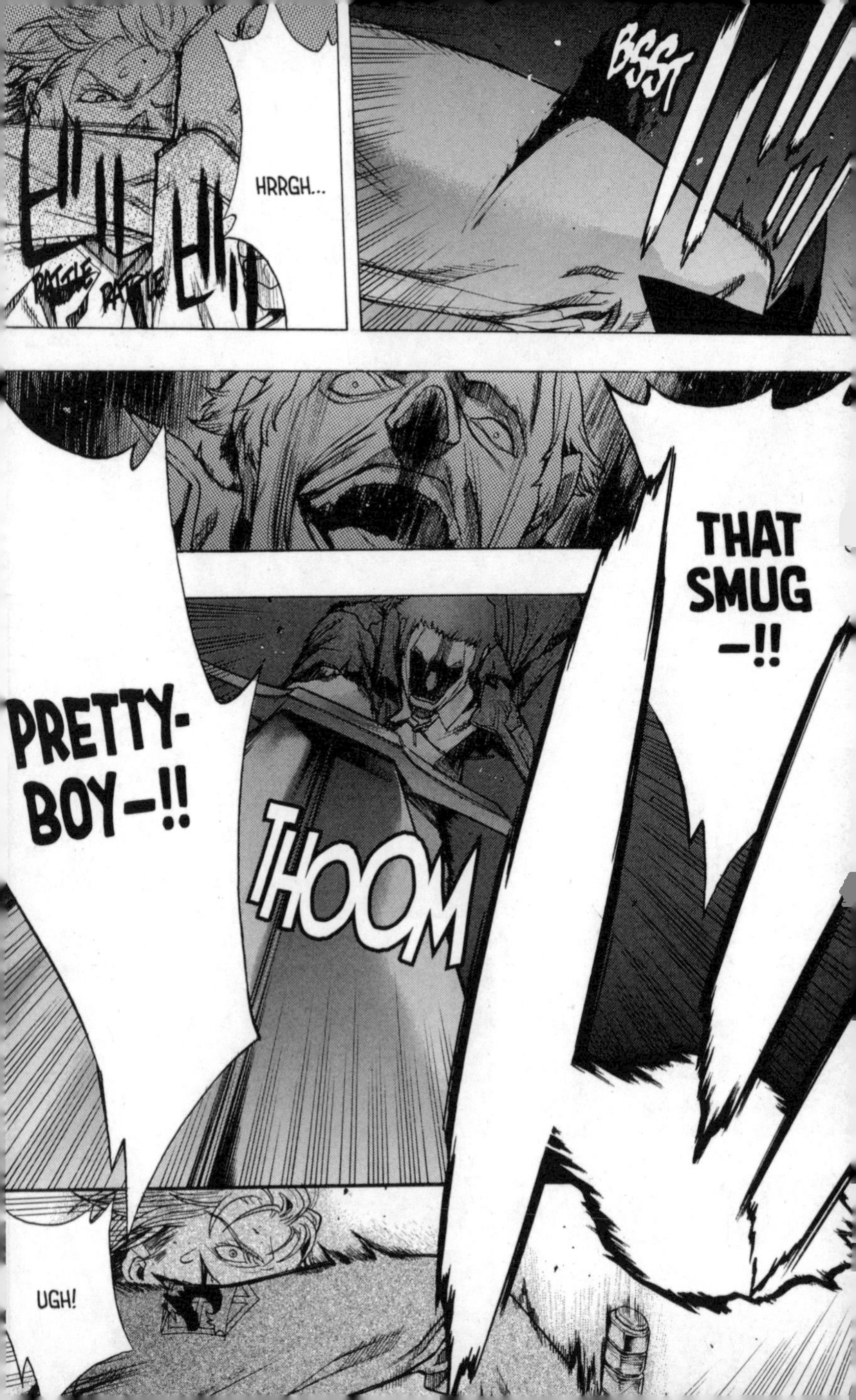
BSST
RATTLE RATTLE
HRRGH...
THAT SMUG—!!
PRETTY-BOY—!!
THOOM
UGH!

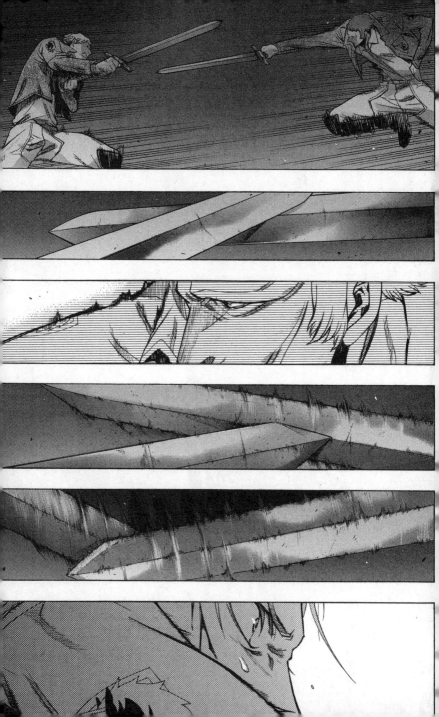

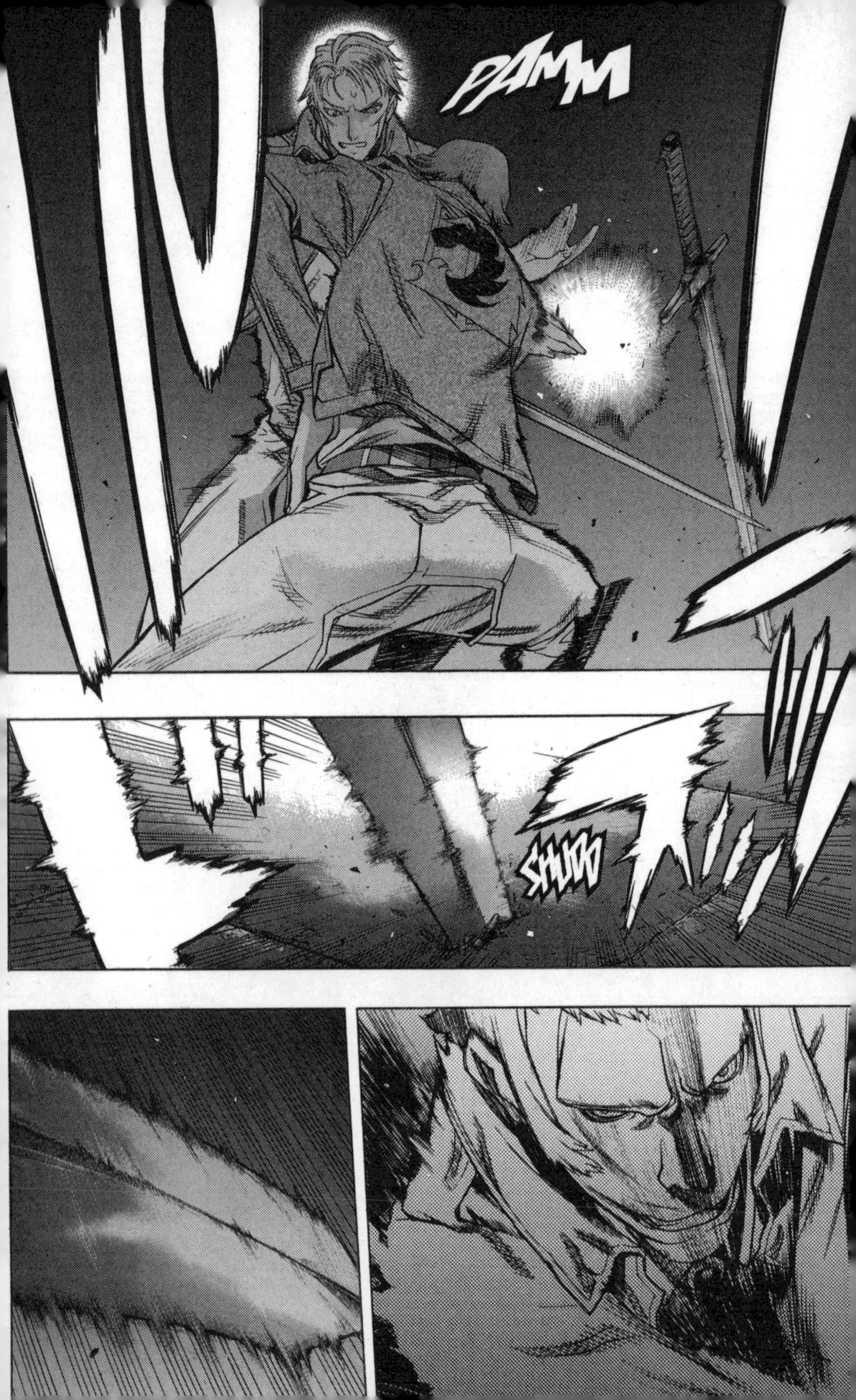
PAMM
SHUOO

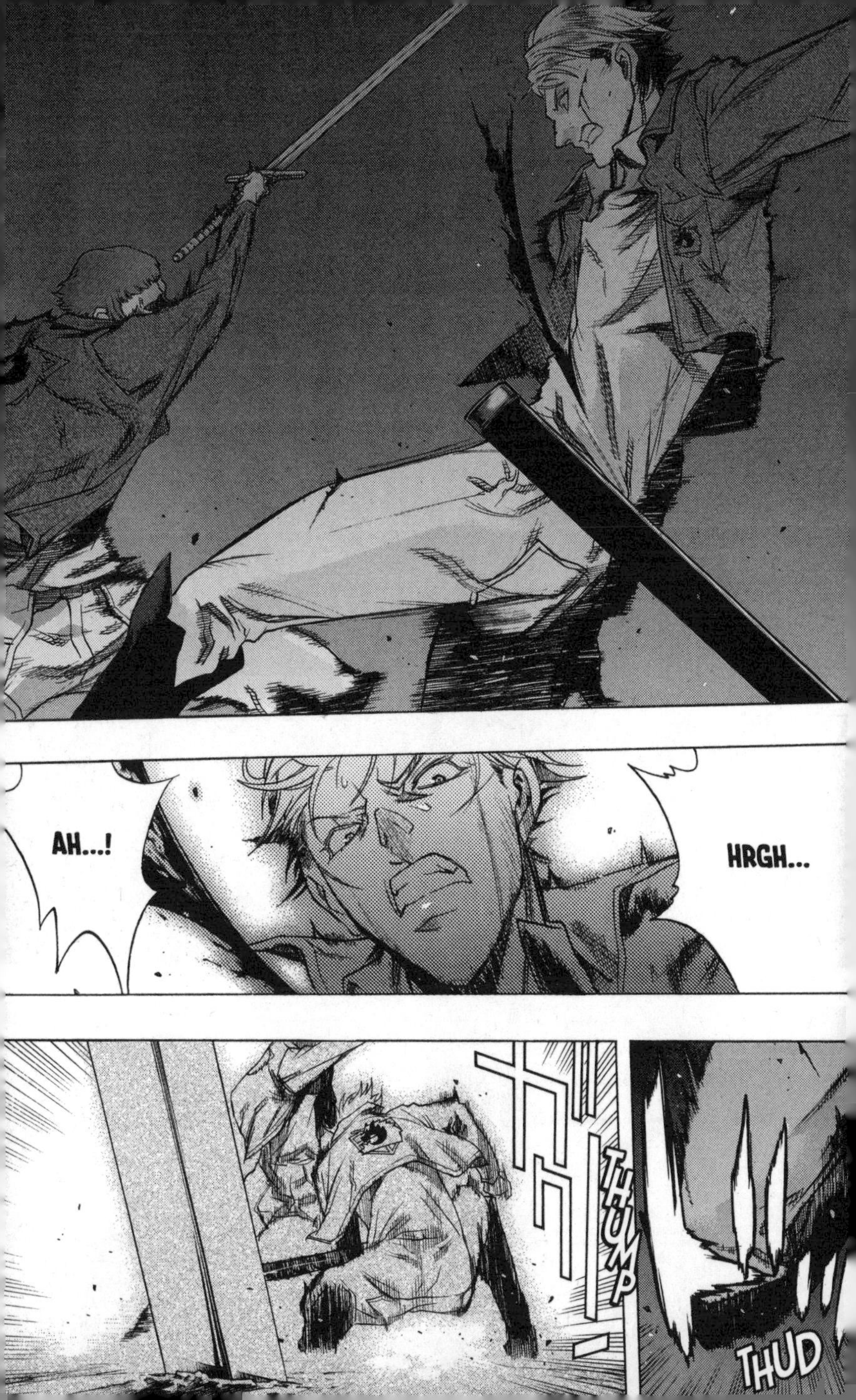
HRGH...
AH...!
THUD
THUMP

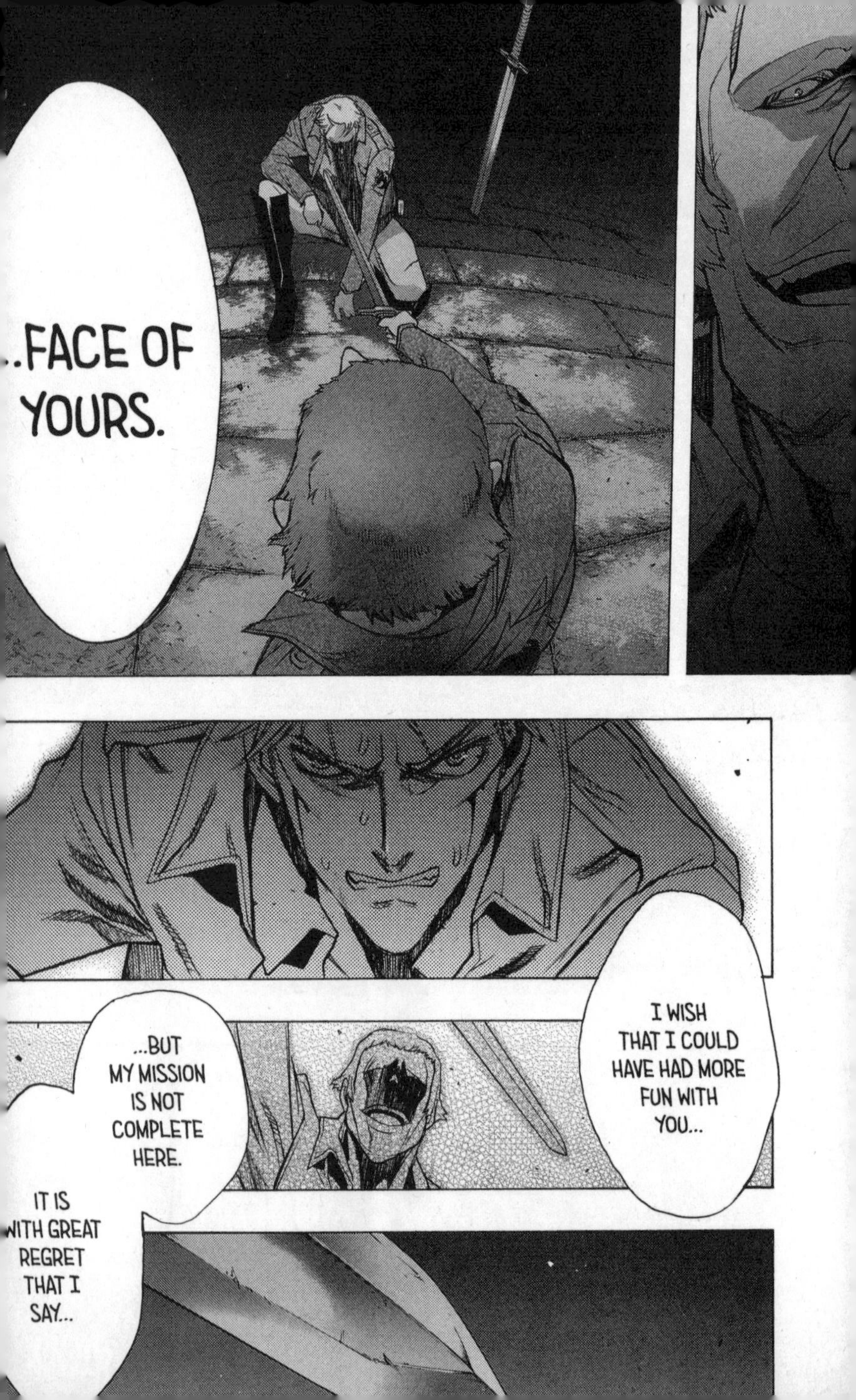
..FACE OF YOURS.
I WISH THAT I COULD HAVE HAD MORE FUN WITH YOU...
...BUT MY MISSION IS NOT COMPLETE HERE.
IT IS WITH GREAT REGRET THAT I SAY...

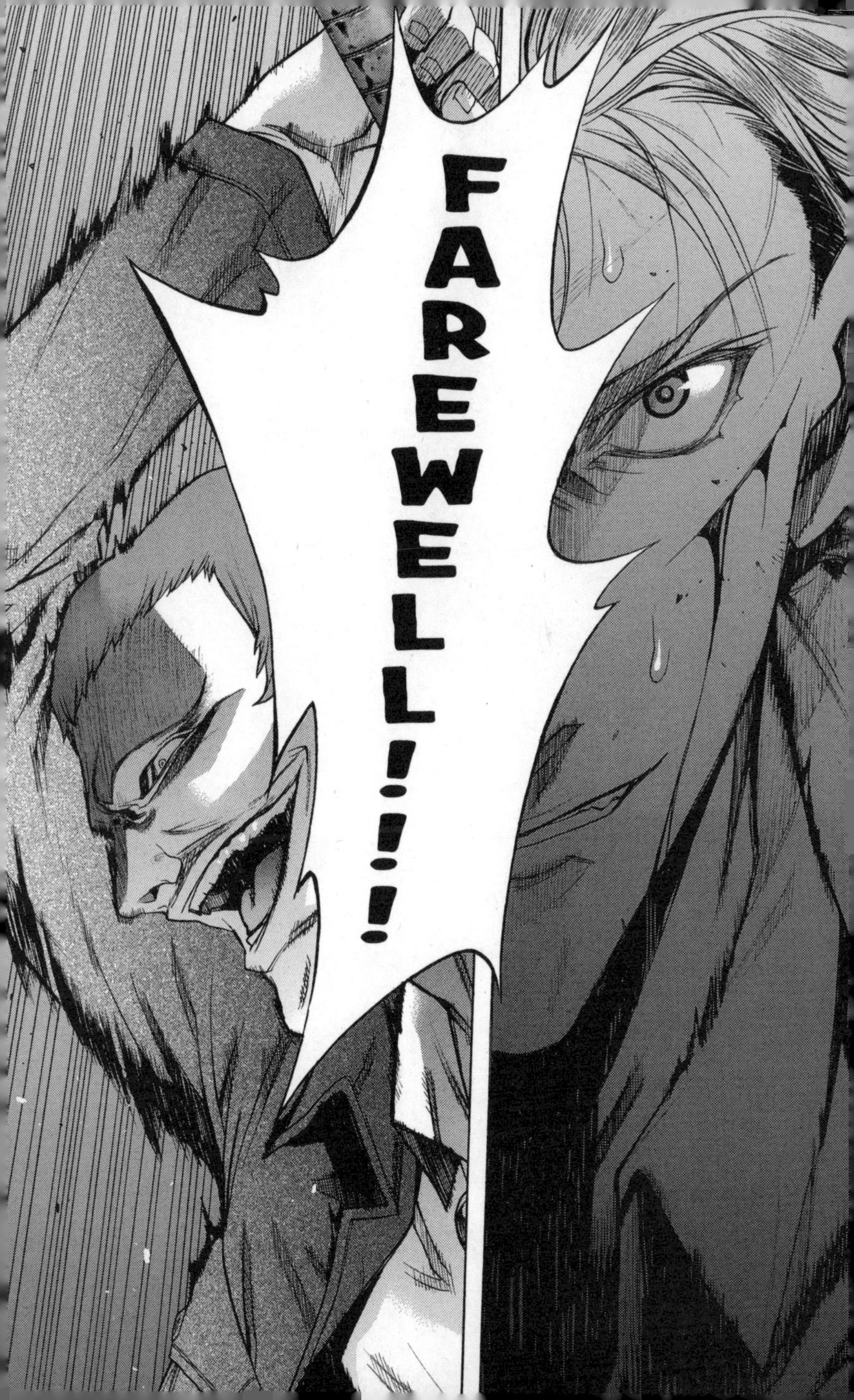
FAREWELL!!!!

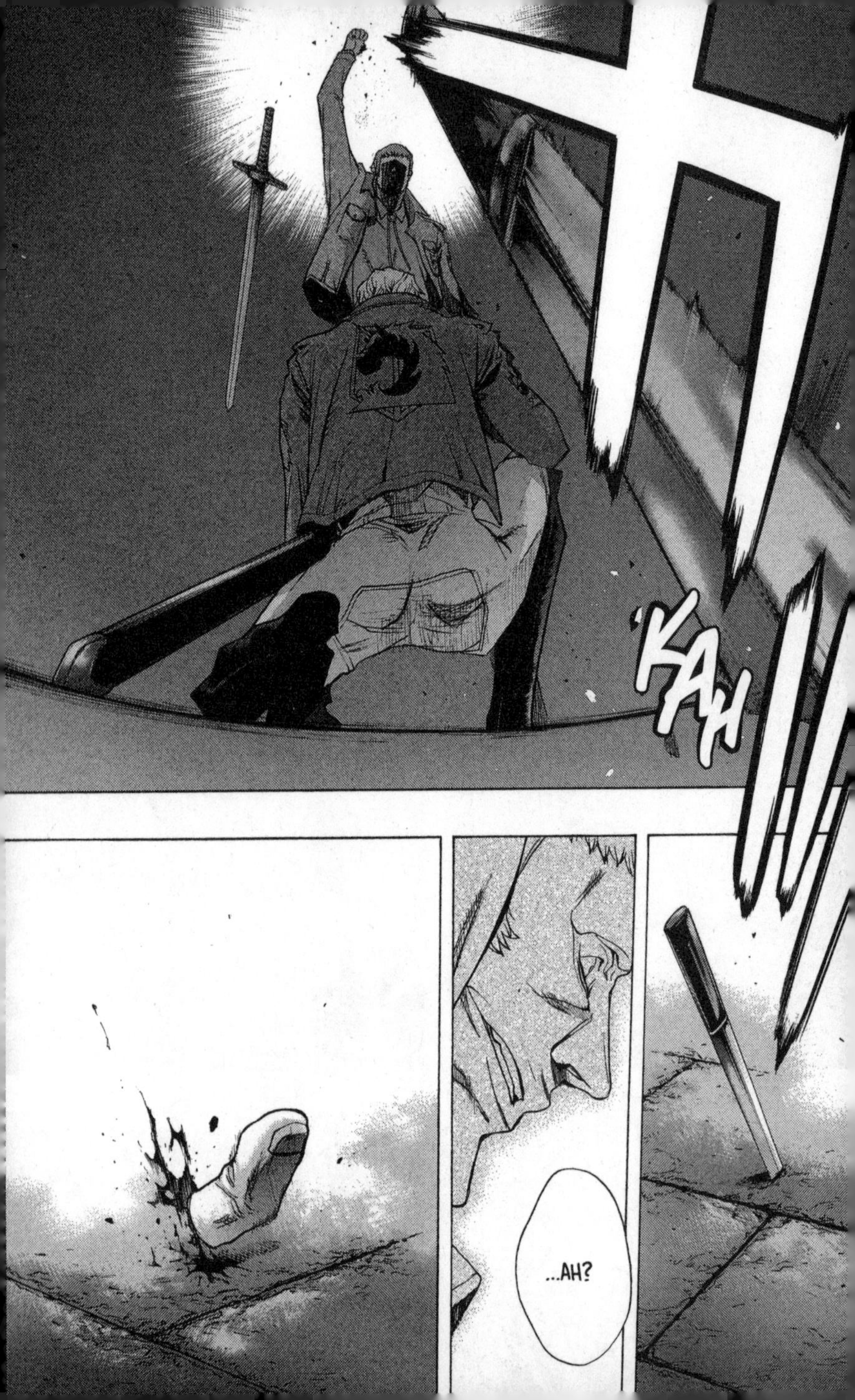
'KAH
...AH?

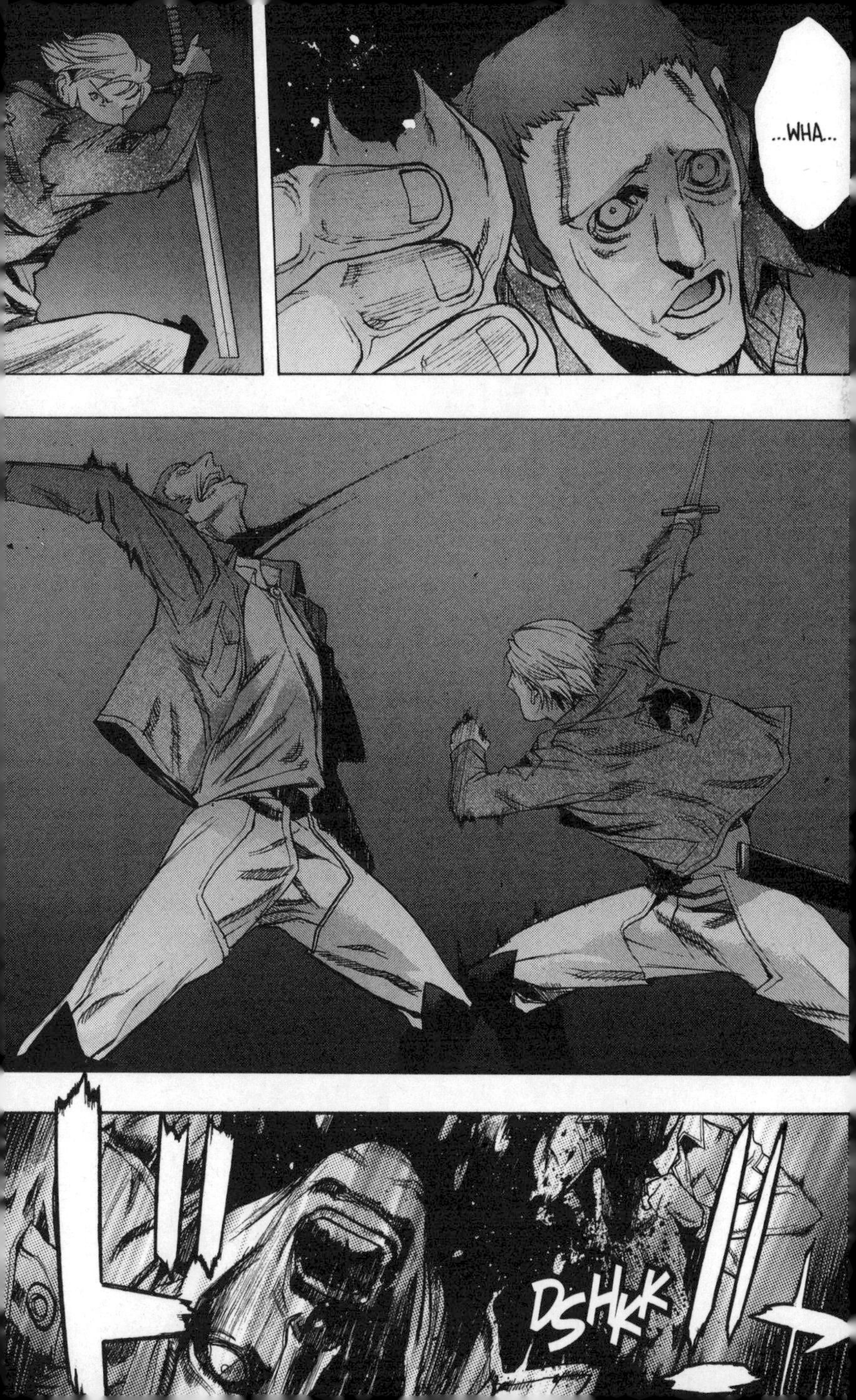
...WHA...
DSHKK

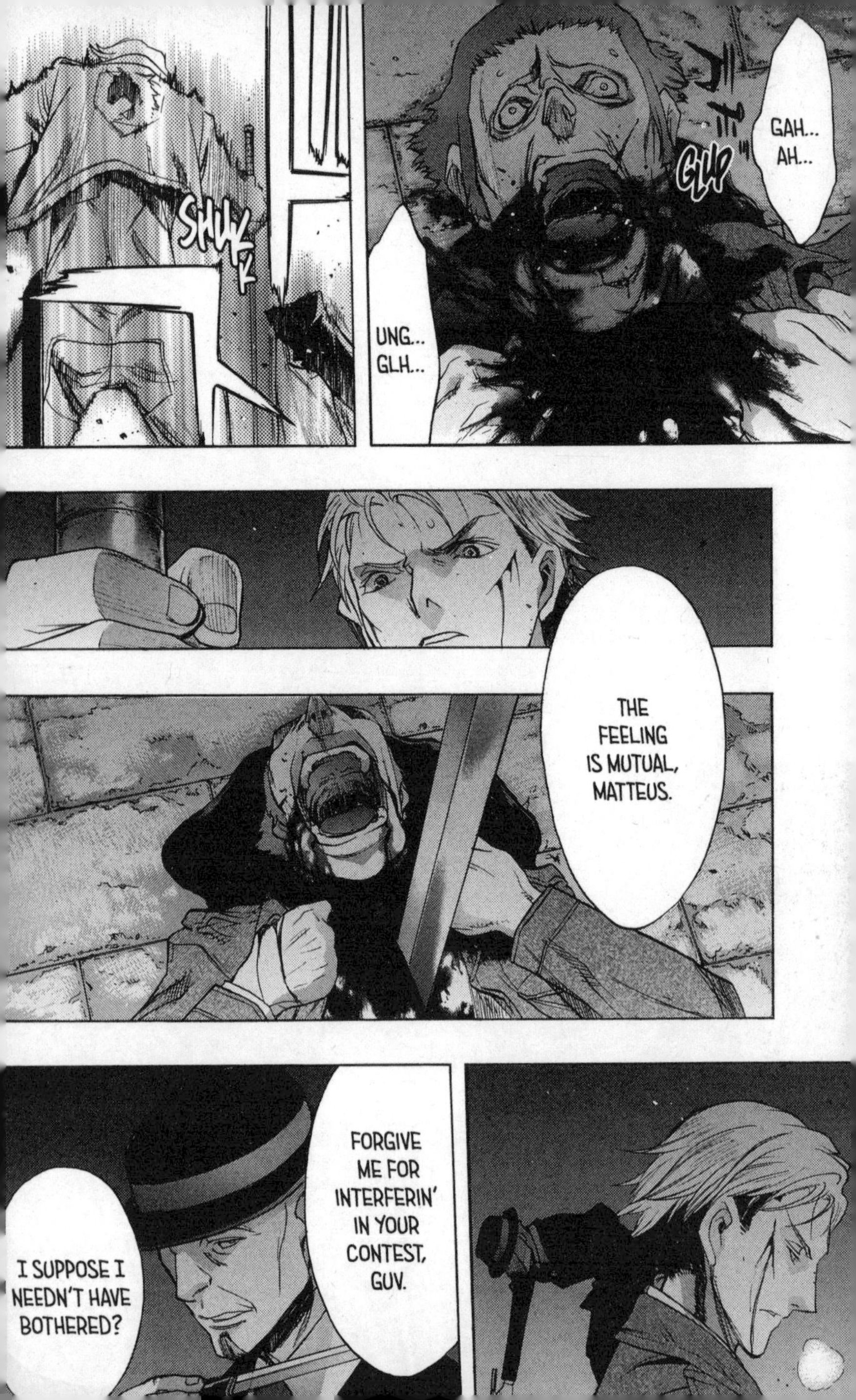
GAH... AH...
GLUP
UNG... GLH...
SHUKK
THE FEELING IS MUTUAL, MATTEUS.
FORGIVE ME FOR INTERFERIN' IN YOUR CONTEST, GUV.
I SUPPOSE I NEEDN'T HAVE BOTHERED?

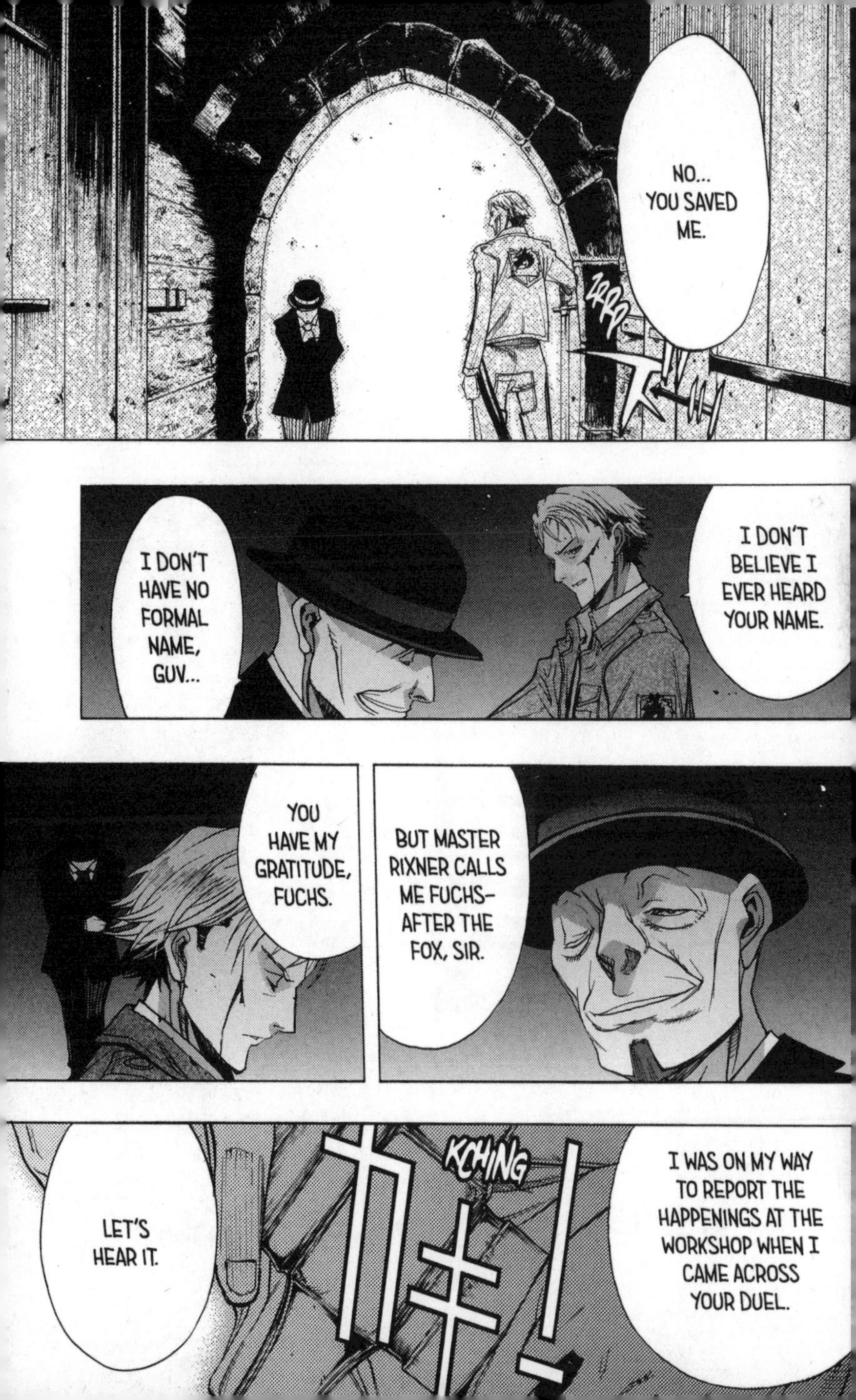
NO... YOU SAVED ME.
I DON'T BELIEVE I EVER HEARD YOUR NAME.
I DON'T HAVE NO FORMAL NAME, GUV...
BUT MASTER RIXNER CALLS ME FUCHS– AFTER THE FOX, SIR.
YOU HAVE MY GRATITUDE, FUCHS.
I WAS ON MY WAY TO REPORT THE HAPPENINGS AT THE WORKSHOP WHEN I CAME ACROSS YOUR DUEL.
KCHING
LET'S HEAR IT.

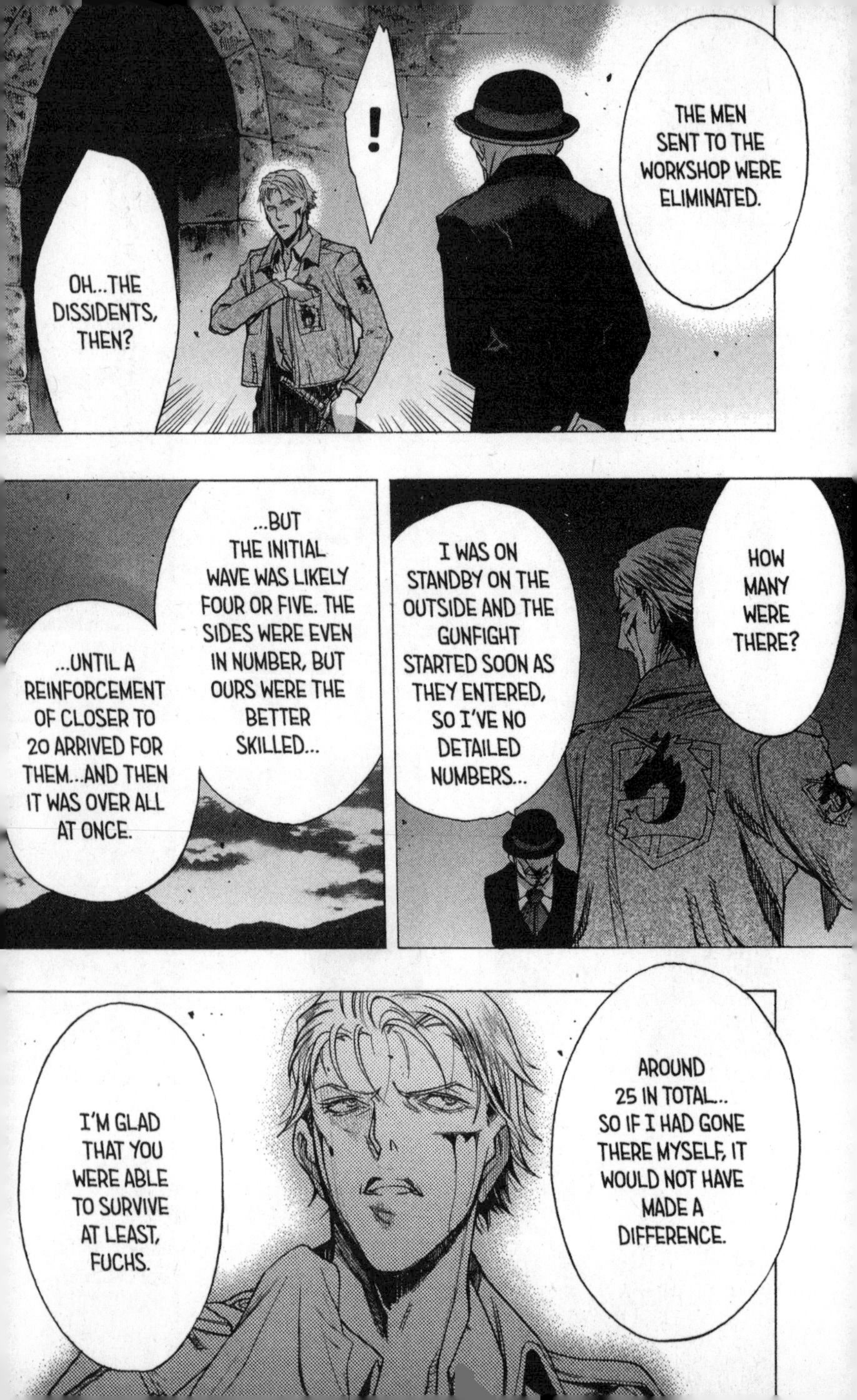
THE MEN SENT TO THE WORKSHOP WERE ELIMINATED.
!
OH...THE DISSIDENTS, THEN?
HOW MANY WERE THERE?
I WAS ON STANDBY ON THE OUTSIDE AND THE GUNFIGHT STARTED SOON AS THEY ENTERED, SO I'VE NO DETAILED NUMBERS...
...BUT THE INITIAL WAVE WAS LIKELY FOUR OR FIVE. THE SIDES WERE EVEN IN NUMBER, BUT OURS WERE THE BETTER SKILLED...
...UNTIL A REINFORCEMENT OF CLOSER TO 20 ARRIVED FOR THEM...AND THEN IT WAS OVER ALL AT ONCE.
AROUND 25 IN TOTAL... SO IF I HAD GONE THERE MYSELF, IT WOULD NOT HAVE MADE A DIFFERENCE.
I'M GLAD THAT YOU WERE ABLE TO SURVIVE AT LEAST, FUCHS.

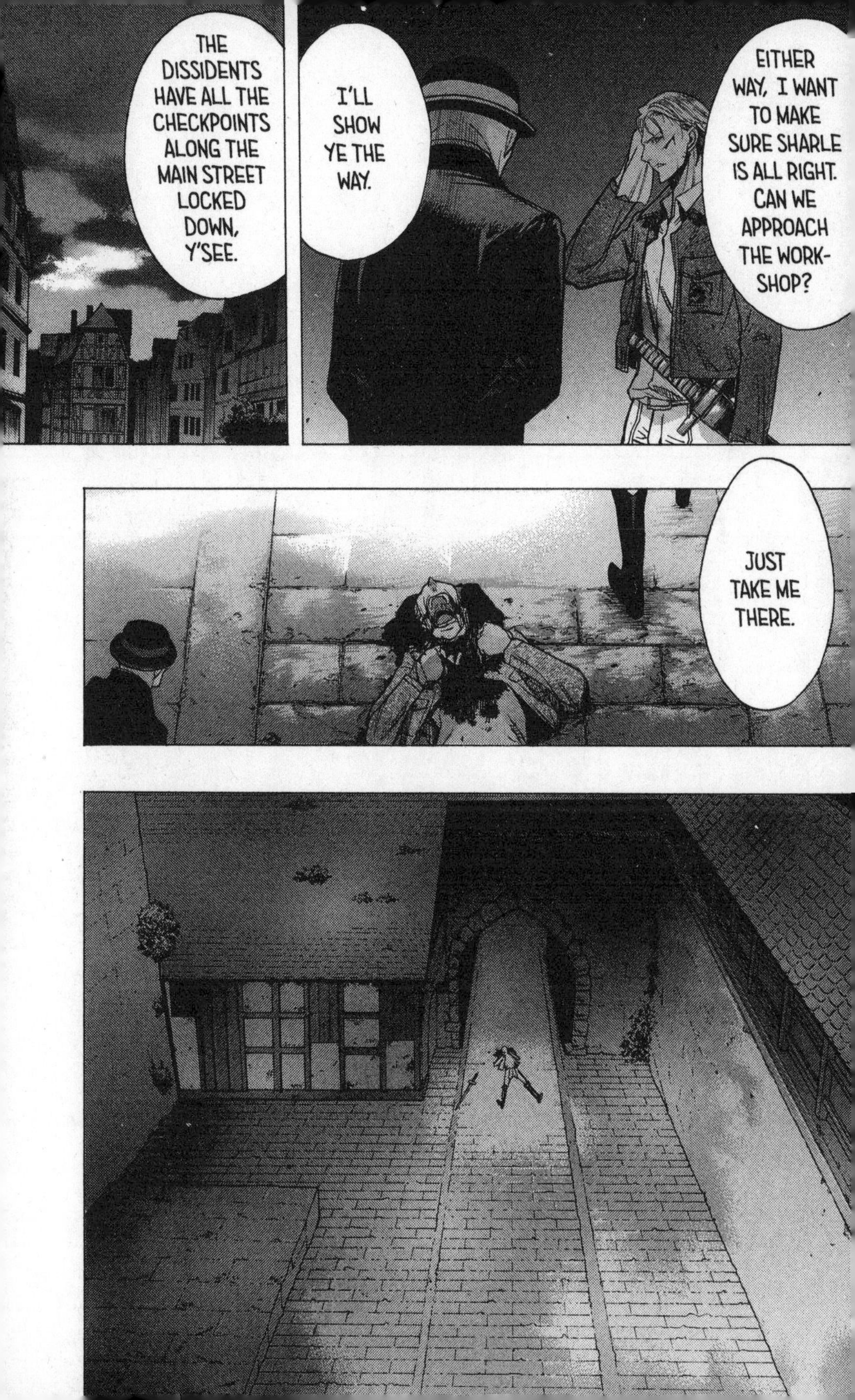
EITHER WAY, I WANT TO MAKE SURE SHARLE IS ALL RIGHT. CAN WE APPROACH THE WORK-SHOP?
I'LL SHOW YE THE WAY.
THE DISSIDENTS HAVE ALL THE CHECKPOINTS ALONG THE MAIN STREET LOCKED DOWN, Y'SEE.
JUST TAKE ME THERE.

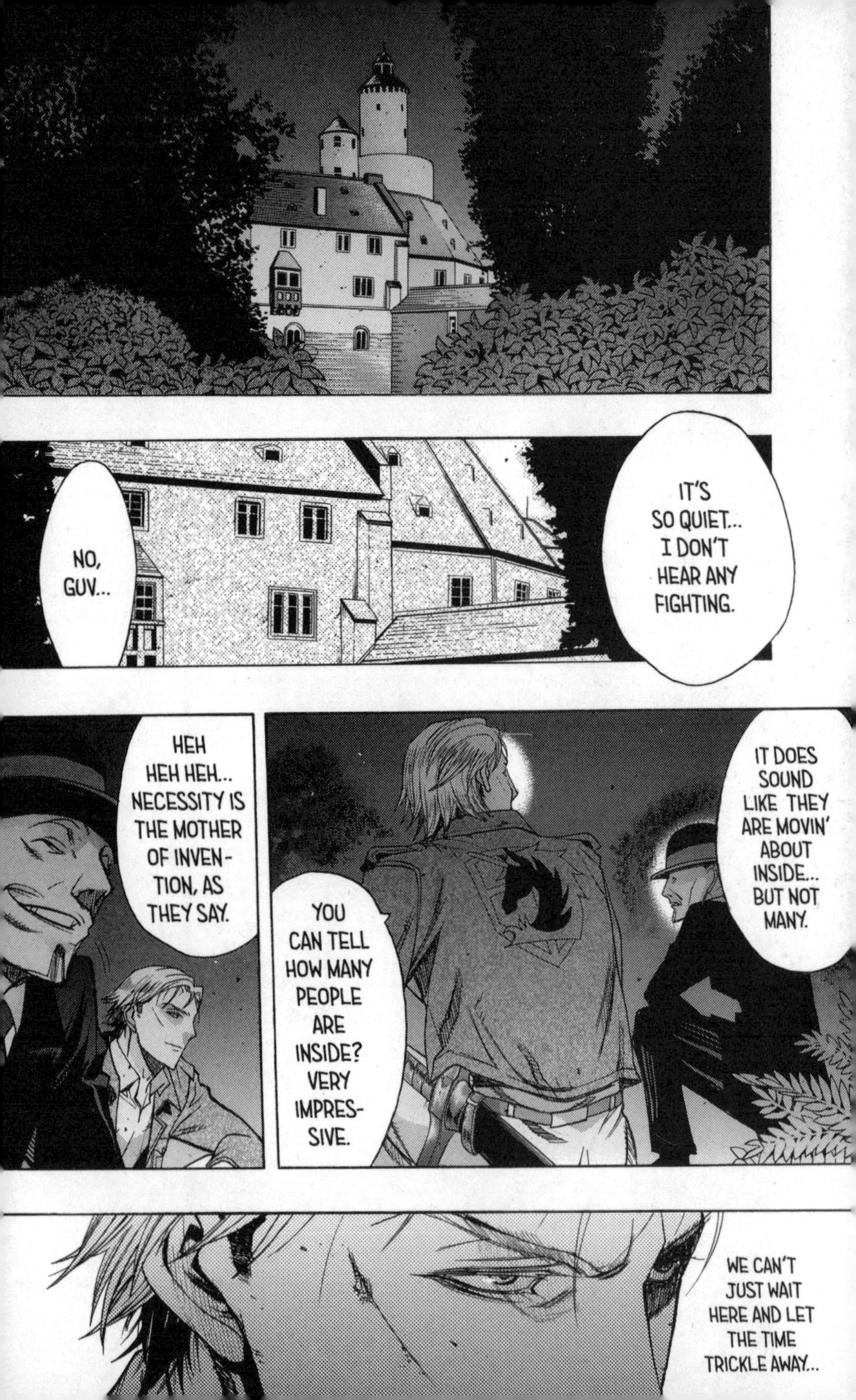
IT'S SO QUIET... I DON'T HEAR ANY FIGHTING.
NO, GUV...
IT DOES SOUND LIKE THEY ARE MOVIN' ABOUT INSIDE... BUT NOT MANY.
YOU CAN TELL HOW MANY PEOPLE ARE INSIDE? VERY IMPRESSIVE.
HEH HEH HEH... NECESSITY IS THE MOTHER OF INVEN-TION, AS THEY SAY.
WE CAN'T JUST WAIT HERE AND LET THE TIME TRICKLE AWAY...

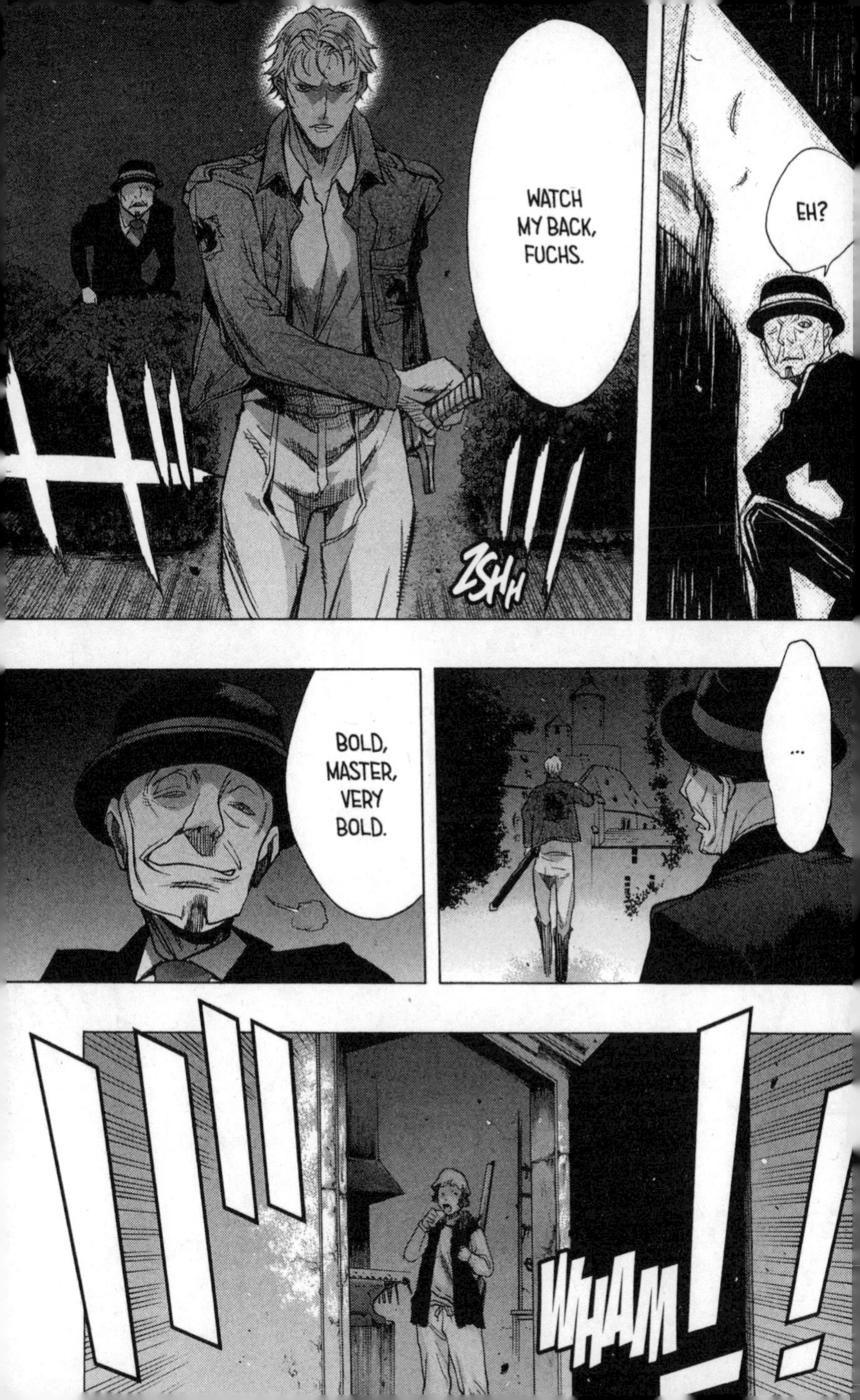
EH?
WATCH MY BACK, FUCHS.
ZSHH
...
BOLD, MASTER, VERY BOLD.
WHAM!!

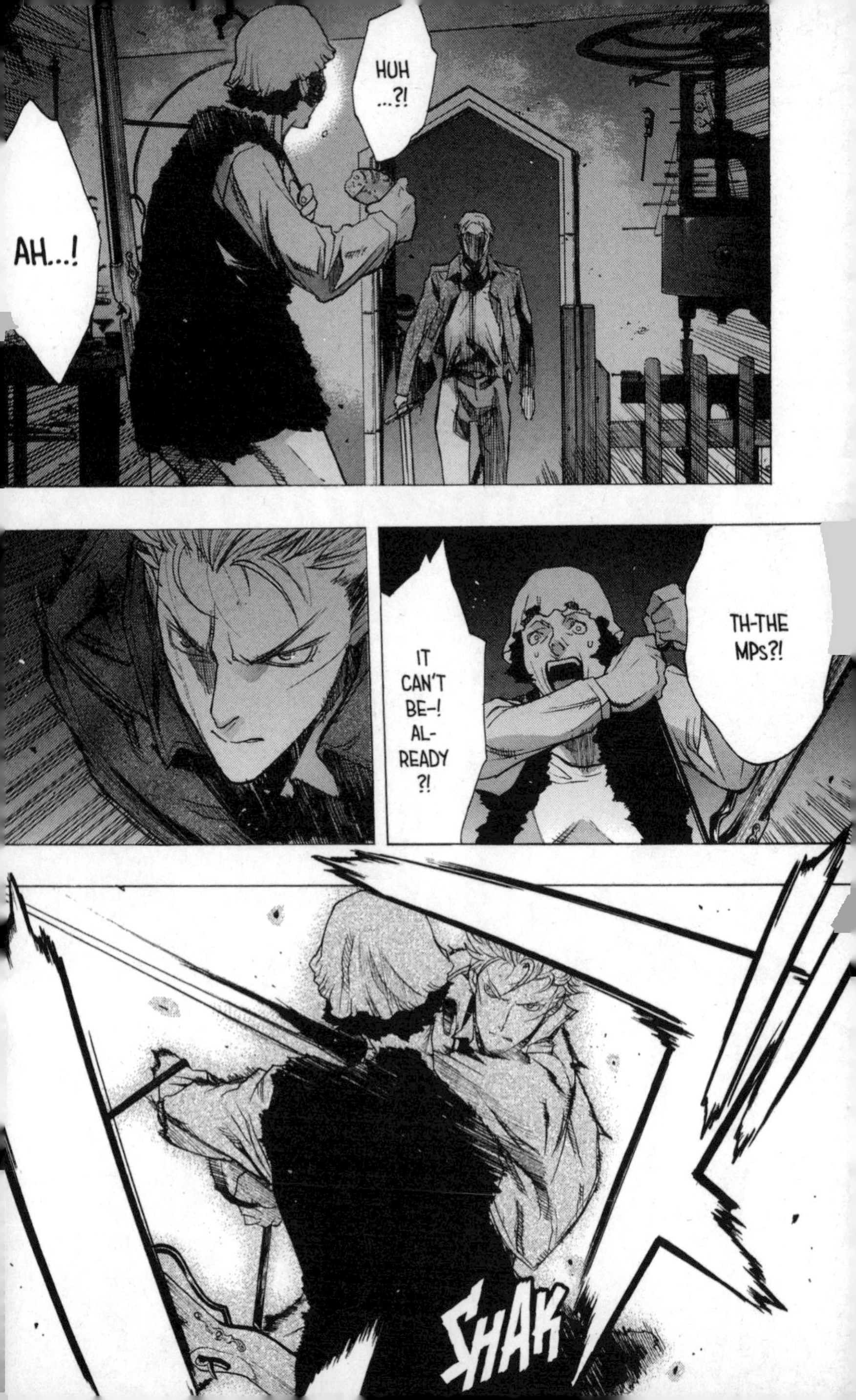
HUH ...?!
AH...!
TH-THE MPs?!
IT CAN'T BE-! AL-READY ?!
SHAK

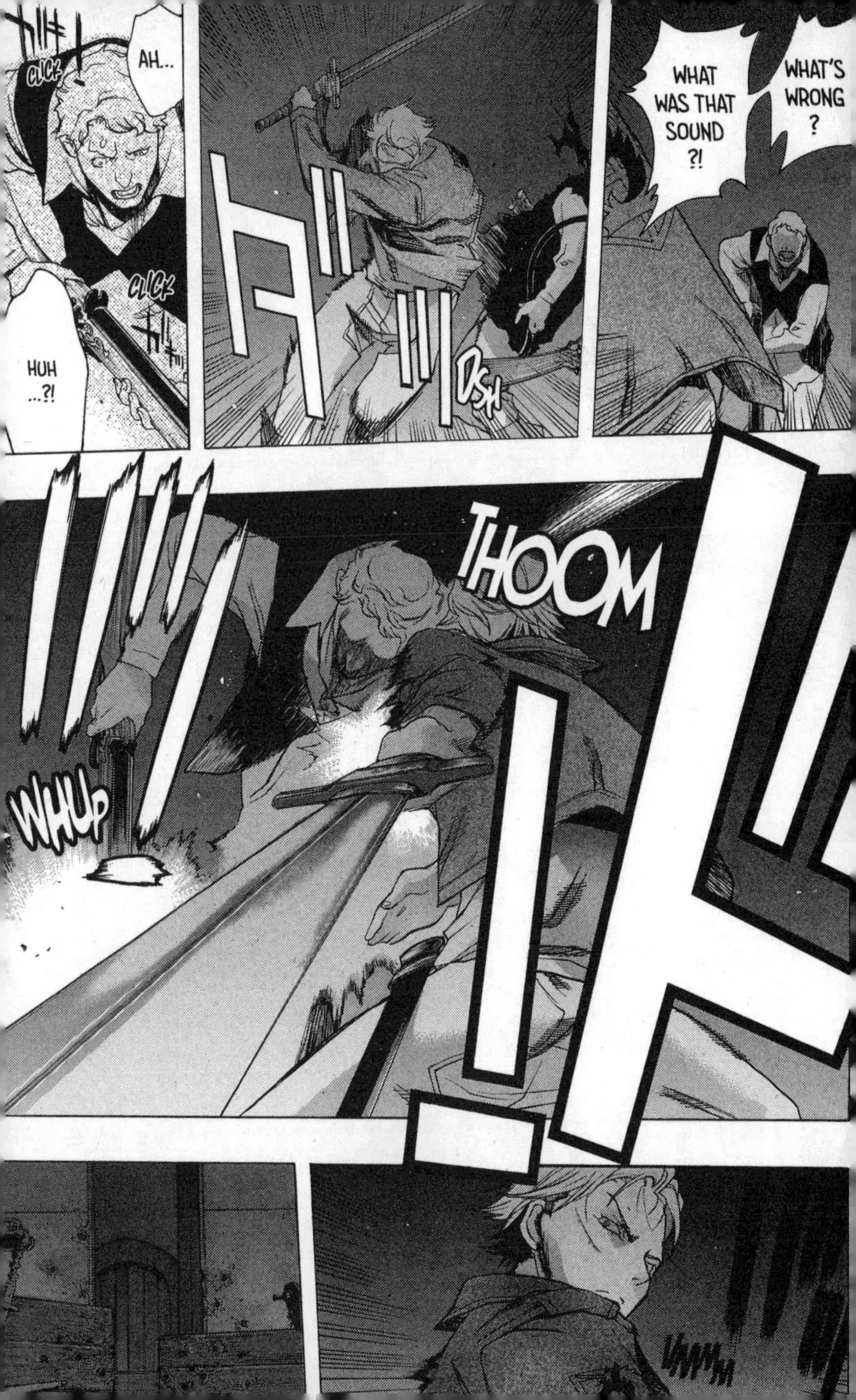
WHAT'S WRONG ?
WHAT WAS THAT SOUND ?!
DSH
AH...
CLICK
CLICK
HUH ...?!
THOOM
WHUP
VMMM

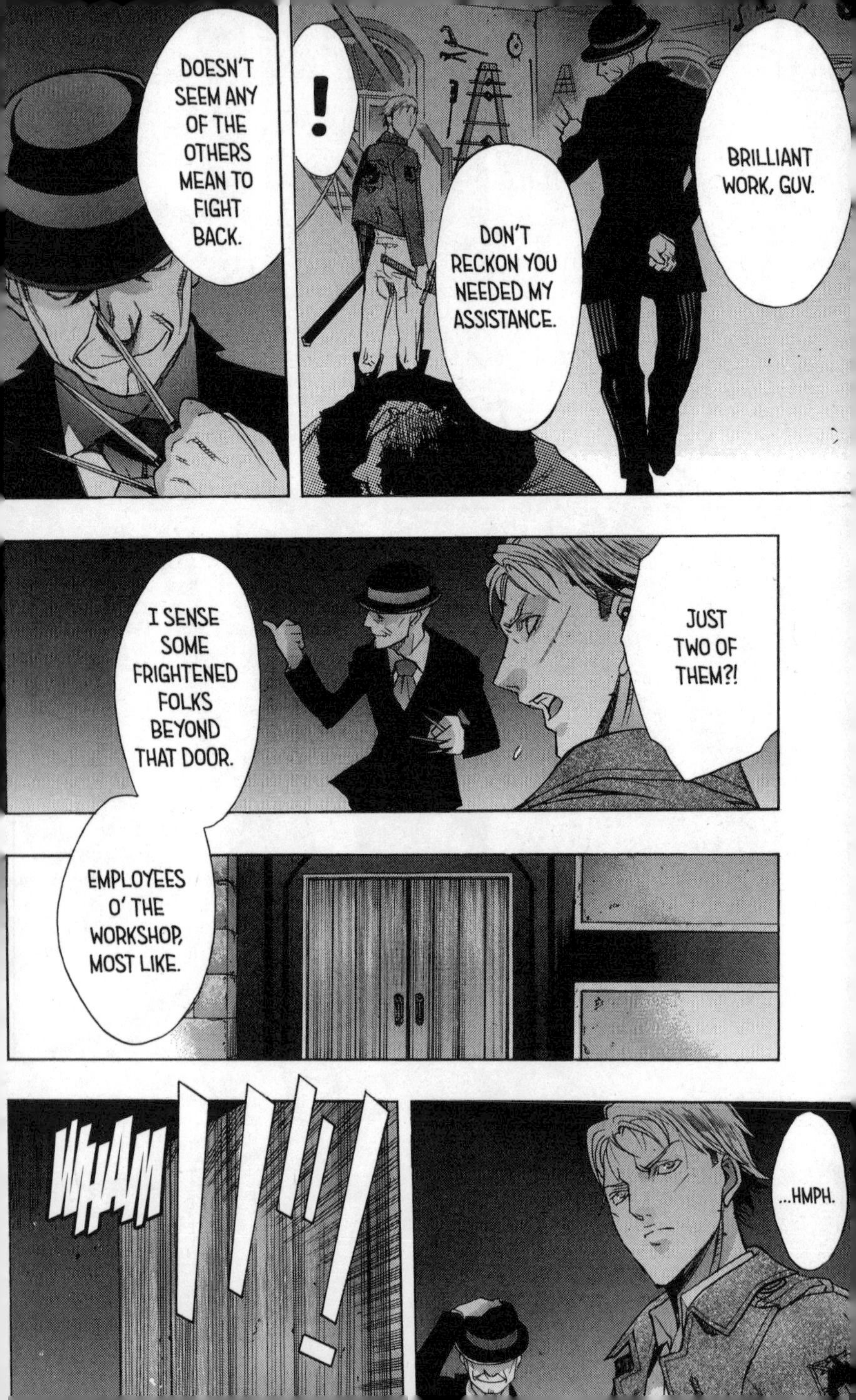
BRILLIANT WORK, GUV.
DON'T RECKON YOU NEEDED MY ASSISTANCE.
!
DOESN'T SEEM ANY OF THE OTHERS MEAN TO FIGHT BACK.
JUST TWO OF THEM?!
I SENSE SOME FRIGHTENED FOLKS BEYOND THAT DOOR.
EMPLOYEES O' THE WORKSHOP, MOST LIKE.
...HMPH.
WHAM

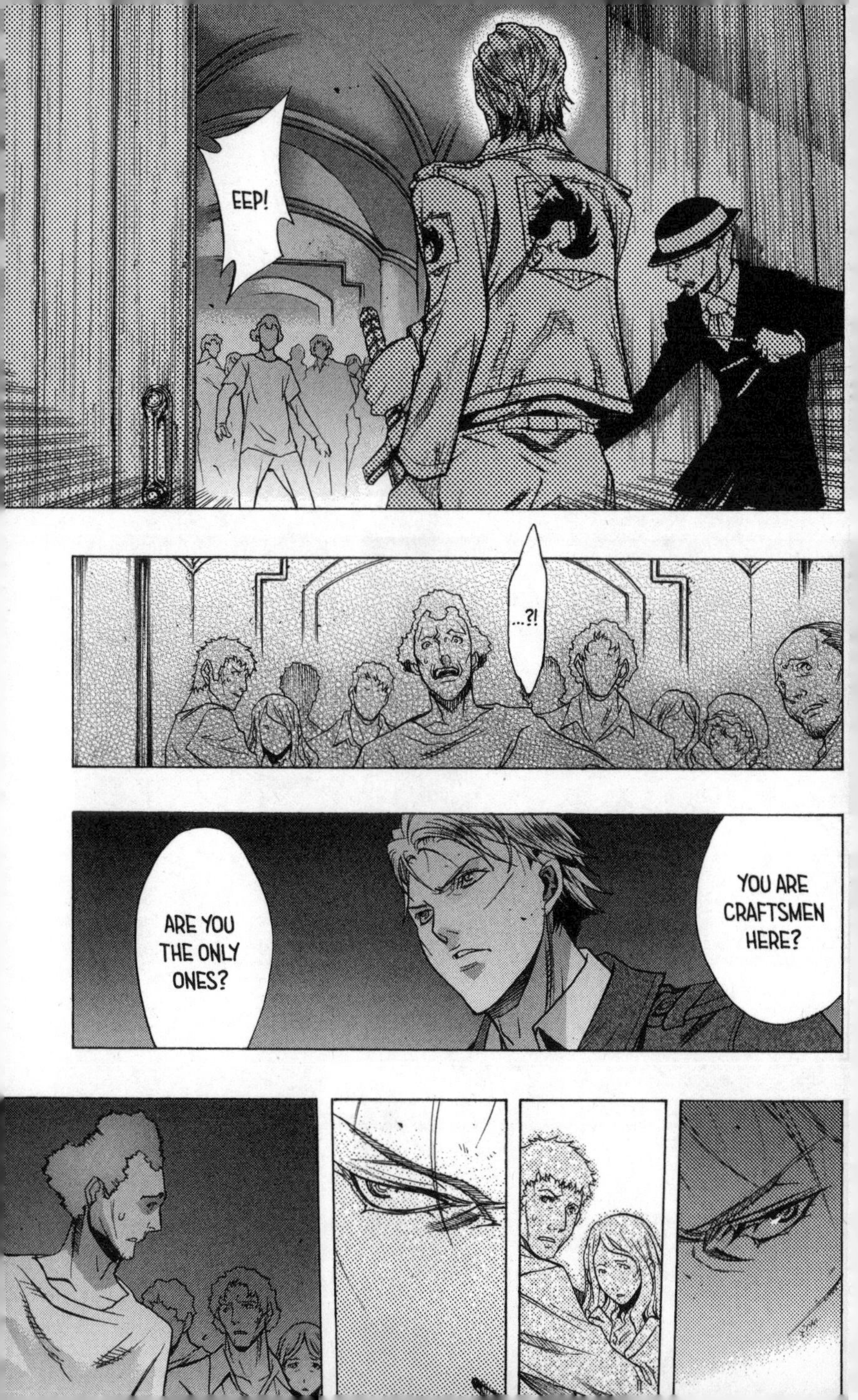
EEP!
...?!
YOU ARE CRAFTSMEN HERE?
ARE YOU THE ONLY ONES?

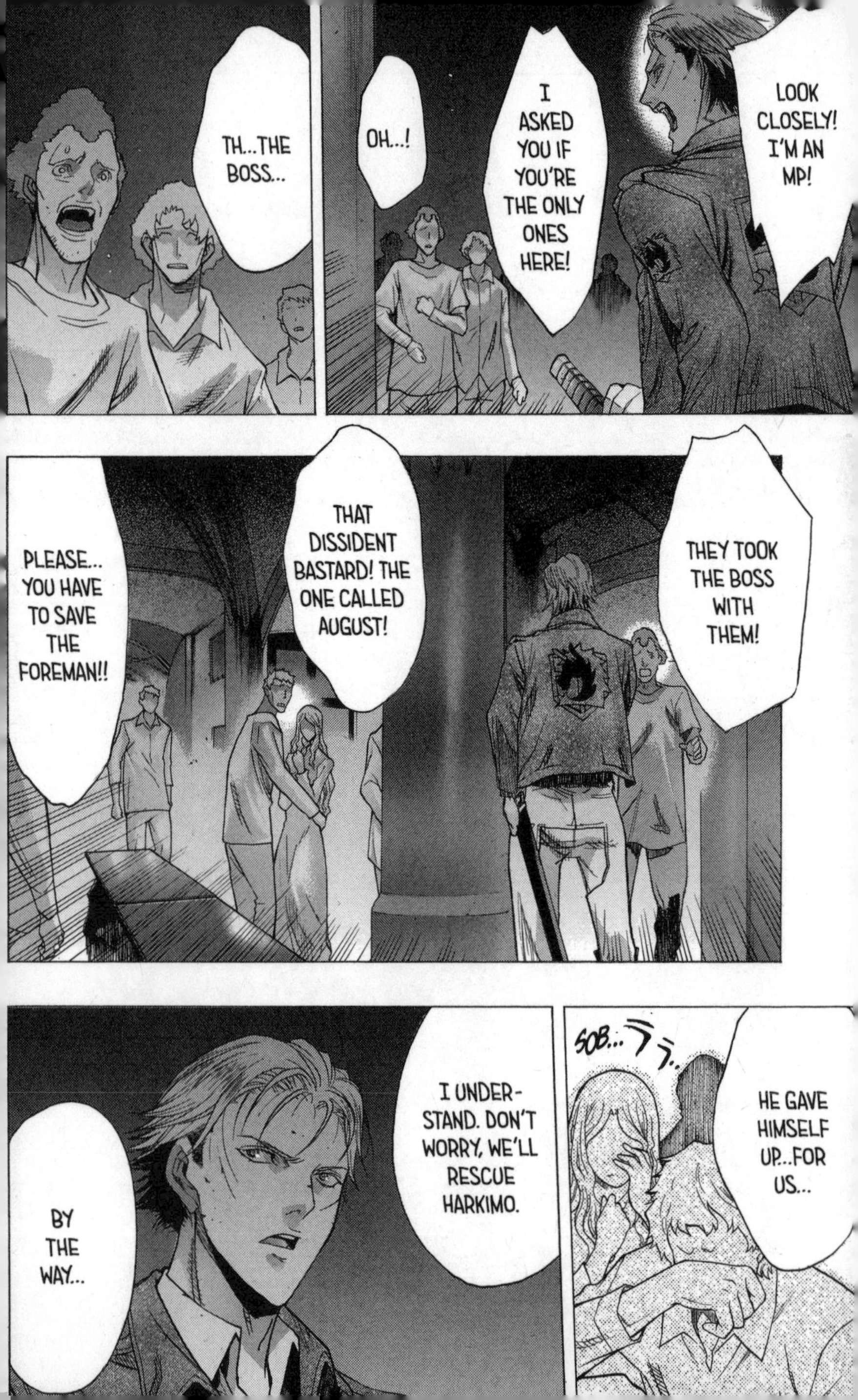
LOOK CLOSELY! I'M AN MP!
I ASKED YOU IF YOU'RE THE ONLY ONES HERE!
OH...!
TH...THE BOSS...
THEY TOOK THE BOSS WITH THEM!
THAT DISSIDENT BASTARD! THE ONE CALLED AUGUST!
PLEASE... YOU HAVE TO SAVE THE FOREMAN!!
HE GAVE HIMSELF UP...FOR US...
SOB...
I UNDER-STAND. DON'T WORRY, WE'LL RESCUE HARKIMO.
BY THE WAY...

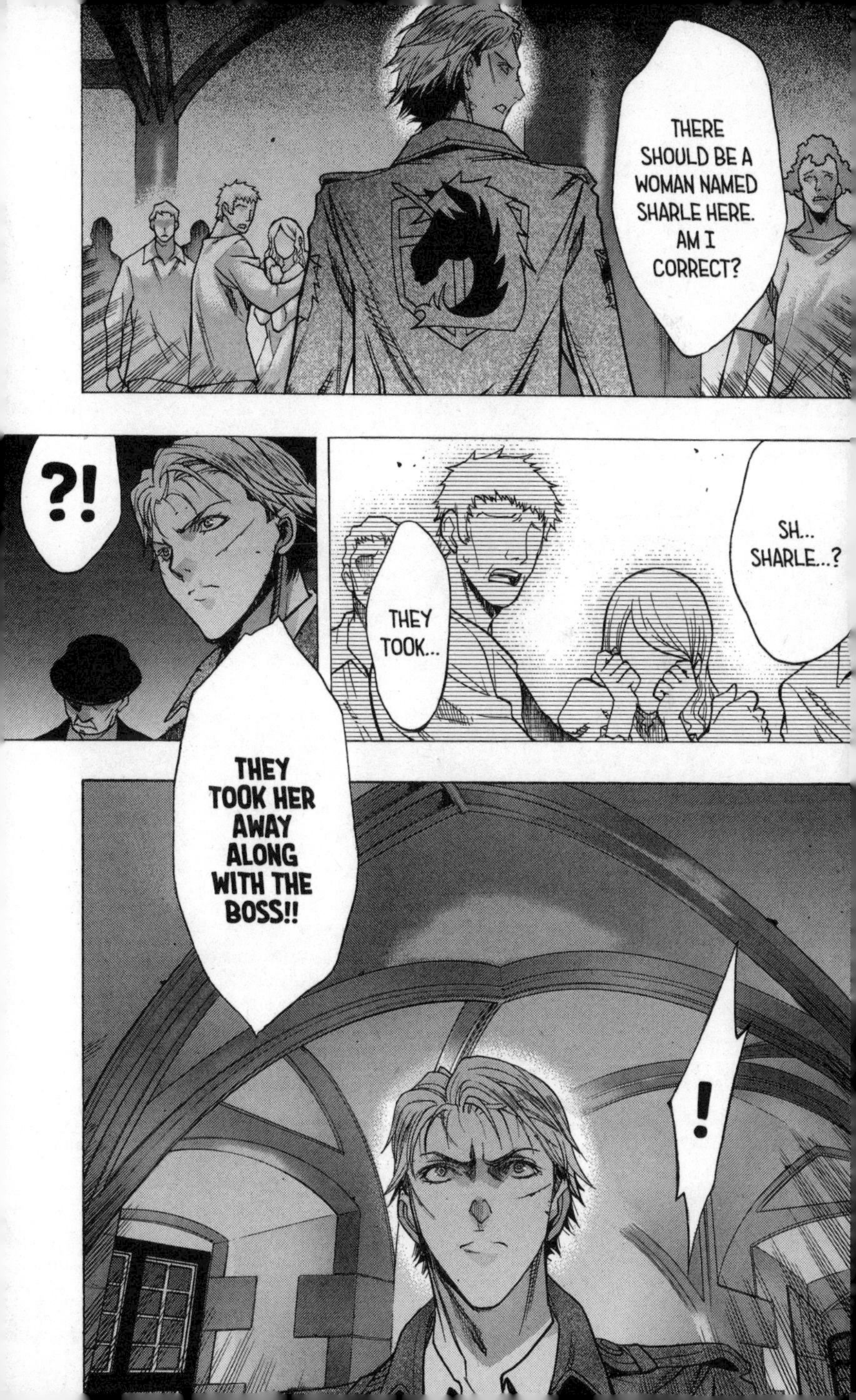
THERE SHOULD BE A WOMAN NAMED SHARLE HERE. AM I CORRECT?
SH... SHARLE...?
THEY TOOK...
?!
THEY TOOK HER AWAY ALONG WITH THE BOSS!!
!

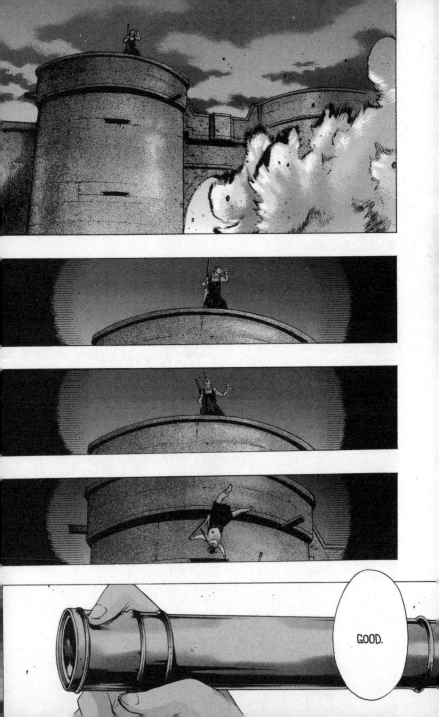

GOOD.

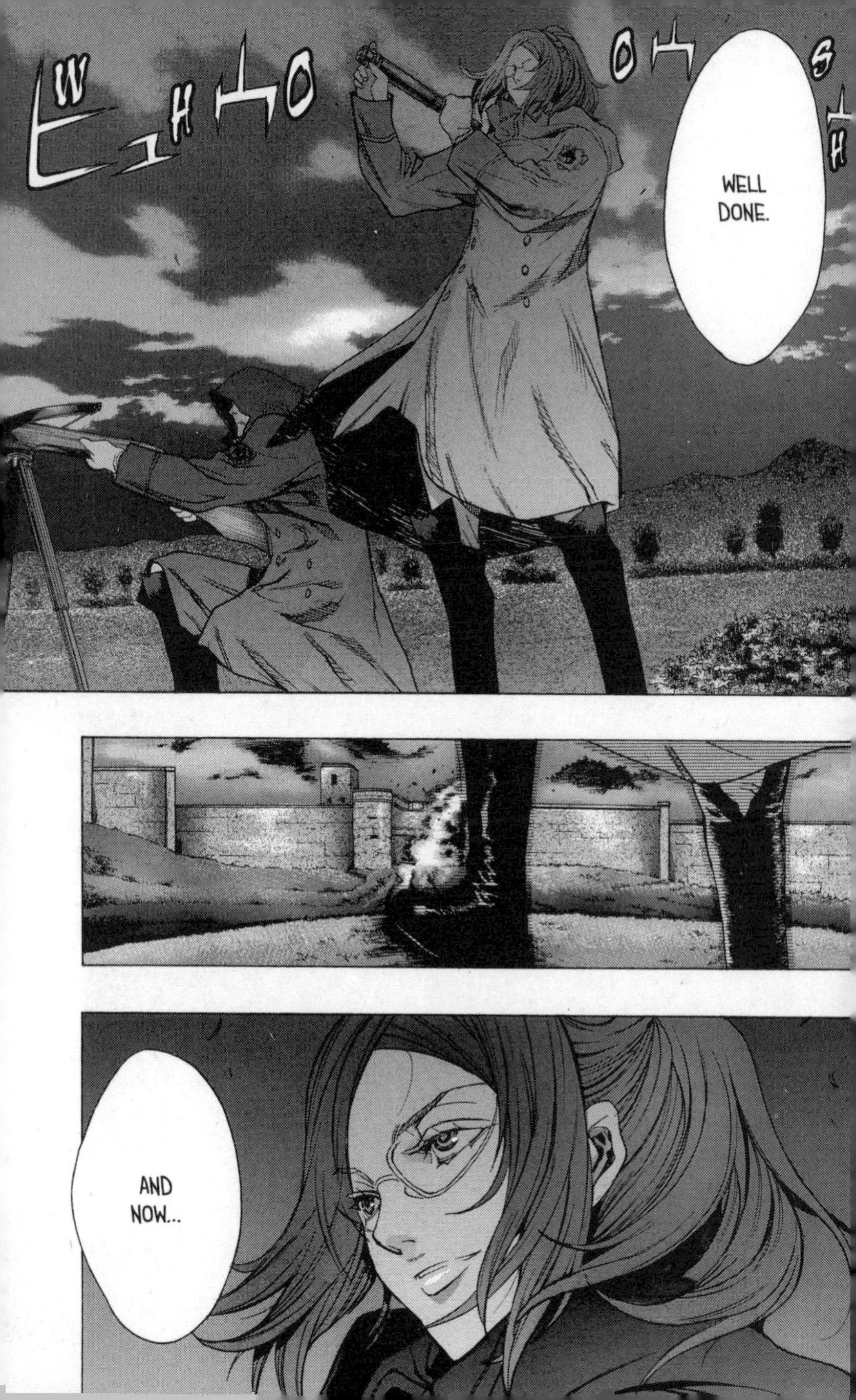
WELL DONE.
WHOOSH
AND NOW...

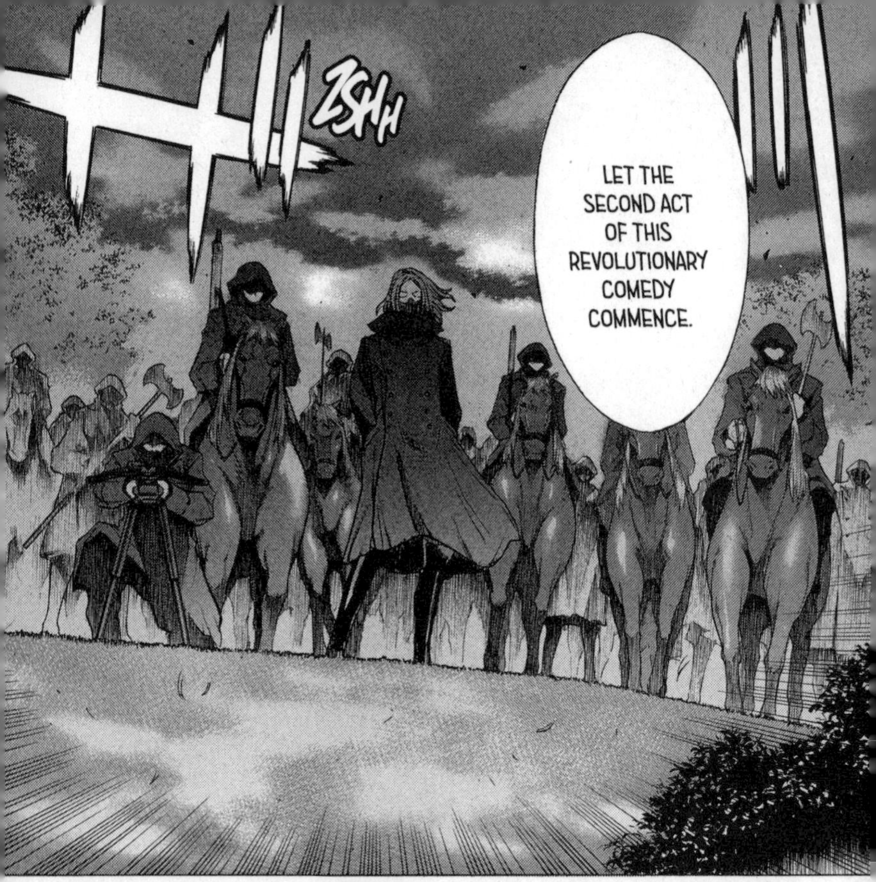
LET THE SECOND ACT OF THIS REVOLUTIONARY COMEDY COMMENCE.
ZSHH
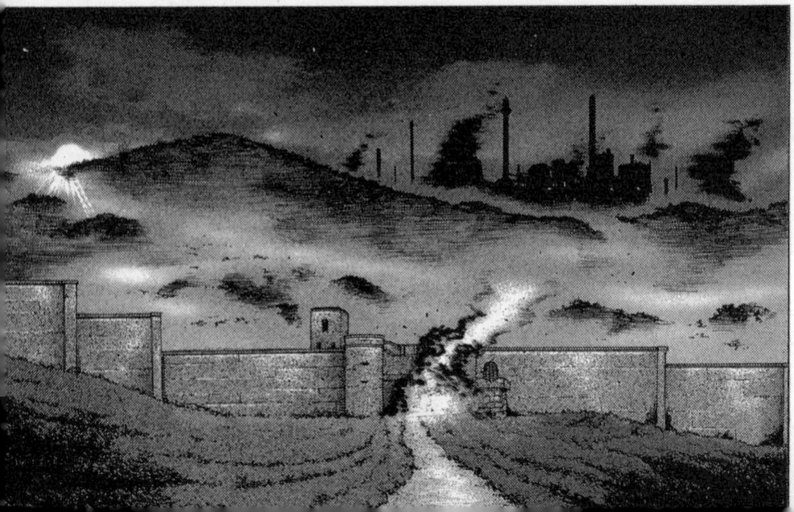

Chapter 27: The Rivalry's Outcome · End

ATTACK on TITAN
BEFORE THE FALL

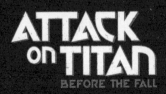

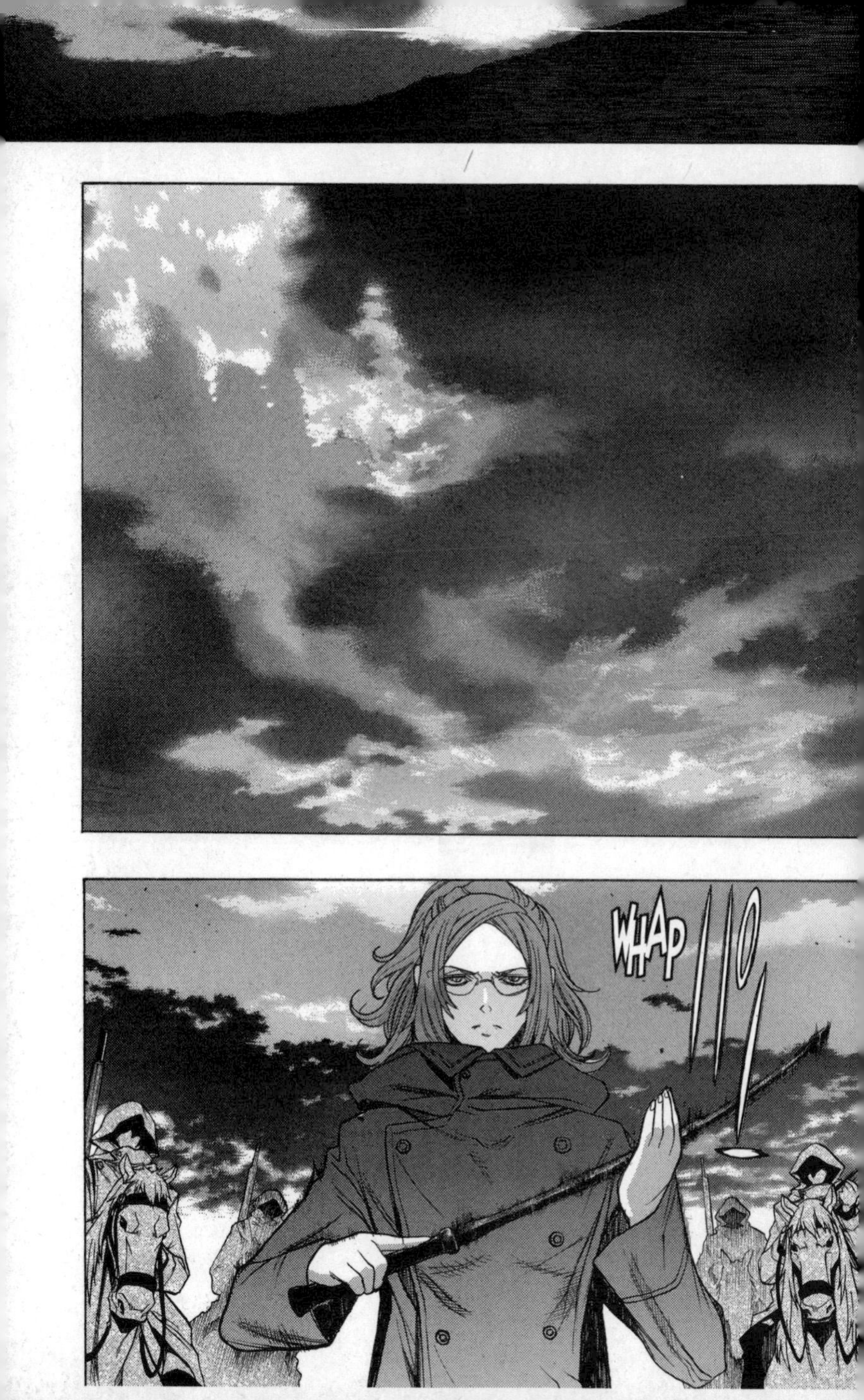
WHAP

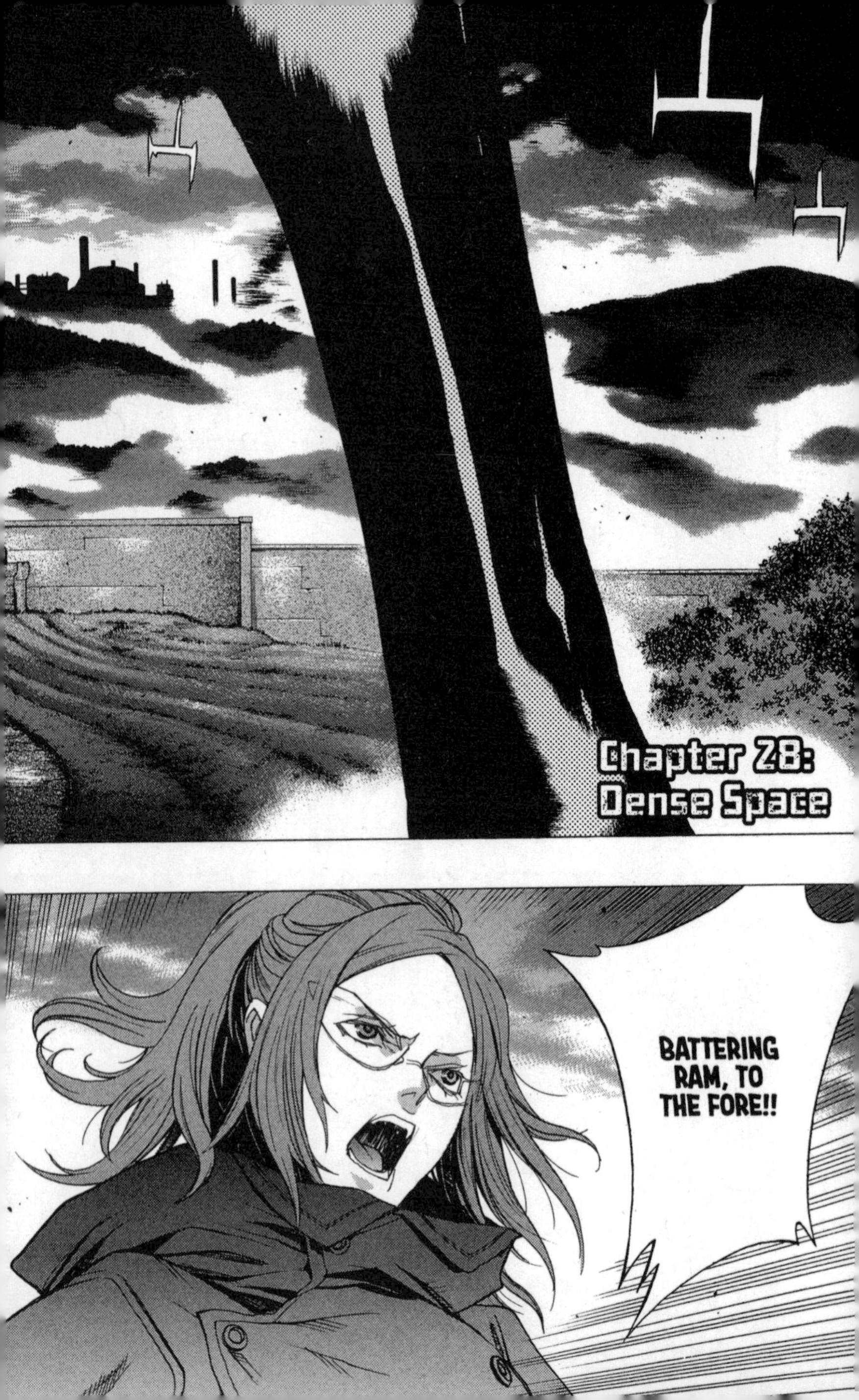
Chapter 28:
Dense Space
BATTERING RAM, TO THE FORE!!

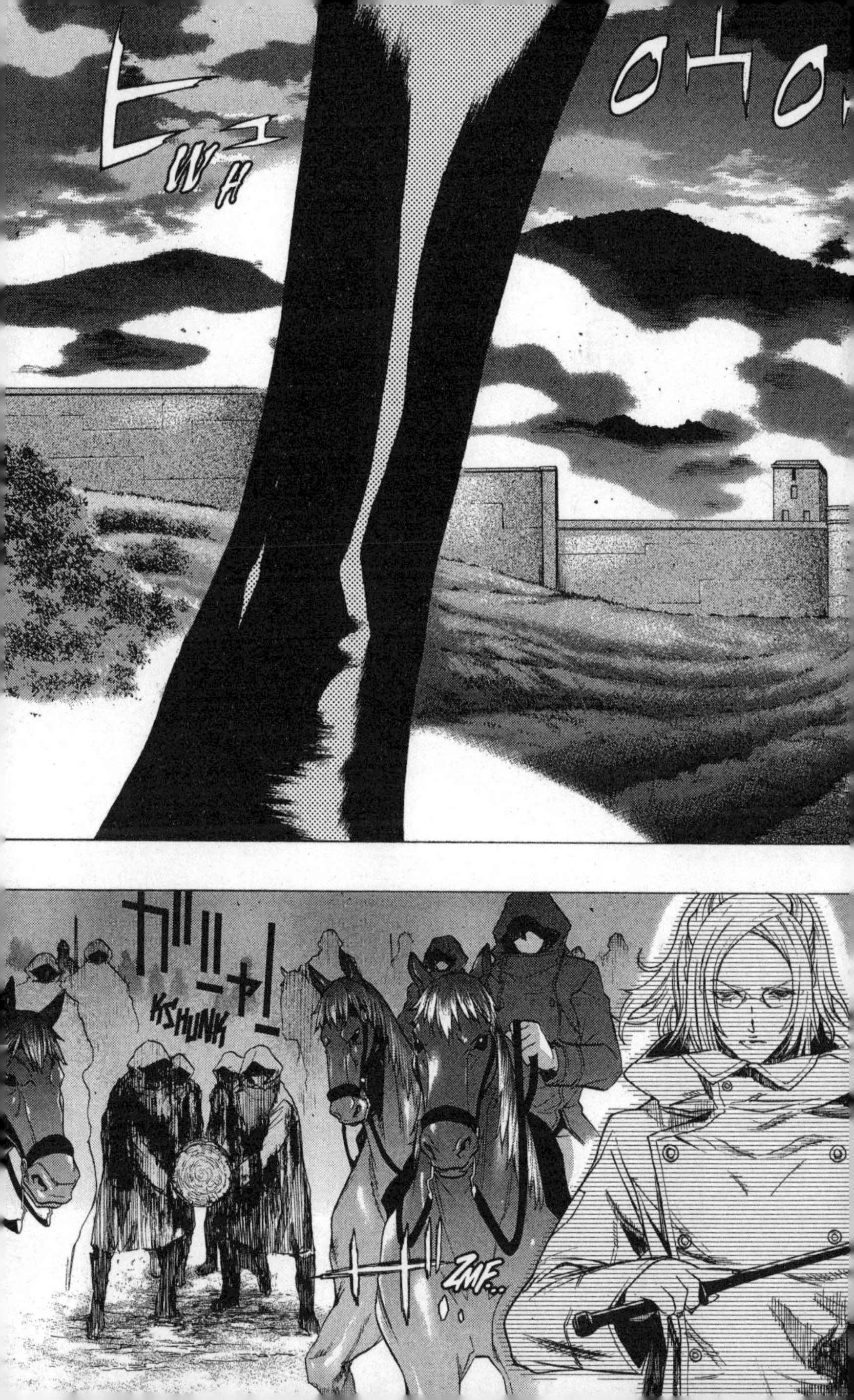
ヒュ
WH
ガシャ!
KSHUNK
ZMF...

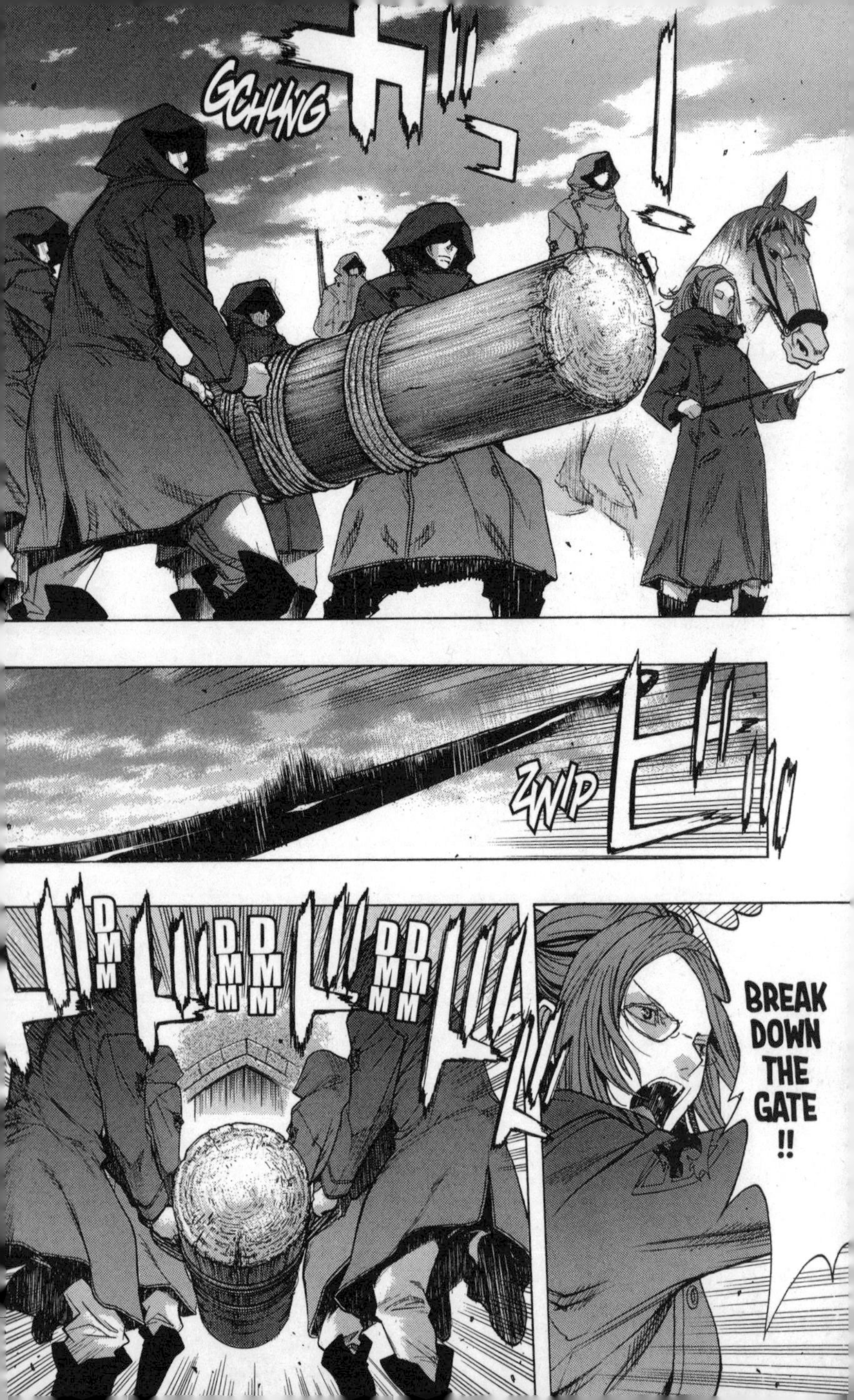
GCHUNG
ZWIP
BREAK DOWN THE GATE !!
DMM
DMMM
DMMM
DMMM
DMMM

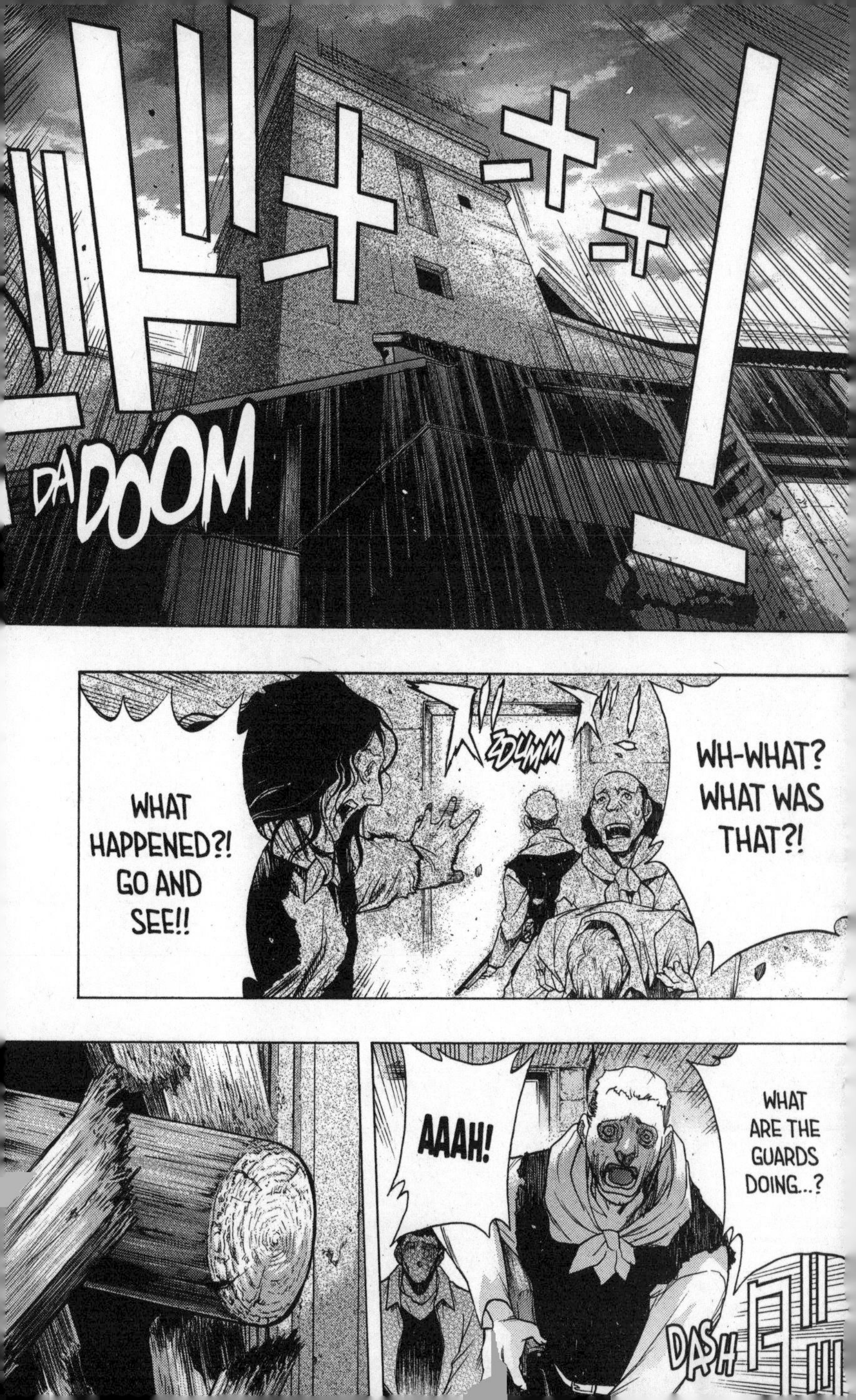
DA DOOM
WH-WHAT? WHAT WAS THAT?!
ZDUMM
WHAT HAPPENED?! GO AND SEE!!
WHAT ARE THE GUARDS DOING...?
AAAH!
DASH

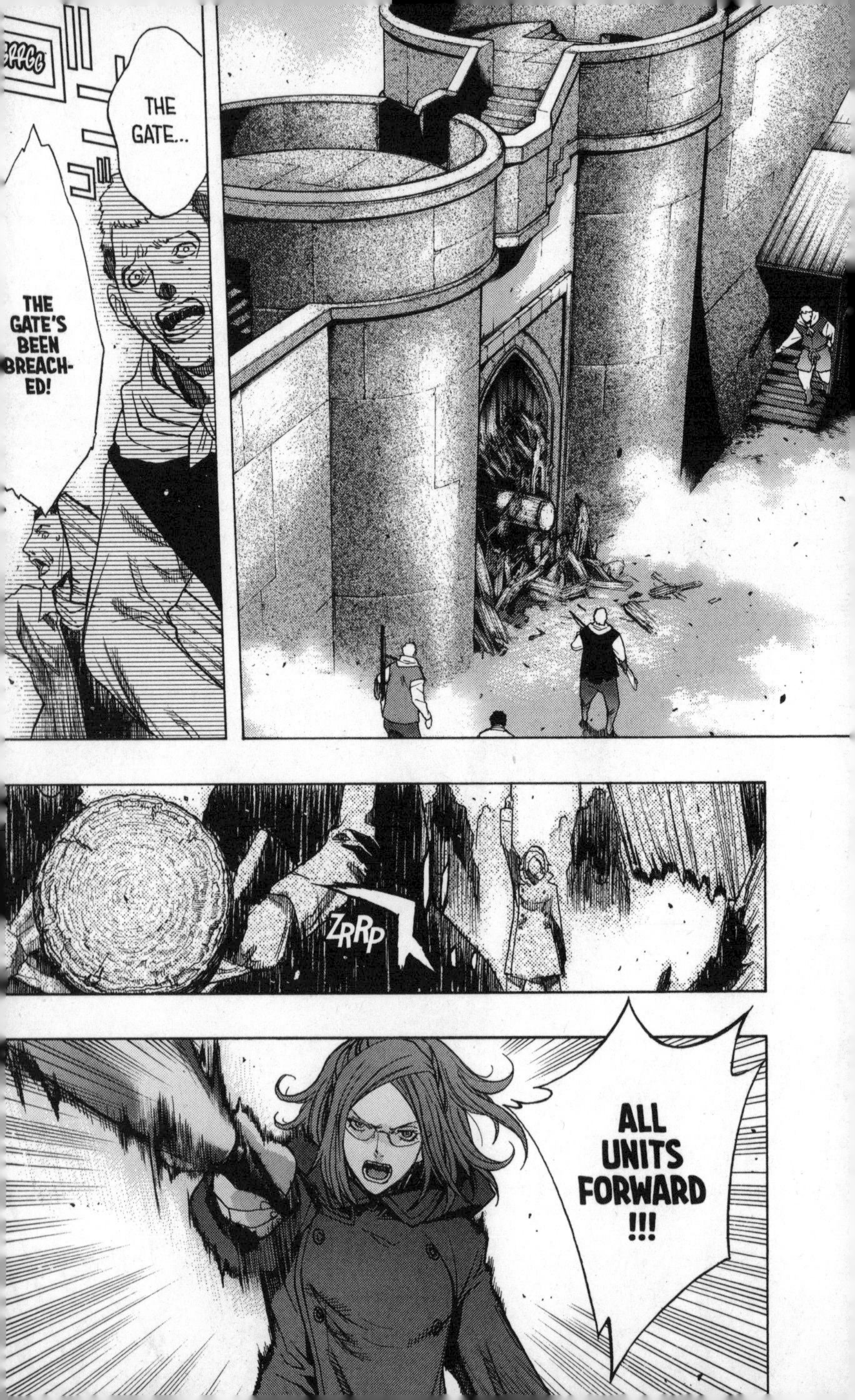
THE GATE...
THE GATE'S BEEN BREACH-ED!
ZRRP
ALL UNITS FORWARD!!!

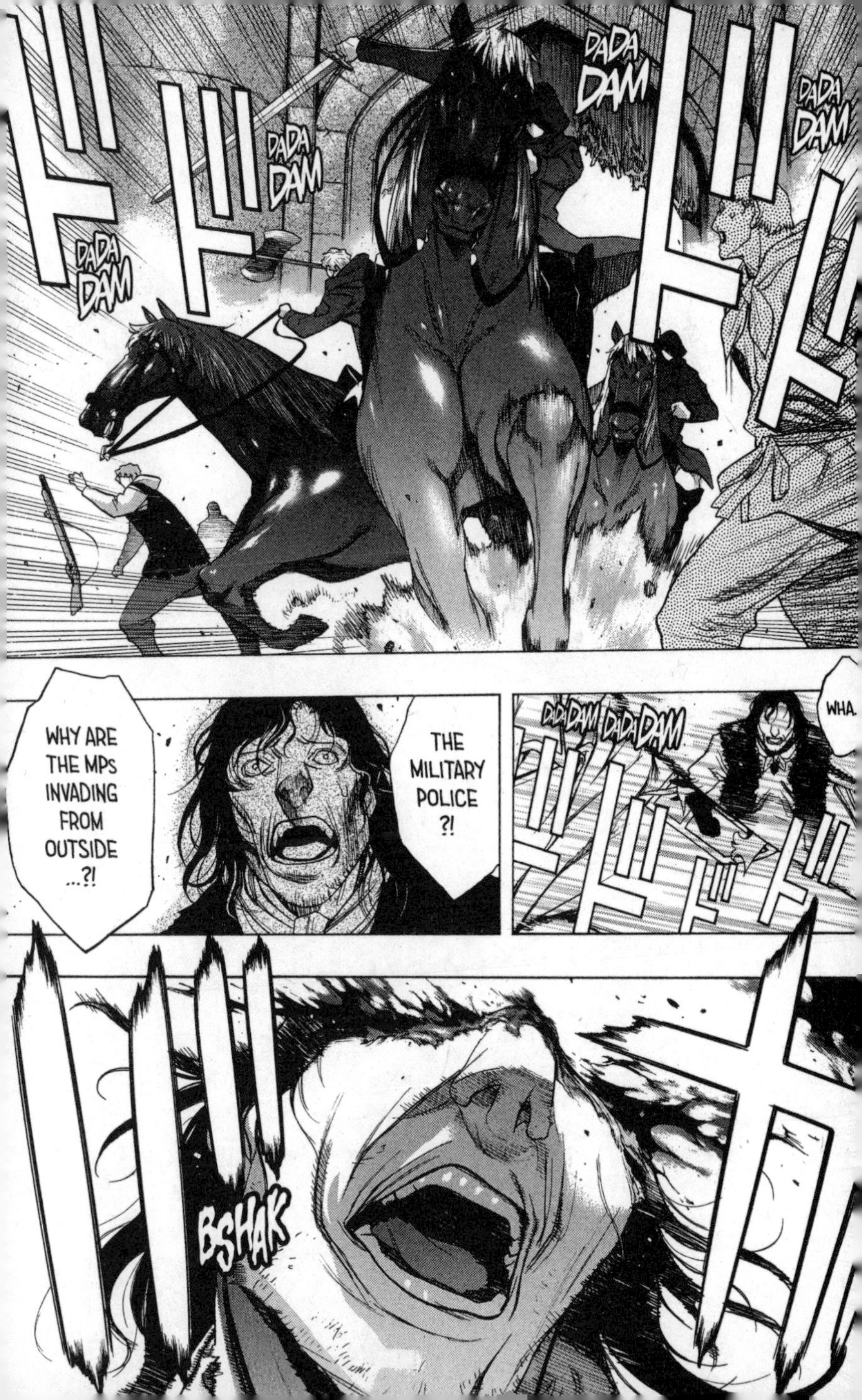
DADA DAM
DADA DAM
DADA DAM
DADA DAM
WHA.
DADA DAM DADA DAM
THE MILITARY POLICE ?!
WHY ARE THE MPs INVADING FROM OUTSIDE ...?!
BSHAK

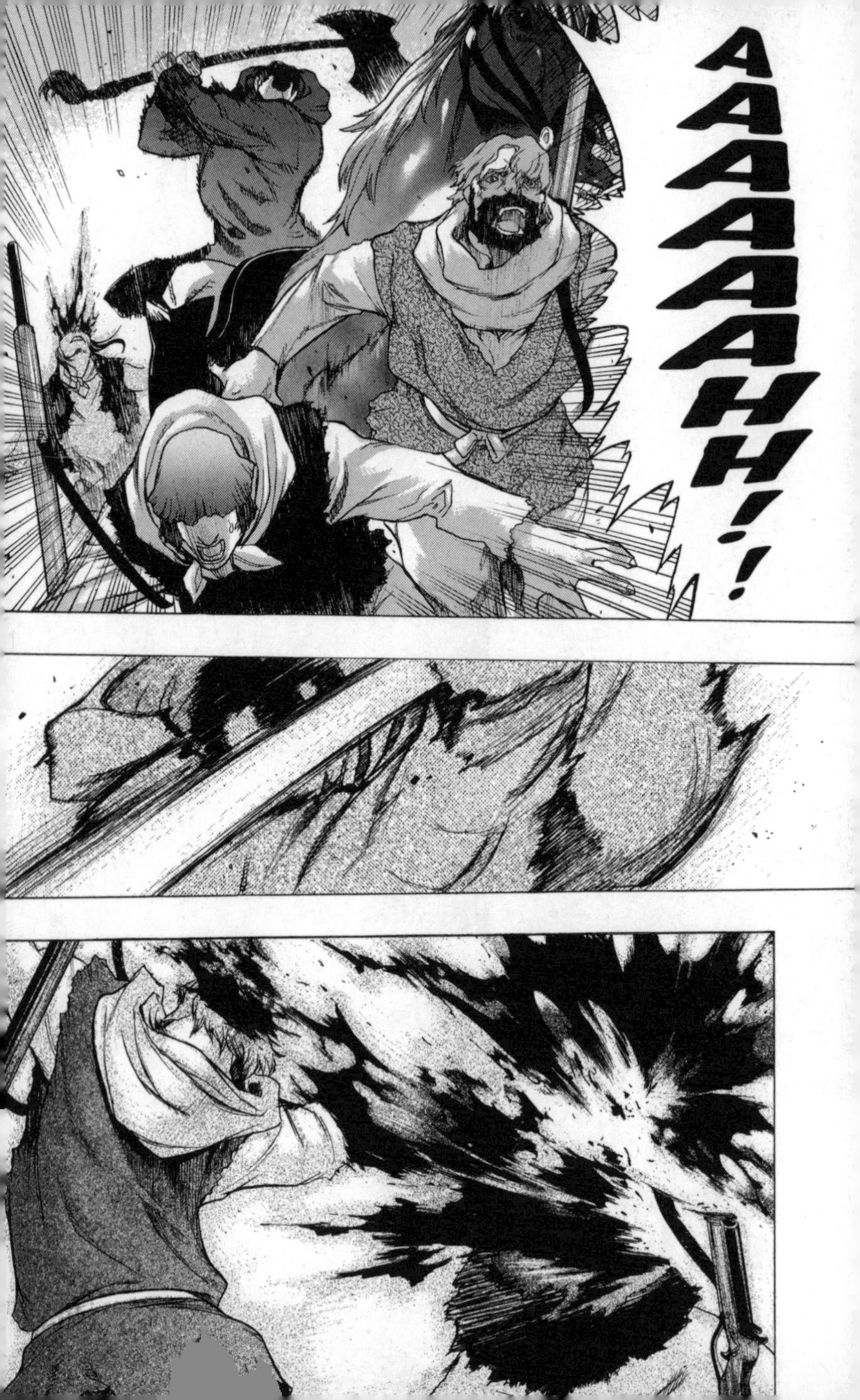
AAAAAAHH!!

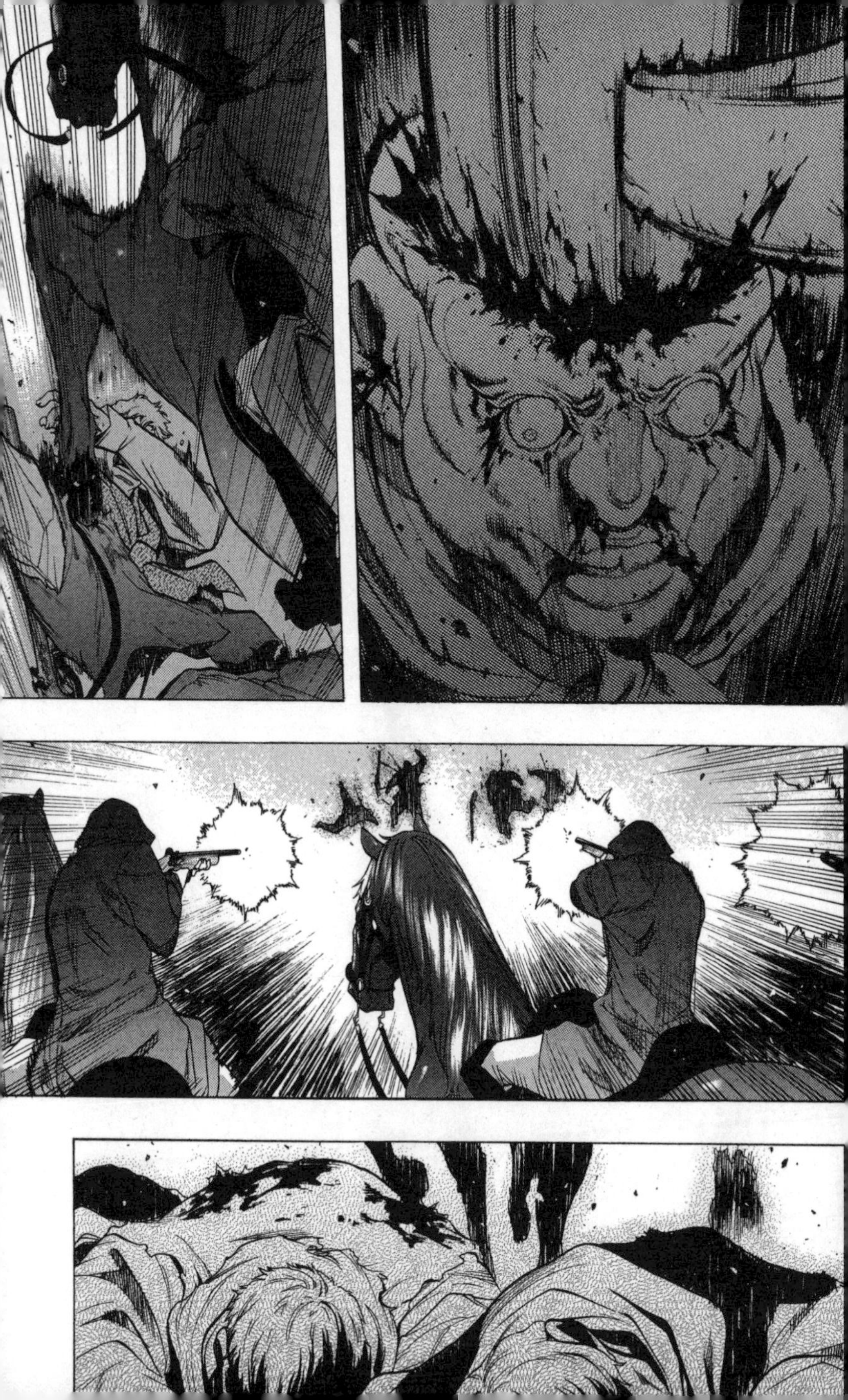

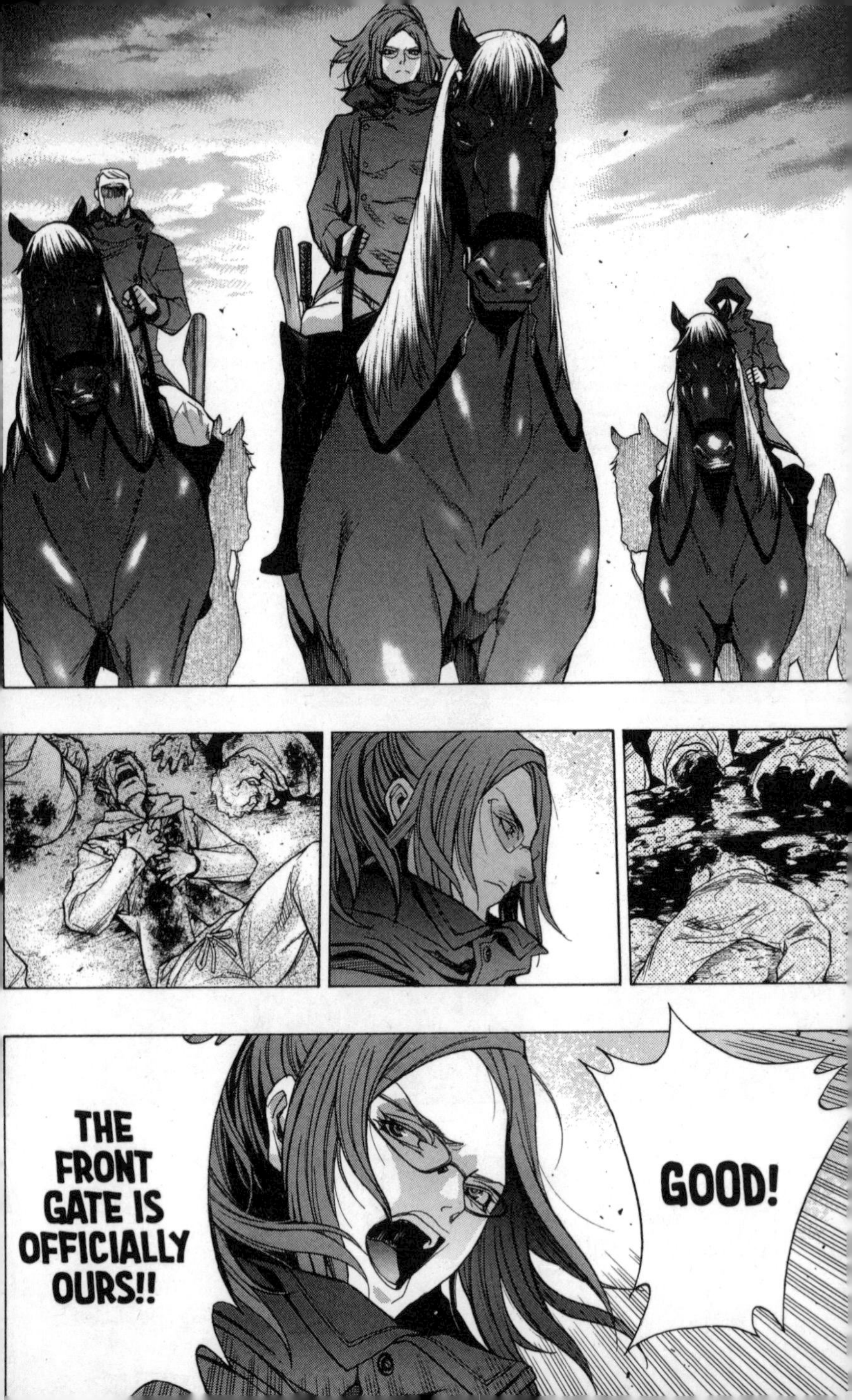
GOOD!
THE FRONT GATE IS OFFICIALLY OURS!!

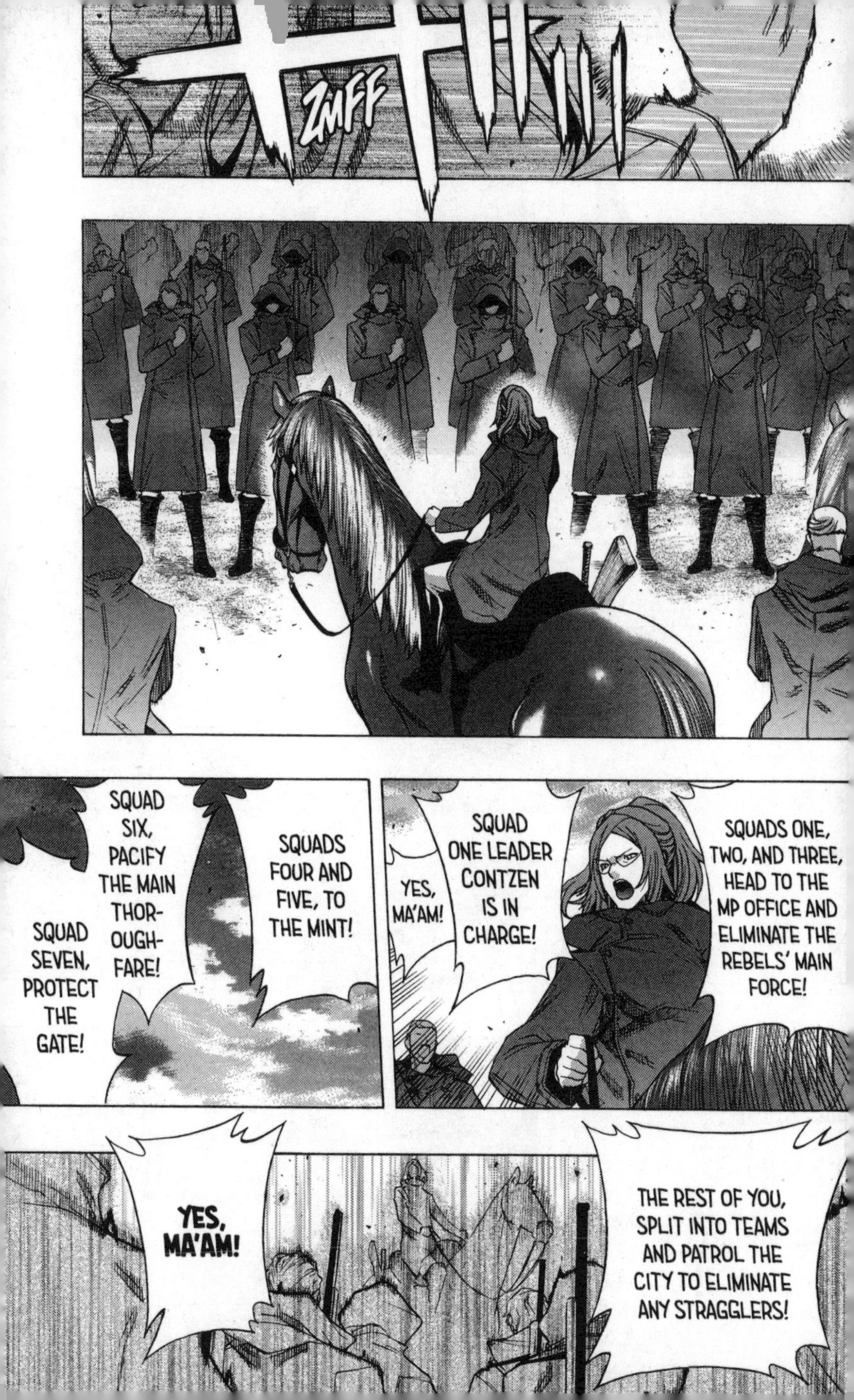
ZMFF
SQUADS ONE, TWO, AND THREE, HEAD TO THE MP OFFICE AND ELIMINATE THE REBELS' MAIN FORCE!
SQUAD ONE LEADER CONTZEN IS IN CHARGE!
YES, MA'AM!
SQUADS FOUR AND FIVE, TO THE MINT!
SQUAD SIX, PACIFY THE MAIN THOR-OUGH-FARE!
SQUAD SEVEN, PROTECT THE GATE!
THE REST OF YOU, SPLIT INTO TEAMS AND PATROL THE CITY TO ELIMINATE ANY STRAGGLERS!
YES, MA'AM!

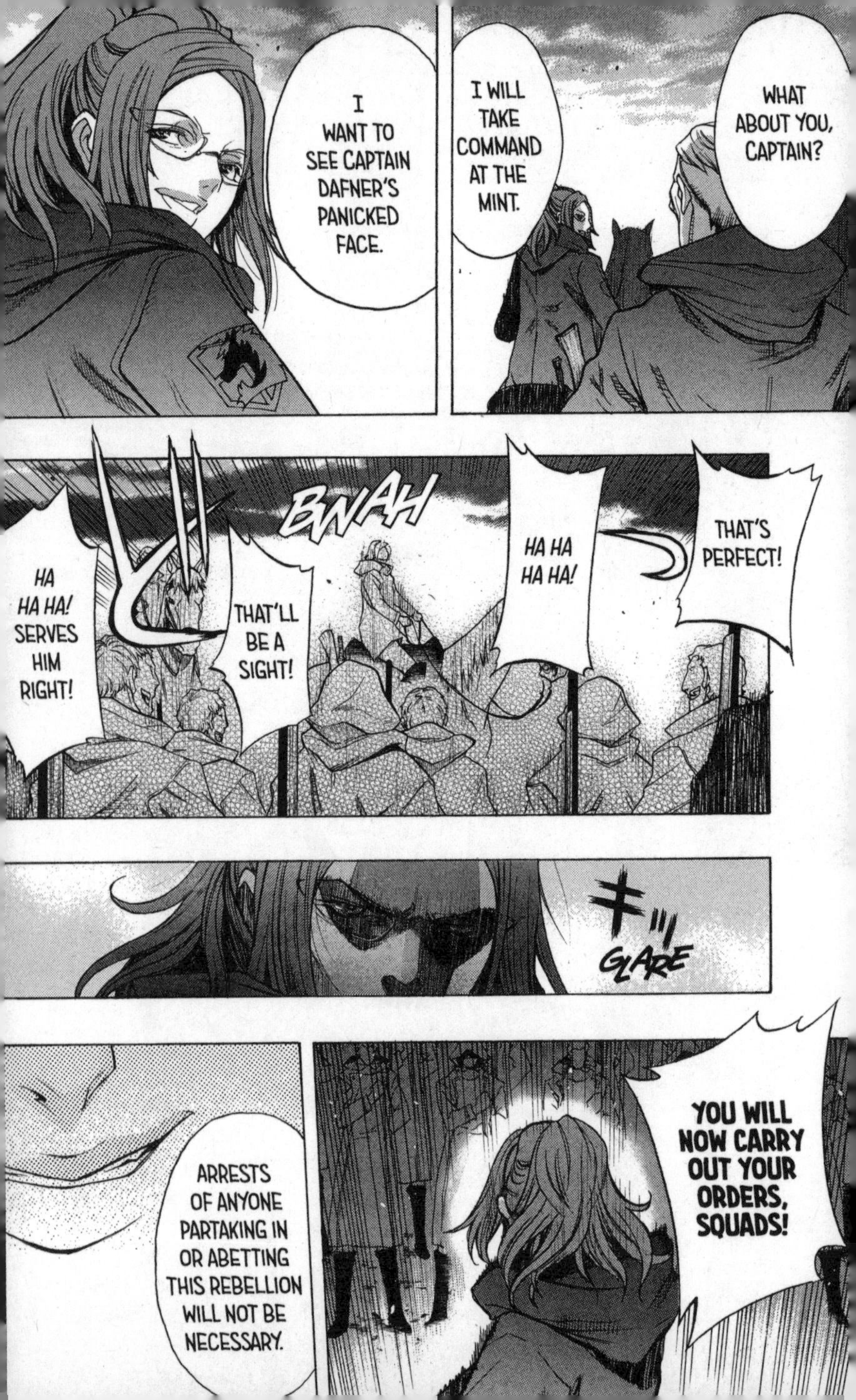
WHAT ABOUT YOU, CAPTAIN?
I WILL TAKE COMMAND AT THE MINT.
I WANT TO SEE CAPTAIN DAFNER'S PANICKED FACE.
THAT'S PERFECT!
HA HA HA HA!
BWAH
THAT'LL BE A SIGHT!
HA HA HA! SERVES HIM RIGHT!
GLARE
YOU WILL NOW CARRY OUT YOUR ORDERS, SQUADS!
ARRESTS OF ANYONE PARTAKING IN OR ABETTING THIS REBELLION WILL NOT BE NECESSARY.

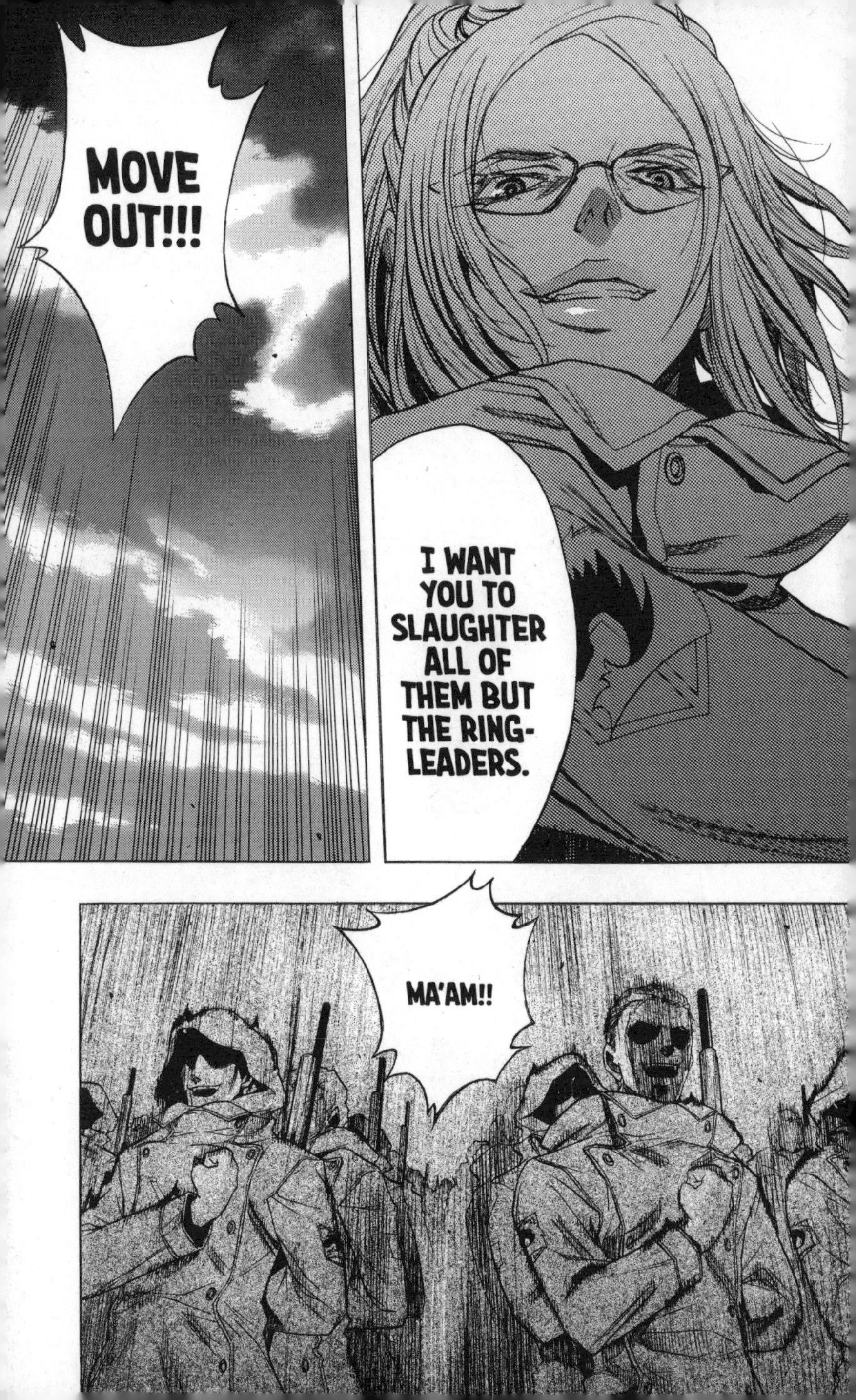
I WANT YOU TO SLAUGHTER ALL OF THEM BUT THE RING-LEADERS.
MOVE OUT!!!
MA'AM!!

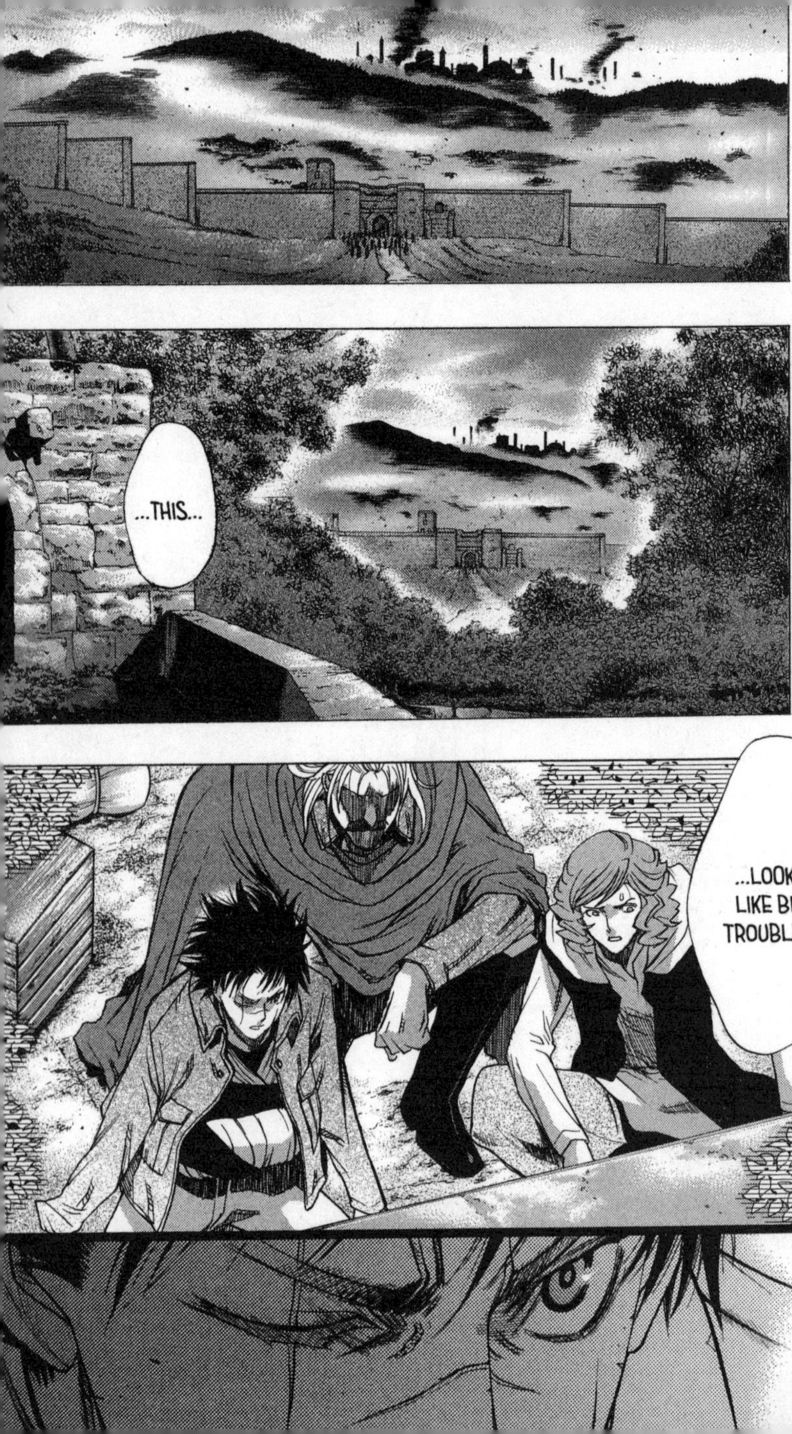
...THIS...
...LOOKS LIKE BIG TROUBLE...

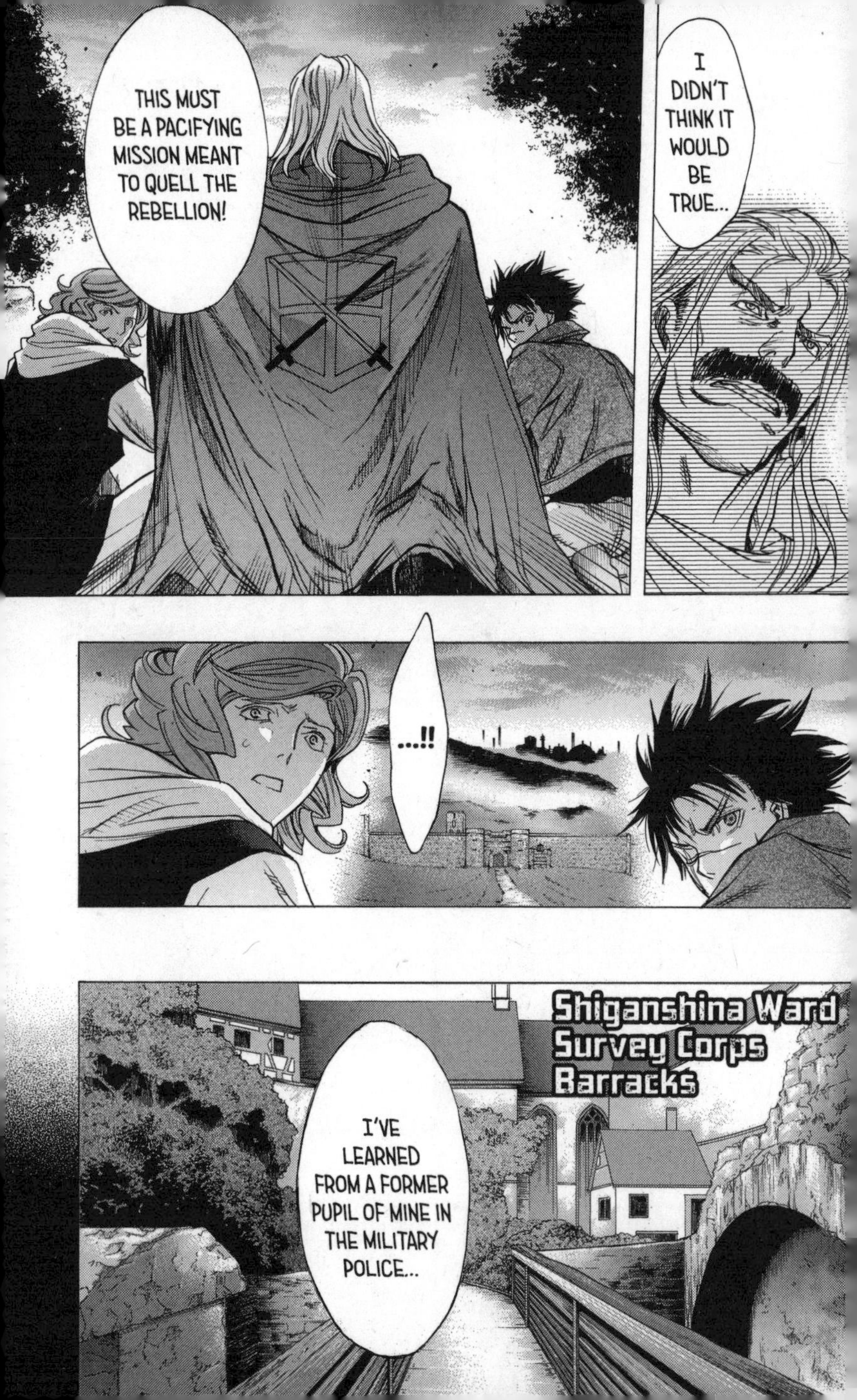
I DIDN'T THINK IT WOULD BE TRUE...
THIS MUST BE A PACIFYING MISSION MEANT TO QUELL THE REBELLION!
...!!
Shiganshina Ward Survey Corps Barracks
I'VE LEARNED FROM A FORMER PUPIL OF MINE IN THE MILITARY POLICE...

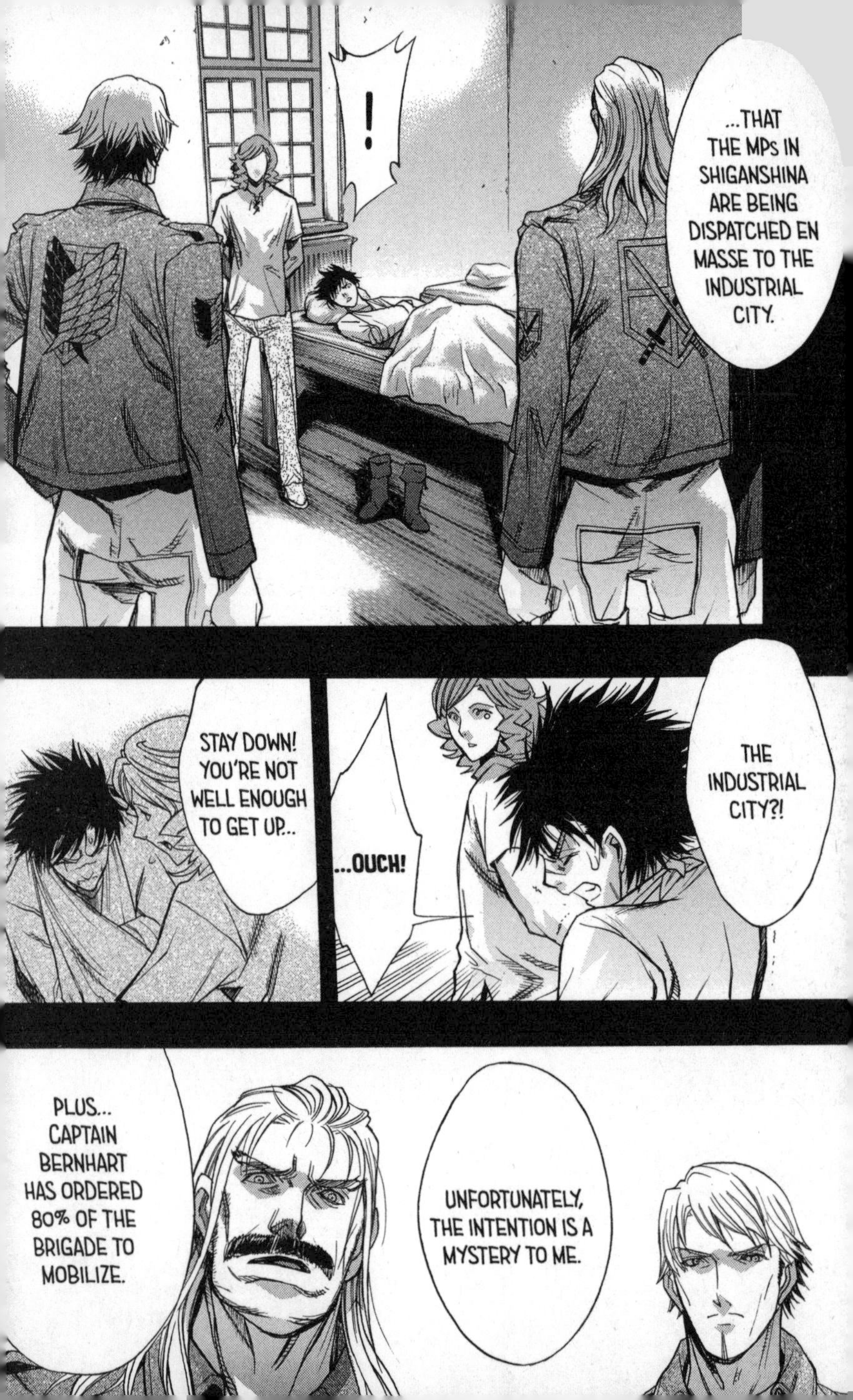
...THAT THE MPs IN SHIGANSHINA ARE BEING DISPATCHED EN MASSE TO THE INDUSTRIAL CITY.
!
THE INDUSTRIAL CITY?!
...OUCH!
STAY DOWN! YOU'RE NOT WELL ENOUGH TO GET UP...
UNFORTUNATELY, THE INTENTION IS A MYSTERY TO ME.
PLUS... CAPTAIN BERNHART HAS ORDERED 80% OF THE BRIGADE TO MOBILIZE.

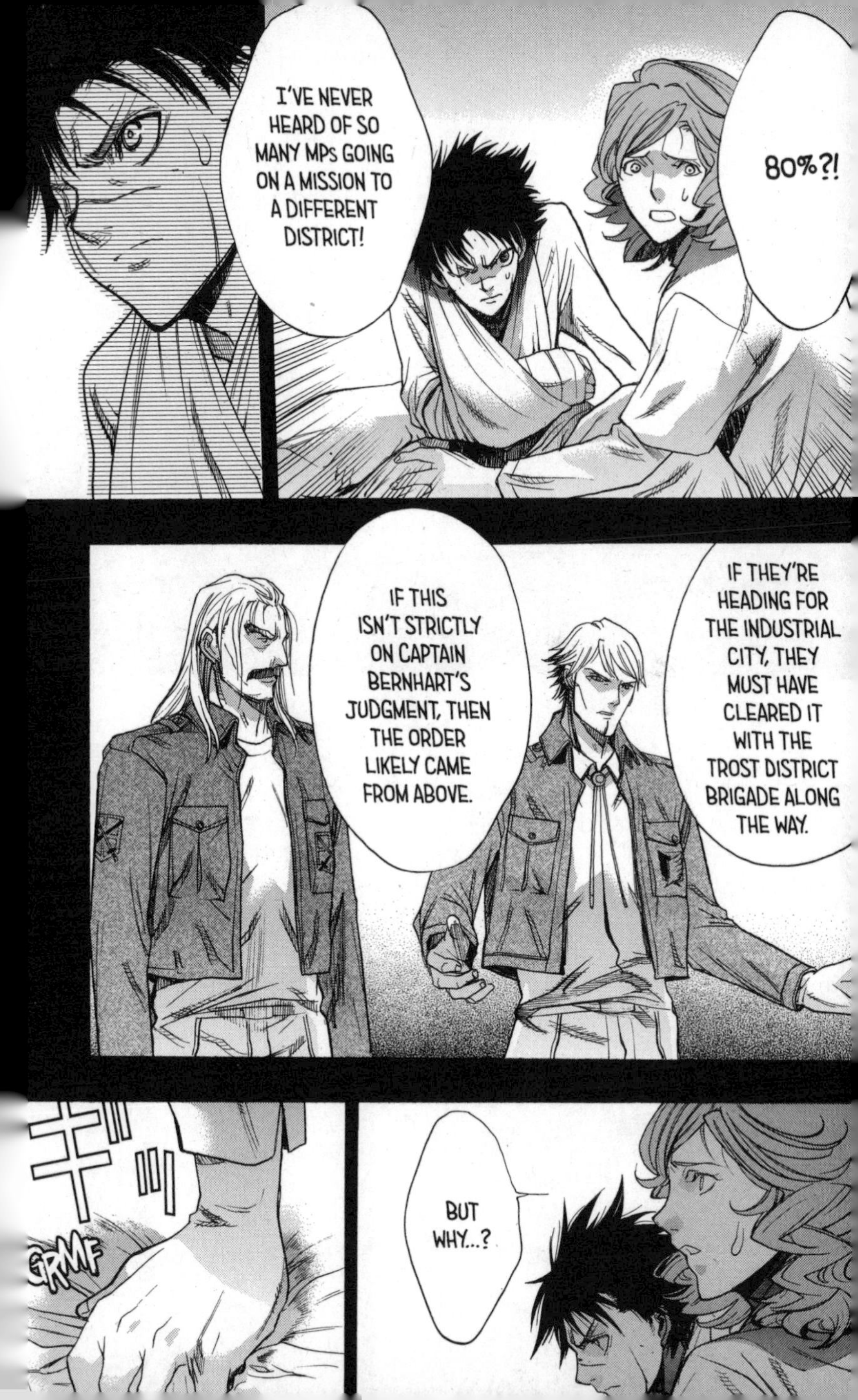
80%?!
I'VE NEVER HEARD OF SO MANY MPs GOING ON A MISSION TO A DIFFERENT DISTRICT!
IF THEY'RE HEADING FOR THE INDUSTRIAL CITY, THEY MUST HAVE CLEARED IT WITH THE TROST DISTRICT BRIGADE ALONG THE WAY.
IF THIS ISN'T STRICTLY ON CAPTAIN BERNHART'S JUDGMENT, THEN THE ORDER LIKELY CAME FROM ABOVE.
BUT WHY...?
GRMF

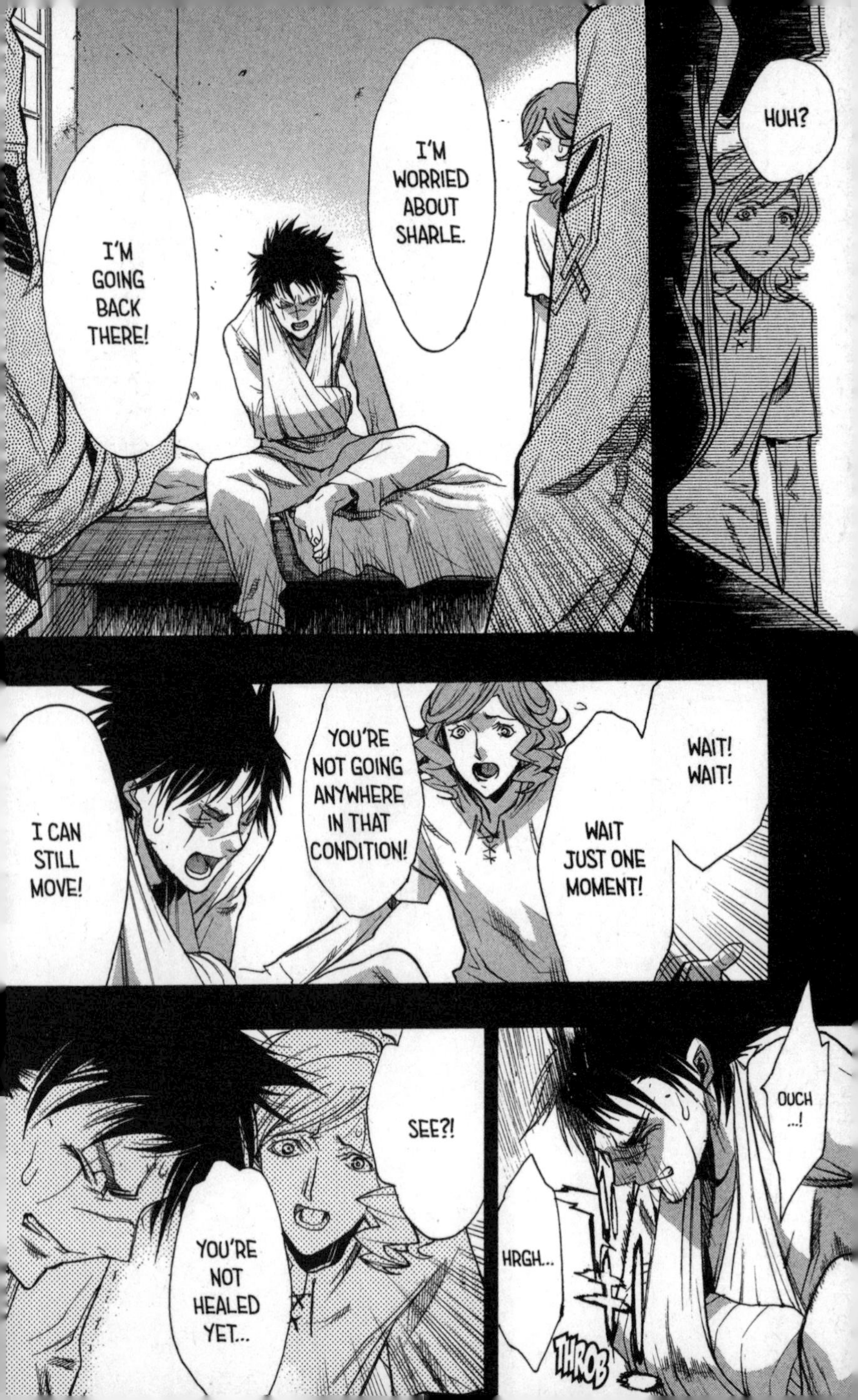
HUH?
I'M WORRIED ABOUT SHARLE.
I'M GOING BACK THERE!
WAIT! WAIT!
WAIT JUST ONE MOMENT!
YOU'RE NOT GOING ANYWHERE IN THAT CONDITION!
I CAN STILL MOVE!
OUCH ...!
HRGH...
THROB
SEE?!
YOU'RE NOT HEALED YET...

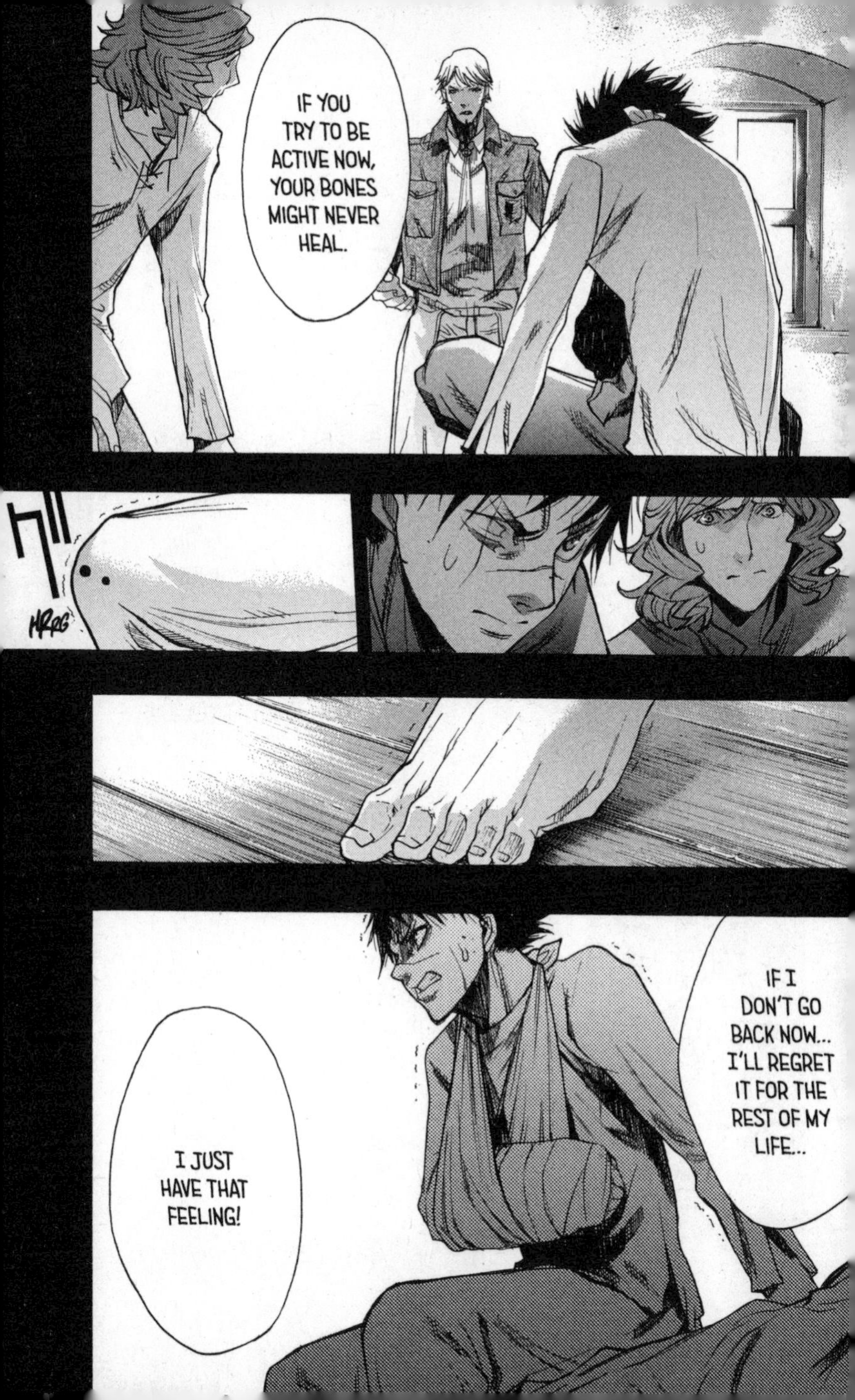
IF YOU TRY TO BE ACTIVE NOW, YOUR BONES MIGHT NEVER HEAL.
HRRG
IF I DON'T GO BACK NOW... I'LL REGRET IT FOR THE REST OF MY LIFE...
I JUST HAVE THAT FEELING!

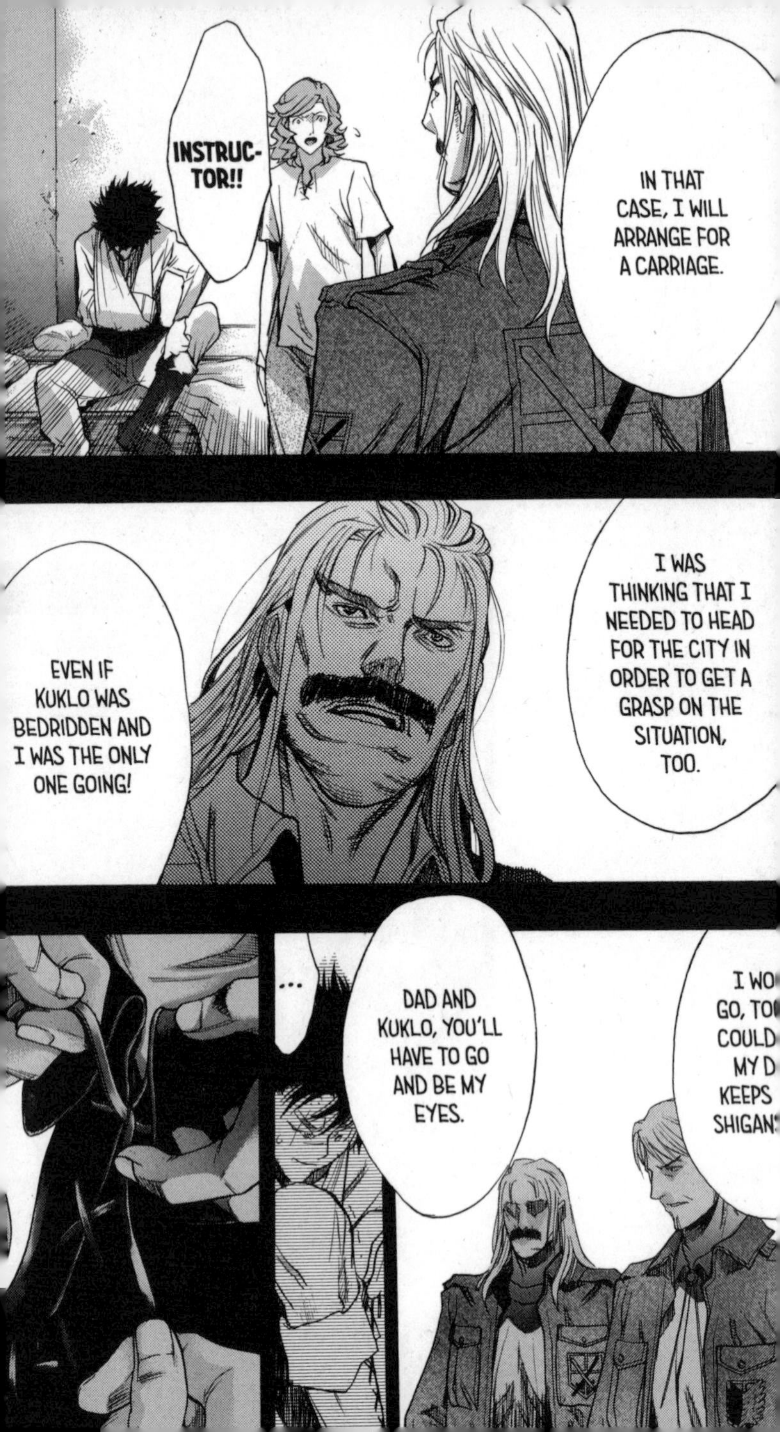
IN THAT CASE, I WILL ARRANGE FOR A CARRIAGE.
INSTRUCTOR!!
I WAS THINKING THAT I NEEDED TO HEAD FOR THE CITY IN ORDER TO GET A GRASP ON THE SITUATION, TOO.
EVEN IF KUKLO WAS BEDRIDDEN AND I WAS THE ONLY ONE GOING!
I WO
GO, TO
COULD
MY D
KEEPS
SHIGAN
DAD AND KUKLO, YOU'LL HAVE TO GO AND BE MY EYES.
...

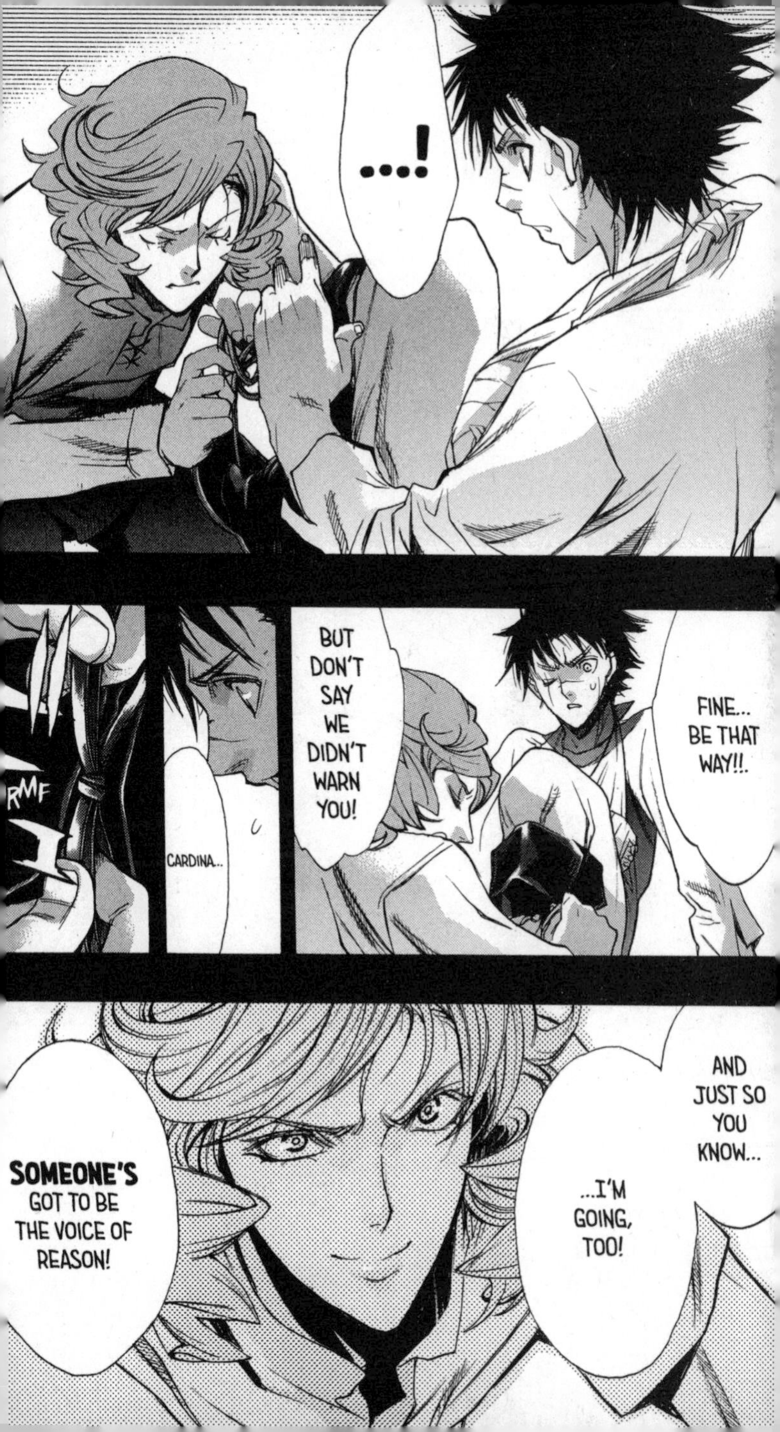
...!
FINE... BE THAT WAY!!.
BUT DON'T SAY WE DIDN'T WARN YOU!
CARDINA...
RMF
AND JUST SO YOU KNOW...
...I'M GOING, TOO!
SOMEONE'S GOT TO BE THE VOICE OF REASON!

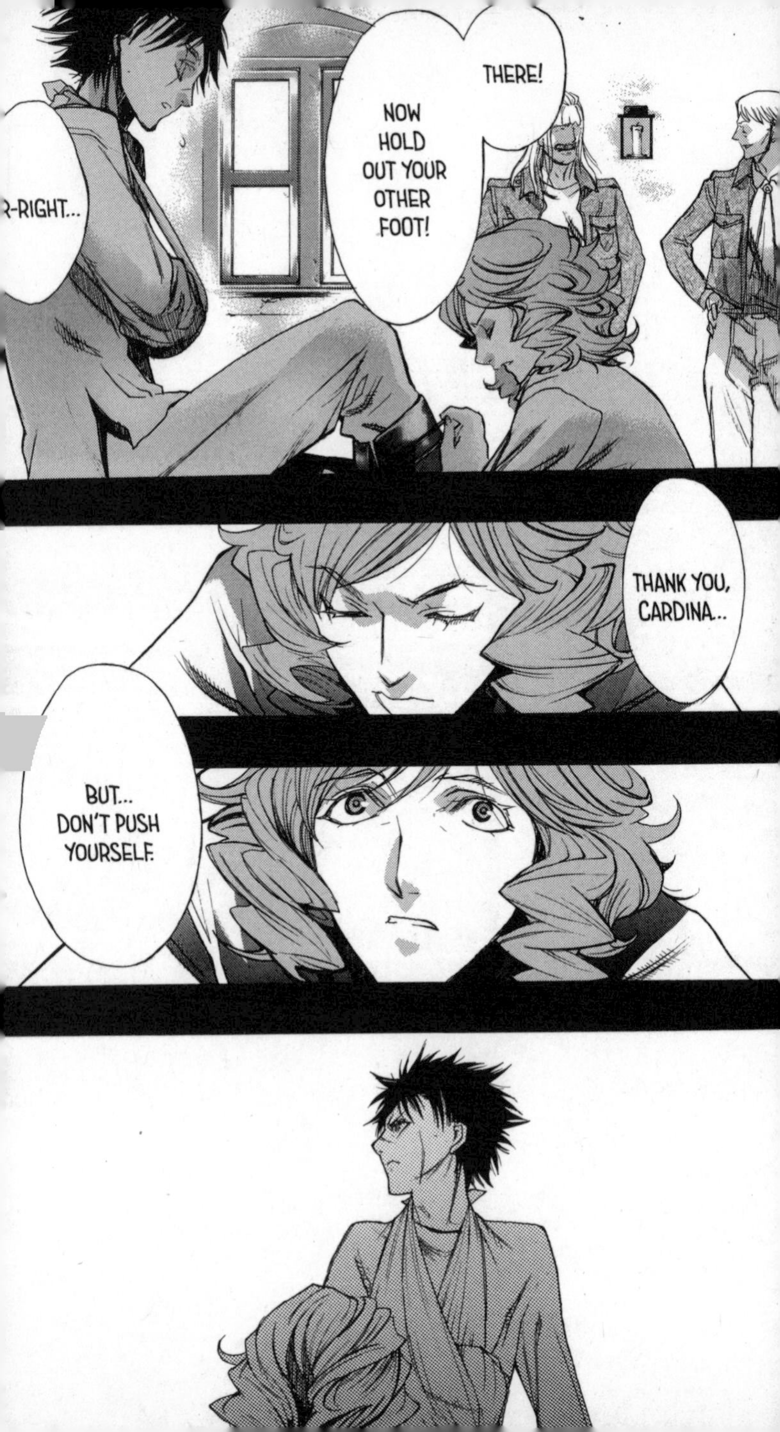
THERE!
NOW HOLD OUT YOUR OTHER FOOT!
R-RIGHT...
THANK YOU, CARDINA...
BUT... DON'T PUSH YOURSELF.

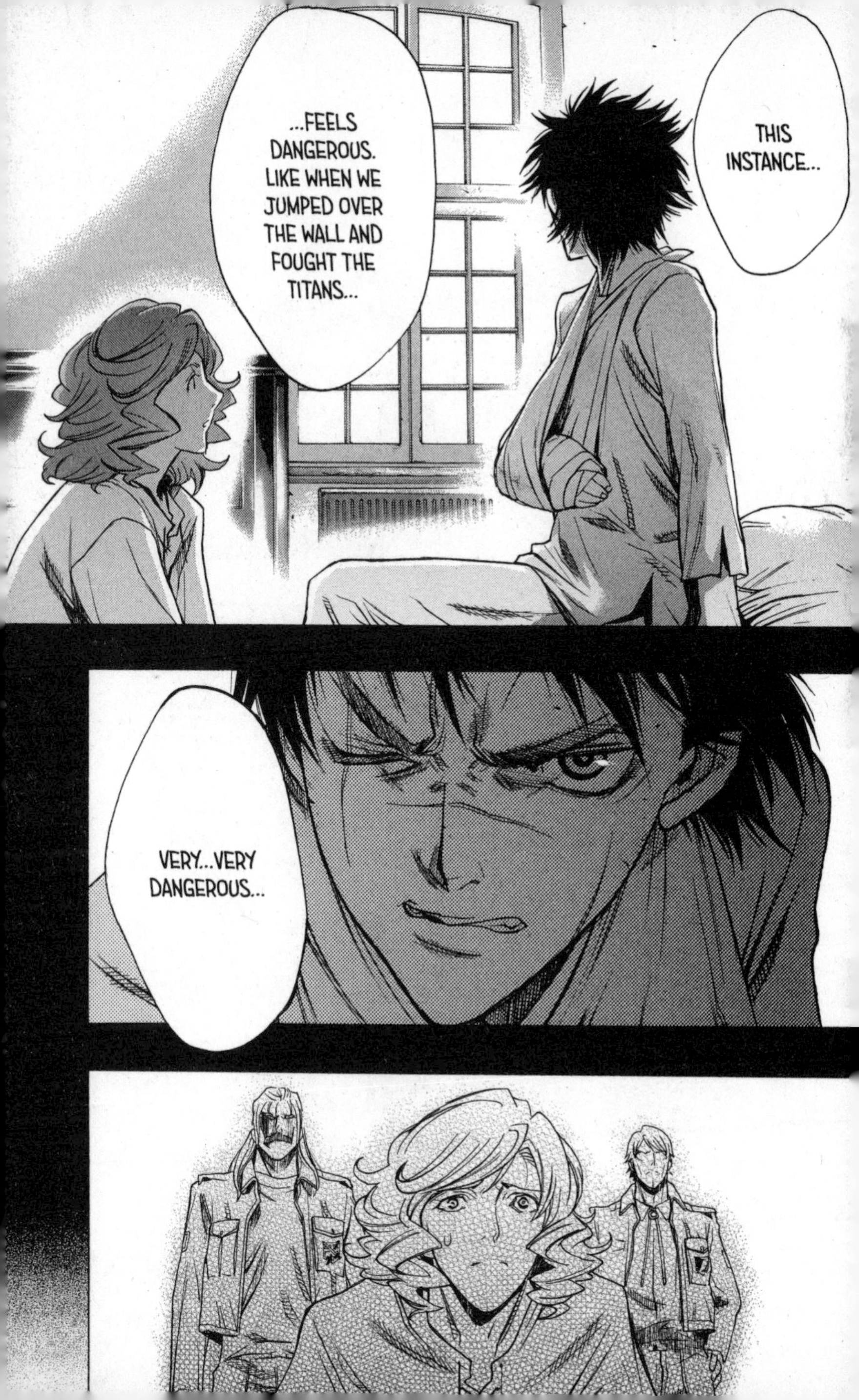
THIS INSTANCE...
...FEELS DANGEROUS. LIKE WHEN WE JUMPED OVER THE WALL AND FOUGHT THE TITANS...
VERY...VERY DANGEROUS...

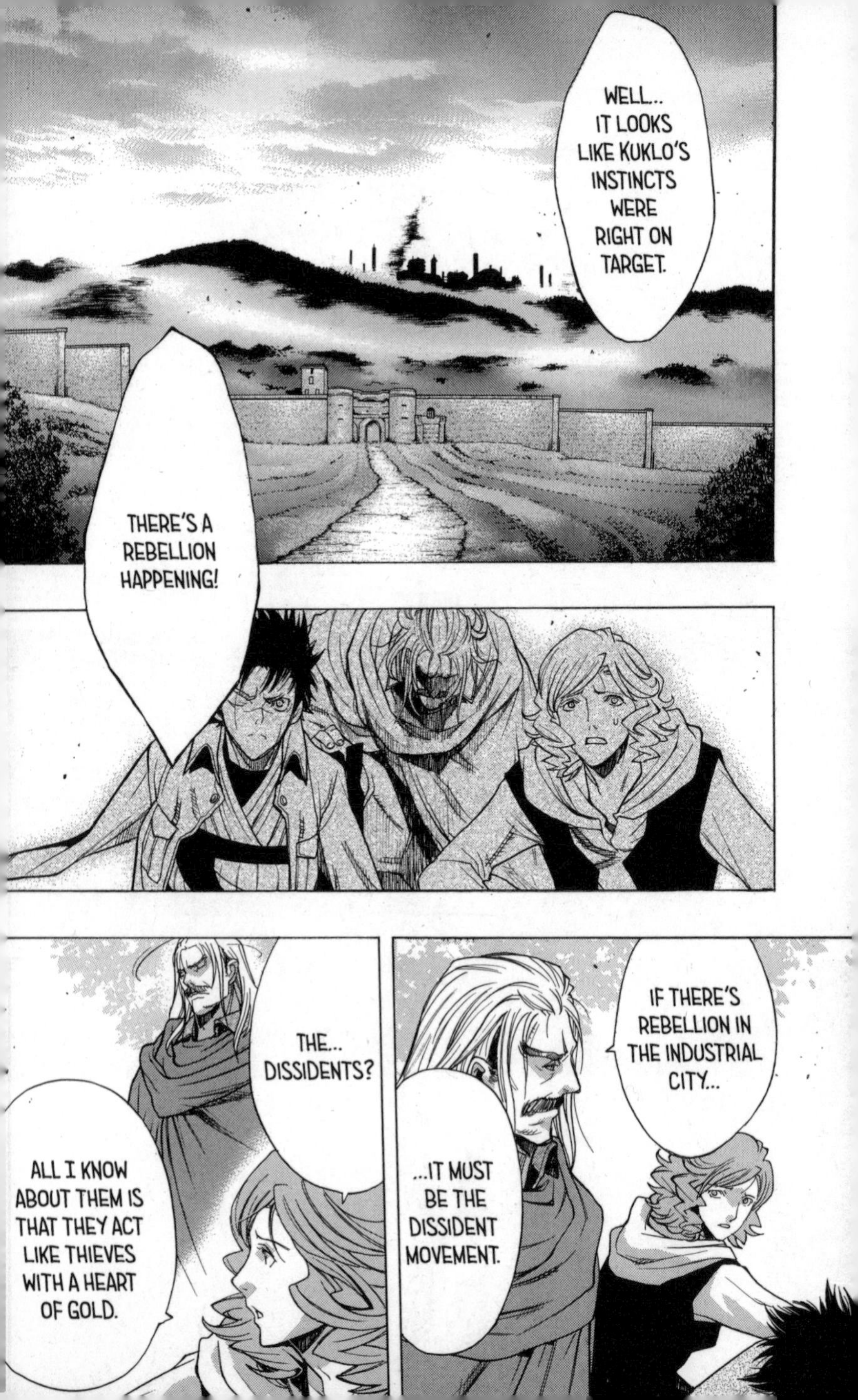
WELL... IT LOOKS LIKE KUKLO'S INSTINCTS WERE RIGHT ON TARGET.
THERE'S A REBELLION HAPPENING!
IF THERE'S REBELLION IN THE INDUSTRIAL CITY...
...IT MUST BE THE DISSIDENT MOVEMENT.
THE... DISSIDENTS?
ALL I KNOW ABOUT THEM IS THAT THEY ACT LIKE THIEVES WITH A HEART OF GOLD.

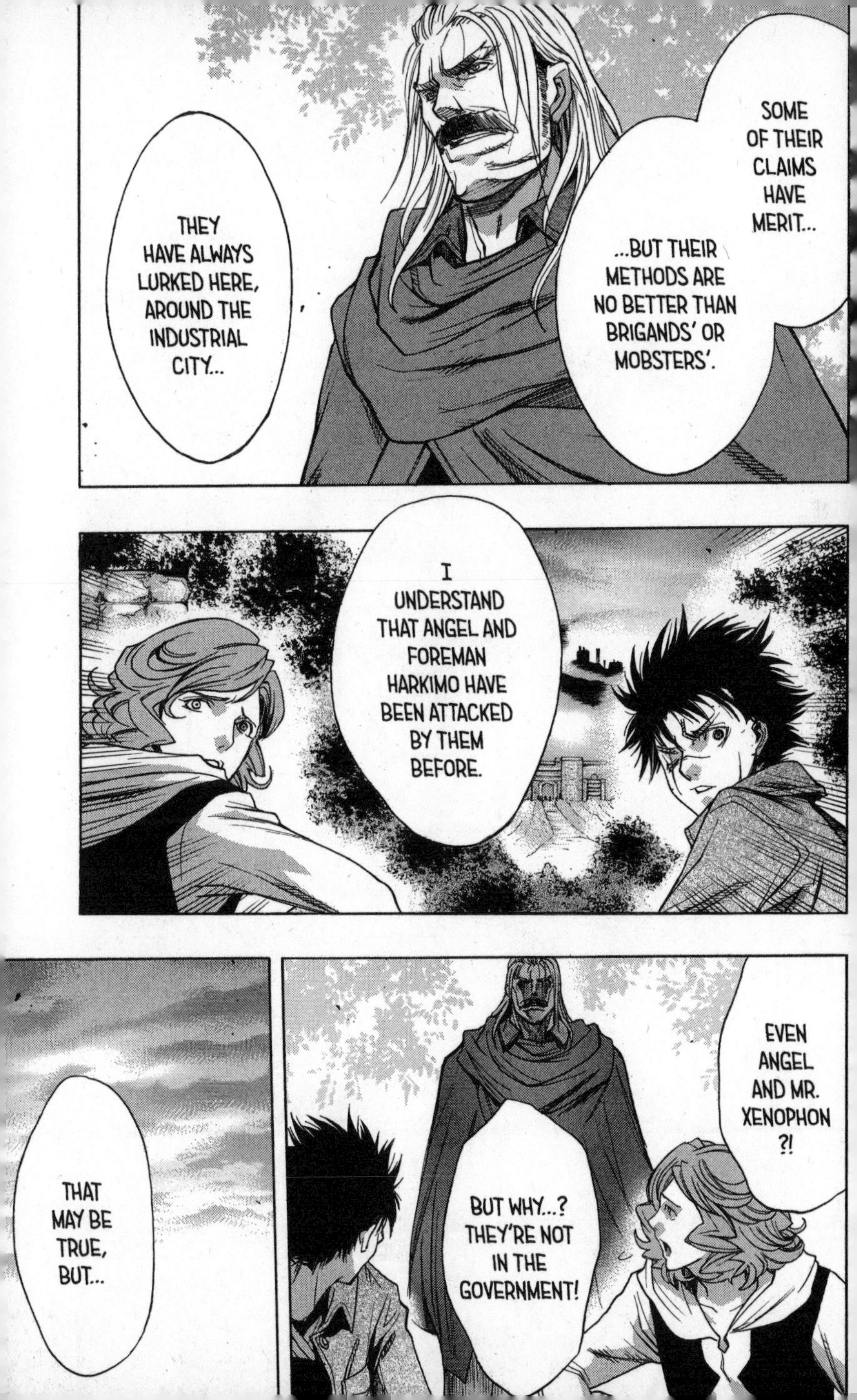
SOME OF THEIR CLAIMS HAVE MERIT...
...BUT THEIR METHODS ARE NO BETTER THAN BRIGANDS' OR MOBSTERS'.
THEY HAVE ALWAYS LURKED HERE, AROUND THE INDUSTRIAL CITY...
I UNDERSTAND THAT ANGEL AND FOREMAN HARKIMO HAVE BEEN ATTACKED BY THEM BEFORE.
EVEN ANGEL AND MR. XENOPHON?!
BUT WHY...? THEY'RE NOT IN THE GOVERNMENT!
THAT MAY BE TRUE, BUT...

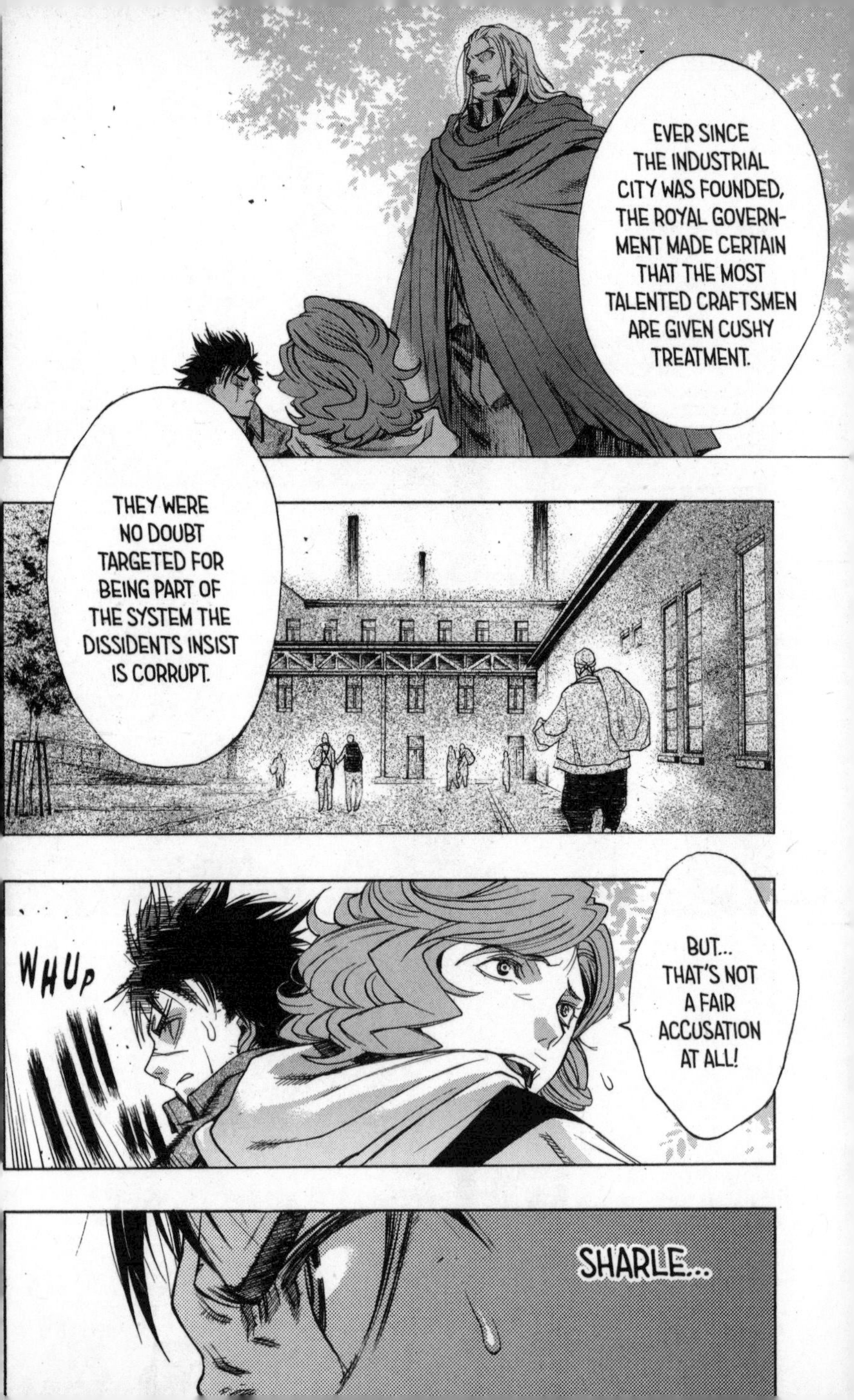
EVER SINCE THE INDUSTRIAL CITY WAS FOUNDED, THE ROYAL GOVERNMENT MADE CERTAIN THAT THE MOST TALENTED CRAFTSMEN ARE GIVEN CUSHY TREATMENT.
THEY WERE NO DOUBT TARGETED FOR BEING PART OF THE SYSTEM THE DISSIDENTS INSIST IS CORRUPT.
BUT... THAT'S NOT A FAIR ACCUSATION AT ALL!
WHUP
SHARLE...

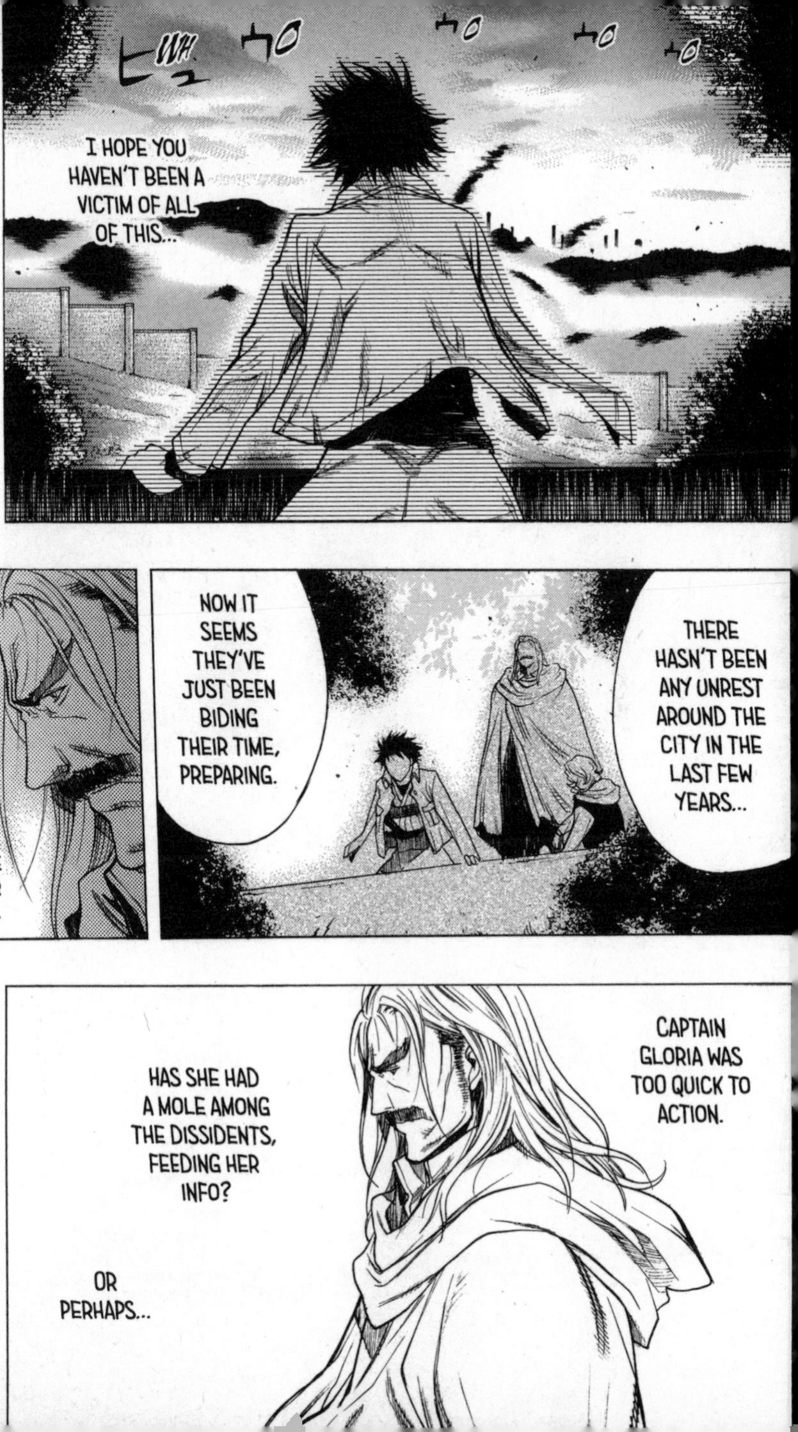
ヒュウウウウ
WH
I HOPE YOU HAVEN'T BEEN A VICTIM OF ALL OF THIS...
THERE HASN'T BEEN ANY UNREST AROUND THE CITY IN THE LAST FEW YEARS...
NOW IT SEEMS THEY'VE JUST BEEN BIDING THEIR TIME, PREPARING.
ON THE OTHER HAND...
CAPTAIN GLORIA WAS TOO QUICK TO ACTION.
HAS SHE HAD A MOLE AMONG THE DISSIDENTS, FEEDING HER INFO?
OR PERHAPS...

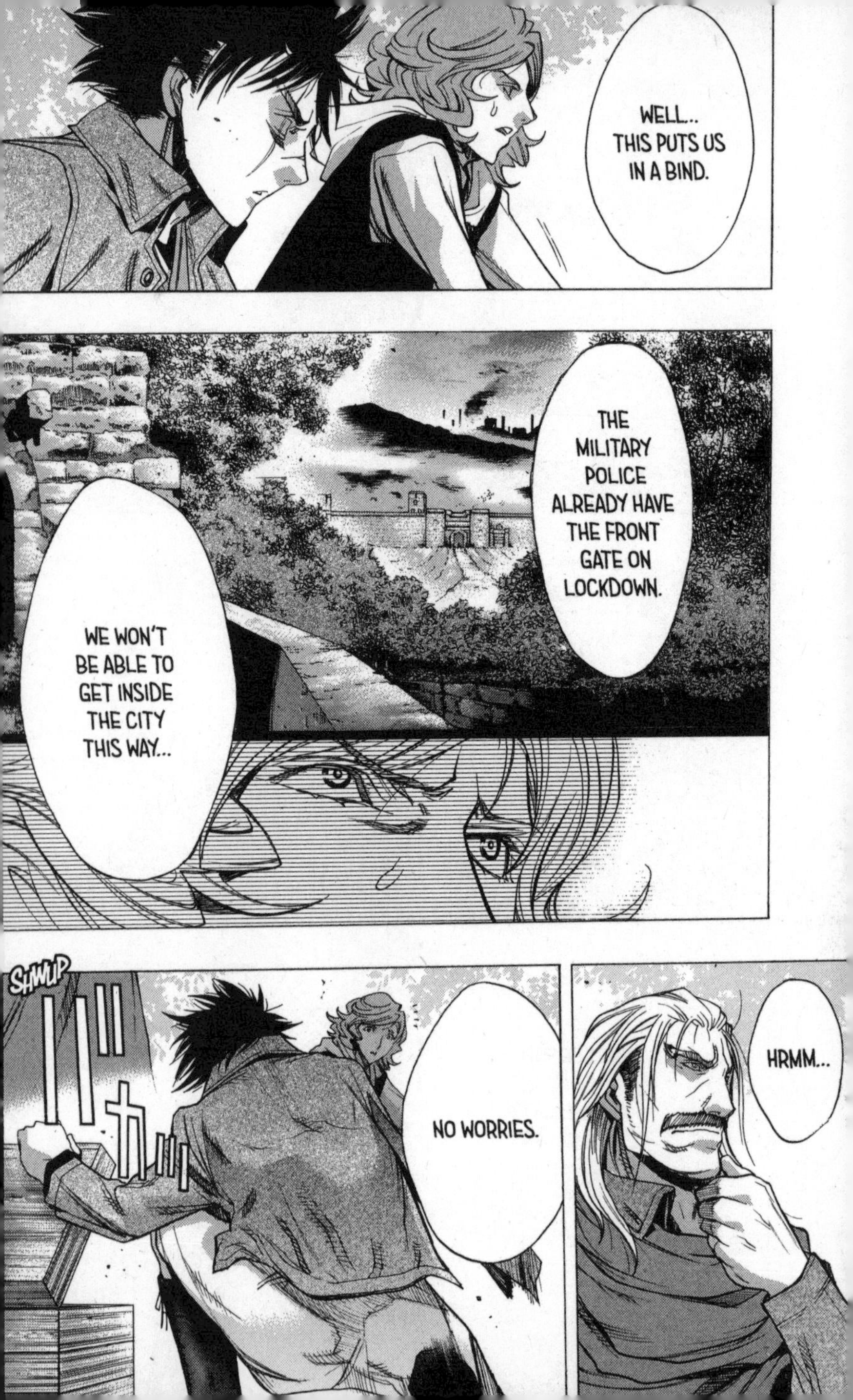
WELL... THIS PUTS US IN A BIND.
THE MILITARY POLICE ALREADY HAVE THE FRONT GATE ON LOCKDOWN.
WE WON'T BE ABLE TO GET INSIDE THE CITY THIS WAY...
HRMM...
NO WORRIES.
SHWUP

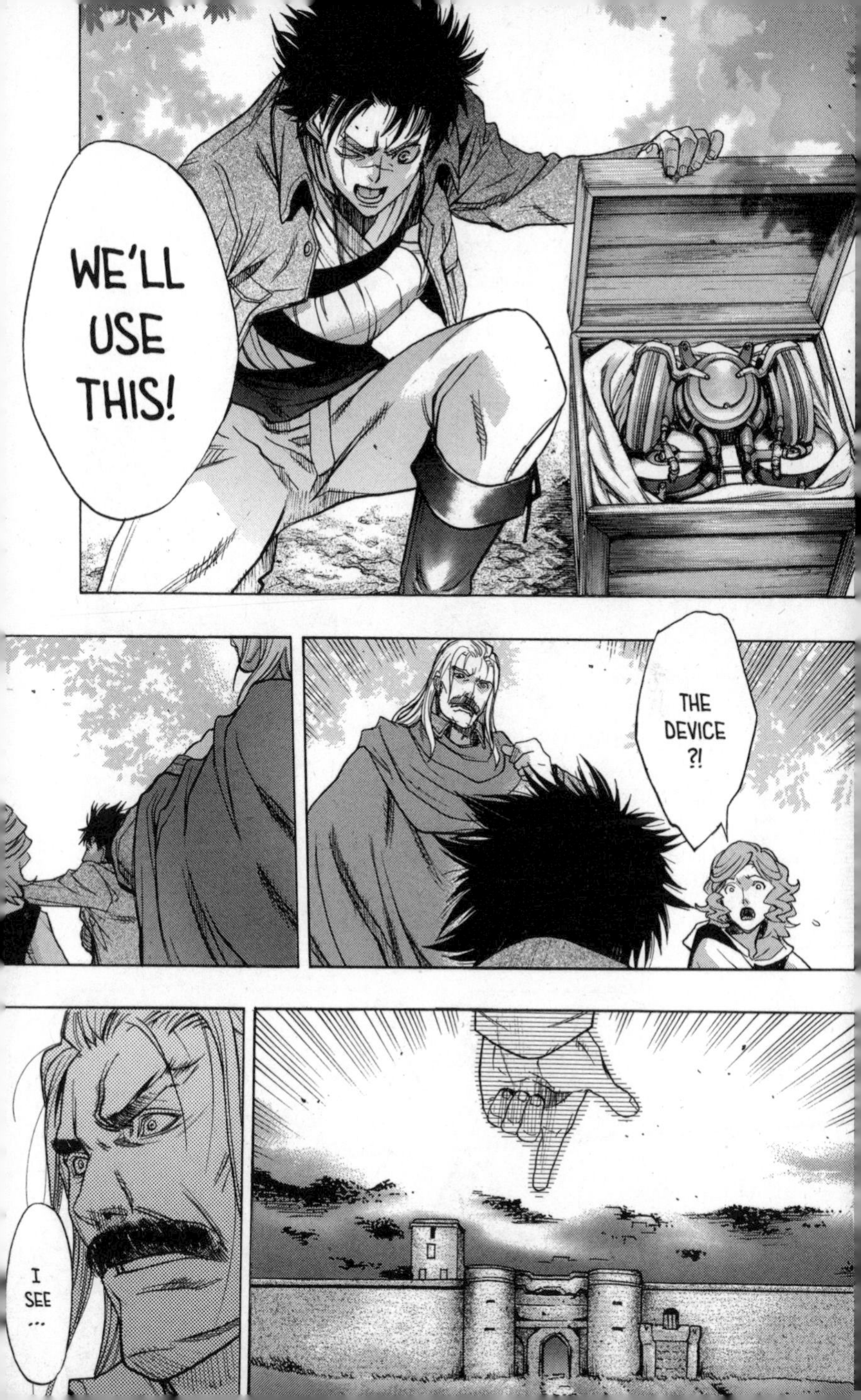
WE'LL USE THIS!
THE DEVICE ?!
I SEE ...

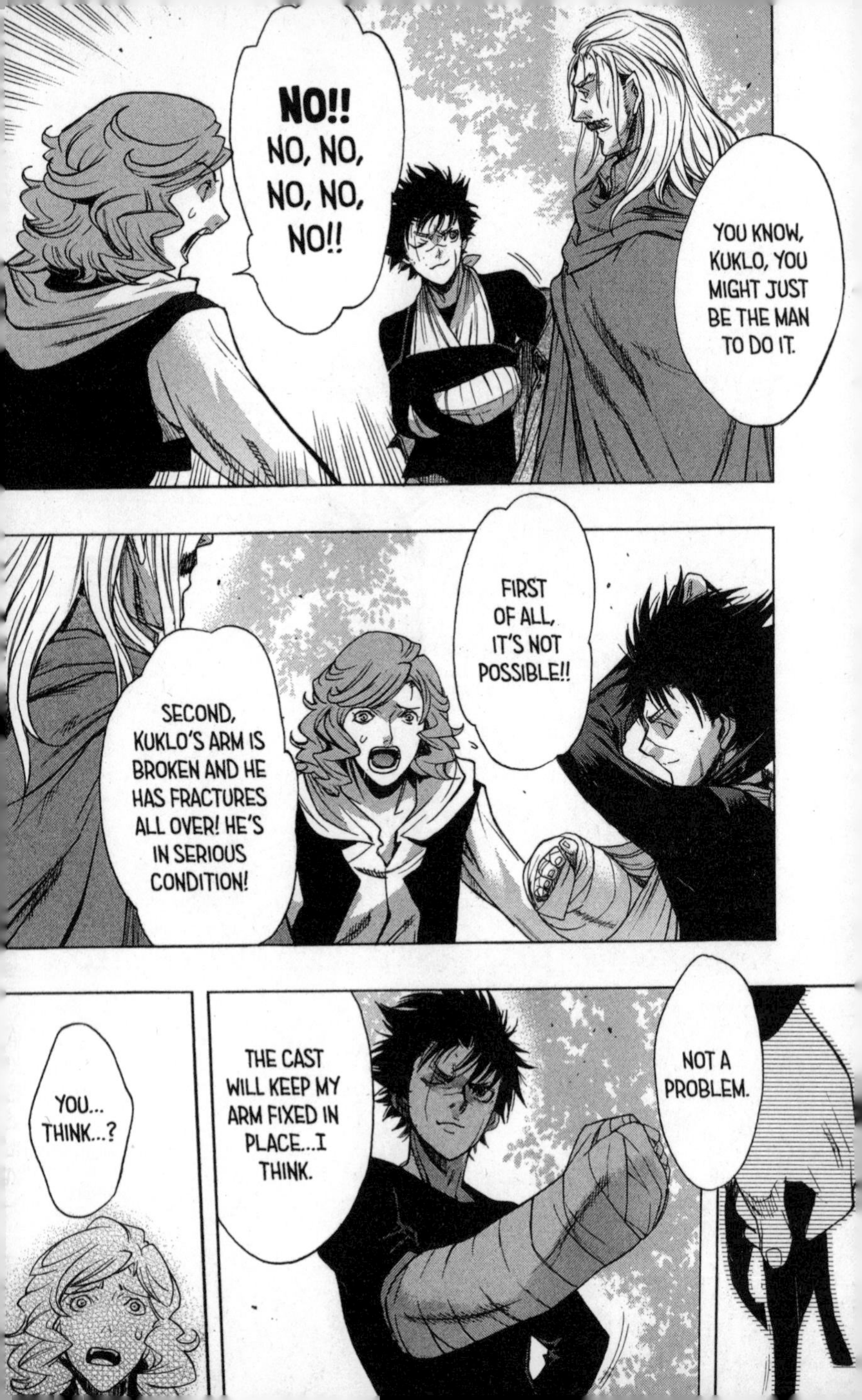
YOU KNOW, KUKLO, YOU MIGHT JUST BE THE MAN TO DO IT.
NO!! NO, NO, NO, NO, NO!!
FIRST OF ALL, IT'S NOT POSSIBLE!!
SECOND, KUKLO'S ARM IS BROKEN AND HE HAS FRACTURES ALL OVER! HE'S IN SERIOUS CONDITION!
NOT A PROBLEM.
THE CAST WILL KEEP MY ARM FIXED IN PLACE...I THINK.
YOU... THINK...?

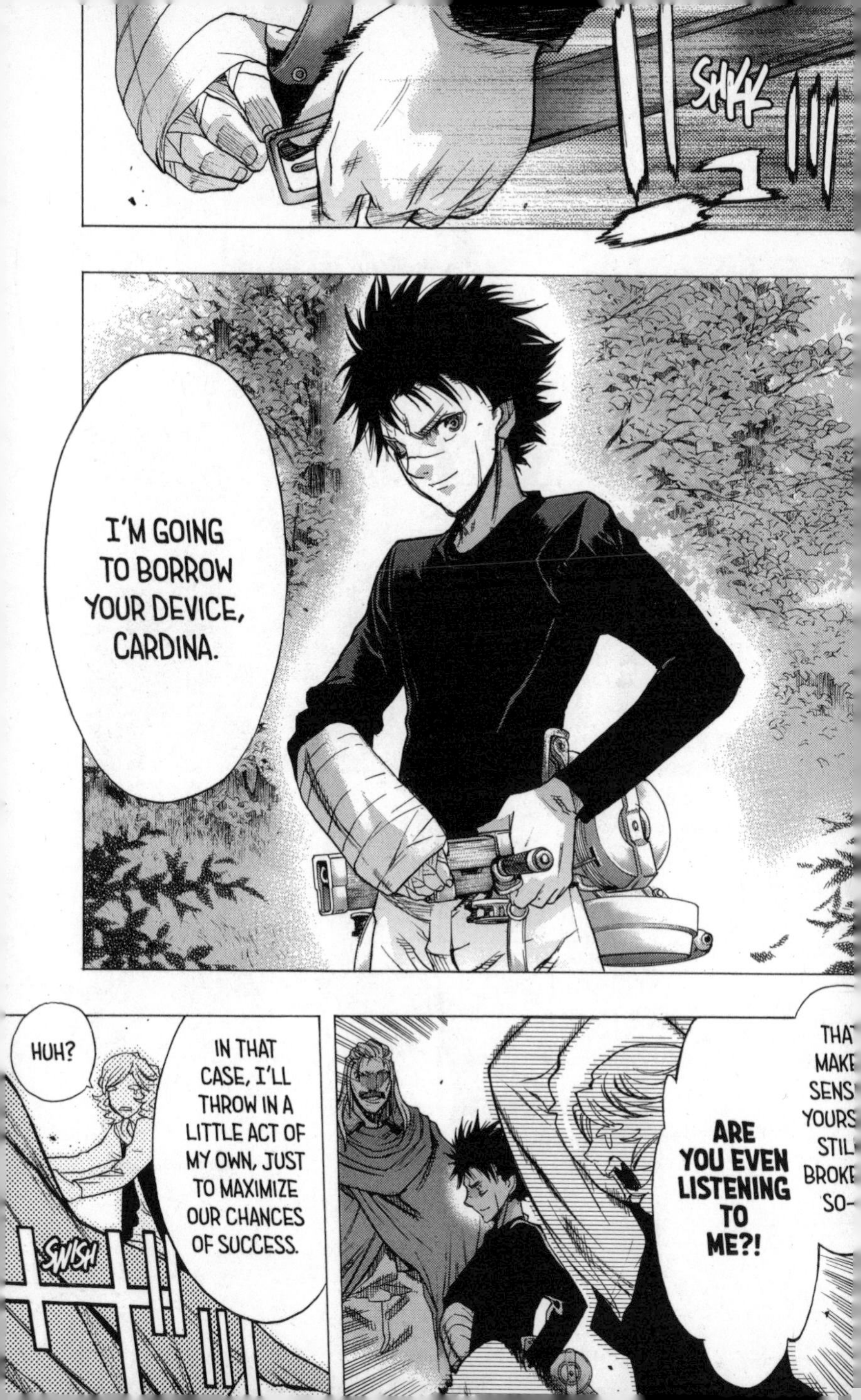
SHKK
I'M GOING TO BORROW YOUR DEVICE, CARDINA.
THAT MAKE SENS YOURS STIL BROKE SO-
ARE YOU EVEN LISTENING TO ME?!
IN THAT CASE, I'LL THROW IN A LITTLE ACT OF MY OWN, JUST TO MAXIMIZE OUR CHANCES OF SUCCESS.
HUH?
SWISH

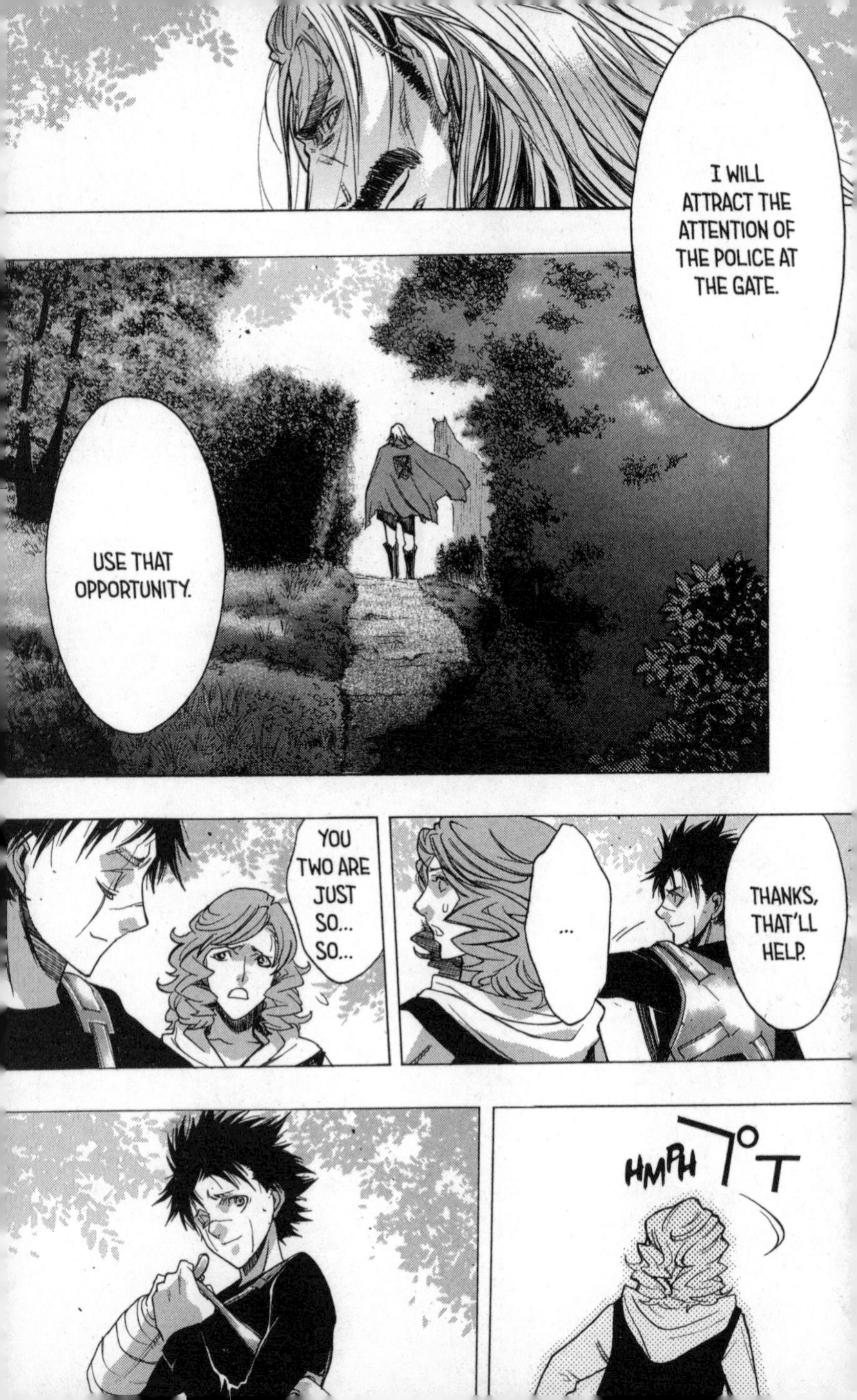
I WILL ATTRACT THE ATTENTION OF THE POLICE AT THE GATE.
USE THAT OPPORTUNITY.
THANKS, THAT'LL HELP.
...
YOU TWO ARE JUST SO... SO...
HMPH

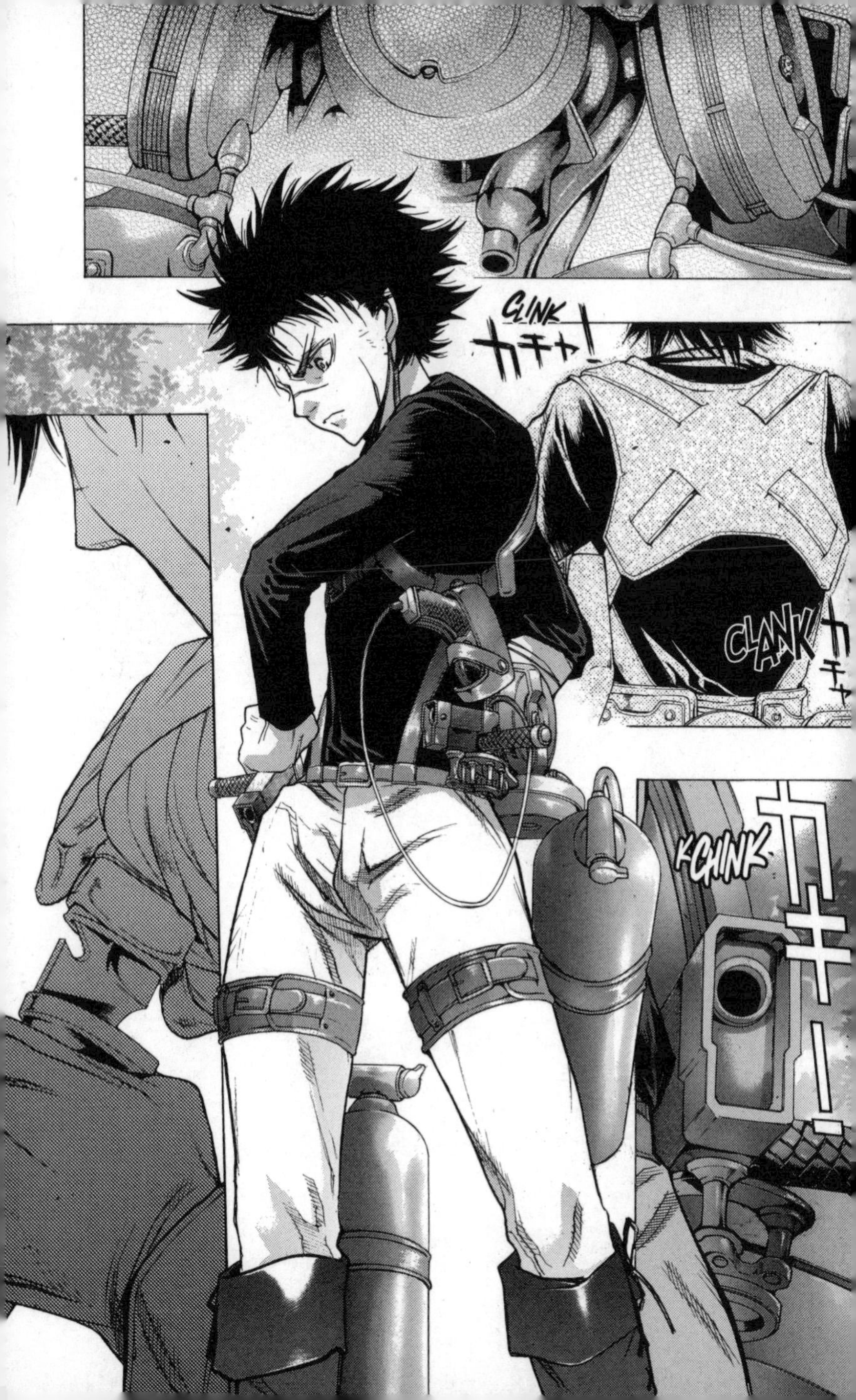
CLINK
カチャ!
CLANK
カチャ
K-CHINK
カキー!

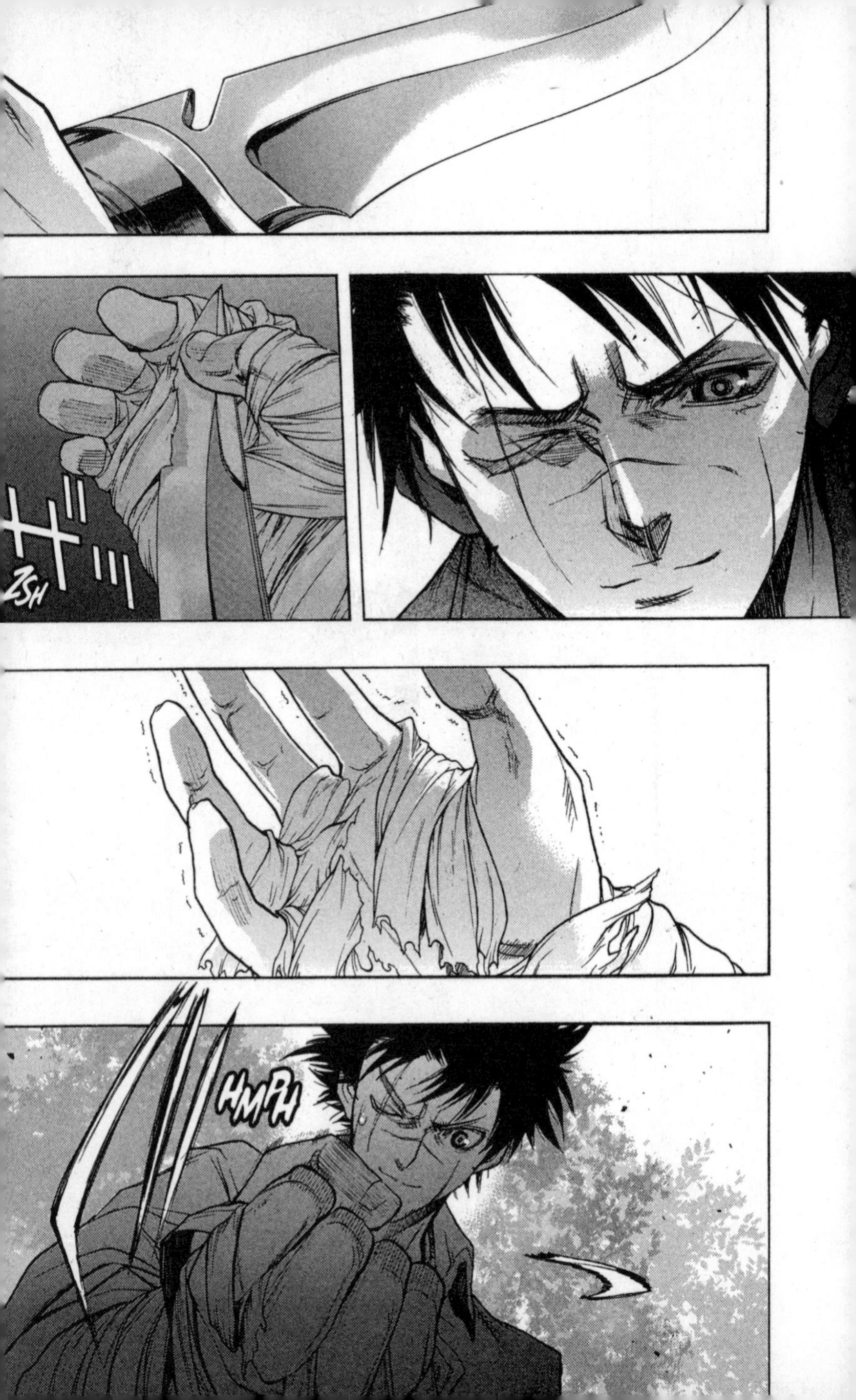
ZSH
HMPH

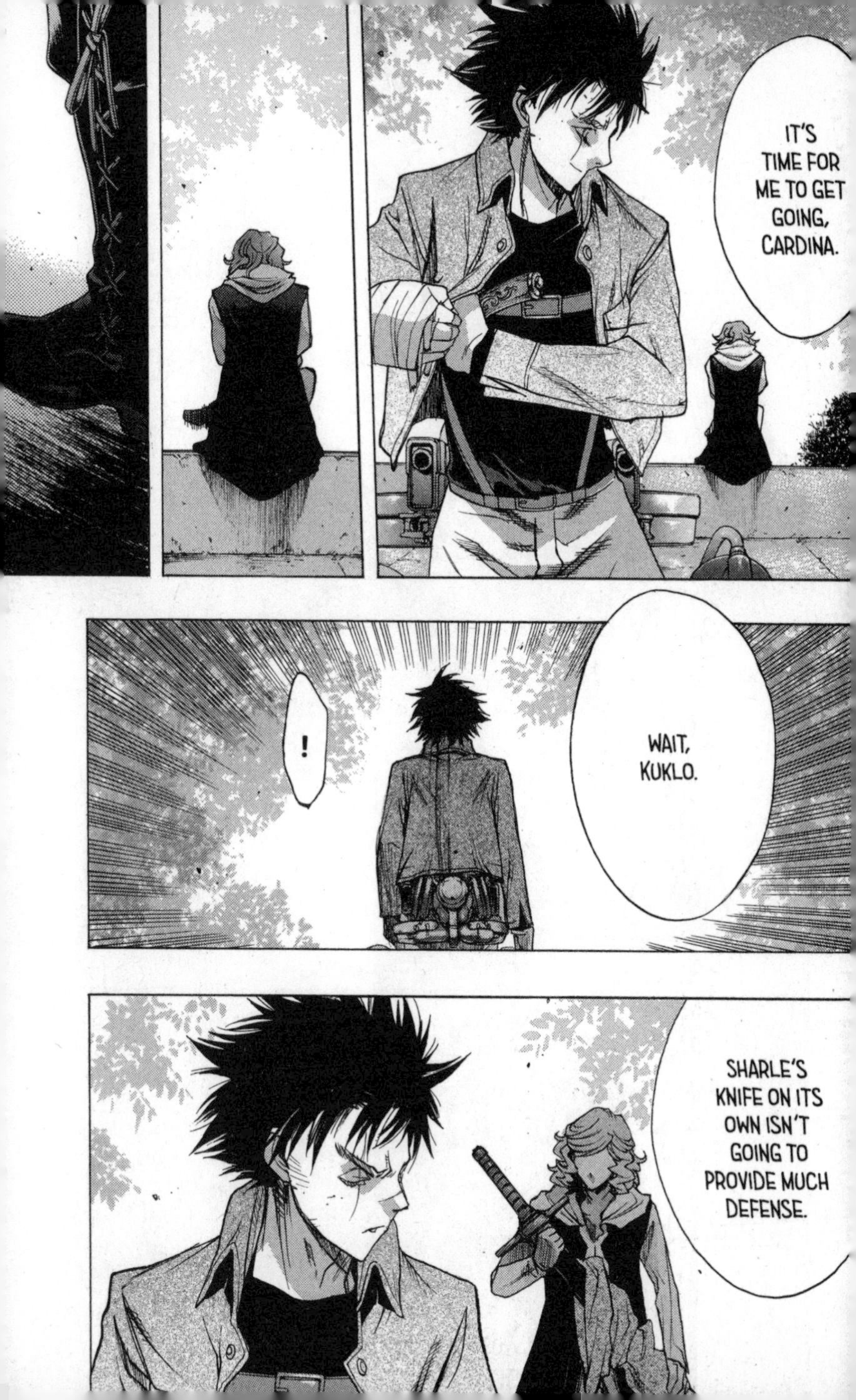
IT'S TIME FOR ME TO GET GOING, CARDINA.
WAIT, KUKLO.
!
SHARLE'S KNIFE ON ITS OWN ISN'T GOING TO PROVIDE MUCH DEFENSE.

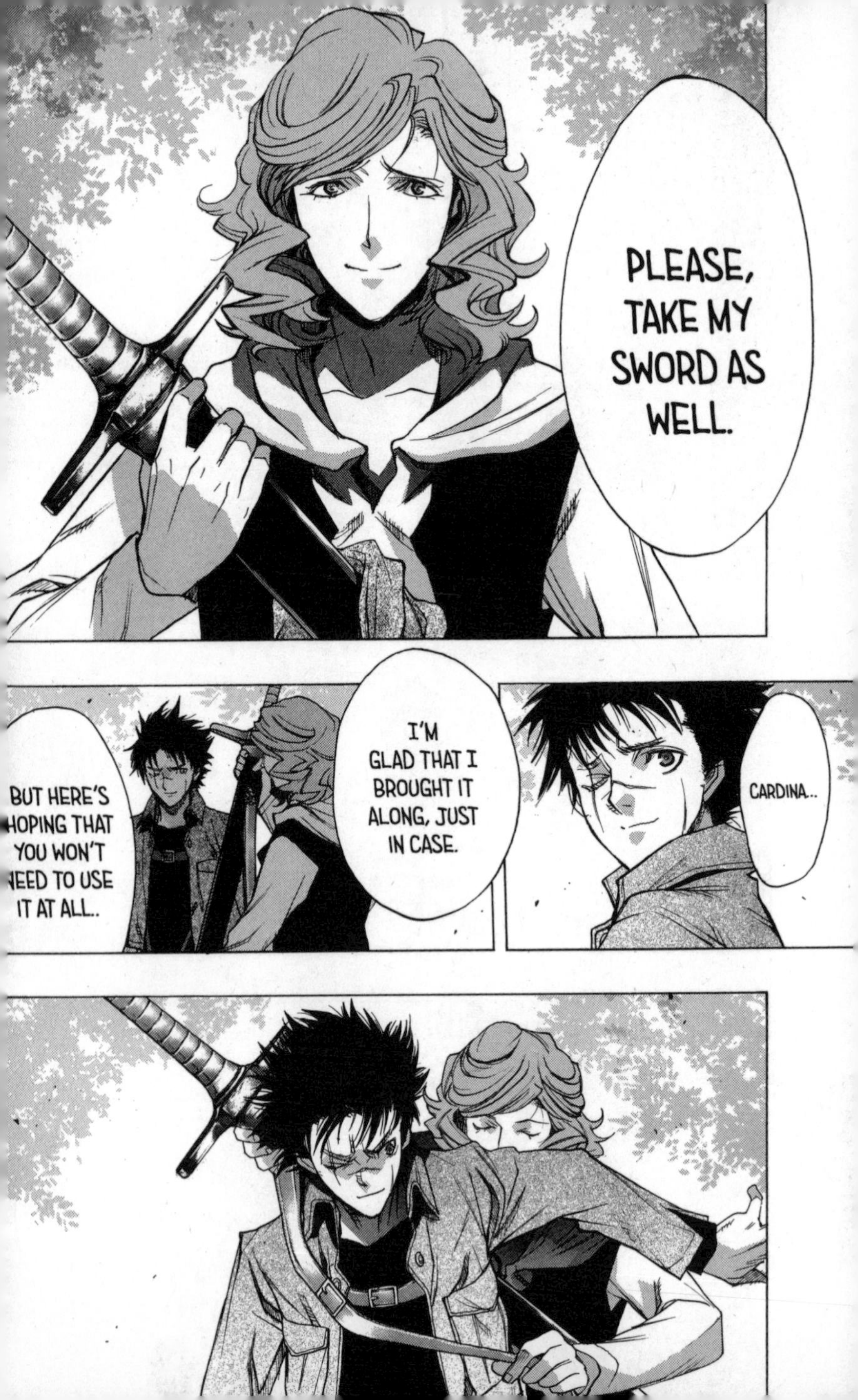
PLEASE, TAKE MY SWORD AS WELL.
CARDINA...
I'M GLAD THAT I BROUGHT IT ALONG, JUST IN CASE.
BUT HERE'S HOPING THAT YOU WON'T NEED TO USE IT AT ALL..

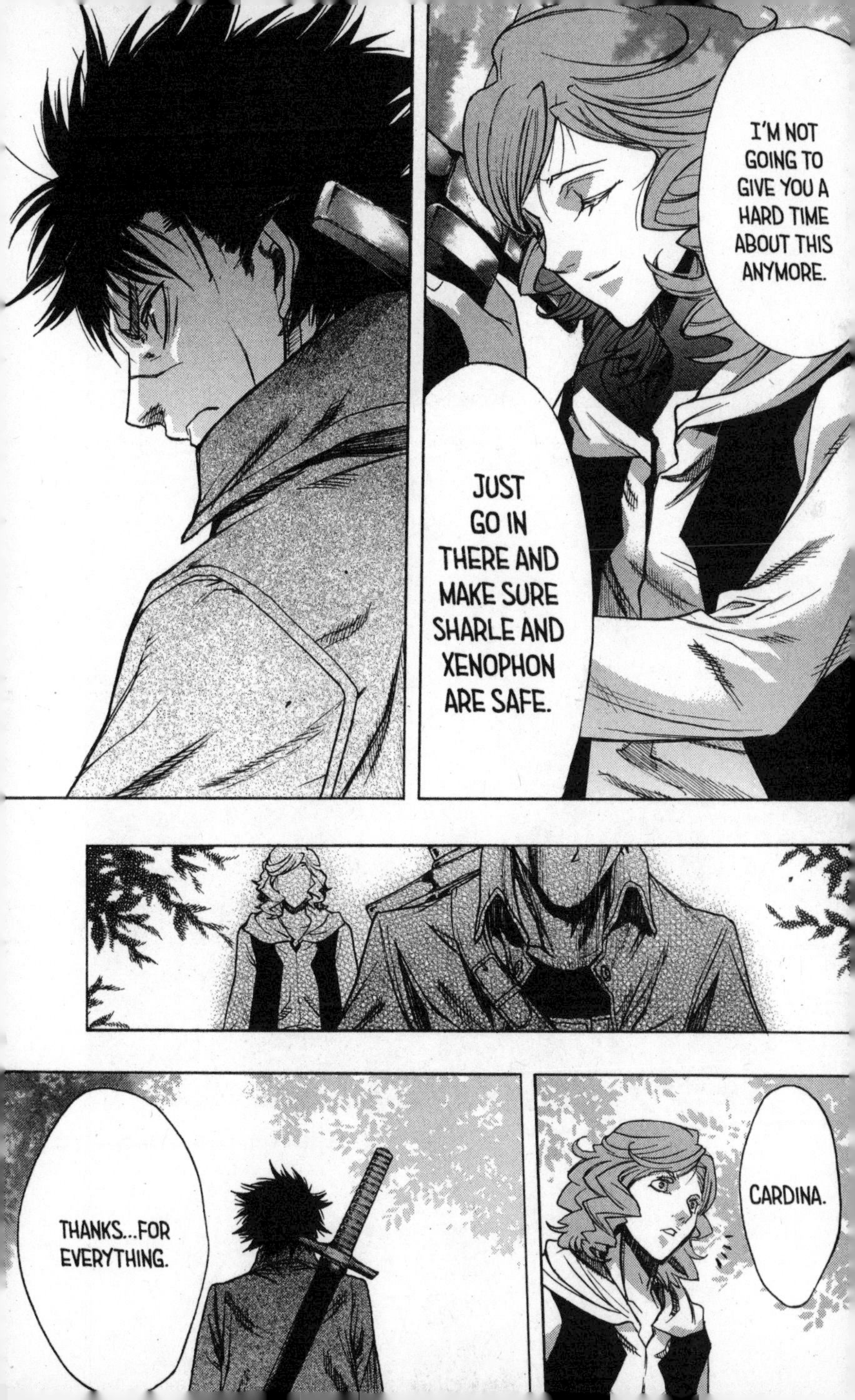
I'M NOT GOING TO GIVE YOU A HARD TIME ABOUT THIS ANYMORE.
JUST GO IN THERE AND MAKE SURE SHARLE AND XENOPHON ARE SAFE.
CARDINA.
THANKS...FOR EVERYTHING.

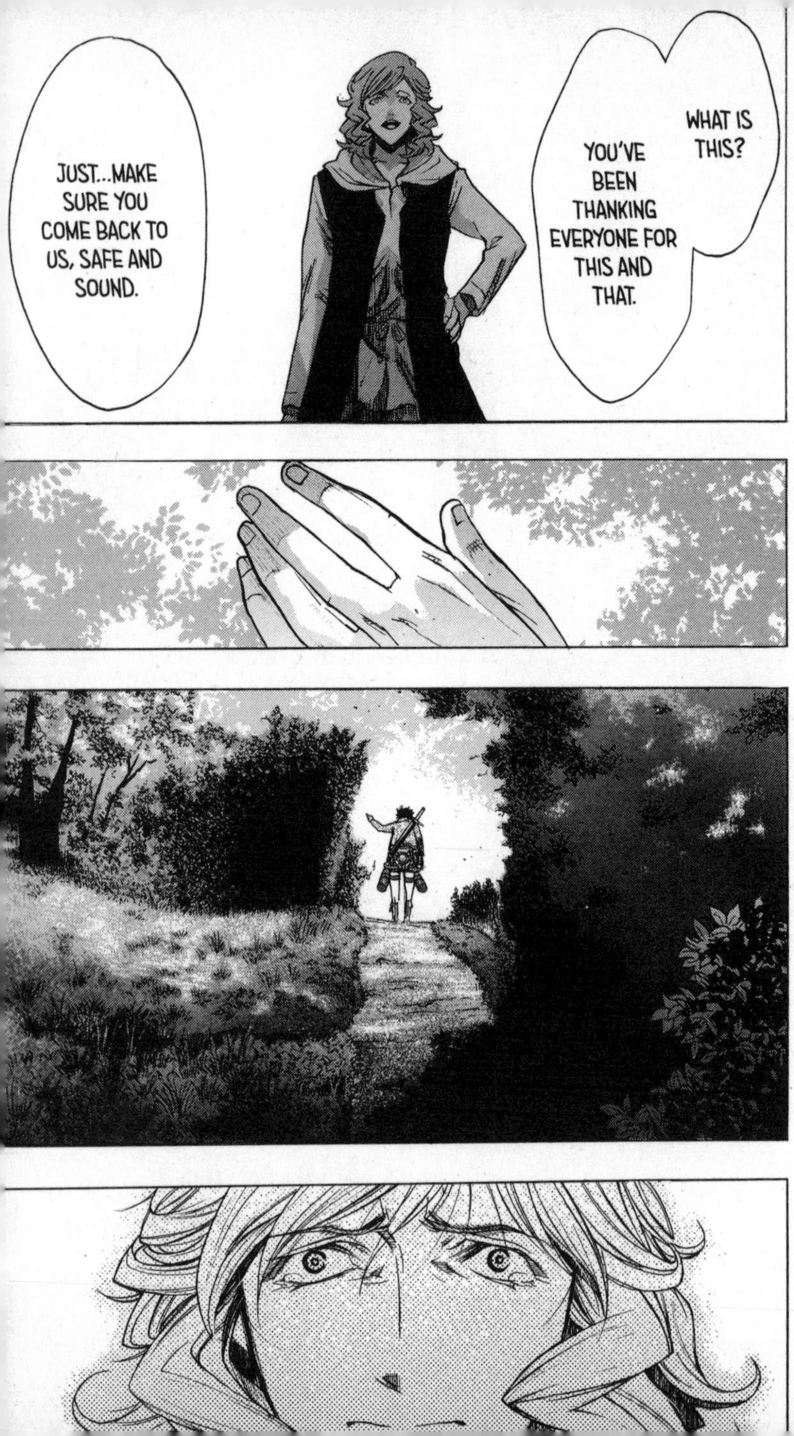
WHAT IS THIS? YOU'VE BEEN THANKING EVERYONE FOR THIS AND THAT.
JUST...MAKE SURE YOU COME BACK TO US, SAFE AND SOUND.

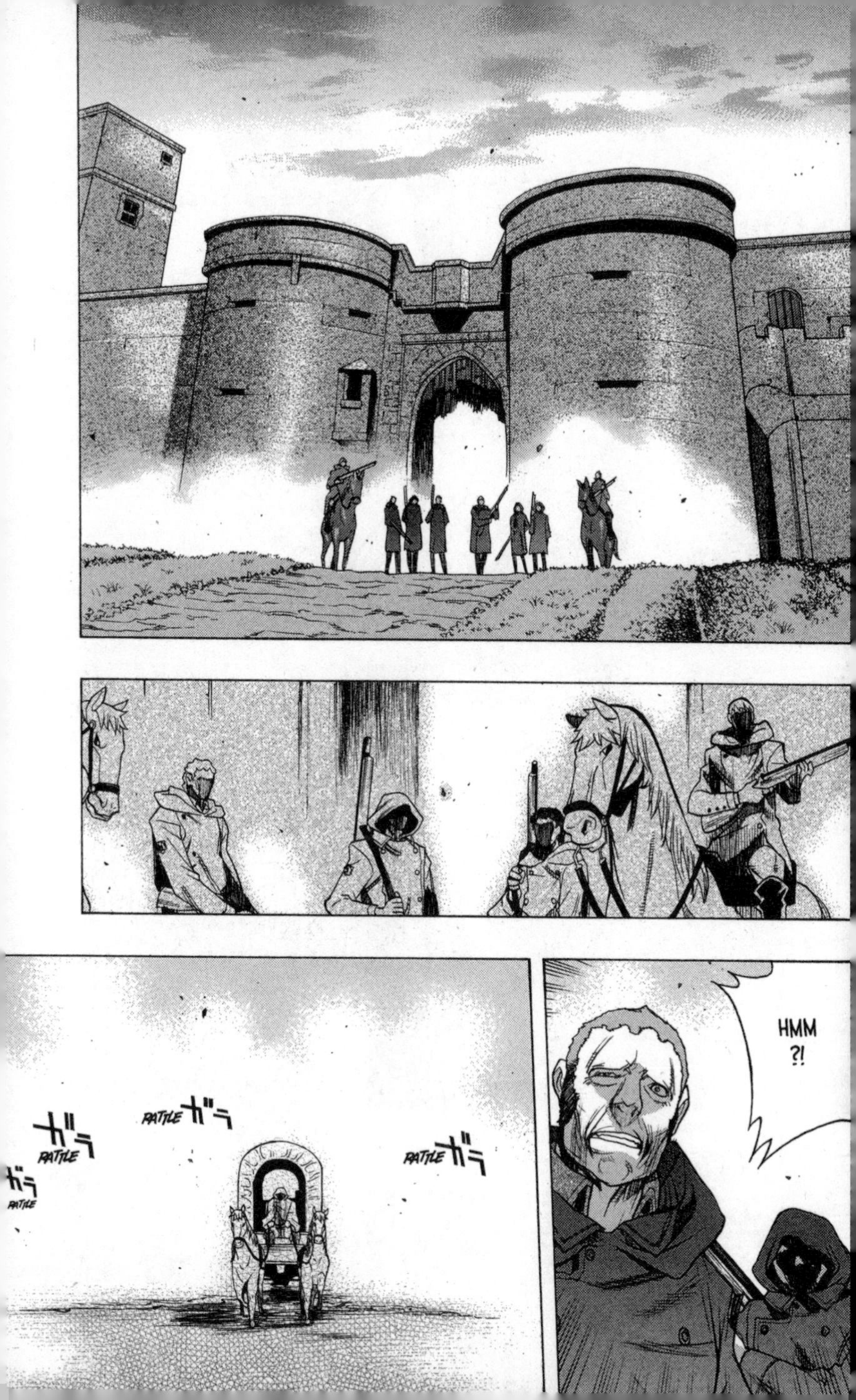
HMM ?!
ガラ RATTLE
ガラ RATTLE
ガラ RATTLE
ガラ RATTLE

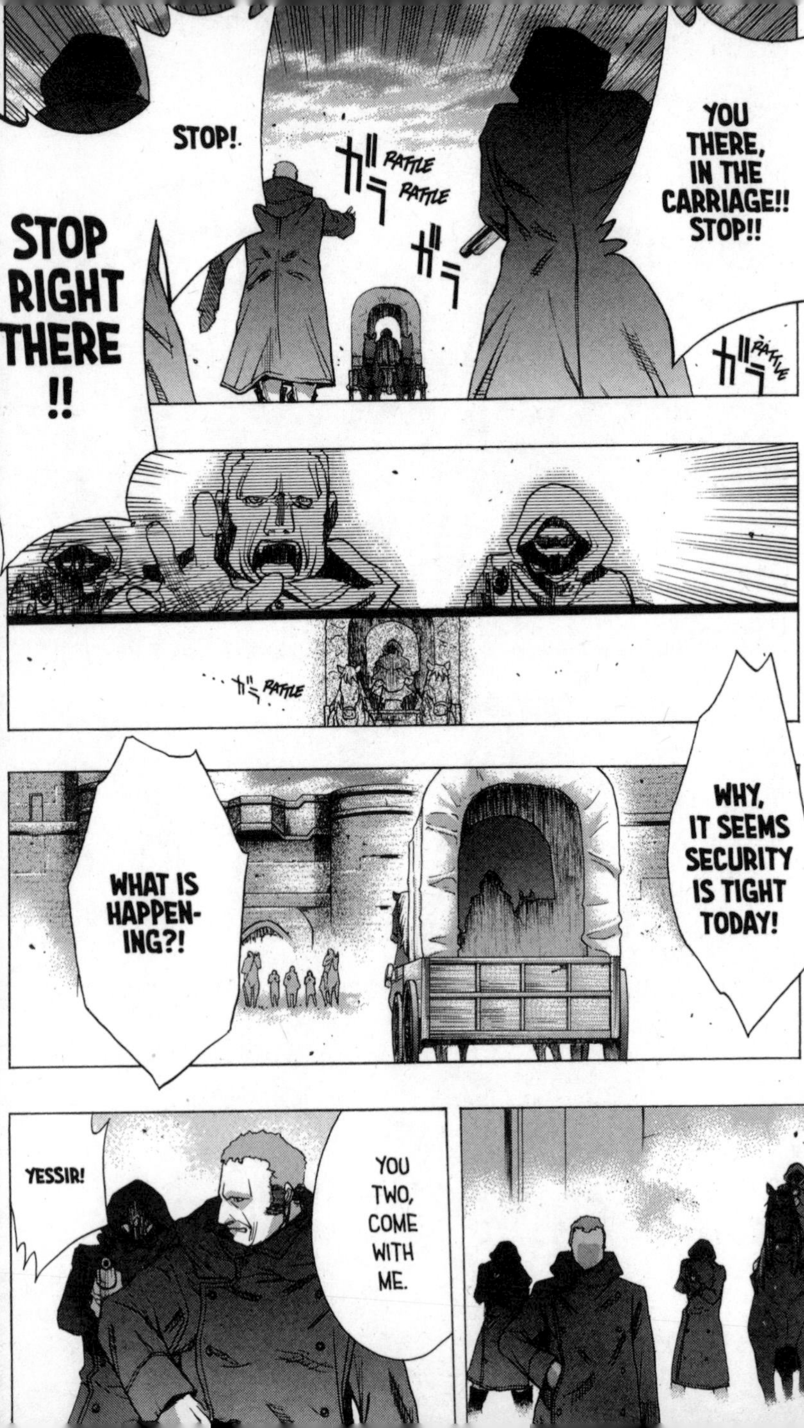
YOU THERE, IN THE CARRIAGE!! STOP!!
ガラ RATTLE
ガラ
ガラ RATTLE RATTLE
STOP!.
STOP RIGHT THERE !!
ガラ RATTLE
WHY, IT SEEMS SECURITY IS TIGHT TODAY!
WHAT IS HAPPEN-ING?!
YOU TWO, COME WITH ME.
YESSIR!

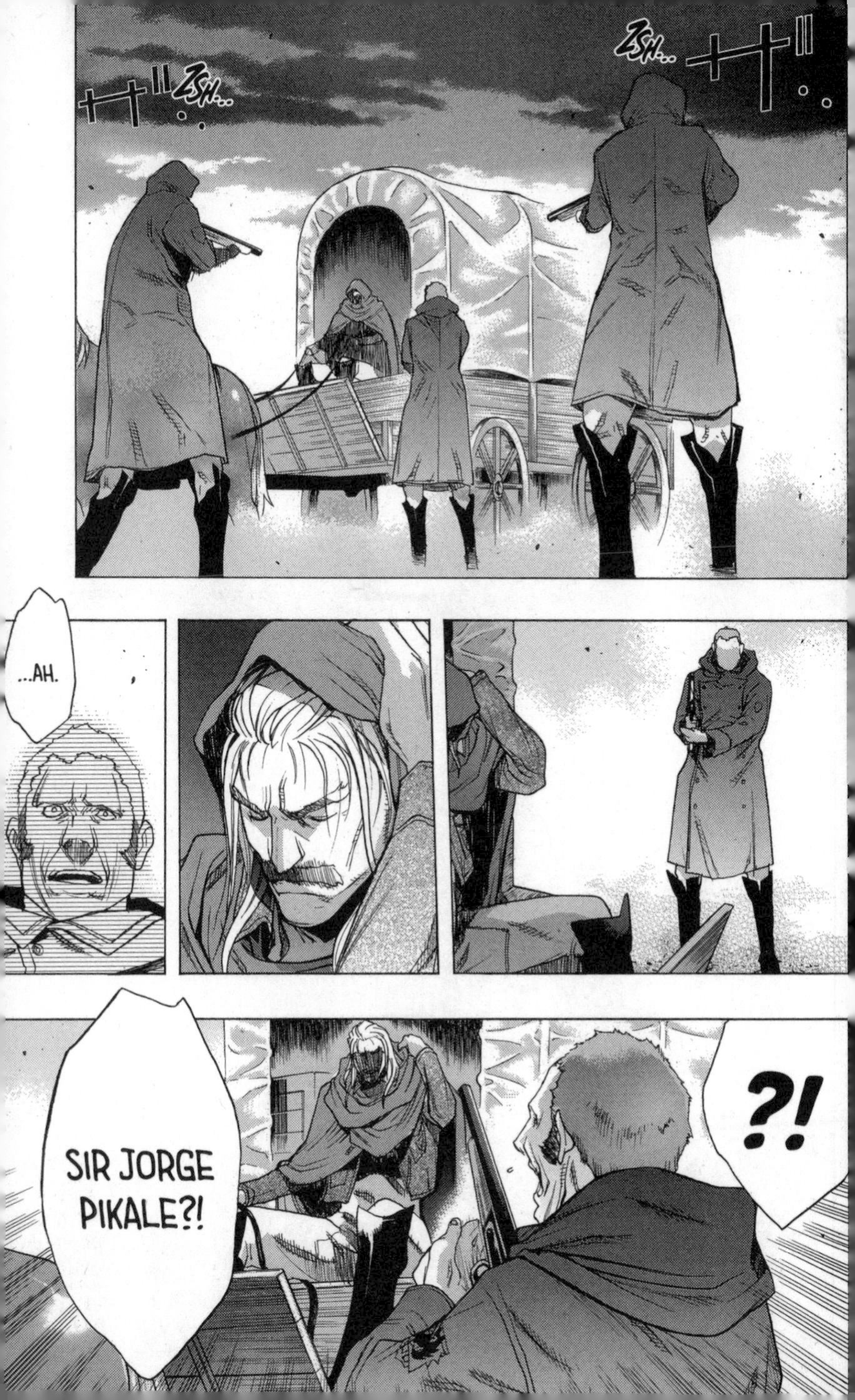
ZSH...
ZSH...
...AH.
?!
SIR JORGE PIKALE?!

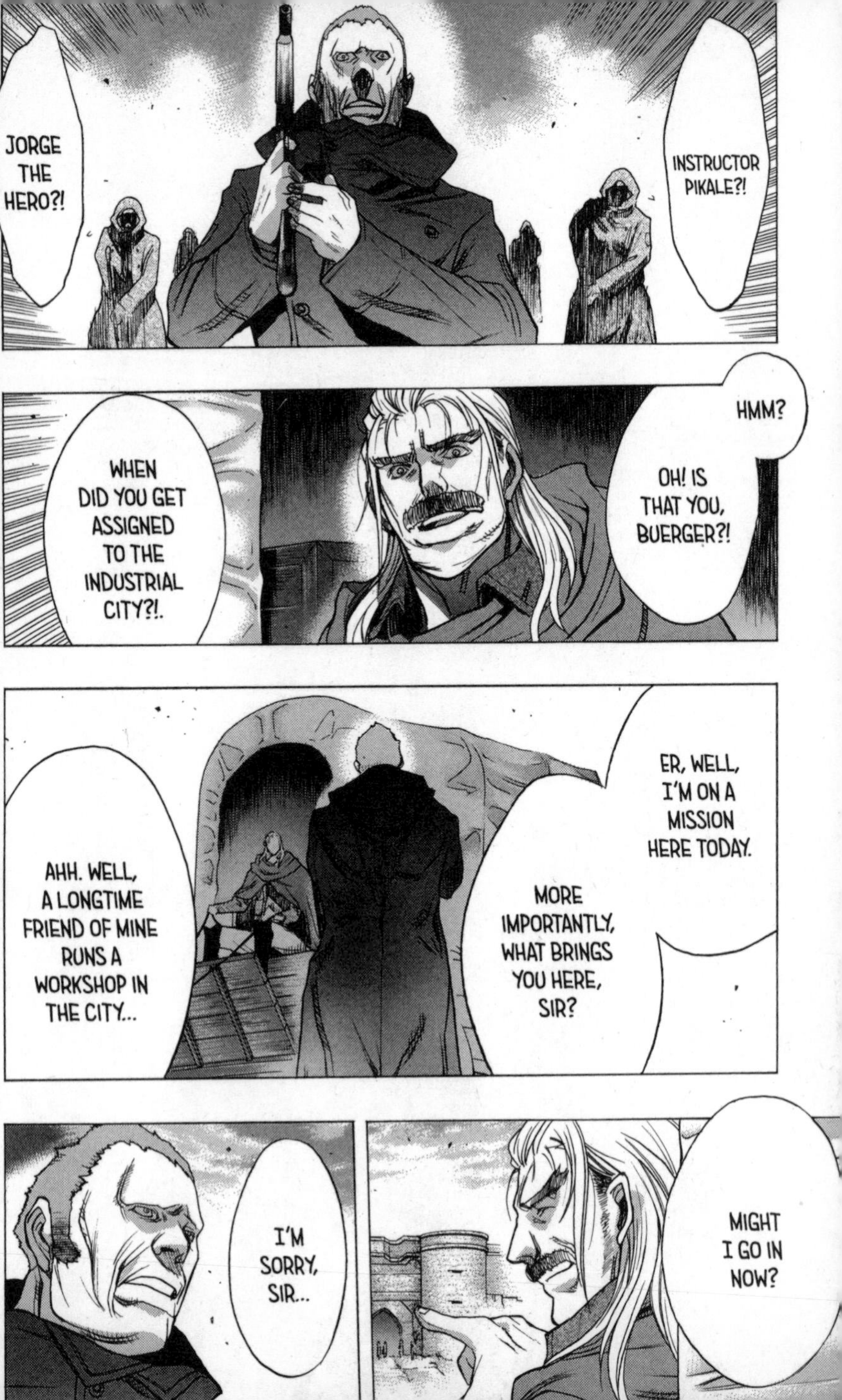
INSTRUCTOR PIKALE?!
JORGE THE HERO?!
HMM?
OH! IS THAT YOU, BUERGER?!
WHEN DID YOU GET ASSIGNED TO THE INDUSTRIAL CITY?!.
ER, WELL, I'M ON A MISSION HERE TODAY.
MORE IMPORTANTLY, WHAT BRINGS YOU HERE, SIR?
AHH. WELL, A LONGTIME FRIEND OF MINE RUNS A WORKSHOP IN THE CITY...
MIGHT I GO IN NOW?
I'M SORRY, SIR...

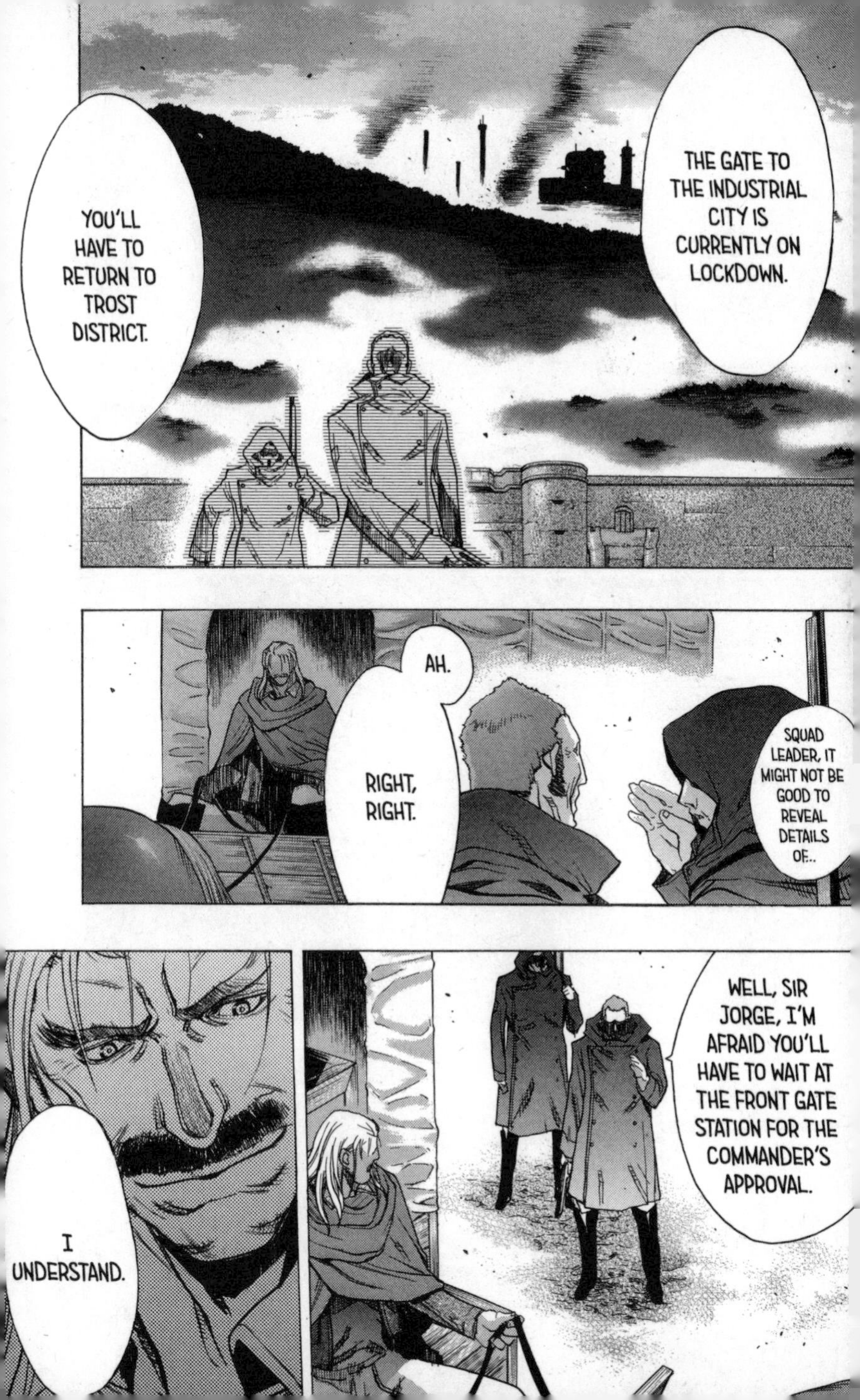
THE GATE TO THE INDUSTRIAL CITY IS CURRENTLY ON LOCKDOWN.
YOU'LL HAVE TO RETURN TO TROST DISTRICT.
SQUAD LEADER, IT MIGHT NOT BE GOOD TO REVEAL DETAILS OF..
AH.
RIGHT, RIGHT.
WELL, SIR JORGE, I'M AFRAID YOU'LL HAVE TO WAIT AT THE FRONT GATE STATION FOR THE COMMANDER'S APPROVAL.
I UNDERSTAND.

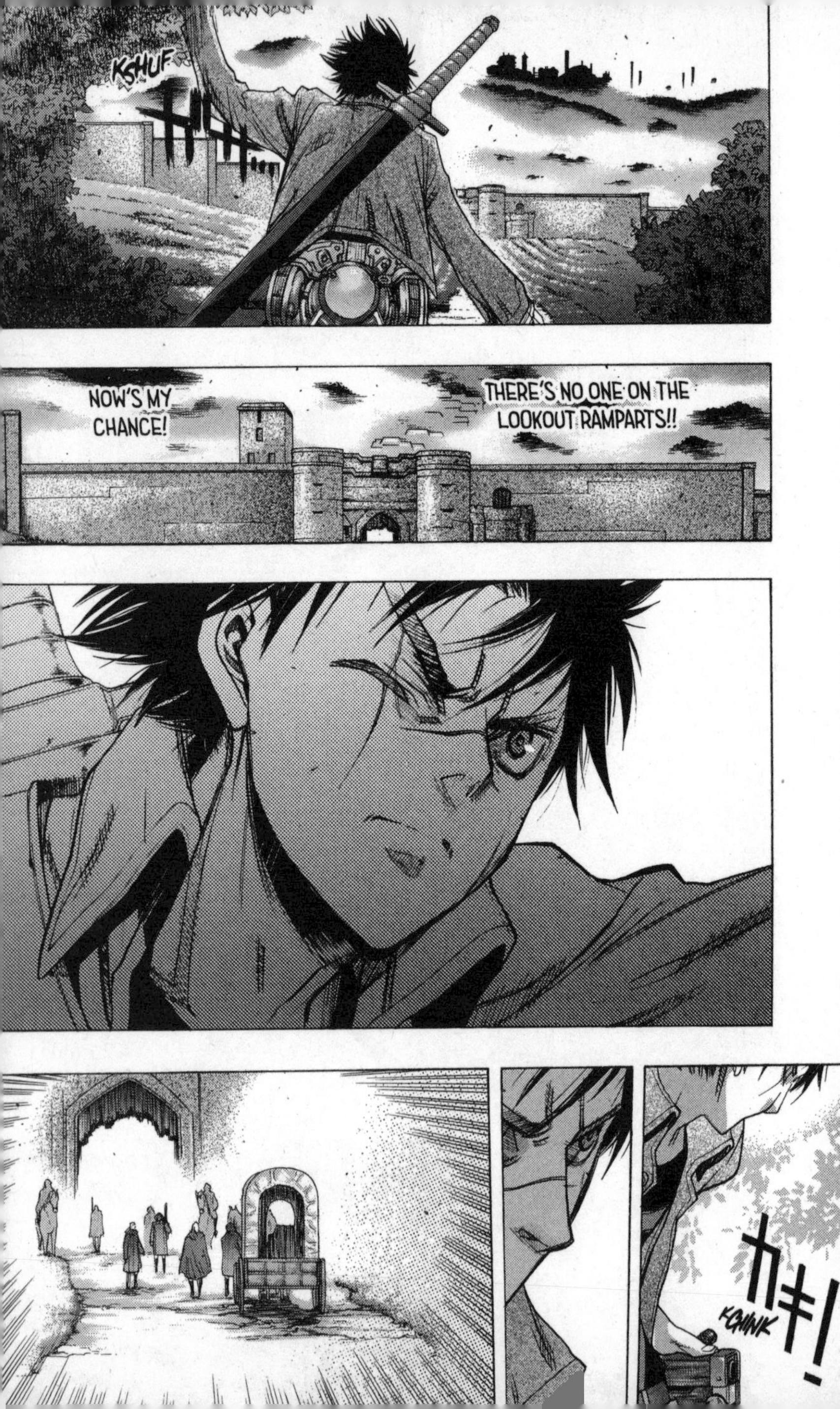
KSHUF
THERE'S NO ONE ON THE LOOKOUT RAMPARTS!!
NOW'S MY CHANCE!
カキ!
K-CHINK

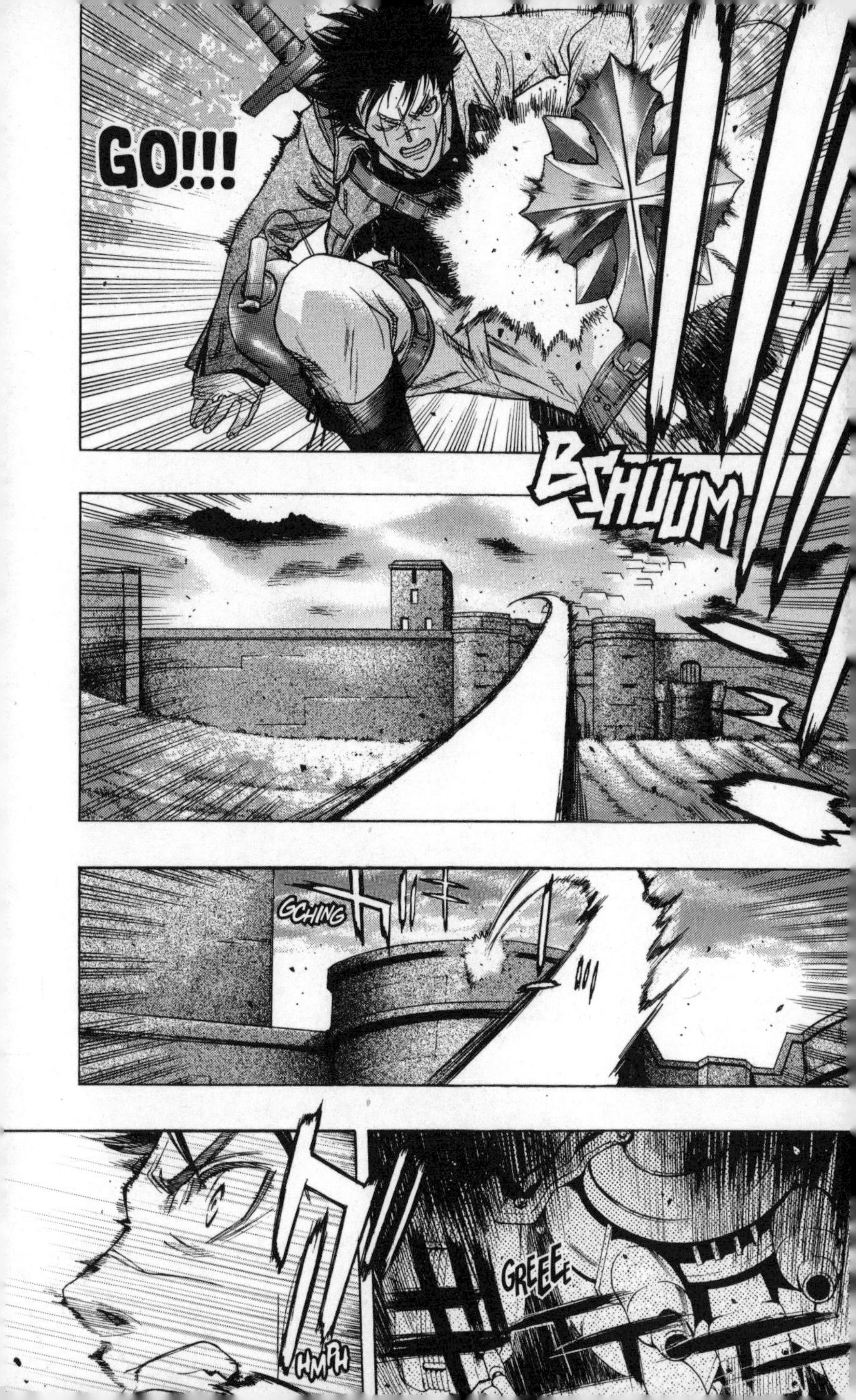
GO!!!
BSHUUM
GCHING
HMPH
GREEEE

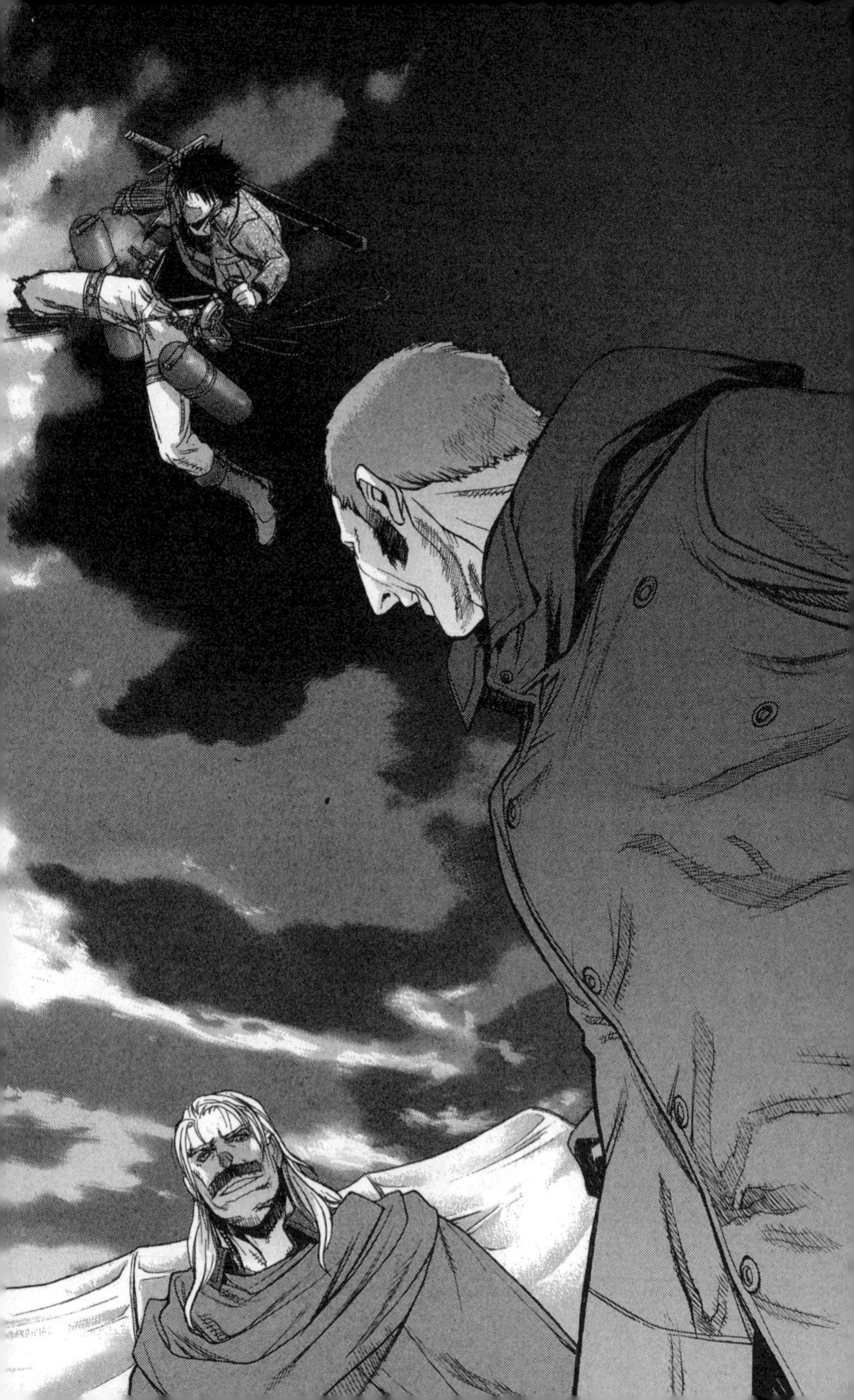

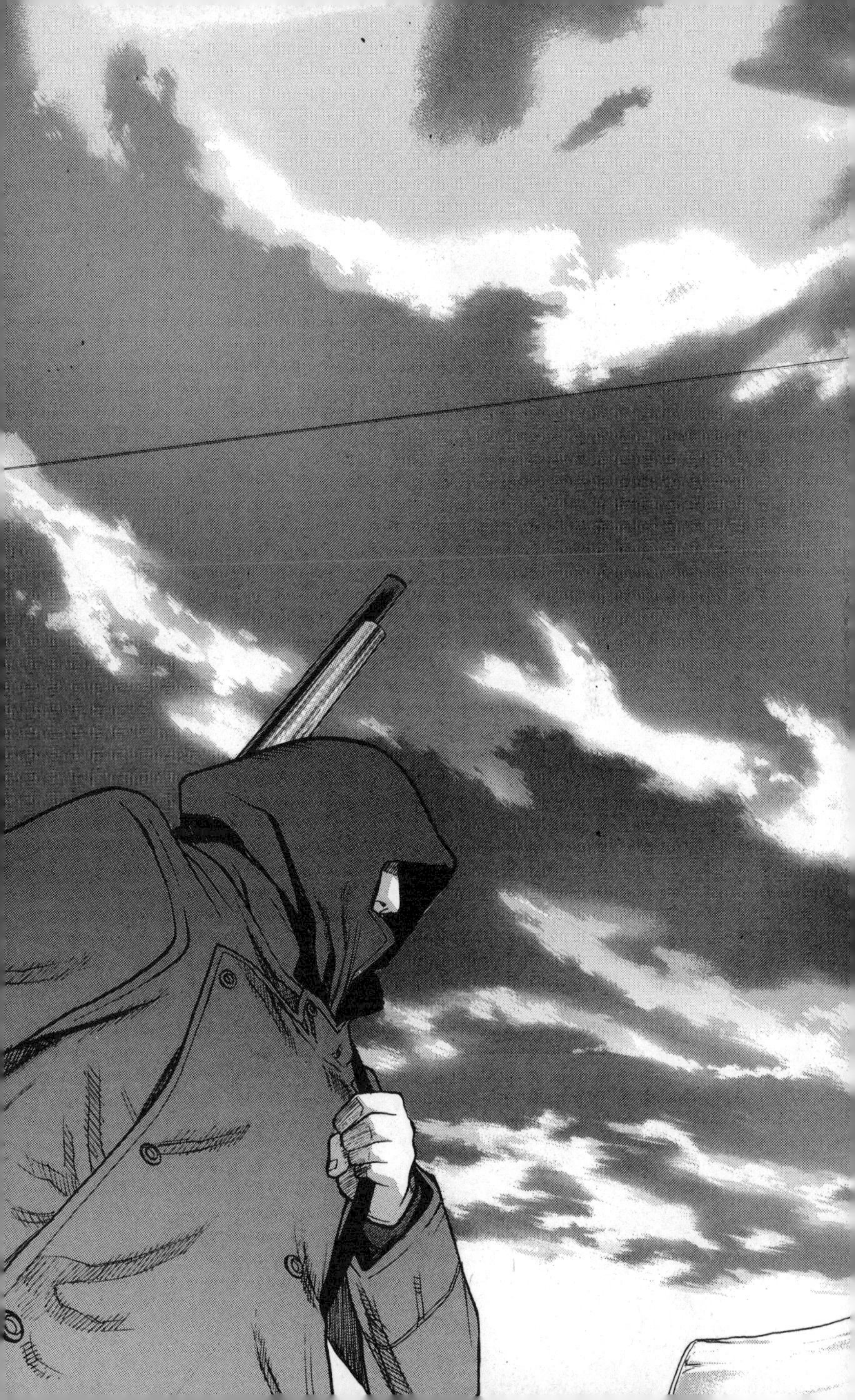

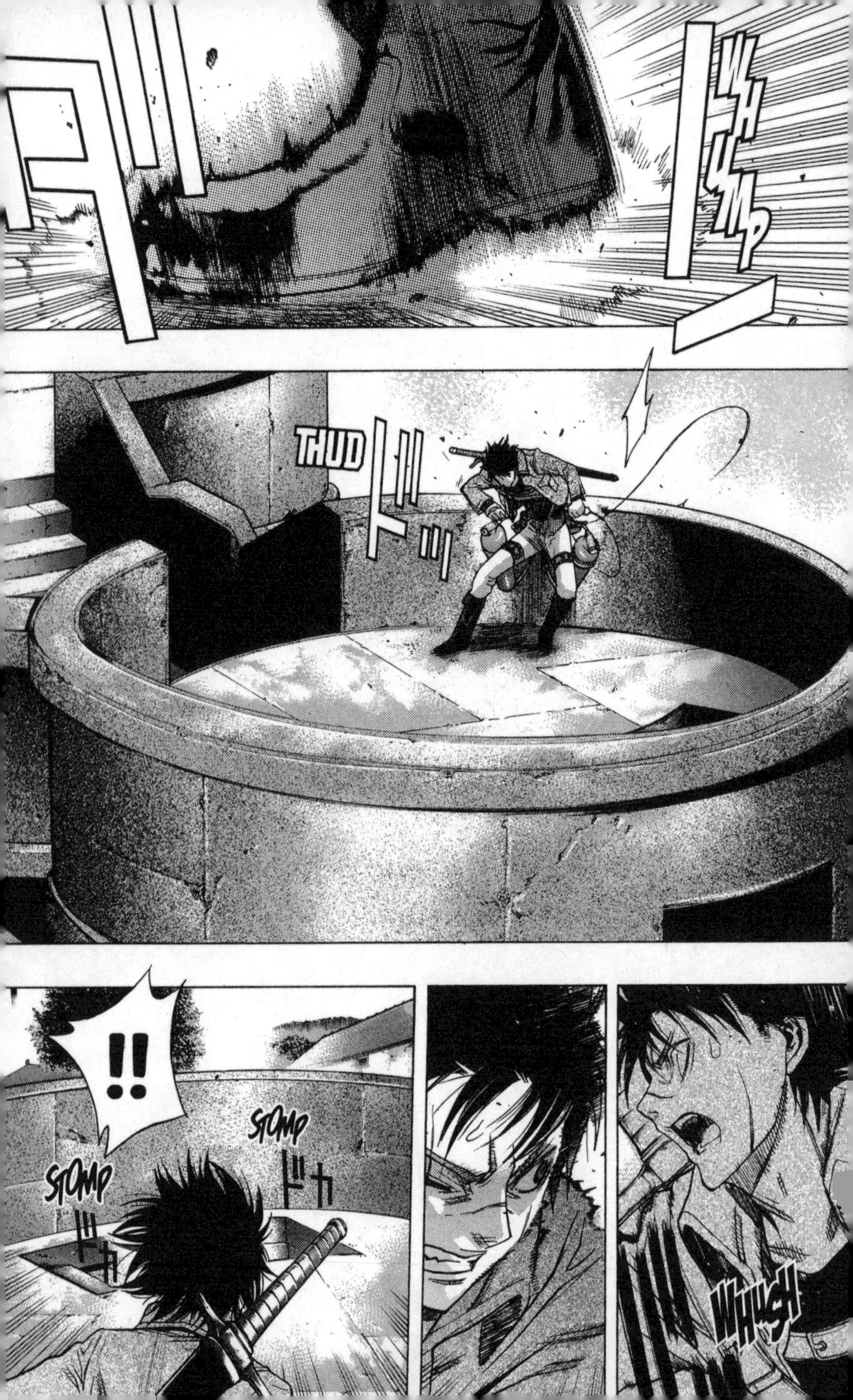
WHUMP
THUD
!!
STOMP
STOMP
WHUSH

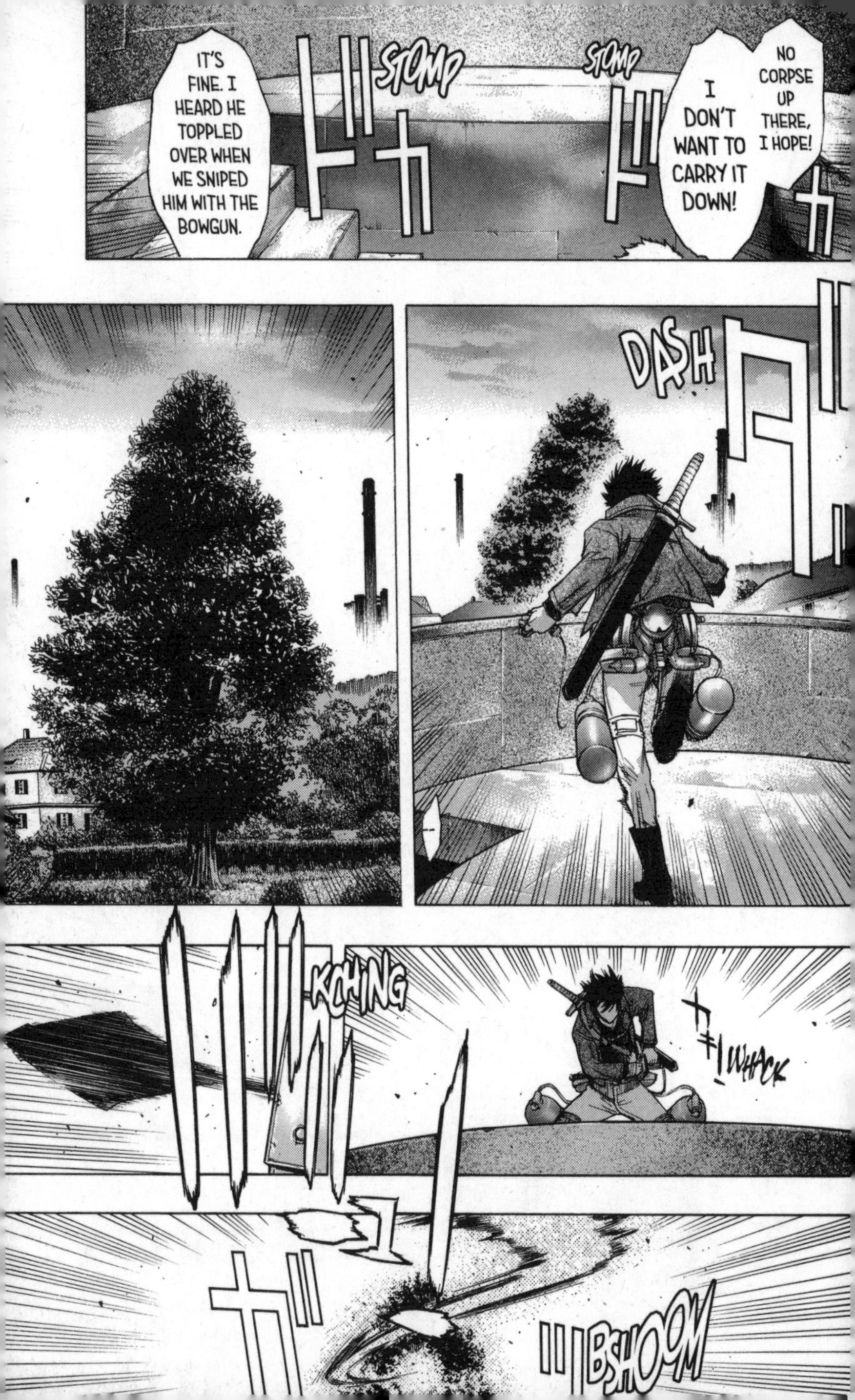
NO CORPSE UP THERE, I HOPE!
I DON'T WANT TO CARRY IT DOWN!
STOMP
STOMP
IT'S FINE. I HEARD HE TOPPLED OVER WHEN WE SNIPED HIM WITH THE BOWGUN.
DASH
WHACK
KCHING
BSHOOM

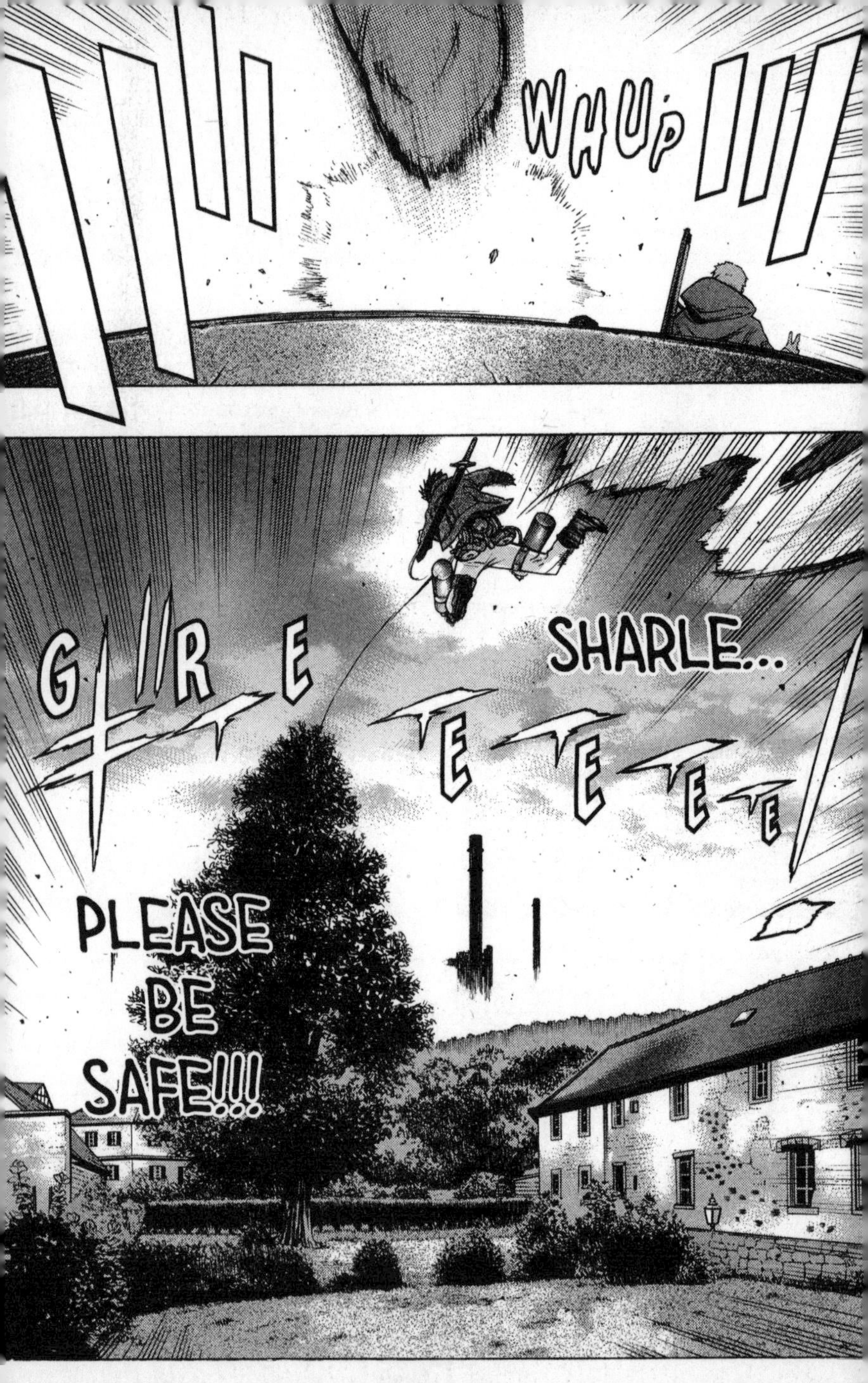
WHUP
SHARLE...
GREEEEE
PLEASE BE SAFE!!!

ATTACK on TITAN
BEFORE THE FALL

TO BE CONTINUED

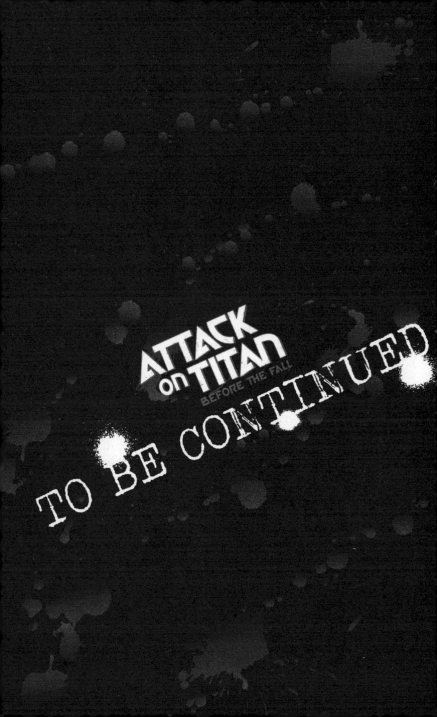

ᴀSTER OF VERTICAL MANEUVERING

ᴐlume 7, Kuklo used the new model of the Device to become the first human to battle a Titan
ᴢing Vertical Maneuvering methods. This little event during the day before he headed beyond
ᴡall that night might have given him a hint about how to utilize Vertical Maneuvering...

inally published: Bessatsu Shonen Magazine, January 2016 issue

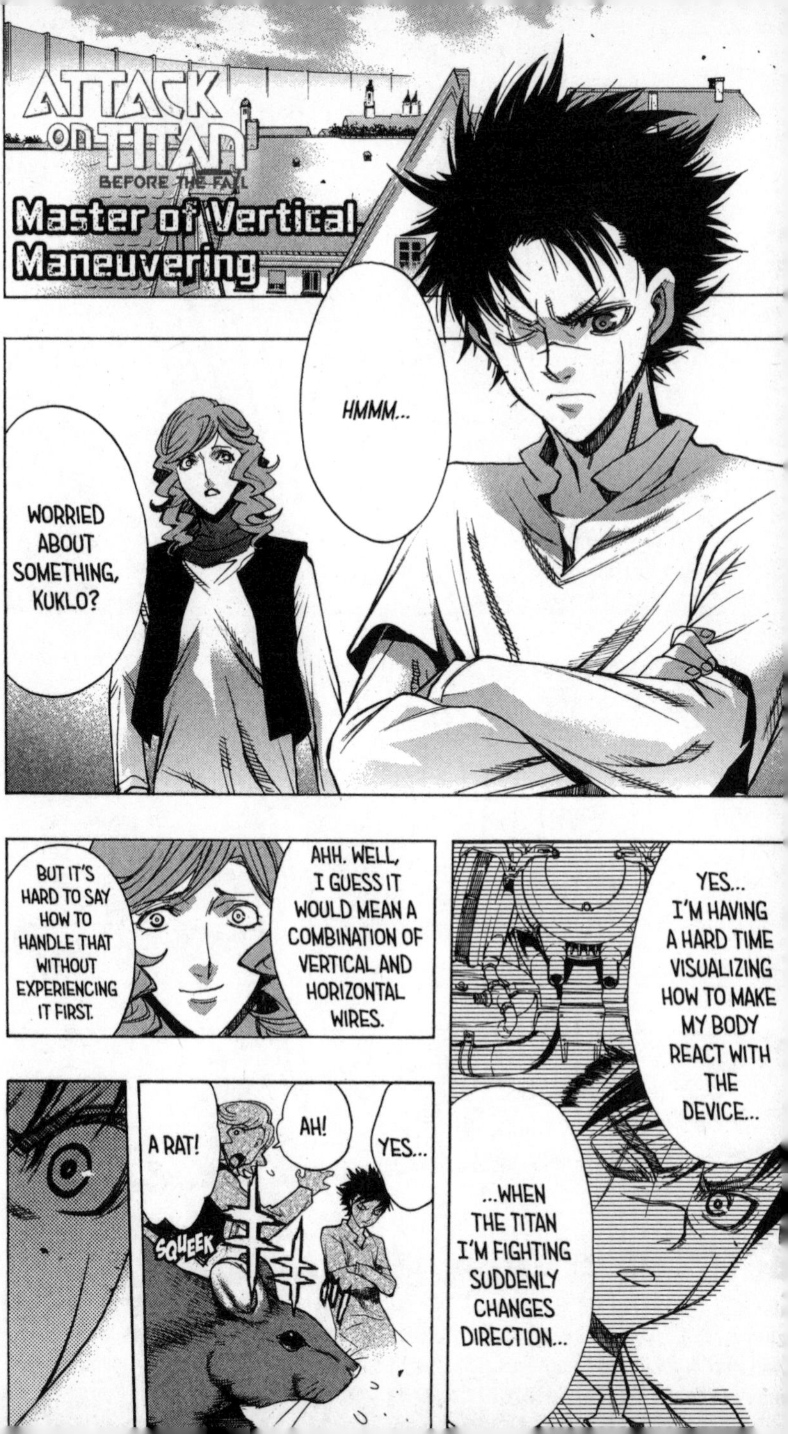
ATTACK on TITAN
BEFORE THE FALL
Master of Vertical Maneuvering
HMMM...
WORRIED ABOUT SOMETHING, KUKLO?
YES... I'M HAVING A HARD TIME VISUALIZING HOW TO MAKE MY BODY REACT WITH THE DEVICE...
...WHEN THE TITAN I'M FIGHTING SUDDENLY CHANGES DIRECTION...
AHH. WELL, I GUESS IT WOULD MEAN A COMBINATION OF VERTICAL AND HORIZONTAL WIRES.
BUT IT'S HARD TO SAY HOW TO HANDLE THAT WITHOUT EXPERIENCING IT FIRST.
YES...
AH!
A RAT!
SQUEEK

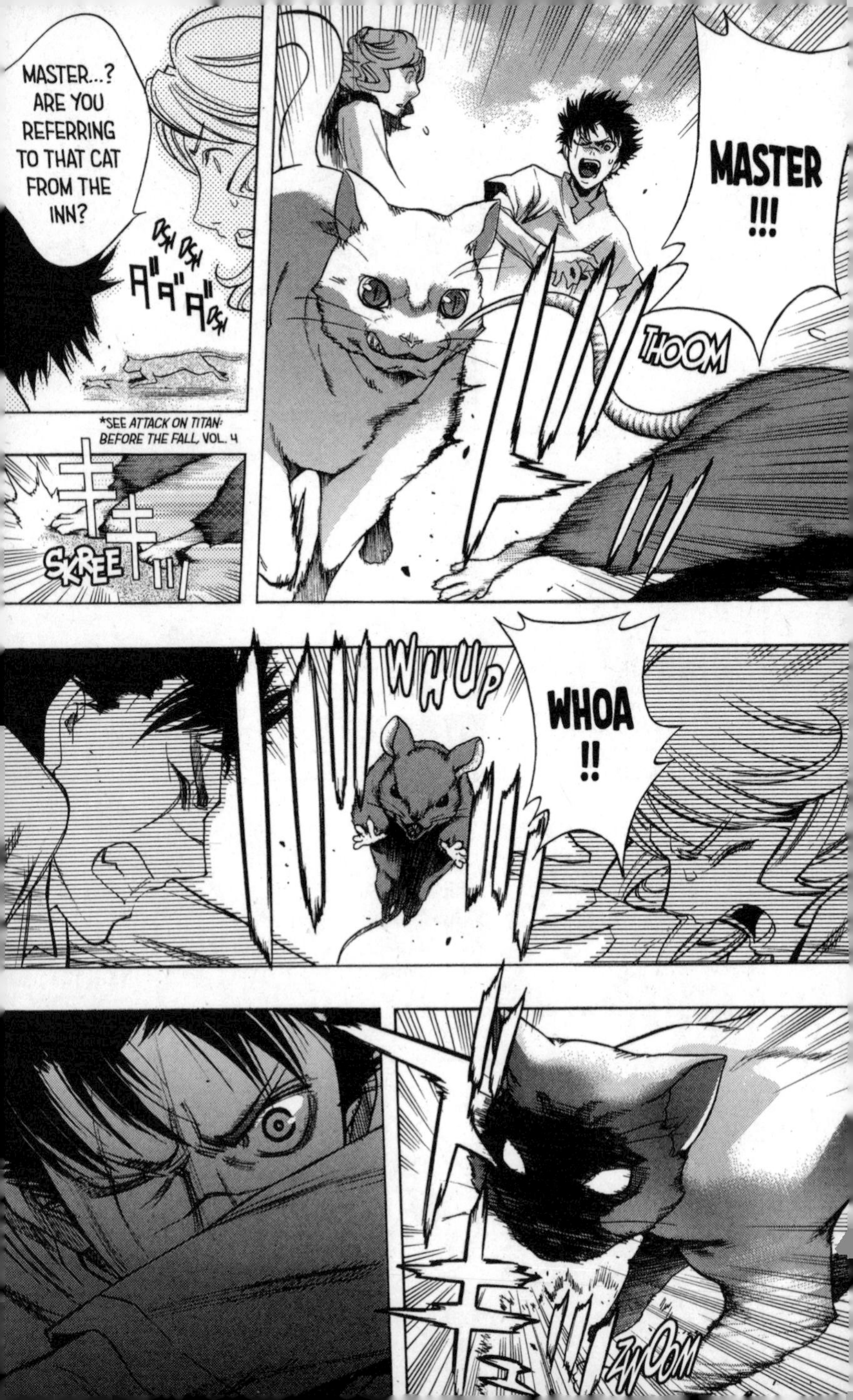
MASTER !!!
THOOM
MASTER...? ARE YOU REFERRING TO THAT CAT FROM THE INN?
DSH DSH
DSH
*SEE ATTACK ON TITAN: BEFORE THE FALL, VOL. 4
SKREE
WHUP
WHOA !!
ZWOOM

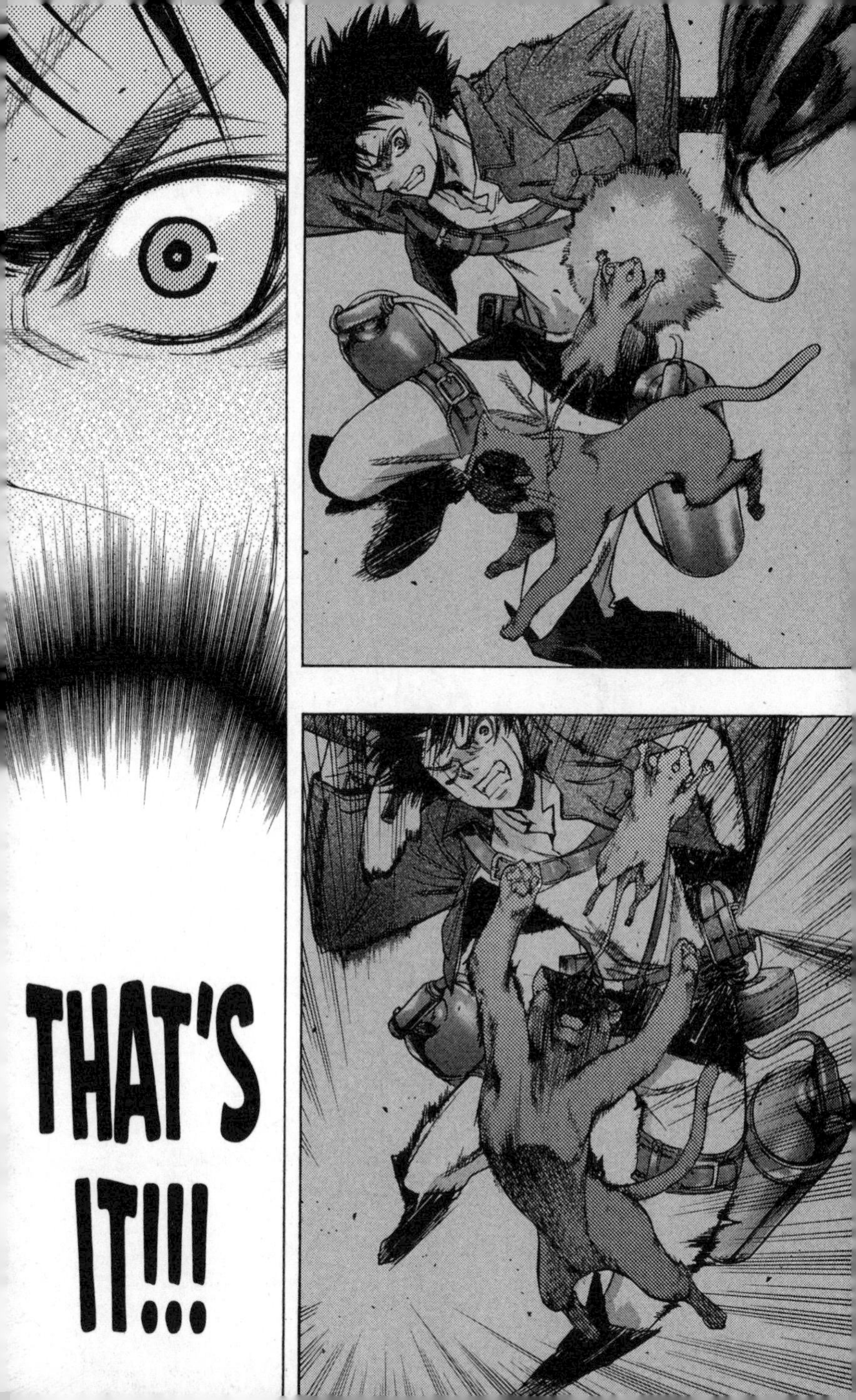
THAT'S IT!!!

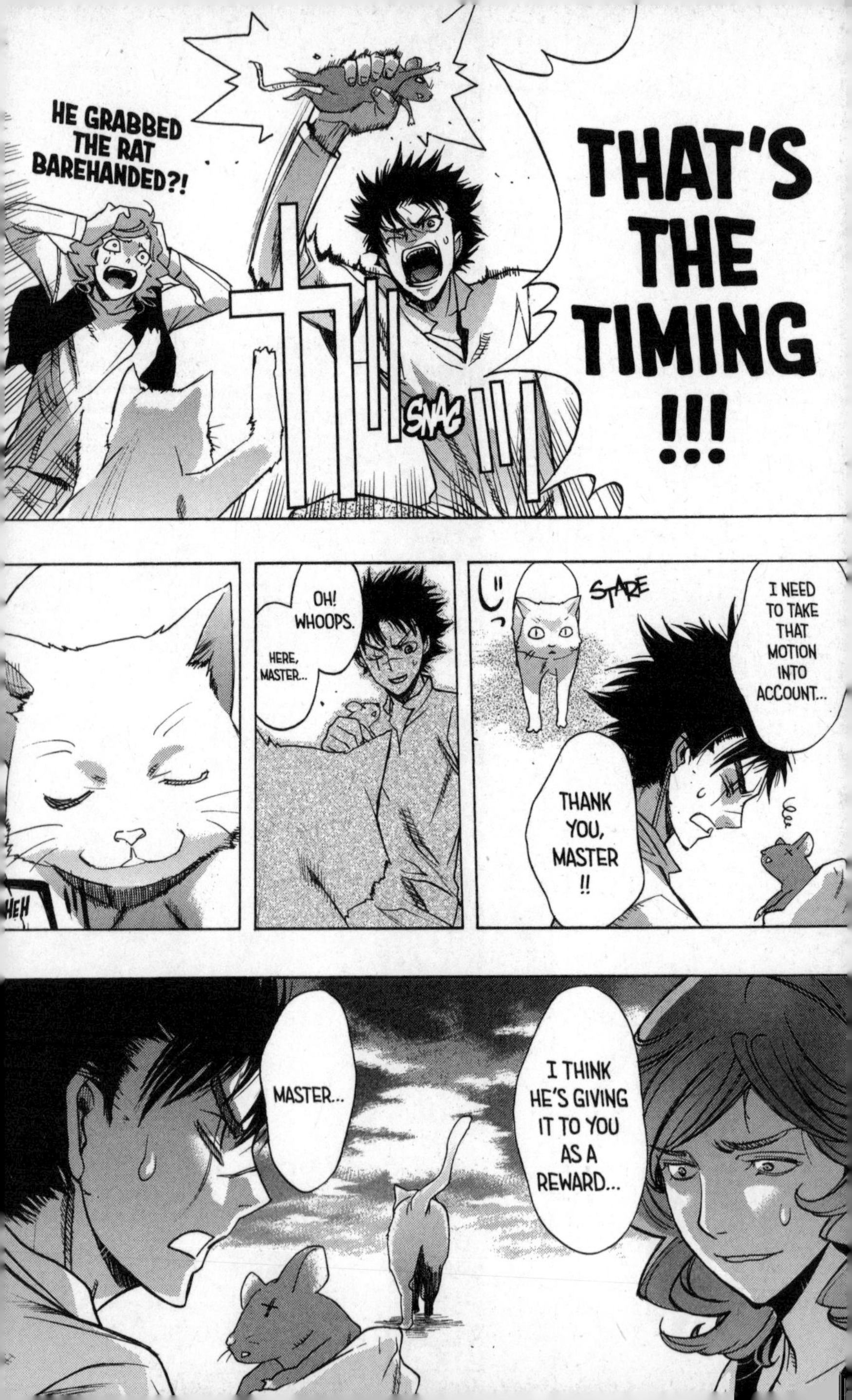
THAT'S THE TIMING!!!
SNAG
HE GRABBED THE RAT BAREHANDED?!
I NEED TO TAKE THAT MOTION INTO ACCOUNT...
STARE
THANK YOU, MASTER!!
OH! WHOOPS.
HERE, MASTER...
HEH
I THINK HE'S GIVING IT TO YOU AS A REWARD...
MASTER...

Master of Vertical Maneuvering · End

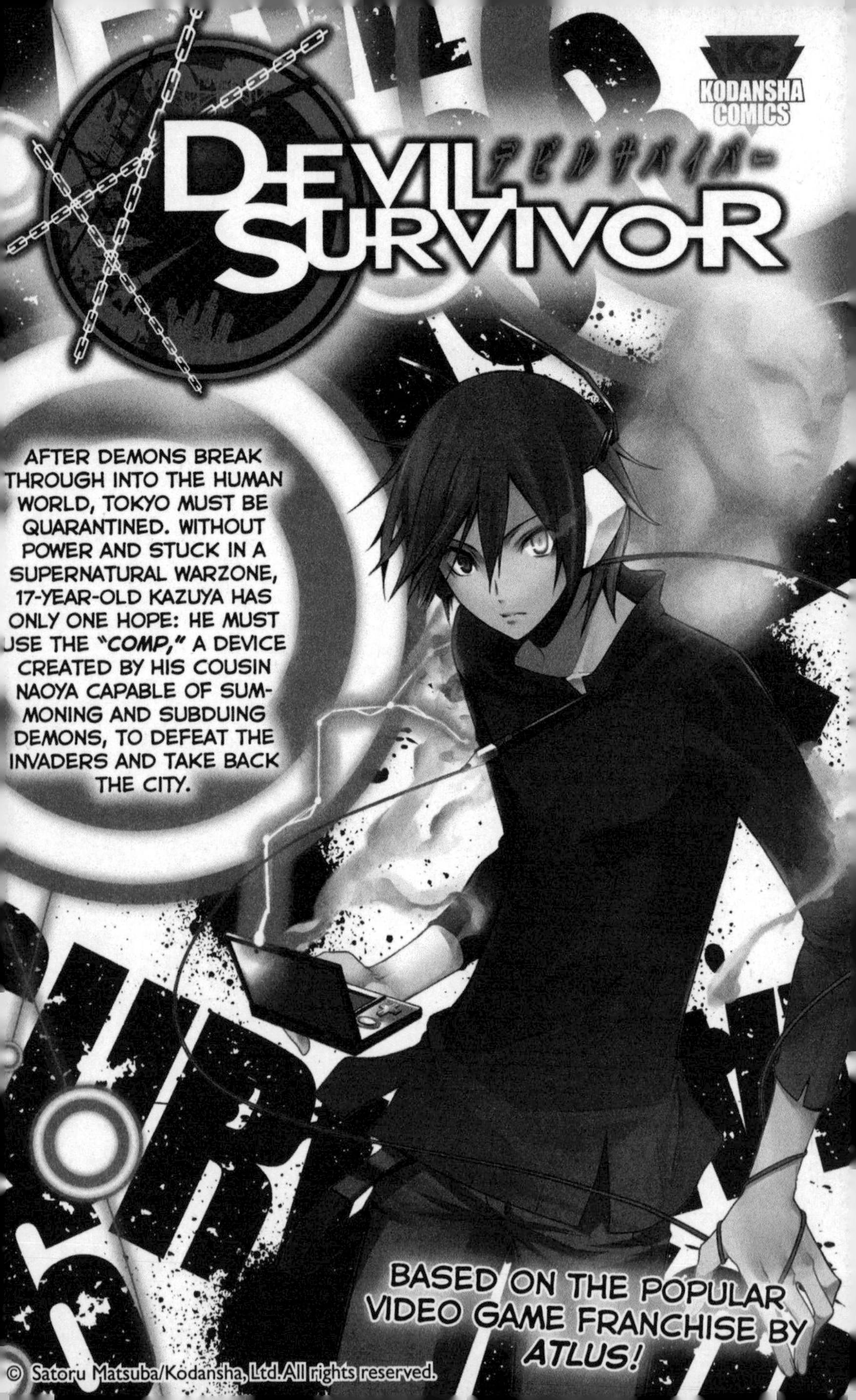
KC
KODANSHA COMICS
DEVIL SURVIVOR
デビルサバイバー
AFTER DEMONS BREAK THROUGH INTO THE HUMAN WORLD, TOKYO MUST BE QUARANTINED. WITHOUT POWER AND STUCK IN A SUPERNATURAL WARZONE, 17-YEAR-OLD KAZUYA HAS ONLY ONE HOPE: HE MUST USE THE *"COMP,"* A DEVICE CREATED BY HIS COUSIN NAOYA CAPABLE OF SUMMONING AND SUBDUING DEMONS, TO DEFEAT THE INVADERS AND TAKE BACK THE CITY.
BASED ON THE POPULAR VIDEO GAME FRANCHISE BY *ATLUS!*
© Satoru Matsuba/Kodansha, Ltd. All rights reserved.

INUYASHIKI

A superhero like none you've ever seen, from the creator of "Gantz"!

ICHIRO INUYASHIKI IS DOWN ON HIS LUCK. HE LOOKS MUCH OLDER THAN HIS 58 YEARS, HIS CHILDREN DESPISE HIM, AND HIS WIFE THINKS HE'S A USELESS COWARD. SO WHEN HE'S DIAGNOSED WITH STOMACH CANCER AND GIVEN THREE MONTHS TO LIVE, IT SEEMS THE ONLY ONE WHO'LL MISS HIM IS HIS DOG.

THEN A BLINDING LIGHT FILLS THE SKY, AND THE OLD MAN IS KILLED... ONLY TO WAKE UP LATER IN A BODY HE ALMOST RECOGNIZES AS HIS OWN. CAN IT BE THAT ICHIRO INUYASHIKI IS NO LONGER HUMAN?

COMES IN EXTRA-LARGE EDITIONS WITH COLOR PAGES!

KODANSHA COMICS

Yamada-kun AND THE Seven Witches

"A very funny manga with a lot of heart and character."
—Adventures in Poor Taste

SWAPPED WITH A KISS?!

Class troublemaker Ryu Yamada is already having a bad day when he stumbles down a staircase along with star student Urara Shiraishi. When he wakes up, he realizes they have switched bodies—and that Ryu has the power to trade places with anyone just by kissing them! Ryu and Urara take full advantage of the situation to improve their lives, but with such an oddly amazing power, just how long will they be able to keep their secret under wraps?

Available now in print and digitally!

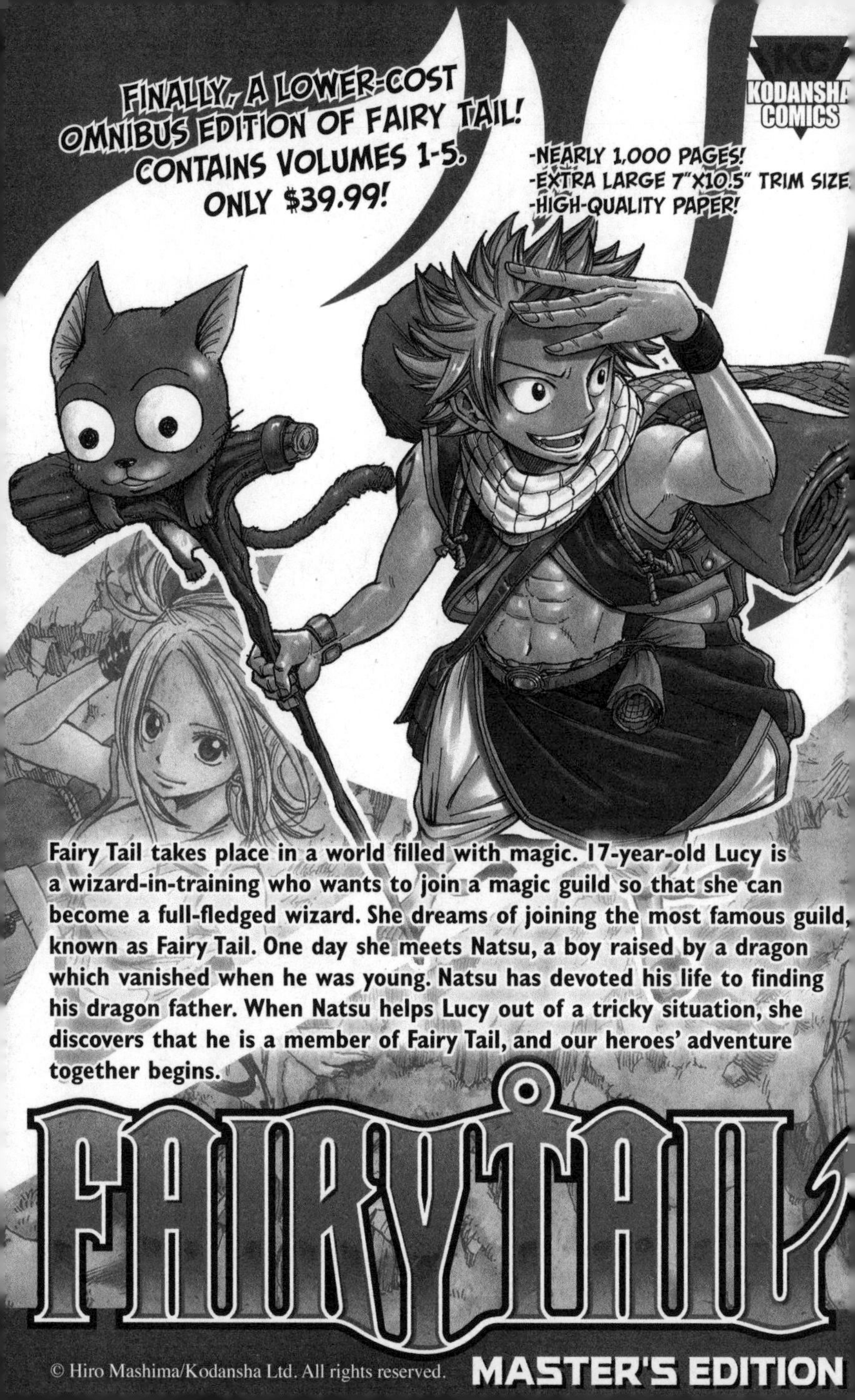
FINALLY, A LOWER-COST OMNIBUS EDITION OF FAIRY TAIL! CONTAINS VOLUMES 1-5. ONLY $39.99!
KODANSHA COMICS
-NEARLY 1,000 PAGES!
-EXTRA LARGE 7"X10.5" TRIM SIZE!
-HIGH-QUALITY PAPER!
Fairy Tail takes place in a world filled with magic. 17-year-old Lucy is a wizard-in-training who wants to join a magic guild so that she can become a full-fledged wizard. She dreams of joining the most famous guild, known as Fairy Tail. One day she meets Natsu, a boy raised by a dragon which vanished when he was young. Natsu has devoted his life to finding his dragon father. When Natsu helps Lucy out of a tricky situation, she discovers that he is a member of Fairy Tail, and our heroes' adventure together begins.
FAIRY TAIL
© Hiro Mashima/Kodansha Ltd. All rights reserved.
MASTER'S EDITION

Maria
THE VIRGIN WITCH

"Maria's brand of righteous justice, passion and plain talking make for one of the freshest manga series of 2015. I dare any other book to top it."
—UK Anime Network

PURITY AND POWER

As a war to determine the rightful ruler of medieval France ravages the land, the witch Maria decides she will not stand idly by as men kill each other in the name of God and glory. Using her powerful magic, she summons various beasts and demons —even going as far as using a succubus to seduce soldiers into submission under the veil of night— all to stop the needless slaughter. However, after the Archangel Michael puts an end to her meddling, he curses her to lose her powers if she ever gives up her virginity. Will she forgo the forbidden fruit of adulthood in order to bring an end to the merciless machine of war?
Available now in print and digitally!

KC
KODANSHA
COMICS

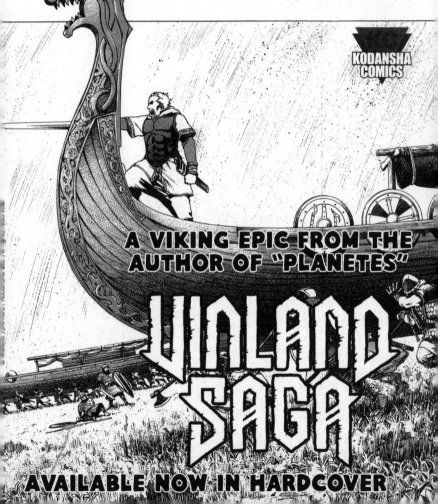

A Kodansha Comics Trade Paperback Original
Attack on Titan: Before the Fall volume 8 copyright © 2016 Hajime Isayama/
Ryo Suzukaze/Satoshi Shiki
English translation copyright © 2016 Hajime Isayama/Ryo Suzukaze/Satoshi Shiki

Published in the United States by Kodansha Comics, an imprint of
Kodansha USA Publishing, LLC, New York.

Publication rights for this English edition arranged through
Kodansha Ltd, Tokyo.

First published in Japan in 2016 by Kodansha Ltd., Tokyo
as *Shingeki no kyojin Before the fall*, volume 8.

ISBN 978-1-63236-260-5

Character designs by Thores Shibamoto
Original cover design by Takashi Shimoyama (Red Rooster)

Printed in the United States of America.

www.kodanshacomics.com

9 8 7 6 5 4 3 2 1
Translation: Stephen Paul
Lettering: Steve Wands
Editing: Lauren Scanlan
Kodansha Comics edition cover design by Phil Balsman

STOP!

You are going the *wrong way!*

Manga is a *completely* different type of reading experience.

To start at the *BEGINNING*, go to the *END!*

That's right! Authentic manga is read the traditional Japanese way–from right to left, exactly the opposite of how American books are read. It's easy to follow: just go to the other end of the book, and read each page–and each panel–from the right side to the left side, starting at the top right. Now you're experiencing manga as it was meant to be.